PENGUIN BOOKS
NOT A NICE MAN TO KNOW

Khushwant Singh is India's best-known writer and columnist. He has been founder–editor of *Yojana*, and editor of the *Illustrated Weekly of India*, the *National Herald* and the *Hindustan Times*. He is the author of classics such as *Train to Pakistan*, *I Shall Not Hear the Nightingale*, *Delhi*, *The Company of Women*. His latest novel, *The Sunset Club*, written when he was ninety-five, was published by Penguin Books in 2010. His non-fiction includes the classic two-volume *A History of the Sikhs*, a number of translations and works on Sikh religion and culture, Delhi, nature, current affairs and Urdu poetry. His autobiography, *Truth, Love and a Little Malice*, was published by Penguin Books in 2002.

Khushwant Singh was a member of Parliament from 1980 to 1986. He was awarded the Padma Bhushan in 1974, but returned the decoration in 1984 in protest against the storming of the Golden Temple in Amritsar by the Indian Army. In 2007, he was awarded the Padma Vibhushan.

Among the other awards he has received are the Punjab Ratan, the Sulabh International award for the most honest Indian of the year, and honorary doctorates from several universities.

MY DATELESS DIARIES

NOT A NICE MAN TO KNOW

The Best of Khushwant Singh

Edited and with an Introduction by Nandini Mehta

Foreword by Vikram Seth

PENGUIN BOOKS

PENGUIN BOOKS
Published by the Penguin Group
Penguin Books India Pvt. Ltd, 11 Community Centre, Panchsheel Park, New Delhi 110 017, India
Penguin Group (USA) Inc., 375 Hudson Street, New York, New York 10014, USA
Penguin Group (Canada), 90 Eglinton Avenue East, Suite 700, Toronto, Ontario, M4P 2Y3, Canada (a division of Pearson Penguin Canada Inc.)
Penguin Books Ltd, 80 Strand, London WC2R 0RL, England
Penguin Ireland, 25 St Stephen's Green, Dublin 2, Ireland (a division of Penguin Books Ltd)
Penguin Group (Australia), 250 Camberwell Road, Camberwell, Victoria 3124, Australia (a division of Pearson Australia Group Pty Ltd)
Penguin Group (NZ), 67 Apollo Drive, Rosedale, Auckland 0632, New Zealand (a division of Pearson New Zealand Ltd)
Penguin Group (South Africa) (Pty) Ltd, 24 Sturdee Avenue, Rosebank, Johannesburg 2196, South Africa

Penguin Books Ltd, Registered Offices: 80 Strand, London WC2R 0RL, England

First published in Viking by Penguin Books India 1993
Published in Penguin Books 1993
This edition published in Penguin Books 2011

Copyright © Khushwant Singh 1993, 2011
Foreword copyright © Vikram Seth 1993

Pages ix and x are an extension of the copyright page

ISBN 9780143417392

Typeset in Minion by InoSoft Systems, Noida
Printed at Chaman Offset Printers, Delhi

To
Sadia Dehlvi
Who gave me more
affection and notoriety
than I deserved

CONTENTS

ACKNOWLEDGEMENTS

While every effort has been made to ensure that permission to reproduce copyright material included in the book was obtained, in the event of any inadvertent omission, the publishers should be notified and formal acknowledgements will be included in all future editions of this book. Some of the essays in this book have appeared in different form in the columns 'With Malice Towards One and All . . .' and 'This Above All' in *Hindustan Times* and the *Tribune* respectively and in *Outlook* and the *Telegraph*. The editor and publisher would like to specially acknowledge the following:

- For 'Seeing Oneself', Konark Publishers, 1987
- For 'Why I Am an Indian', *The Illustrated Weekly,* February 1970
- For 'The Haunted Simla Road', *The Observer,* London
- For 'Manzur Qadir', *The Illustrated Weekly,* October 1974
- For 'Prabha Dutt', *The Hindustan Times,* March 1984
- For 'Phoolan Devi', *The Hindustan Times,* 1981
- For 'Nirad Chaudhuri', *The Illustrated Weekly*
- For 'Krishna Menon', *Opinion* magazine, Bombay
- For 'Shraddha Mata', *New Delhi* magazine, September 1979
- For 'Doomsday in Yogiland', *The New York Times*
- For 'Holy Men and Holy Cows', *The New York Times*
- For 'Going Gaga Over Yoga', *The New York Times*

- For 'The Romance of New Delhi', *The Statesman,* Calcutta
- For 'The Hanging of Bhutto', *New Delhi* magazine, April and June, 1979
- For 'The Monsoon in Indian Literature and Folklore', from *Monsoons,* edited by Jay S. Fein and Pamela L. Stephens, John Wiley & Sons, New York, 1987
- For 'The Sikh Homeland', from *A History of the Sikhs, Vol. I and 2, 1839-1988,* Oxford University Press, 1991
- For excerpt from Iqbal's *Shikwa,* Oxford University Press, 1981
- For 'Bara Mah', from *Hymns of Guru Nanak,* Sangam Books, Orient Longman, 1978
- For 'Exchange of Lunatics', by Saadat Hasan Manto, from *Land of the Five Rivers,* Jaico Publishing House, 1965
- For 'The Death of Sheikh Burhanuddin', by Khwaja Ahmed Abbas, from *Land of the Five Rivers,* Jaico Publishing House, 1965
- For 'A Bride for the Sahib', 'Portrait of a Lady' and 'Posthumous' from *The Short Stories of Khushwant Singh,* Ravi Dayal Publisher
- For chapter from *Train to Pakistan,* Ravi Dayal Publisher
- For chapter from *I Shall Not Hear the Nightingale,* IBH Publishing Company, Bombay, 1970

FOREWORD

For Khushwant: An Acrostic Sonnet

King of the columnists and prince of hosts,
Hero of cats (twenty at least) who feed
Under your aegis, trencherman of toasts—
Scotch, naturally, not French—God knows we need
Humour and courage, tolerance and wit
When hope is scarce and murder's blessed by prayer,
And every bully, oaf, and hypocrite
Nurtures his flock on hatred and hot air.
Threats to your life have not made you less bold.
Sexcess can't spoil you. May you scatter your words
inimitably on for decades more—
No less amused and generous than your old
Grandmother, standing by the courtyard door,
Halting her prayers to feed and chide the birds.

Vikram Seth

INTRODUCTION

I first met Khushwant Singh as a college friend of his daughter Mala nearly fifty years ago. Khushwant Singh had already published the first volume of his scholarly and much-acclaimed *History of the Sikhs*, but nevertheless his public image was that of an irreverent iconoclast, and his second novel, *I Shall Not Hear the Nightingale*, had, according to the university grapevine, 'some damn sexy passages, yaar' (Mala extracted a promise from all her friends not to read *Nightingale*, otherwise she would be mortified each time we met her father. I kept my word, and read the novel for the first time only when selecting material for the first edition of this book, in 1992).

But to get back to that first meeting and that first impression almost fifty years ago . . . Khushwant Singh was engrossed in a book and looked none too pleased at being disturbed when we walked in. He quizzed us sharply on our Ancient Indian history syllabus, quickly plumbed the depth of our ignorance on the subject of Asokan edicts and, with a dismissive shrug, went back to his reading. My first impression was that of a bookish and rather strict paterfamilias, with little time to waste on small talk—definitely not a hearty Sardarji.

The next time I met him was as a junior member of his editorial staff at *New Delhi* magazine. Khushwant Singh had installed a special black glass partition between his office and the hall in which we worked and through this, he informed us triumphantly, he could see what we were up to, though we couldn't see him! A constant stream of visitors went in and out of his room every morning—comely ladies with literary aspirations, elderly men pushing a worthy cause or an obscure book for review; politicians and godmen; starlets and film makers; and every foreign writer or journalist who visited Delhi. Loud guffaws issued forth, and tantalizing whispers of gossip, while we strained our ears to overhear. Here then was Khushwant Singh as the Sardarji-in-the-Bulb, raconteur *par excellence* of ribald jokes and malicious gossip.

And then there was Khushwant Singh as Boss—kindly, avuncular, incredibly generous in the help and encouragement he gave younger journalists, and cheerfully taking the rap for all our mistakes. He also had, as we soon discovered, an enormous appetite for work—and no patience with shirkers.

But which is the real Khushwant Singh? The inspired translator of Guru Nanak's hymns or the irreverent chronicler of human foibles and vanities? The erudite historian who has written some of the most enduring books on the Sikhs and Punjab, or the best-selling author of full-blooded novels and short stories (many of them with 'damn sexy' passages)? The sensitive, observant nature-watcher and animal-lover, or the intrepid reporter on the trail of saints and sinners? The reflective introvert or the exuberant extrovert?

As this collection bears out, he is, of course, all of these; but through all his different avatars run several common threads—his total lack of humbug, hypocrisy and prudishness (the 'sexy passages' are, I am sure, part of his long-running crusade to rid Indians of their prudery and inhibitions); the vivid, lively style which makes him compulsively readable on any subject; and above all, the hugely infectious zest for life, for living and learning, that infuses all his work.

One of the aims of this anthology is to introduce the 'Complete Khushwant Singh' to his readers, many of whom, alas, know him only through his weekly 'Malice' column. For though it is the most widely-read column in India, and guaranteed to give a hefty boost to the circulation of any journal that carries it, it simply does not do justice to the range and depth of Khushwant Singh's talents and interests.

A typical Malice column would contain an entertaining vignette from Khushwant Singh's latest freebie junket abroad ('In the last thirty-five years I have not spent a single *naya paisa* of my own either towards travel or hospitality,' he confesses gleefully); a provocative comment on something in the news that week; a pithy book review; an indulgent plug for some young woman's artistic or literary endeavours; an obituary (perhaps speaking ill of the dead); an Urdu couplet and a Punjabi joke. But as I discovered when working with Khushwant Singh at the *Hindustan Times*, this weekly offering is like a tray of *hors-d'oeuvres* that he dishes up quickly and easily, even as he labours long and hard over a rich and substantial main course—it could be a long personality profile, an essay on religion or literature, or a new novel.

So while pieces from the Malice column have, of course, been included (among them a couple of obituaries to die for), the greater part of this book consists of selections from other genres. One of them is a lively play, *Tyger, Tyger Burning Bright* which lay buried and unpublished among piles of old manuscripts at Khushwant Singh's home, until he suddenly remembered it and dug it out when I was selecting material for the first edition of *Not a Nice Man to Know*. Inexplicably, it has never been performed, though there are plans for its stage debut to mark his ninety-sixth birthday in August 2011. The fiction selection also includes four short stories and excerpts from four novels—*Train to Pakistan*, widely accepted as one of the great novels on Partition; *I Shall Not Hear the Nightingale*; *Delhi*, and his most recent one, *The Sunset Club*. All of them bear eloquent testimony to Khushwant Singh's mastery of the art of story-telling—his narrative skill; his unerring ear for dialogue; his ability to create authentic, memorable characters; and his powerful evocation of time, mood and place. They also reveal a writer of depth.

Then, there are excerpts from his translations. Khushwant Singh professes to being an agnostic but his interest in religion has given rise to some fine translations, notably of Iqbal's *Shikwa* and Guru Nanak's *Bara Mah* which, retaining all the poetry and passion of the originals, for the first time bring these works to life in the English language.

The selections from Khushwant Singh's longer articles and essays for journals and newspapers cover a wide range of subjects—from the hanging of Bhutto (he was the only Indian journalist in Pakistan on that fateful day), to a profile of Mother Teresa, written under somewhat bizarre circumstances. Some time in the eighties, when Mother Teresa lay critically ill in a Calcutta nursing home, I phoned Khushwant Singh one morning from the *Indian Express* where I then worked. It seemed unlikely that she would survive the night, and the paper wanted him to write her obituary for the next day's front page. Late that night, after working non-stop all day to meet his deadline, Khushwant Singh delivered his article, and no sooner had it been typeset than Mother Teresa took a miraculous turn for the better—aided, perhaps, by his whole-hearted labour of love. The non-fiction selection also includes extracts from his autobiography, *Truth, Love and a Little Malice* and from *History of the Sikhs*; a marvellous treatise on the monsoon and a provocative essay on religion.

Last, but by no means least, are the jokes, selected by Khushwant Singh himself. My own favourite Khushwant Singh jokes have, alas, not been included—they are the ones he tells at his own expense. As editor of the *Hindustan Times* he usually came to work in a rumpled, paan-stained Pathan suit, driving his battered Ambassador himself. One evening, as he was driving out of the Hindustan Times building near Connaught Place, two attractive American women hailed him. Khushwant Singh immediately stopped, beaming at this stroke of luck, and speculating happily on why they seemed so eager to catch his attention. 'Taxi! Taj Hotel!' they said, rudely shattering his fantasies as they opened the back door and got in. Khushwant Singh obligingly—and silently—drove them to their destination, charged a fare of seven rupees (half the metered rate), accepted a two-rupee tip, and then sped back to the office—this was too good a story not to be shared immediately. But to really savour it, you had to have heard Khushwant Singh tell it himself—and it got better each time he retold it.

In 1992, when I was preparing the first edition of *Not a Nice Man to Know*, Khushwant Singh declared that his life's work was done, that he was living on borrowed time, and that apart from his autobiography he was unlikely to write anything more of substance. Over the last two decades, he's had to eat those words many times over (no doubt chasing them down with shots of his favourite Single Malt). His prolific and sparkling output since 1992 includes new collections of essays, translations and short stories, and no fewer than three novels; the last one, *The Sunset Club*, written in 2010, when he was ninety-five. All of them remain bestsellers. At ninety-six, he continues to follow a punishing daily schedule, rising at dawn and working without a break until sunset, turning out two weekly newspaper columns, apart from regular book reviews and essays. Last year, as he handed me the completed manuscript of *The Sunset Club*, he said he was thinking of starting on a new novel, set in Sujan Singh Park where he lives, and with characters based on some of his neighbours. With an impish twinkle in his eye, he added: 'I think I'll call it "Love Thy Neighbour".'

Of the original selection of thirty-three pieces in the first edition of this book, we have retained thirty, and added as many as eighteen new ones. Still, there is much that I reluctantly had to leave out for reasons of space; and many readers will, no doubt, complain that some of their own favourites are missing from this collection. We'll include those in the next edition of this book, that we hope to bring out to celebrate his 100th birthday.

Nandini Mehta
April 2011

COLUMNS

SEEING ONESELF

The gods in their wisdom did not grant me the gift of seeing myself as others see me. They must have thought knowing what others thought of me might engender suicidal tendencies in me and decided to let me stew in my own self-esteem. Now I am up against the formidable task of having to write about myself.

It is a daunting assignment. Have you ever tried to look at yourself squarely in the eyes in your own mirror? Try it and you will understand what I mean. Within a second or two you will turn your gaze from your eyes to other features—as women do when they are making-up or men do when they are shaving. Looking into the depths of one's own eyes reveals the naked truth. The naked truth about oneself can be very ugly.

I know I am an ugly man. Physical ugliness has never bothered me nor inhibited me from making overtures to the fairest of women. I am convinced that only empty-headed nymphomaniacs look out for handsome gigolos. They have no use for the likes of me; I have no use for the likes of them. My concern is not with my outward appearance, my untidy turban, unkempt beard or my glazed look (I have been told that my eyes are those of a lustful budmaash) but what lies behind the physical, the real me compounded of conflicting emotions like love and hate, general irritability and occasional equipoise, angry denunciation and tolerance of another's point of view, rigid adherence to self-prescribed regimen and accommodation of others' convenience. And so on. It is on these qualities that I will dwell in making an estimate of myself.

First, I must dispose of the question which people often ask me: 'What do you think of yourself as a writer?' Without appearing to wear the false cloak of humility, let me say quite honestly that I do not rate myself very highly. I can tell good writing from the not so good, the first rate from the passable. I know that of the Indians or the Indian-born, Nirad Chaudhuri, V.S. Naipaul, Salman Rushdie, Amitav Ghosh and Vikram Seth handle the English language better than I. I also know I can, and have, written as well as any of the others—R.K. Narayan, Mulk Raj Anand, Manohar Malgonkar, Ruth Jhabvala, Nayantara Sahgal or Anita Desai. What is more, unlike most in the first or the second category, I have never laid claim to being a great writer. I regard self-praise to be the utmost form of vulgarity. Almost every Indian writer I have met is prone to laud his or her achievements. This is something I have never done. Nor ever solicited awards or recognition. Nor ever spread false stories of being considered for the Nobel Prize for literature. The list of prominent Indians who spread such canards about themselves is formidable: Vatsyayan (Agyeya), G.V. Desani, Dr Gopal Singh Dardi (former Governor of Goa), Kamla Das and many others.

Am I a likeable man? I am not sure. I do not have many friends because I do not set much store by friendship. I have found that friends, however nice and friendly they may be, demand more time than I am willing to spare. I get easily bored with people and would rather read a book or listen to music than converse with anyone for too long. I have had a few very close friends in my time. I am ashamed to admit that when some of them dropped me, instead of being upset, I felt relieved. And when some died, I cherished their memory more than I did their company when they were alive.

I have the same attitude towards women whom I have liked or loved. It does not take much for me to get deeply emotional about women. Often at the very first meeting I feel I have found the Helen I was seeking, and like Majnoon sifting the sands of desert wastes my quest for Laila was over. None of these infatuations lasted very long. At times betrayal of trust hurt me deeply but nothing left lasting scars on my psyche. The only lesson I learnt was that as soon as you sense the others cooling off, be the one to drop them. Dropping people gives you a sense of triumph; being dropped one of defeat which leaves the ego wounded. I do not have the gift of friendship. Nor the gift of loving or being loved.

Hate is my stronger passion. Mercifully, it has never been directed against a community but only against certain individuals. I hate with a passion unworthy of anyone who would like to describe himself as civilized. I try my best to ignore them but they are like an aching tooth which I am periodically compelled to feel with my tongue to assure myself that it still hurts. My hate goes beyond people I hate. I drop people who befriend them. My enemy's friends become my enemies.

Hate does not always kill the man who hates, as is maintained by the sanctimonious. Unrepressed hate can often be a catharsis. Shakespeare could gnash his teeth with righteous hatred:

> You common cry of cours whose breath I hate
> As reek O' the rotten fens, whose loves I prize
> As the dead carcasses of unburied men
> That do corrupt the air.

Fortunately there are not many people I hate. I could count them on the tips of the fingers of one hand—no more than four or five. And if I told you why I hate them, you may agree that they deserve contempt and hatred.

I hate name-droppers. I hate self-praisers. I hate arrogant men, I hate liars. Is there anything wrong in hating them? People ask me, why can't you leave them alone? Why can't you ignore their existence? Now, that is something I cannot do. I cannot resist making fun of name-droppers, calling liars liars to their faces. And I love abusing the arrogant. I have been in trouble many times because of my inability to resist mocking these types. And since most name-droppers, self-praisers and arrogant men go from success to success, become ministers, Governors and win awards they don't deserve, my anger often explodes into denouncing them in print. I have been dragged into courts and before the Press Council. This can be a terrible waste of time and money. I think I will have wax images of my pet hates and vent my spleen on them by sticking pins in their effigies. May the fleas of a thousand camels infest their armpits!

I am not a nice man to know.

WHY I AM AN INDIAN

Why am I an Indian? I did not have any choice: I was born one. If the good Lord had consulted me on the subject I might have chosen a country more affluent, less crowded, less censorious in matters of food and drink, unconcerned with personal equations and free of religious bigotry.

Am I proud of being an Indian? I can't really answer this one. I can scarcely take credit for the achievements of my forefathers. And I have little to be proud of what we are doing today. On balance, I would say, 'No, I am not proud of being an Indian.'

'Why don't you get out and settle in some other country?' Once again I have very little choice. All the countries I might like to live in have restricted quotas for emigrants. Most of them, are white and have a prejudice against coloured people. In any case I feel more relaxed and at home in India.

I dislike many things in my country, mostly the government. I know the government is not the same thing as the country, but it never stops trying to appear in that garb. This is where I belong and this is where I intend to live and die. Of course I like going abroad. Living is easier, wine and food are better, women more forthcoming—it's more fun. However, I soon get tired of all those things and want to get back to my dung-heap and be among my loud-mouthed, sweaty, smelly countrymen. I am like my kinsmen in Africa and England and elsewhere. My head tells me it's better to live abroad, my belly tells me it is more fulfilling to be in 'phoren', but my heart tells me 'get back to India'. Each time I return home, and drive through the stench of bare-bottomed defecators that line the road from Santa Cruz airport to the city, I ask myself:

Breathes there the man with soul so dead
Who never to himself hath said
This is my own, my native land?

I can scarcely breathe, but I yell, 'Yeah, this is my native land. I don't like it, but I love it.'

Are you an Indian first and a Punjabi or Sikh second? Or is it the other way round? I don't like the way these questions are framed and if I am denied my Punjabiness or my community tradition, I would refuse to call myself Indian. I am Indian, Punjabi and Sikh. And even so I have a patriotic kinship with one who says I am 'Indian, Hindu and Haryanvi' or 'I am Indian, Moplah Muslim and Malayali.' I want to retain my religious and linguistic identity without making them exclusive in any way.

I am convinced that our guaranteed diversity is our strength as a nation. As soon as you try to obliterate regional language in favour of one 'national' language or religion, in the name of some one Indian credo, you will destroy the unity of the country. Twice was our Indianness challenged. In 1962 by the Chinese; in 1965 by the Pakistanis. Then, despite our many differences of language, religion and faith, we rose as one to defend our country. In the ultimate analysis, it is the consciousness of frontiers that makes a nation. We have proved that we are one nation.

What then is this talk about Indianizing people who are already Indian? And has anyone any right to arrogate to himself the right to decide who is and who is not a good Indian?

FAREWELL TO THE *ILLUSTRATED WEEKLY*

This column, written as Khushwant Singh's 'Farewell' to the *Illustrated Weekly,* was never published. On 25 July 1978, one week before he was to retire (and the week before this column was scheduled to appear), he was abruptly asked to leave 'with immediate effect'. Khushwant quietly got up, collected his umbrella, and without a word to his staff, left the office where he had worked for nine years, raising the *Illustrated Weekly's* circulation from 65,000 to 4,00,000. The new edition was installed the same day, and ordered by the *Weekly's* management to kill the 'Farewell' column.

I took over as editor of the *Illustrated Weekly of India* in June 1969. At the time I had no intention of staying at the job for more than two years. I found Bombay too large, too crowded and dirty. I deliberately avoided making friends so that the leaving would not be painful. I have been here nine long years; I thoroughly enjoyed my job and despite my resolution not to get too close to people, I made deep emotional attachments, the closest being to my journal which I nurtured as my own child. And now the time has come to say farewell I am unable to put on a false smile to say it.

I have no illusions of having been a 'distinguished' editor; the epithet is willy-nilly attached to everyone who holds the post. All my predecessors and I have done our jobs to the best of our abilities. Nevertheless each one left the stamp of his personality on the journal. Under the English editors it was a society magazine with a lot of tittle-tattle of cocktail parties and the goings-on in the brown sahibs' circles. Under its first two Indian editors it

9

became a vehicle of Indian culture, devoting most of its pages to art, sculpture, classical dance and pretty pictures of flowers, birds and dancing belles. It did not touch controversial subjects, was strictly apolitical and asexual (save occasional blurred reproductions of Khajuraho or Konarak). It earned a well-deserved reputation for dull respectability. I changed all that. What was a four-wheeled victoria taking well-draped ladies out to eat the Indian air I made a noisy, rumbustious, jet-propelled vehicle of information, controversy and amusement. I tore up the unwritten norms of gentility, both visual and linguistic. The initial reaction was like that of a maiden whose modesty had been outraged. Many representations were made to the management to sack me, the journal was blacklisted by many institutions and irate parents wrote to tell me that they were embarrassed to leave it lying about the house lest their children were corrupted by its contents. Mercifully, the denigrators were vastly outnumbered by those who were stimulated by the change. And circumstances took a fortuitous turn and there was no one who could have sacked me earlier. By then I was able to establish a rapport even with my detractors. However harsh and unmerited their criticism, I published it. And slowly the circulation built up, till the *Weekly* did become a weekly habit of the English-reading pseudo-elite of the country. It became the most widely read journal in Asia (barring Japan) because it reflected all the contending points of view on every conceivable subject: politics, economics, religion and the arts. My own views I confined to the one page which I reserved for myself. I did not say anything of world-shattering importance. Some readers were amused, some irritated—most ignored it. It was my ambition to make the *Weekly* into a national institution with a readership running into tens of millions. And I was supremely confident I could and would do that. Alas! that was not to be.

What more is there to say in a speech of farewell? Ah! Yes, I will miss Bombay—the sun coming up over Elephanta and lighting the harbour with its ships and sailing boats; the spectacular display of lights from Malabar Hill round the Bay to Nariman Point and beyond; the turbulent angry sea during the monsoons with waves dashing over Marine Drive; the jingle of dancers' bells practising into the late hours for the Ganpati immersion; the sun-drenched lawns of Azad and Cross Maidans with cricketers in white flannels like confetti on the green. The full moon shimmering on a placid sea. All these sights and much more: the men and women I cross on my way to the office. We do not know each other, no smiles of recognition are exchanged, but if I don't cross them at the usual point, I feel something will go wrong that day. It will be the same with *mian bhais* from whom I buy my fruit and paan, the Makapaw from whom I buy my *pao* and *unda,* the Bawaji who presses fresh papaya juice and the old Sardar who fries fish on the pavement. I will miss the ladies and pimps of the Colaba lanes whose bawdy language has enriched my vocabulary and the pye-dogs who wag their tails when they see me.

Then there are my colleagues with whom I have spent most hours of the day. All of us became members of the *Weekly* joint family of which I was *karta* for all these years. I will recall their sense of belonging and dedication with nostalgia for it was they more than I who took the *Illustrated Weekly* from the doctors'– dentists'–barbers' waiting-rooms into the homes of people who matter. I wish I was with them when the journal celebrates its centenary in 1980.

And I will miss my readers. Their letters of abuse, criticism and praise were my daily sustenance. It is curious that though I got to know only a few personally I was aware of their censorious and applauding presence all the time. Whatever success the *Weekly* achieved was largely due to the readers feeling that it was their magazine and they could say whatever they liked or disliked about it.

The old order changeth, yielding place to new, and god fulfils himself in many ways lest one editor perpetuate himself beyond the years prescribed to him. I had a good innings for which I give thanks to those who let me play it. I opened my score with an invocation to the god of auspicious beginnings, *Sri Ganesheya Namah*; I end with a reminder from the Mahabharata:

> As two pieces of wood floating in the ocean come together at one time and are again separated, even such is the union of living creatures in this world.

So farewell! I switch off the bulb in which I have sat with my Scotch and my scribbling pad.

The Haunted Simla Road

Many years ago the bells of St Crispins woke up the people of Mashobra on Sunday mornings. We threw open our windows and let the chimes flood into the room along with the sunlight. We watched the English folk coming from the hotels and houses for service. It was the only day in the week they were up before the local inhabitants. All morning, visitors continued to pour in from Simla in rickshaws, on horseback and on foot. At evensong when the religious were at prayer once more, the road to Simla echoed with the songs and laughter of people returning to the city.

The bells of St Crispins do not toll any more. The lychgate is padlocked and there is mildew on the golden letters of the church notice board. The haunts of the English holiday-makers, 'Wild Flower Hall' and 'Gables', have not had their shutters up since they were put down in the autumn of 1947. The only white people around are a couple of elderly missionary ladies who walk about briskly, stopping occasionally to inspect a wild flower, inhale the crisp mountain air holding their arms stiff at their sides with beatific expressions on their upturned faces. There is a young English writer in khaki shorts and sandals getting the feel of the country at the country liquor shop. Sometimes Italian priests from the monastery of San Damiano stray into the bazar to buy provisions.

Apart from the people little else has changed. There is the deckle-edged snow-line beyond the peaks of Shali in the north, and the vast plains of Hindustan towards the south; one can see the Sutlej winding its silvery serpentine course through the orange haze. There are the dense forests of deodar, fir and mountain hemlocks. There are the terraced fields with clusters of villages in their midst—and flat roofs with corn drying on them. All day long the lammergeyers circle in the deep blue of the sky or sit on crags amongst the rhododendrons, sunning themselves with their wings stretched out. Barbets call in the valleys and the cicadas drown the distant roar of the stream with their chirpings. Convoys of mules bell their way endlessly into the Himalayas with the muleteer's plaintive flute receding in the distance. A hill-woman's song rises above all other sounds and for one ecstatic minute fills the hills and valleys with its long melodious monotone. It ends abruptly and there again are the barbet, cicada, mule bells, the flute and the roar of the stream.

There are things that make you pause and wonder whether the British have really left. Houses which look like English country homes are still unoccupied and give the impression that they await their departed masters. Local inhabitants never tire of gassing about memsahibs who did their shopping in the bazar. Even now the bania will slip into quoting price for the pound instead of the seer or kilogram. An asthmatic old Sinhalese who made jams and pickles for hotel residents still refers wheezily to England as home and presses his syrupy rhubarb wines on his listeners with a toothless 'doch and dorres'. One comes across names and pierced hearts on trunks of trees that tell tales of romance which lichen and moss have not obliterated. Then there is the cuckoo—the English cuckoo—with its two distinct notes which people say was imported by an Englishman in a fit of nostalgia.

In the evening when the mules are tethered and muleteers sip tea or smoke their hookahs they tell of the many foreigners who had lived in and around Mashobra. The eccentric American missionary who converted the whole of the apple-growing valley of Kotgarh to Christianity and then converted them back to Hinduism; of an ayah who still haunts the house in which she was murdered by her master's wife; of the people who had simply abandoned homes they had built and lived in for many years because they could not be bothered to come back from England; of phantom rickshaws and phantom ladies riding side-saddle on phantom horses.

It is a long walk back from Mashobra to Simla. The road is deserted after sunset and only the lights of the city scattered in profusion on Jacko Hill keep your spirits up. On the right is the Koti Valley with its stream glistening like quick-silver and the soft glow of oil lamps that come on unnoticed in distant farmsteads. There is something which makes you keep looking back over your shoulder. You hear the stamp of rickshaw-pullers' feet and whiffs of perfume and cigar-smoke steal mysteriously across the moon-flecked road—and your heart is too full for words.

ME AND MY FILTHY LUCRE

I did not know why money is called filthy lucre. There is nothing filthy about a wad of crisp, new currency notes; nor shining silver rupee or five-rupee coins. Now I know. At the first World Punjabi Conference in Chandigarh, the convenors gave me a copy of the citation stating why I had been among the chosen Punjabis of the millennium, a silver plaque with two coins of the earliest Sikh currency depicting both sides with inscriptions in Persian. And a blue velvet pouch with a golden string—it contained the prize money of Rs 1,00,000. I expected it to be a crossed cheque; it was cash, a bundle of 500-rupee notes. My troubles began. I hurried back to Hotel Shivalik View, I had invited A.S. Deepak and Vandana Shukla to join me for lunch. I put the velvet bag containing the notes on the table so that I could keep my eyes on it.

'You want me to count them?' asked Deepak. 'It may be more than one lakh.'

I declined his offer. 'It will take you all afternoon to do so. It may be less than the promised one lakh.'

After lunch, I went to my room to have a siesta. I locked the room door from the inside, put my things in my bag but held the velvet bag under my pillow and dozed off. I woke up to make sure the bag was still there. And then dozed off again.

The room bell rang. I opened the door to let in two janitors. They said they had come to check if all the light bulbs were functioning. I had not complained about any having fused. They changed one bulb. I became suspicious.

I had to go to dine with the Kaushiks—Anil, who was in the Indian police service, and his wife, Sharda. I took the money with me. I could not put all of it in my pockets and so gave some of it to Deepak, who had come to fetch me, to put in his coat pocket.

In the Kaushiks's home, I mentioned the problem of having so much cash on my person. 'Let's have a look,' said Anil. He felt the wad of currency notes. 'Have you counted them?' he asked.

'No,' I replied, 'I will do that in Delhi.'

Back in my hotel room, I bolted the door from the inside, put the velvet pouch under my pillow and switched off the lights. I slept fitfully. Every little noise outside woke me up. I switched on the lights to make sure no one had broken into my room. I felt under my pillow to make sure the velvet pouch was still there. I must have got up at least four times that night, the longest of the year. I was finally woken up by the operator announcing it was 6 a.m. and the room bearer bringing in a tray with a glass of fresh orange juice and coffee. My throat was sore. I went down with a heavy cold. It was the one lakh rupees in cash which brought it on.

On the train to Delhi, I hugged the pouch against my chest. It was very awkward with a running nose and streaming eyes. However, I managed to get the money safely home. I dumped the pouch in my granddaughter's lap and said, 'Take the bloody lucre as a New Year gift.' And soon my nose stopped dripping and my eyes stopped watering. That proves how filthy lucre can be.

On Old Age

Whenever my son, living in Mumbai, was asked why he was going to Delhi, his reply was 'to see my A. Pees'. A.P. stood for aged parents. Now that he is himself what in modern parlance is described as a senior citizen, and his mother has passed away, he answers the same question, saying 'to see old Pop'.

With the passing of generations, younger people's attitude towards the old has changed. When I was a young man, we used to describe aged people as oldies, or worse sattreah bahattreah (feeble-minded in his seventies). Now persons in their seventies are not considered old. New attitudes and a sizeable vocabulary have been evolved to describe them. For one, their way to show respect to the aged is to keep a respectful distance from them. So we have old people's homes, a good distance from the homes they once lived in and ruled over. There is much to be said in favour of old people's homes. The few that I have visited in England and USA are as luxurious as any five-star hotel; separate cottages with modern amenities like world radio and TV, spacious dining and sitting rooms where you can meet and chat with others in your own age group; light, tasty food and wines, billiards rooms, card tables for bridge, rummy or patience. There are spacious lawns and flower beds. Above all, there are nurses and doctors in attendance round the clock. They cost a packet. Inmates are happy blowing up their life's savings to live out their last days in comfort because they are aware they can't take anything with them when they go. Their offspring don't grudge pitching in because they are relieved of the responsibility of looking after their parents and can get on with their own lives. The notion of a family gathered around the bed of a dying patriarch or matriarch is as dead as a dodo.

However much I approve of old people's homes, I resent being described as a gerry (for geriatric), old boomer, fuddy-duddy, gaffer or old fogey (for god father), codger, coot, geezer, etc. Some new coinages like dinosaur, fossil, cotton top, cranky, crumbly are downright offensive. Eighty years ago Chesterton wrote in his essay, 'The Prudery of Slang': 'There was a time when it was customary to call a father a father . . . Now, it appears to be considered a mark of advanced intelligence to call our father a bean or a scream. It is obvious to me that calling the old gentleman "father" is facing the facts of nature. It is also obvious that calling him a "bean" is merely weaving a graceful fairytale to cover the facts of nature.' Call us oldies or what you will, but bear in mind that just as a *saas bhi kabhi bahu thhi* (the mother-in-law was once a bride), you too will one day become an old person and slang words like codger, geezer or fuddy-duddy can be hurtful even to an oldie who is hard of hearing.

I am not quite deaf but getting more hard of hearing by the day. Friends are too polite to draw my attention to my growing infirmity but members of my family are more outspoken. My wife who, has been dead for many years, never spared me when I asked her to repeat what she had said with a question, 'Hain?' She would snap back and exclaim: 'Dora! Why don't you have your ears examined?'

Now everytime a stranger calls on me, my son, if he is around, tells him or her, 'Speak a little loudly. My pop is hard of hearing.' And the other day my daughter asked me, 'Aren't you thinking of getting a hearing aid?'

There are pros and cons about hearing aids. I had a Canadian friend, a well-known art critic who had one connected to a battery tucked into his front pocket. I asked him if it was a nuisance. 'No,' he replied firmly. 'I have it switched on when I am out on the road so that I can hear cars hoot to get out of their way.

I also have it on when attending musical concerts. It's only at parties when people begin to bore me that I switch it off and switch on a smile to appear as if I am all ears.'

Two of my friends acquired hearing aids: Prem Kirpal, at ninety-six, got one from Paris at the enormous price of Rs 1.5 lakh. He hardly ever used it. When I asked him why, he replied: 'The battery will run out and I'll have to get another one from Paris.'

Bharat Ram, who is the same age as me, also uses a hearing aid but has to cup his ears to catch what anyone is saying. The artist Satish Gujral lost his hearing as a child and was more than able to cope with life: he was able to teach himself to speak in English without being able to hear what he was saying. Then he found a living hearing aid in his comely wife, Kiran, who has taught him to read her lips and hand gestures. He gets over his handicap by doing most of the talking and reducing what he has to hear to the minimum. Some years ago he went to Australia for an ear surgery which would restore his hearing to normal. For some months he kept up the pretence that he could hear sounds he hadn't heard before. Actually the surgery did nothing for him. He is back to his more reliable hearing aid—his wife.

I am not yet a gone case. I can hear people sitting close to me without much difficulty. I have problems hearing people who speak too softly, go on at the speed of machine-gun fire or go on interminably mimi, mim, mimi. Then I assume the mien of the smiling Buddha and occasionally grunt to indicate I am following what is being said. My only fear is that the person might ask me a question. I answer it with a benign smile. I also have problem answering telephone calls. Young people, mainly girls, are awed, as if they were talking to an ogre, and say what they have to at a breathless speed. I have to admonish them, 'Please speak slowly and clearly as I am hard of hearing. It would be better if you spelt out what you have to say on paper. I can see better than I can hear.'

So far I have got away with it. I still enjoy classical music on my satellite radio, follow the news and comments on TV channels. If I am hard of hearing, it's other people's problem, not mine. But use a hearing aid to help them out? No. I often wonder if deaf people are cremated or buried with ear plugs and batteries or sent to the other world as deaf, as they were on the day they died.

Sometimes old people in their eighties write to me about the problems of life in its decline. They complain about increasing helplessness, being neglected by their sons, daughters-in-law and grandchildren. Their chief complaint is loneliness: they do not know how to pass their time. Being old, they get little sleep and are up well before dawn. They believe in god, say their prayers, go to temples, gurdwaras and churches or offer namaaz five times a day; and yet time hangs heavy on them. What are they to do?

I am older than most of them. I have old-age problems like rotting teeth having to be replaced by false ones, glasses changed periodically because my vision is getting poorer by the day, having to use hearing aids, carrying a walking stick to prevent myself from falling, taking dozens of pills against fluctuating blood pressure, an enlarged prostrate, an irregular heartbeat etc. But I manage to get at least six hours of sleep at night, despite having to get up twice or thrice to empty my bladder, and another hour in the afternoon. I too get up before dawn.

Since I do not believe in god or prayers, my mind turns to more earthly problems. Will my bowels move properly this morning? Should I drink more orange-carrot juice and glasses of water to help me clear my stomach? When I get a good clearing, I am relieved and happy. When I do not, it weighs on my mind. I am edgy and ill-tempered. It affects my work. I do not grumble about being neglected by my children and grandchild. They do their best to look after my needs—see that I eat what I want, take me to doctors, dentists and opticians. They know I prefer to be left alone, so they leave me alone. Time does not hang heavy on me because I always have something to occupy my mind. My days pass as swiftly as a weaver's shuttle.

What advice do I give them? First, reduce your dependency on others to the very minimum and do your best to be as self-sufficient as you can. Fill your time by doing things that occupy your mind and time. Don't waste time on muttering prayers you don't understand but meditate by stilling your mind from wandering. A minute or two will be good enough. If you can't read or watch TV because they strain your eyes, listen to good music on your radio with complete attention. Sit in a park and watch birds, butterflies and insects—not just look at them but watch them closely, try to identify them, read about them and add to your knowledge of nature. Cultivate hobbies like collecting stamps, preserving leaves and flowers, origami—whatever you fancy. Even learn how to knit your own sweaters and socks. Free yourself of the hunger for human company. Befriend dogs, cats, birds—they will respond to your affection more than human beings. Equally important is to cut down on your food intake. Get up from your dining table with hunger unfulfilled: you will then look forward to enjoying your next meal and keep thinking about it. What you eat and drink will taste better. When fully occupied mentally, time will never hang heavy on you. You wake up and before you realize it the day is over and it is time to retire to bed for the night. You will enjoy sound sleep.

Both Zohra Sehgal, who is two years older than me, and her Pakistani sister Uzra Butt, who is two years my junior, are fitter than I am, both in mind and body. Zohra has a phenomenal memory. She can recite reams of Urdu poetry by the hour without looking at a scrap of paper; I learnt Uzra does much the same in Lahore. The two sisters conceived, concocted and enacted a dialogue between them, *Ek Thee Nani* (Once There Was a Grandmother), which draws packed houses in India and Pakistan. What is the secret of their physical and mental fitness? From Zohra I gathered she eats very little and lives largely on soups and broths. She spends an hour every morning on the roof strolling about and refreshing her memory of Urdu poetry. She has cut down her social life to the minimum and refuses to give interviews either on the phone or in person unless it is paid for. I chided her when she came to wish me on my ninetieth birthday. I said, 'Zohra, I hear you charge a fee for talking to anyone. Is that true?' She beamed a smile and held out the open palm of her hand, 'Haan—yes, lao fees do, pay me at once.'

From Uzra I picked up another clue to longevity. The sisters had been with Prithvi Theatre and then with Uday Shanker's dance troupe doing Bharatanatyam. I asked Uzra whether she was still dancing. 'There are not many takers for Bharatanatyam in Pakistan. But this time in India I have been learning Odissi—it is less mechanical and more sensuous. I find it more fulfilling.' I was amazed: to learn a new form of dance at the age of eighty-eight is truly defying the passage of the years. Clearly, if you want to prolong your life, look forward to doing something in the tomorrows to come.

It is most important that an old person reconciles himself to the fact that he has become old and does not try to behave like a young man; if he does so, he will only make an ass of himself. It has been truly said: *Jawaanee jaatee rahee / Aur hamein pataa bhee na chalaa / Usee ko dhoond rahey hain / Kamar jhukai hooey* (Youth had fled / And I did not know about it / I seek for it on the ground / With my back bent double).

No matter how well a person may look after himself, with age, parts of his body begin to decay. Teeth rot and have to be replaced with dentures. That necessitates radical changes in our diet. No more tough meat or vegetables or fruit that need to be bitten into with sharp teeth. So in every home that has an old man, a parallel menu has to be made to cater to his needs. Eyes go bleary. Lucky is an old man who does not have to wear spectacles and is able to read newspapers or watch television. I still do both but only just.

Hearing becomes defective and one may need a hearing aid. I am sure my hearing is sound but my friends tell me it is not. Memory begins to play tricks. I still pride mine: I can recite passages of poetry by the yard and hardly ever consult the telephone directory to dial a number. But I do forget faces, even those of pretty girls, and have problems recalling names. It does not bother me very much.

What bothers me is having to slow down, and my inability to walk without the help of a walking stick. I recall the days of my youth when I walked from Simla to Narkanda and back non-stop—72 miles. Now I am reduced to doing a few rounds of my little garden and am scared of walking on an uneven path lest I stumble and break one of my bones. That is often the prelude to the end of an old man's life. Old people become slothful, slovenly and lazy. I never suffered from the daily bath fetish. I find rubbing the vital parts of my body with a damp towel as cleansing as immersing myself in a tub or pouring lota-fulls of water on my body. I no longer bother to change for the night and sleep in the same clothes I wear all day long. When I eat, soup, daal and curry drip on my beard and on to my shirt. People around me find it repulsive. I could not care less.

More serious is the problem created by an enlarged prostate gland. The urge to empty one's bladder often does not give one the time to get to a urinal. You wet your trousers or salwar. It is best to pretend you splashed water carelessly. Others know the truth but maintain a polite silence.

With old age, values change. Bowel movements become sluggish. One has to resort to laxatives to ensure proper evacuation. It's odd but an old man's day begins with worrying about his bowels. If he gets a clear evacuation he feels as if he has conquered the fort of Chittorgarh. If he does not, he remains cranky for the rest of the day.

I keep going with the help of a variety of pills, twenty every day. I grumble but I know they keep me alive and kicking.

It is true that a person is himself not aware of the passage of years: he may have turned grey, lost his teeth, become hard of hearing and may barely be able to see, but his vanity prevents him from accepting that he has grown old and senile.

It is other people, mostly children, who rudely remind him

that he has aged. Boys and girls who used to called him uncle start addressing him daadoo or naanoo. The other day a family accosted me in Lodhi park. The mother asked her four-year-old son to touch my feet. The child looked me up and down, shouted 'buddha'—old fellow—and ran away. I was mortified.

I delude myself that I have not really become a buddha. My friends have but I still have a sparkle in my eyes and my heart is as young as it ever was. One of my lady friends, twenty years younger than me, is now a grandmother and has turned grossly fat. I continue to pay her compliments as I did thirty years ago when she was fair and saucy. The truth is encapsulated in another couplet:

Begum, teri husn ke hukkey mein aanch nahin;
Ik ham hee hain
Ki phir bhee gudgudai jaatey hain.
(Begum, there is no fire left
In the hookah of your beauty;
It is only I who still keeps drawing on it.)

You can't do very much about old age. It creeps up on you at a snail's pace to start with, then gathers speed in your middle age, and before you know it, you are an old man or woman. The symptoms appear in different people at different times: hair starts turning grey; some people start greying in their thirties, others in their fifties or sixties; some manage to have black hair into their seventies.

Many dye their hair and beards to appear younger than they are and manage to fool others for some time, but not themselves. There are changes in the body that make you aware of the relentless march of time. Your teeth begin to decay. Everytime you visit your dentist, he yanks one out till all are gone and he fits you with dentures that look whiter than the originals.

Once again, the age when people start losing their teeth varies enormously. Some lose them in their forties, others go to their graves or funeral pyres in their eighties or nineties taking all their thirty-two originals with them. The same applies to the eyes and ears; some wear glasses while still at school; others need no visual aid till the end of their days.

Some begin to turn hard of hearing by middle age and need hearing aids; others never have hearing problems. The most important milestone in people's lives is the state of their libido.

Both men and women regard a declining interest in sex as a sure indicator of ageing. With men this is more dramatic than with women, who can enjoy sex long after their menopause. Men continue to fantasize about it all their lives but sometime after they have completed the biblical span of seventy years, they find their bodies unable to fulfill their desire; their minds remain as potent as ever, their organs let them down.

And they have to accept that they are into old age and the fun has gone out of their lives. This is what men need most—as Nazeer Akbara Bedi put it: *Har cheez se hota hai bura burhaapa/ Aashiq ko to Allah na dikhlaaye burhaapa.* (Of all things that happen, the worst is old age / May Allah never afflict a lover with old age.)

Men never give up the hope of recovering their youth. They try all sorts of elixirs, aphrodisiacs (kushtas) and now Viagra to retain their potency. They may succeed in restoring a little self-confidence and ability to perform. Women find it harder than men to accept old age. They are prone to lying about it and use cosmetics liberally to hide their wrinkles. It takes a brave man to go on paying compliments to an old flame in her older incarnation.

Very reluctantly men give up hope of recovering their youth. The French comedian and singer, Maurice Chevalier, very rightly remarked, 'When you hit seventy, you eat better, you sleep more soundly, you feel more active than when you were thirty. Obviously, it is healthier to have women on your mind than on your knees.'

Chevalier also has the ultimate answer to growing old: 'Old age isn't bad when you consider the alternative.'

Old age need not be an unmitigated curse. It has many advantages. You are freed of ambition to achieve more. 'Of making many books, there is no end and much study is weariness of the flesh,' says the Bible. One can take liberties with young girls because they know and you know it will never go beyond a warm hug. One can get away with bad manners; people forgive you as a cranky, old grey-beard.

In my late eighties, I enjoy reading pornography. Old bawdy songs come back to my mind. One favourite used to be a Punjabi doggerel about a white bearded lusty bony. It began with '*toomba vajdaee na, taar bina* (she cannot live without her lover)'. It went on to describe the antics of the buddha baba who was '*vadda bajogee*' (great miracle man, very clever). He made love to a she-camel by climbing a ladder; he spent the night in the brothel and left his companion with a counterfeit four-anna piece ('*chavanni khotee*'). Old age need not be dull or boring.

Eighteen years ago when I was editor of the *Hindustan Times*, I was usually the first to be in office and the last of the editorial staff to return home, often after midnight. K.K. Birla who owned the paper once asked me, '*Sardar sahib, aap ka* retire *hone ka koi* programme *nahin hai?*' I replied, '*Birlaji*, retire *to main Nigambodh Ghat mein hee hoonga*'—meaning that I would give up work only when I was carried feet first to the cremation ground. I was then in my seventies. Now I am past my eighties and am having second thoughts on the subject. I still manage to rise at 4.30 a.m. and work almost non-stop till 7 p.m. Not being religious I do not waste time on prayer or meditation. My motto still remains 'Work is worship but worship is not work'. I hope I will be able to stick to this motto till the last day of my life.

However, I am coming around to the view that there may be something in the traditional Hindu belief of the four stages of human existence—Brahmacharya (bachelorhood), Grihastha (house-holder), Vaanprastha (retiring to a forest abode) and Sanyasa (solitude) each of a span of twenty-five years. Guru Nanak described what happens to person who lives into the nineties. In a hymn in Raga Mauha, he wrote (I use G.S. Makin's translation from *The Essence of Sri Guru Granth Sahib*): 'A human being spends the first ten years of his life in childhood, up to 20 years in growing up, at 30 he blossoms into a handsome youth, at 40 he attains full growth: at 50 he starts feeling weak: at 60 he feels old, at 70 he feels the weakening of his senses, at 80 he is not capable of doing any work and at 90 he keeps lying down and does not understand the basic reasons of all the weaknesses.'

Nature has its own calendar of ageing. Human societies in different parts of the world have evolved norms to suit their social structure. By nature's calendar both males and females may be regarded to be in their infancy till they are old enough to procreate, that is in the case of the female when she begins to menstruate and in that of the male when he is able to fertilize the female. However, human societies prescribe different ages for when they are allowed to do so. So we have legal bars against marriages below certain ages and we provide deterrents against having too many children. The common use of contraceptives makes this possible. The reproductive phase of females comes to an end with menopause, while that of males lasts much longer but with rapidly decreasing capability. Both males and females are at the peak of their physical prowess between the ages of eighteen and thirty-five. Thereafter their bodies begin to decline but their mental faculties remain unimpaired for many more years to come. Nevertheless, man-made rules require them to retire by the time they are sixty. So is human nature in conflict with human rites and laws throughout a person's existence? In addition, medical sciences have made spectacular advances which ensure us much longer lives in good health than our ancestors could have envisaged. Their neatly made-up calendars of the spans and stages of life no longer hold good.

Guru Nanak lived for seventy years (1469–1539). With the kind of medicines and medical expertise available at that time, one can well understand that by fifty, a man started feeling weak, at sixty old, at seventy his senses (sight, hearing, taste etc.)

began to deteriorate, by eighty he was unfit to do any work and at ninety he was largely confined to his charpoy. As one of the Guru's followers, I can cite my own case. I am close to being ninety. Although my vision is poor, I am hard of hearing and can only hobble around my house, I do not spend most of my time lying in bed. I work much harder than I have ever before. Among my present-day pre-occupations is to read the Guru's bani and translate it into English.

As for the Hindu division of life into four periods, I have been in the fourth, i.e. sanyasa, for quite some time. But it has my own definition. It means having contact with the outside world to the minimum but enjoying all the creative comforts at home (*ghar hi main udaasa*). I have no intention of entering the actual sanyasa. Where in the jungle will I find a doctor or a dentist when I need one?

In view of advances made in the standards of hygiene and medicine I think the period of grihastha should be doubled, as most men are capable of producing their best upto their seventies. For them Vaanprastha should not necessarily mean retiring to an ashram or its modern counterpart, an old people's home, but while staying with their families gradually withdraw from decision-making—let their sons and / or daughters take over the family business, give up directorships of companies and being on the governing bodies of clubs, schools, colleges, hospitals etc. Also, cut down travel and their social life to the necessary minimum. That will give them more time to be with themselves and prepare them for the fourth and final stage of their life's journey.

Sanyasa no longer requires them to become a lonely wanderer. I do not recommend spending time in places of worship as that amounts to an admission of inability to be alone. If they need the solace of religion or prayer, let them indulge in them at home. There are other things they could do to distract their minds: work in the garden if they have one, grow potted plants, paint, listen to music, best of all, immerse themselves in books, all kinds of books, and if so inclined, write. I am quite happy living in sanyasa without becoming a sanyasi. I mean to keep reading books, all kinds of books, till my eyes give up on me. And I mean to keep writing till the pen drops out of my hand.

My youngest brother, who among other things owned a restaurant and made it a point to be the last to leave, would often tell me, 'K. Singh, of two things you can never be sure: one, when a person may drop in to have a meal, and two, when death will come to you.'

A vaidji whom I often visited in his shop while taking an after-dinner stroll disagreed. He said death gives you many signals before it finally arrives to take you away. He quoted an anecdote of a wealthy man who became a friend of Yama, the messenger of death. One day he made a request to Yama, 'You and I have been close friends for many years. I ask you for just one favour: please give me timely warning that my time on earth will soon be over so that I can arrange my worldly affairs before I go.' Yama agreed to do so. However, one day the wealthy man suddenly died, leaving his business in a mess. When he met Yama he complained bitterly of having been let down by his friend. 'Not at all,' protested Yama, 'instead of one warning I gave you several. First I made your hair turn grey, then I deprived you of your teeth; then I made you hard of hearing and impaired your vision. Finally I made you feeble of mind. If you still chose to ignore these warning signals, you can only blame yourself.'

It is true that an enfeebled mind is, as it were, the final alarm bell for the start of a long march to the unknown. Other things you may learn to live with, but a mindless existence is like being dead while continuing to breathe. Alec Douglas Home summed it up in a doggerel:

To my deafness I'm accustomed,
To my dentures I'm resigned,
I can manage my bi-focals,
But oh how I miss my mind.

This view is confirmed by a physiotherapist:

Man is not old when his hair turns grey
Man is not old when his teeth decay,
But man is approaching his long last sleep
When his mind makes appointments
His body cannot keep.

The trouble with us humans is that we begin to think of death only in our old age. In our young years time hangs heavy and we delude ourselves into believing it will go on for ever and ever.

Time picks up speed as we grow old:

When as a child I laughed and wept
Time crept
When as a youth I dreamt and talked
Time walked.
When I became a full-grown man
Time ran.
And later as older I grew
Time flew.
Soon shall I find when travelling on
Time gone.
Will Christ have saved my soul by then?
Amen!

Happy Families

Much has been written about what it takes to make a happy family. It is like casting pearls of wisdom before swine. I can count the number of happy families I know on half the fingers of one hand; unhappy families, by the score. Also, happy families tend to be self-centred, unwelcoming towards outsiders, and uniformly boring. On the other hand, however awkward it may be to visit an unhappy family, you will find a lot of individuality amongst its members (which is why they find it difficult to get on with each other) and they are usually more interesting.

I can think of only one family which was held out as an example of an ideally integrated home. I stayed with them many times. I was always made to feel like an intruder and a poor relation. They spent their time praising each other and running down everyone else. The children, far from growing up into healthy, successful men and women, fell by the roadside as non-entities.

The base of every family is its children. Neglect them, and you erode the very foundations on which the family edifice is built. You achieve the same negative result by mollycoddling them. The family tree is meant to shelter them from the rain and the scorching sun while they are juveniles. Once they are adults, the umbilical cord must be finally cut, they must be exposed to the harsh world, learn to make their own decisions, make their own mistakes and pay for them. But make sure that the nucleus of the family home remains intact so that they can return to it to lick their wounds till they are ready to face the world again.

No one can prescribe rules for a happy family. There must be some kind of bonding like being together at meals, going out together to the pictures or picnics, and if you are believers, worshipping together. I have found that in families which have books in their homes for different age groups, there is usually more interaction between its members, less contention and more harmony. A bookless home is no home. A bookless family is less likely to hang together than one in which members have other things than making money and scandals on their minds.

We all know by experience that families whose members are at variance with each other are the most unhappy because it does not take much to change bonds of affection into bitter hatred. In such situations, it is best to break the family up and let everyone go his or her own way.

PREPARE FOR DEATH WHILE ALIVE

I do not know when I was born, because in my village, no records of births or deaths were maintained. And in my part of western Punjab, no one bothered with such things as horoscopes. My father was away in Delhi; my mother, who was barely literate, did not think birthdays were of any importance. My year of birth was put down later as 1915—it could as well have been 1914 or 1916—and my father put down 2 February as my date of birth. His mother, who was there when I was born, told me later that her son had got it all wrong and that I was born in mid-August. So I am right in saying that I am not sure when I was born. And I cannot say when I will die except that it will not be too long from now. By any reckoning I am eighty-five years old, give or take a year.

Humra Qureshi had come to interview me on what she assumed was my eighty-fifth birthday, for a column she writes for the *Times of India*. After putting me through the usual routine of questions about my past and present, she came to the final 'What now?' I did not give a very coherent answer on what I planned to do in the years left to me. However, after she left I pondered over the matter for a long time. Socrates had advised, 'always be occupied in the practice of dying'. How does one practice dying? The Dalai Lama, then only fifty-eight, advised meditating on it. I am not sure how thinking about it can help. It is particularly difficult for someone like me who has rejected belief in god and the possibility of another life after death, be it reincarnation or the Day of Judgement followed by heaven or hell. However, there

34

comes a time when one stops regarding death as something that comes to other people with the realization that you too are on the waiting list. If you are taken ill, you begin to think about it sooner than if you are in good physical shape. In either case, by the time you are in your eighties, it begins to preoccupy your mind more and more. You think of what you could have done in your life but failed to do. You wanted to become a millionaire but did not go beyond accumulating a modest bank balance; you wanted to become prime minister of India, a champion tennis player, cricketer, golfer, athlete etc., but did not get beyond being part of the second eleven of your college team or a mediocre club player. Or, in my case, I wanted to win many literary awards, earn huge royalties but ended up as a second-rate book writer who would be forgotten a few years after he was gone. So the first thing to get over through meditation or just pondering, is the feeling of regret over your failures—you did your best but it was not good enough to get you to the top. So what?

Equally important is to get over the sense of guilt for having wronged other people. Everyone of us causes hurt to someone or the other in our lives. This rankles in our minds. It is advisable to make amends by expressing regret. Having peace of mind should be a person's top priority in the final years of his life. Prayers, pilgrimages and religious rituals are not as effective as candid confession and seeking forgiveness. There also comes a time when you begin to regard your body as no more than something which encases your real self, like an envelope that contains a letter with a vital message. The body will perish when the envelope is torn open; will anything survive after the body is gone? Will the letter inside the torn envelope be something worth reading after the envelope ceases to exist? I do not have answers to these questions, and none of the answers given by people who believe that something of us survives after death, makes sense to me.

All I hope for is that when death comes to me, it comes swiftly, without much pain; like fading away in sound slumber. Till that time I will strive to live as full a life as I did in my younger days. My inspirations are Dylan Thomas's immortal lines:

> Do not go gentle into that good night,
> Old age should burn and rage at close of day;
> Rage, rage against the dying of the light.

One should prepare oneself to die like a man; no moaning, groaning or crying for reprieve. Allama Iqbal put it beautifully:

> Nishaan-e-mard-e-Momin ba to goyam?
> Choon margaayad, tabassum bar lab-e-ost

(You ask me for signs of a man of faith? When death comes to him, he has a smile on his lips.)

PROFILES

Amrita Shergil

I am hardly justified in describing Amrita Shergil as a woman in my life. I met her only twice. But these two meetings remain imprinted in my memory. Her fame as an artist, her glamour as a woman of great beauty which she gave credence to in some of her self-portraits, and her reputation for promiscuity, snowballed into a veritable avalanche which hasn't ended to this day, gives me an excuse to include her in my list.

One summer, her last, I heard that she and her Hungarian cousin–husband who was a doctor had taken an apartment across the road from where I lived in Lahore. He meant to set up a medical practice; she, her painting studio. Why they chose to make their home in Lahore, I have no idea. She had a large number of friends and admirers in the city. She also had rich, landowning relatives on her Sikh father's side who regularly visited Lahore. It seemed as good a place for them to start their lives as any in India.

It was June 1941. My wife had taken our seven-month-old son, Rahul, for the summer to my parents' house 'Sunderban' in Mashobra, seven miles beyond Simla. I spent my mornings at the High Court gossiping with lawyers over cups of coffee or listening to cases being argued before judges. I had hardly any case to handle myself. Nevertheless, I made it a point to wear my black coat, white tabs around the collar and carry my black gown with me to give others an appearance of being very busy. I returned home for lunch and a long siesta before I went to play tennis at the Cosmopolitan Club.

One afternoon I came home to find my flat full of the fragrance of expensive French perfume. On the table in my sitting room-cum-library was a silver tankard of chilled beer. I tiptoed to the kitchen and asked my cook about the visitor. 'A memsahib in a sari,' he informed me. He had told her I would be back any moment for lunch. She had helped herself to a bottle of beer from the fridge and was in the bathroom freshening up. I had little doubt my uninvited visitor was none other than Amrita Shergil.

For several weeks before her arrival in Lahore I had heard stories of her exploits during her previous visits to the city before she had married her cousin. She usually stayed in Faletti's Hotel. She was said to have made appointments with her lovers with two-hour intervals—at times six to seven a day—before she retired for the night. If this was true (men's gossip is less reliable than women's) love formed very little part of Amrita's life. Sex was what mattered to her. She was a genuine case of nymphomania, and according to her nephew Vivan Sundaram's published account, she was also a lesbian. Her modus vivendi is vividly described by Badruddin Tyabji in his memoirs. One winter when he was staying in Simla, he invited Amrita to dinner. He had a fire lit for protection from the cold and European classical music was playing on his gramophone. He wasted the first evening talking of literature and music. He invited her again. He had the same log fire and the same music. Before he knew what was happening, Amrita simply took her clothes off and lay stark naked on the carpet. She did not believe in wasting time. Even the very proper Badruddin Tyabji got the message.

Years later Malcolm Muggeridge, the celebrated author, told me that he had spent a week in Amrita's parents' home in Summer Hill, Simla. He was then in the prime of his youth—his early twenties. In a week she had reduced him to a rag. 'I could not cope with her,' he admitted. 'I was glad to get back to Calcutta.'

A woman with the kind of reputation Amrita enjoyed drew men towards her like iron filings to a magnet. I was no exception. As she entered the room, I stood up to greet her. 'You must be

Amrita Shergil,' I said. She nodded. Without apologizing for helping herself to my beer she proceeded to tell me why she had come to see me. They were mundane matters which robbed our first meeting of all romance. She wanted to know about plumbers, dhobis, carpenters, cooks, bearers etc. in the neighbourhood whom she could hire. While she talked I had a good look at her. Short, sallow-complexioned, black hair severely parted in the middle, thick sensual lips covered in bright red lipstick, stubby nose with blackheads visible. She was passably good looking but by no means a beauty.

Her self-portraits were exercises in narcissism. She probably had as nice a figure as she portrayed herself in her nudes but I had no means of knowing what she concealed beneath her sari. What I can't forget is her brashness. After she had finished talking, she looked around the room. I pointed to a few paintings and said, 'These are by my wife; she is an amateur.' She glanced at them and scoffed, 'That is obvious.' I was taken aback by her disdain but did not know how to retort. More was to come.

A few weeks later I joined my family in Mashobra. Amrita was staying with the Chaman Lals who had rented a house above my father's. I invited them for lunch. The three of them—Chaman, his wife Helen and Amrita, came at midday. The lunch table and chairs were lined on a platform under the shade of a holly oak which overlooked the hillside and a vast valley. My seven-month-old son was in the playpen teaching himself how to stand up on his feet. He was a lovely child with curly brown locks and large questioning eyes. Everyone took turns to talk to him and compliment my wife for producing such a beautiful boy. Amrita remained lost in the depths of her beer mug. When everyone had finished, she gave the child a long look and remarked, 'What an ugly little boy!' Everyone froze. Some protested at the unkind remark. But Amrita was back to drinking her beer. After our guests had departed, my wife said to me very firmly, 'I am not having that bloody bitch in my house again.'

Amrita's bad behaviour became the talk of Simla's social circle. So did my wife's comment on her. Amrita got to know what my wife had said and told people, 'I will teach that bloody woman a lesson she won't forget; I will seduce her husband.'

I eagerly awaited the day of seduction. It never came. We were back in Lahore in the autumn. So were Amrita and her husband. One night her cousin Gurcharan Singh (Channi) who owned a large orange orchard near Gujranwala turned up and asked if he could spend the night with us, as Amrita, who had asked him over for the weekend, was too ill to have him stay with her. The next day, other friends of Amrita's dropped in. They told us that Amrita was in a coma and her parents were coming down from Summer Hill to be with her. She was an avid bridge player and in her semi-conscious moments mumbled bridge calls. The next morning I heard that Amrita was dead.

I hurried to her apartment. Her father, Sardar Umrao Singh Shergil, stood by the door in a daze, mumbling a prayer. Her Hungarian mother went in and out of the room where her daughter lay dead unable to comprehend what had happened. That afternoon no more than a dozen men and women followed Amrita's coretge to the cremation ground. Her husband lit her funeral pyre. When we returned to her apartment, the police were waiting for her husband. Britain had declared war on Hungary as an ally of its enemy, Nazi Germany. Amrita's husband was therefore considered an enemy because of his nationality, and had to be detained in prison.

He was lucky to be in police custody. A few days later, his mother-in-law, Amrita's mother, started a campaign against him accusing him of murdering her daughter. She sent letters to everyone she knew asking for a full investigation into the circumstances of her daughter's sudden death. I was one of those she sent a letter to. Murder it certainly was not; negligence, perhaps. I got details from Dr Raghubir Singh who was our family doctor and the last person to see Amrita alive. He told me that he had been summoned at midnight. Amrita had peritonitis caused perhaps by a clumsy abortion. She had bled profusely. Her husband asked Dr Raghubir Singh to give her blood transfusion. The doctor refused to do so without fully examining his patient. While the two doctors were arguing with each other, Amrita quietly slipped out of life. But her fame liveth evermore.

R.K. Narayan

It must be over forty years ago that I first met R.K. Narayan in his hometown, Mysore. I had read some of his short stories and novels. I marvelled how a storyteller of modern times could hold a reader's interest without injecting sex or violence in his narratives. I found them too slow-moving, without any sparkling sentences or memorable descriptions of nature or of his characters. Nevertheless, the one-horse town of his invention, Malgudi, had etched itself on my mind. And all my South Indian friends raved about him as the greatest of Indians writing in English. He certainly was among the pioneers comprising Raja Rao, Govind Desani and Mulk Raj Anand. Whether or not he was the best of them is a matter of opinion.

Being with Narayan on his afternoon strolls was an experience. He did not go to a park but preferred walking up to the bazaar. He walked very slowly and after every few steps he would halt abruptly to complete what he was saying. He would stop briefly at shops to exchange namaskaras with the owners, introduce me and exchange gossip with them in Kannada or Tamil, neither of which I understood. I could sense these gentle strolls in crowded bazaars gave him material for his novels and stories. I found him very likeable and extremely modest despite his achievements.

We saw a lot more of each other during a literary seminar organized by the East-West Centre in Hawaii. Having said our pieces and sat through discussions that followed, we went out for our evening walks, looking for a place to eat. It was the same kind of stroll as we had taken in Mysore, punctuated by abrupt halts in the middle of crowded pavements till he was ready to resume walking. Finding a suitable eatery posed quite a problem. Narayan was a strict teetotaller and a vegetarian; I was neither. We would stop at a grocery store where he bought himself a carton of yoghurt. Then we would go from one eatery to another with R.K. Narayan asking, 'Have you got boiled rice?' Ultimately we could find one. Narayan would empty his carton of yoghurt on the mound of boiled rice. The only compromise he made was to eat it with a spoon instead of his fingers which he would have preferred. Such eateries had very second-rate food and no wines. Dining out was no fun for me.

One evening I decided to shake off Narayan and have a ball on my own. 'I am going to see a blue movie. I don't think you will like it,' I told him. 'I'll come along with you, if you don't mind,' he replied. So we found ourselves in a sleazy suburb of Honolulu watching an extremely obscene film depicting all kinds of sexual deviations. I thought Narayan would walk out, or throw up. He sat stiffly without showing any emotion. It was I who said, 'Let's go.' He turned to me and asked kindly: 'Have you had enough?'

We should get Narayan in the proper perspective. He would not have gone very far but for the patronage of Graham Greene who also became a kind of literary agent. He also got the enthusiastic patronage of *The Hindu* of Madras. N. Ram and his former English wife Susan wrote an excellent biography of Narayan. Greene made Narayan known to the English world of letters; *The Hindu* made him a household name in India.

Narayan was a very loveable man, but his humility was deceptive. Once when All India Radio invited a group of Indian writers to give talks and offered them fees far in excess of their usual rates, while all others accepted the offer Narayan made it a condition that he should be paid at least one rupee more than the others. In his travelogue, *My Dateless Diary*, he writes about a dialogue at a luncheon party given in his honour. 'I blush to record this, but do it for documentary purposes. After the discussions (between two publishers declaring which of Narayan's novels is their favourite one, and rank him with Hemingway and Faulkner as the world's three greatest living writers) have continued on these lines for a while, I feel I ought to assert my modesty—I interrupt them to say, "Thank you, but not yet . . ." They brush me aside and repeat, "Hemingway, Faulkner and Narayan, the three greatest living . . .'" Narayan goes on at some length about the argument between the publishers over whether to include Greene or Hemingway, besides Narayan himself, among the three greatest.

I was foolish enough to write about this in my column. Narayan never spoke to me again.

R.K. Laxman

Long before I got to know him, I had sensed that Laxman had a touch of the genius. I had sent a story, 'Man, How does the Government of India Run?' to the then editor of the *Illustrated Weekly of India*, C.R. Mandy. He sent the story to Laxman for a suitable illustration. Without ever having seen me or my photograph, Laxman drew a caricature of a Sikh clerk (who was the main character of my story) and it bore a startling resemblance to me.

By then he had established the reputation of being India's best cartoonist and most people took the *Times of India* because of his frontpage cartoons and its last-page crossword puzzle. The rest of the paper was like any other national daily. And however distinguished its editors, few people bothered with the contents of its edit page.

I knew Laxman was the youngest of R.K. Narayan's six brothers. His illustrations of his brother's short stories put life into the narrative and highlighted the fact that they were Tamil Brahmins settled in Mysore. We struck up a close friendship almost from the first day I took up the editorship of the *Illustrated Weekly of India*. I told him that in my opinion he was the world's greatest cartoonist. I meant it because I had lived in England, the USA and France for many years and seen the works of cartoonists there. Laxman did not protest: he evidently agreed with my assessment of his worth. Almost every other morning he came to my room and asked me to order coffee for him. He never bothered to ask me if I was busy. Far from resenting his dropping in unannounced, I looked forward to the gossip sessions. However, while he thought nothing of wasting my time every other morning, he never allowed anyone to enter his cabin while he was at work.

Laxman was as witty a raconteur of people's foibles as he was adept in sketching them on paper. I discovered that he was a bit of a snob and did not deign to talk to the junior staff. My son Rahul once told me that he had run into Laxman at a cinema. When Laxman discovered that Rahul was not in the most expensive seats, he ticked him off.

He was a great socializer and could be seen at cocktail parties of consulates, the rich and the famous. He loved driving through congested streets and gladly accepted my invitations for drinks, driving all the way from Malabar Hills where he lived, to Colaba, five miles away from my flat. Unlike his brother who was abstemious, Laxman loved his Scotch. It had to be of premium quality. However, he never returned the hospitality. Other characteristics I noticed about him which he shared with his brother was an exaggerated respect for money. R.K. Narayan was the doyen of Indian authors. He drove a hard bargain.

Once when AIR invited ten of India's top authors to talk about their work and offered what seemed to be more than adequate fees, Narayan accepted only on the condition that he be given at least one rupee more than the others. Likewise, Laxman and I were asked by Manjushri Khaitan of the B.K. Birla family to produce commemoration volumes on Calcutta's 300th anniversary. We were given five-star accommodation. I accepted whatever Manjushri offered me for writing the text. Laxman demanded and got, twice as much. His cartoons sold many more copies than my book did.

Underneath the facade of modesty, both Narayan and Laxman conceal enormous amounts of self-esteem and inflated egos. Once again I have to concede that neither has anything to be modest about. They are at the top in their respective fields.

Manzur Qadir

My closest friend of many years lay dying; I could not go to his bedside. His wife and children were only an hour-and-a-half's flight from me; I could not go to see them. I could not ring them up nor write to them. And when he died, I was not there to comfort them. They are Pakistani, I am Indian. What kind of neighbours are we? What right have we to call ourselves civilized?

I had missed the news in the morning paper. When a friend rang me up and said, 'Your old friend is gone,' the blood in my veins froze. I picked up the paper from the wastepaper basket and saw it in black and white. Manzur Qadir was dead. At the time he was dying in London, I was drinking and listening to Vividh Bharati in Bombay. And when he was being laid to rest in the family graveyard at Lahore, I was wringing my hands in despair in Colaba. He was Pakistani, I am Indian.

It is believed that when a person is dying, all the events of his life flash before his mind's eye. I must have occupied many precious seconds of Manzur Qadir's dying thoughts as he also regarded me as his closest friend. I spent the whole morning thinking of how we met and why I was drawn close to him. At our first meeting thirty years ago we had talked about death. I had quoted lines from the last letter his wife Asghari's brother had written to his father, Mian Fazl-i-Husain:

I am working by candlelight,
It flickers, it's gone.

49

Manzur Qadir was a man of contradictions. He showed little promise as a student; he became much the most outstanding lawyer of Pakistan. Next to law, his favourite reading was the Old Testament and the Quran. Nevertheless he remained an agnostic to the last. He was an uncommonly good poet and wrote some of the wittiest, bawdiest verse known in the Urdu language. At the same time he was extremely conservative, correct in his speech and deportment. Although born a Punjabi he rarely spoke the language and preferred to converse in Hindustani which he did with uncommon elegance. He was long-winded but never a bore; a teetotaller who effervesced like vintage champagne.

The dominant traits of his character were kindliness—he never said a hurtful word about anyone. And integrity which surpassed belief. He made upwards of Rs 50,000 a month; income-tax authorities were constantly refunding tax he had paid in excess. He did not give a tinker's cuss about money. It was commonly said, 'God may lie, but not Manzur Qadir.' Though godless he had more goodness in him than a clutch of saints.

The respect and admiration he commanded amongst his friends was unparalleled. Some years after Partition a group of us were discussing G.D. Khosla's *Stern Reckoning*. The book, as the title signifies, justified the killings that took place in East Punjab in the wake of Partition as legitimate retribution. We were going for Khosla's partisan approach; he and his wife were arguing back. Suddenly a friend asked Khosla, 'Would you present a copy of this book to Manzur?' Khosla pondered for a while and replied, 'No, not to him.' That ended the argument. We came to judge the right or wrong of our actions by how Manzur Qadir would react. He was the human touchstone of our moral pretensions.

Manzur Qadir had no interest in politics and seldom bothered to read newspapers. His ignorance of world affairs was abysmal. Once in London we happened to see a newsreel of Dr Sun Yat Sen. He asked me who this Sen was. When I expressed my amazement at his lack of information, he retorted testily: '*Hoga koee sala Bangali daktar.*' Later in the evening, when I narrated the incident to his daughter Shireen, she chided her father. He made me swear I wouldn't tell anyone about it. I didn't till I read in the papers that President Ayub Khan had made him foreign minister of Pakistan. I sent him a telegram of congratulations, 'Greetings from Dr Sun Yat Sen, the Bengali doctor.'

I spent a short holiday with him when he was foreign minister I stayed as a guest in my own home. (I had put him in possession when I left Lahore in August 1947. He not only saved the life of my Sikh servants whom he brought to the Indian border at night at considerable risk to his life, but sent back every book in my library, every item of furniture and even the remains of liquor in my drink cabinet.) He told me how he had become foreign minister. He had criticized Ayub Khan's dictatorship at a meeting. That evening an army jeep came to fetch him. Believing that he was being arrested he said good-bye to his family. He was driven to the President's residence. Said Ayub Khan: 'It is no good criticizing me and my government unless you are willing to take the responsibility for what you say.' Manzur Qadir returned home as foreign minister.

True to his character, Manzur never canvassed for any job nor showed the slightest eagerness to hold on to power. He strove with none, for none was worth his strife. He allowed himself to be outmanoeuvred by unscrupulous politicians. After four years as foreign minister, during which he made a desperate bid to improve relations with India, he quit the job with no regrets. He was forced to become chief justice and, when he desired to throw that up, persuaded to take up briefs on behalf of the government. He was engaged as government counsel in all the important conspiracy cases and represented his country before international tribunals. Whether it was Iskander Mirza or Ayub Khan, Yahya Khan or Bhutto, no ruler of Pakistan could do without Manzur Qadir.

Last year I spent a day with him in Nathiagali near Murree. He was a very sick man afflicted with phlebitis. But for old times' sake, he drove down to Islamabad to pick me up and drove me back the next evening. I saw for myself the affection and esteem with which he was held by everyone from General Tikka Khan down to the humblest tradesman in the bazar. It was a continuous shaking of hands and salam alaikums.

He bore the pain of his illness with incredible courage and without the slightest attempt to find false props offered by religion. He knew he had a short time to go but had no fear of death. I forget the Urdu couplet he used to quote but it was very much like Wesley's:

> *If I must die, I will encounter darkness as a bride and hug it in my arms.*

At our final farewell, the tears were in my eyes, not his.

> *When summoned hence to thine eternal sleep, oh, mayest thou smile while all round thee weep.*

An English friend kept me informed of his deteriorating state of health in the London hospital. Apparently she too was not with him when the end came. Tributes to such a man as Manzur Qadir can only be written in tears which leave no stain on paper. He shall be forever honoured and forever mourned.

PRABHA DUTT

It would have been more appropriate if Prabha had written this piece on me rather than I on her. Her pen was still rapier sharp; mine is somewhat blunted with age. She would have used royal-blue ink to write my obituary; I can only use my colourless tears to write hers. For Prabha it was not yet time for the noonday prayer; for me bells peal for evensong. None of these considerations counted with the Divine Reaper: early one morning when He set out to gather blossoms from the media's flower-bed of lilies, he plucked one still in the prime of her youth and the fairest of them all.

I knew very little of Prabha Dutt before I became her boss. She was the bossy type and instinctively resented anyone lording over her. When she first came to see me in my office she made it quite clear that she wasn't the kind of person who took orders from anyone; she knew her job better than I and if I minded my business she would mind hers. She regarded me with her large, grey eyes as an insect-collector would examine the latest beetle in his collection and put me several questions framed to find out what kind of editor I would make. I was somewhat overawed by her presence and the *viva-voce* test she put me through. It took me several months to break through her impersonal, no-nonsense attitude toward me and persuade her to accept the hand of friendship I extended to her.

The breakthrough was dramatic. Prabha was as much married to the *Hindustan Times* as she was to her husband and as involved with the paper as she was with her two daughters. And extremely touchy about both. It was after one of her many outbursts against a colleague who got away with very little work that she dissolved in tears of rage. I was able to take the liberty of putting a paternal arm round her shoulders. She shrugged it off but thereafter did me the honour of treating me as her father-in-office to whom she could turn in moments of crisis.

In Prabha's scheme of values work took precedence over everything else. This gave her enormous courage to speak her mind without bothering who she was speaking to and writing without concern of consequences that might follow. In my presence she told K.K. Birla to his face what was wrong with the *Hindustan Times*. She bust financial and social rackets (she had a lady-like disdain for sex scandals) and was often threatened with violence. The one and only time she quarrelled with me was when I tried to withhold her story on S.L. Khurana who had been executive president of the *Hindustan Times* and was then Lieutenant Governor of Delhi. I have little doubt that if she had found out something about my evading taxes, smuggling contraband or involvement in some shady deal, despite her affection for me, she would not have spared me.

Prabha was a very conservative, strait-laced person, passionately devoted to her family, friends, servants and their families. She not only spent every moment she could spare from work teaching her and her servants' children but eagerly took on the problems of her friends on her own shoulders. She was as fierce in her loyalties towards people she befriended as she could be aggressively unfriendly and outspokenly offensive to their detractors. These characteristics gave her the image of one who was hard as nails and quick of temper. Those who knew her better realized how soft she really was: every outburst of temper was followed by a cascade of tears. She was like the cactus, prickly on the outside, sugar-sweet within.

Had Prabha a premonition that she had a short time to go? I am not sure. She certainly crammed in as much activity for her two daughters as any mother would who felt she may soon be parted from them. On the other hand a day before her haemorrhage she went to see a relative in hospital and told him very cheerfully how lucky he was to be lying comfortably in bed without having to bother about going to office. Little did she then know that within a few hours she would be in the same hospital fighting a losing battle for her own life. Her closest friend, Usha Rai, told me that the evening before she died, as Usha was rubbing her hands, Prabha asked her in a feeble voice: 'Are you reading the lines on my palm? Tell me, will I leave this hospital alive?'

In all my years in journalism I have yet to meet as gutsy a girl, with integrity that brooked no compromise, daring that verged on foolhardiness, total dedication to her work with contempt for the kaamchor (shirker), than Prabha Dutt. The most fitting tribute I can pay her is by placing a wreath stolen from Shakespeare:

Now boast thee death, in thy possession lies
A lass unparalleled!

Mother Teresa, Apostle of the Unwanted

It must have been more than twenty years ago that I was asked by the *New York Times* to do a profile of Mother Teresa for its magazine section. I wrote to Mother Teresa, asking her permission to call on her. And having got it, spent three days with her from the early hours of the morning to late at night. Nothing in my long journalistic career has remained as sharply etched in my memory as those three days with her in Calcutta. In my little study in my villa at Kasauli I have only two pictures of the people I admire most—Mahatma Gandhi and Mother Teresa.

Before I met her face to face I read Malcolm Muggeridge's book on Mother Teresa, *Something Beautiful for God*. Malcolm was a recent convert to Catholicism and prone to accept stories of miracles. He had gone to make a film on her for British Broadcasting Corporation (BBC) Television. They first went to the Nirmal Hriday (Sacred Heart) Home for dying destitutes close to the Kalighat temple. The team took some shots of the building from outside and of its sunlit courtyard. The camera crew was of the opinion that the interior was too dark and they had no artificial lights. However, since some footage was left, they decided to use it for interior shots. When the film was developed the shots of the dormitories were found to be clearer than those taken in sunlight. The first thing I asked Mother Teresa was if this was true. She replied, 'But of course, such things happen all the time.' And added with increasing intensity of voice, 'Every day, every hour, every single minute, God manifests himself in some miracle.'

She narrated other miracles of the days when her organization was little known and chronically short of cash. 'Money has never been much of a problem,' she told me. 'God gives through His people.' She told me that when she started her first school in the slums, she had no more than five rupees with her. But as soon as people came to know what she was doing, they brought money and things: 'It was all divine providence.' One winter they ran out of quilts. Her nuns found sheets but there was no money to buy cotton. Just as Mother Teresa was about to rip open her own pillow, the bell rang. Some official who was about to leave Calcutta for a posting abroad had brought his quilts and mattresses to give them away. On another occasion when they had run out of rations, a lady they had never seen before left them a bag of rice. 'We measured the rice with our little tin cup; it was exactly what we required for the day. When I told the lady that, she broke down and cried as she realized that God had used her as an instrument of His will.'

The first institution she took me to was Nirmal Hriday. It was in 1952 that the Calcutta Corporation handed the building to her. Orthodox Hindus were outraged. Four hundred Brahmin priests attached to the Kali temple demonstrated outside the building. 'One day I went out and spoke to them. "If you want to kill me, kill me. But do not disturb the inmates. Let them die in peace."' That silenced them. Then one of the priests staggered in. He was an advanced case of galloping phthisis. The nuns looked after him till he died. That changed the priests' attitude towards Mother Teresa. Later one day another priest entered the Home, prostrated himself at Mother Teresa's feet and said, 'For thirty years I have served the Goddess Kali in her temple. Now the goddess stands before me.'

I went round Nirmal Hriday with Mother Teresa. In the hour we were there, of the 170 men and women lying in rows, two died. Their beds were quickly taken by two lying on the floor of the veranda outside. Mother Teresa went round to everyone of the inmates and asked them how they were. Her only message of cheer to people who knew they had not much longer to go was *Bhoggoban acchen*—there is God.

Mother Teresa did not make an impressive figure—barely five foot tall and very slim, high cheek bones and thin lips. And a face full of wrinkles. It was a homely face without any charisma. Muggeridge was right in describing her as a unique person, 'but not in the vulgar celebrity sense of having neon lighting about her head. Rather in the opposite sense—of someone who has merged herself in the common face of mankind.' The nun's dress she had designed for herself would make the plainest looking woman look plainer.

She spoke with an Indian lilt in her voice. And like most convent-bred Indians ended her sentences with an interrogatory 'No?', meaning 'isn't that so?' She told me how at the age of twelve she had dared to become a nun and left her parental home in Skopje (Yugoslavia.) How she learnt English in a Dublin convent and came to Calcutta in 1929 as a geography teacher in St Mary's High School. She was for many years principal of the school. Then suddenly a strange restlessness came over her; it was, as she describes it 'a special call from Jesus Christ'. 10 September 1946 was her 'day of decision' as well as 'inspiration day'. This is how she put it: 'I was going to Darjeeling to make my retreat. It was in that train I heard the call to give up all and follow Him to the slums and serve Him among the poorest of the poor.' She prepared herself for her mission, receiving an intensive course in nursing at Patna. In 1948 she opened her first school in the slums of Calcutta in a private house donated to her. Her only helper was Subhasini Das (Sister Agnes). A new order, the Missionaries of Charity, was instituted. A male branch, Brothers of Charity, came up some years later, and initiates had to take four vows—poverty, chastity, obedience and whole-hearted service to the poor.

Mother Teresa taught herself Bengali which she soon was able to speak fluently. When India became independent she took Indian nationality. Her strength came from simple convictions. ('She is blessed with certainties,' writes Muggeridge.) When I asked her, 'Who has been the dominant figure in your life—Gandhi, Nehru, Albert Schweitzer?' without a pause she replied, 'Jesus Christ.' When I followed it up with a question about books that might have impressed her, her answer was equally categorical and in the singular: 'The Bible.'

The day I accompanied Mother Teresa on a 'begging' expedition, we boarded a crowded tram car. A man immediately stood up to offer her his seat. Another untied a knot in his dhoti and took out change to buy her ticket. The ticket conductor refused to take money from her and punched a ticket for which he paid himself. We arrived at the office of a large biscuit factory. Mr Mukherjee, the manager, had his excuses ready. His business was not doing well, he was having union problems. And so on. Mother Teresa expressed sympathy with him. 'We only want the broken biscuits you discard. Thank God, we have no union problems. We work for God; there are no unions.' I could see Mr Mukherjee's defences crumble. He picked up his phone and ordered forty large tins of broken biscuits to be delivered to Mother Teresa.

Recognition came to Mother Teresa. In 1962 she was awarded the Padma Shri. Both Pandit Nehru and his sister Vijayalakshmi Pandit who were present at the investiture admitted that they almost broke down with emotion. A few months later came the Magsaysay award. Pope Paul VI presented her with a car; she auctioned it and raised four-and-a-half lakh rupees. In 1971 she was awarded the Pope John XXIII prize of 21,500 US dollars. Then came the Good Samaritans and the Joseph Kennedy awards and the Templeton Foundation Prize. While making the presentation Prince Philip referred to the 'sheer goodness which shines through Mother Teresa's life and work and inspires humility, wonder and admiration'.

Since then till she got the Nobel Prize for peace there was not a month when she was not showered with money and awards of some kind or the other. Every paise went into the upkeep of hospitals, orphanages and leprosaria which she opened in different parts of India as well as in foreign countries.

One evening, returning from Sealdah to her home we had to get out of our car as there was a mammoth funeral procession coming from the opposite direction. It was the cortege of Muzaffar Ahmed, one of the founding fathers of communism in India. As we proceeded on our way, men waving little red flags stepped out of their ranks to touch Mother Teresa's feet, receive her blessings, and then rejoin the procession.

Mother Teresa dropped me at Dum Dum airport. As I was about to take leave of her she said 'So?' meaning if I had anything else to ask. 'Tell me how you can touch people with loathsome diseases like leprosy and gangrene. Aren't you revolted by people filthy with dysentry and cholera vomit?'

She replied, 'I see Jesus in every human being. I say to myself: this is hungry Jesus, I must feed him. This is sick Jesus. This one has gangrene, dysentry and cholera. I must wash him and tend to him. I serve them because I love Jesus.'

The last time I saw Mother Teresa was two years ago when she came to Delhi to receive two Maruti Vans presented to her by my friend H.N. Sikand. There was an enormous crowd in his home. Mother Teresa passed by me without recognizing me. How could she after all those years and the millions of people she must have met? She made a very short speech of thanks in her usually flat voice. I could see through my own tear-filled eyes that almost everyone present was also in tears.

PHOOLAN DEVI, QUEEN OF DACOITS

For two years after this article was written, Phoolan Devi continued to evade capture. Then, in February 1983, she surrendered to the police. On 25 July 2001, Phoolan Devi was shot dead by assailants.

It was the afternoon of Saturday, 14 February 1981. Winter had given way to spring. Amidst the undulating sea of ripening wheat and green lentil were patches of bright yellow mustard in flower. Skylarks rose from the ground, suspended themselves in the blue skies and poured down song on the earth below. Allah was in His heaven and all was peace and tranquillity in Behmai.

Behmai is a tiny hamlet along the river Jamuna inhabited by about fifty families belonging mainly to the Thakur caste, with a sprinkling of shepherds and ironsmiths. Although it is only eighty miles from the industrial metropolis, Kanpur, it has no road connecting it to any town. To get to Behmai you have to traverse dusty footpaths meandering through cultivated fields, and go down narrow, snake-infested ravines choked with camelthorn and elephant grass. It is not surprising that till the middle of February few people had heard of Behmai. After what happened on Saturday the 14th, it was on everyone's lips.

There was not much to do in the fields except drive off wild pig and deer: some boys armed with catapults and loud voices were out doing this; others played on the sand bank while their buffaloes wallowed in the mud. Men dozed on their charpoys: women sat in huddles gossiping as they ground corn or picked lice out of their children's hair.

No one in Behmai noticed a party dressed in police uniforms cross the river. It was led by a young woman with short-cropped hair wearing the khaki coat of a deputy superintendent of police with three silver stars, blue jeans and boots with zippers. She wore lipstick and her nails had varnish on them. Her belt was charged with bullets and had a curved Gurkha knife—a *kokri*—attached to it. A sten-gun was slung across her shoulders and she carried a battery-fitted megaphone in her hand. The party sat down beside the village shrine, adorned with the trident emblem of Shiva, the god of destruction.

The eldest of the party, a notorious gangster named Baba Mustaqeem, instructed the group how to go about their job. A dozen men were to surround the village so that no one could get out; the remaining men, led by the woman, were to search all the houses and take whatever they liked. But no women were to be raped nor anyone except the two men they were looking for were to be slain. They listened in silence and nodded their heads in agreement. They touched the base of Shiva's trident for good luck and dispersed.

The girl in the officer's uniform went up on the parapet of the village well, switched on the megaphone and shouted at the top of her voice: 'Listen you fellows! You *bhosreekey!* (progenies of the cunt) If you love your lives hand over all the cash, silver and gold you have. And listen again! I know those *madarchods* (mother-fuckers) Lal Ram Singh and Shri Ram Singh are hiding in this village. If you don't hand them over to me I will stick my gun into your bums and tear them apart. You've heard me. This is Phoolan Devi speaking. If you don't get cracking, you know what Phoolan Devi will do to you. *Jai* Durga *Mata!* (victory to the Mother Goddess Durga!).' She raised her gun and fired a single shot in the air to convince them that she meant what she said.

Phoolan Devi stayed at the well while her men went looting the Thakurs' homes. Women were stripped of their earrings, nose-pins, silver bangles and anklets. Men handed over whatever cash they had on their persons. The operation lasted almost an hour.

But there was no trace of Lal Ram Singh or Shri Ram Singh. The people of the village denied having ever seen them. 'You are lying!' roared Phoolan Devi. 'I will teach you to tell the truth.' She ordered all the young men to be brought before her. About thirty were dragged to her presence. She asked them again: 'You mother-fuckers, unless you tell me where those two sons of pigs are, I will roast you alive.' The men pleaded with her and swore they had never seen the two men.

'Take these fellows along,' she ordered her men. 'I'll teach them a lesson they will never forget.' The gang pushed the thirty villagers out of Behmai along the path leading to the river. At an embankment she ordered them to be halted and lined up. 'For the last time, will you tell me where those two bastards are or do I have to kill you?' she asked pointing her sten-gun at them. The villagers again pleaded ignorance: 'If we knew, we would tell you.' 'Turn round,' thundered Phoolan Devi. The men turned their faces towards the green embankment. 'Bhosreekey, this will also teach you not to report to the police. Shoot the bloody bastards!' she ordered her men and yelled: 'Jai Durga Mata!' There was a burst of gunfire. The thirty men crumpled to the earth. Twenty were dead; others hit in their limbs or buttocks sprawled in blood-spattered dust.

Phoolan Devi and her murderous gang went down the path yelling: 'Jai Durga Mata! Jai Baba Mustaqeem! Jai Bikram Singh! Jai Phoolan Devi!'

The next morning the massacre of Behmai made front page headlines in all newspapers all over India.

~

Dacoity in India is as old as history. In some regions it is endemic and no sooner are some gangs liquidated than others come up. The most notorious dacoit country is a couple of hundred miles south-west of Behmai, along the ravines of the Chambal river in Madhya Pradesh. In the Bundelkhand district of Uttar Pradesh in

which Behmai is located, it is of comparatively recent origin and
the state police suspect that when things became too hot around
the Chambal some gangs migrated to Bundelkhand where the
terrain was very much like the one they were familiar with. The
river Jamuna, after its descent from the Himalayas, runs a sluggish,
serpentine course past Delhi and Agra into Bundelkhand. Here it
passes through a range of low-lying hills covered with dense forests.
Several monsoon-fed rivulets running through deep gorges join
it as it goes on to meet the holy Ganga at Allahabad. It is wild
and beautiful country: hills, ravines and forests enclosing small
picturesque hamlets. By day there are peacocks and multi-coloured
butterflies: by night, nightjars calling to each other across the pitch
black wilderness flecked by fireflies. Neelgai (blue bull), spotted
deer, wild boar, hyena, jackal and fox abound. It is also infested
with snakes, the commonest being cobras, the most venomous
of the species. Cultivation is sparse and entirely dependent on
rain. The chief produce are lentils and wheat. The peasantry is
amongst the poorest in the country. The two main communities
living along the river banks are Mallahs (boatmen) and Thakurs.
The Thakurs are the higher caste and own most of the land. The
Mallahs are amongst the lowest in the Hindu caste hierarchy, own
little land and live mostly by plying boats, fishing and distilling
liquor. Till recently dacoit gangs were mixed: Thakurs, Mallahs,
Yadavs (cattlemen), Gujjars (milkmen) and Muslims. But now
more and more are tending to becoming caste-oriented. There is
little love lost between the Thakurs and the Mallahs. Behmai is a
Thakur village; Phoolan Devi, a Mallahin (boatwoman).

No stigma is attached to being a dacoit; in their own territory
they are known as *bagis* or rebels. Hindi movies, notably the
box-office hit of all times *Sholay* (Flames), in which the hero is
a dacoit, has added romance to the profession of banditry. It is
said that a song entitled: 'Shall we kill you or shall we let you
go' is Phoolan Devi's favourite.

Dacoit gangs are well-equipped with automatic weapons,
including self-loading rifles mostly acquired through raids. A

police note on anti-dacoity operations records that Jalaun district which includes Behmai has fifteen gangs of between ten to thirty members each operating in the area. Phoolan Devi and her current paramour, Man Singh Yadav, have fifteen men with them. In the last six months the police have had ninety-three encounters with dacoits in which they killed 159, captured 137; forty-seven surrendered themselves. 439 still roam about the jungles and ravines, hunting and being hunted.

I sat on the parapet of the village well on the same spot from where Phoolan Devi had announced her arrival in Behmai a year-and-a-half earlier. In front of me sat village men, women and children and the police escort provided for me. An old woman wailed: 'That Mallahin killed my husband and two sons. May she die a dog's death!' A man stood up and bared his belly which showed gun-shot scars; another bared his buttocks and pointed to a dimple where a bullet had hit him.

'Can any of you tell me why Phoolan Devi came to this village and killed so many people?'

No one answered.

'Is it true that Lal Ram Singh and Shri Ram Singh were in Behmai?'

A chorus of voices answered: 'No, we have never seen them.'

'Is it true that a few months before the dacoity they had brought Phoolan Devi with them, raped her for several weeks before she managed to escape?'

'Ram! Ram,' protested some of them. 'We had never seen the Mallahin in this village before the dacoity.'

'Why then did she ask for the two brothers? How did she know her way about this village?'

No one answered.

'You will not get anything out of these fellows,' said the inspector of police to me in English. 'You know what these villagers are! They never tell the truth.'

I gave up my cross-examination and decided to go round Behmai. I started from the village shrine with the Shiva trident, came back to the well and then to the embankment where she had killed the twenty men. I went up a mound where the police had set up a sentry-box from which I could get a bird's-eye view of the village, the river Jamuna and the country beyond. The police sentinel on duty who had been in the village for several weeks volunteered the following information: 'Sir, I think I can tell you why Phoolan Devi did what she did. You see that village across the Jamuna on top of the hill? It is called Pal, it is a Mallah village. Mallahs used to come through Behmai to take the ferry. Thakur boys used to tease their girls and beat up their men. I am told there were several instances when they stripped the girls naked and forced them to dance. The Mallahs appealed to Phoolan Devi to teach these Thakurs a lesson. She had her own reasons as well. Her lover Bikram Singh had been murdered by Thakurs Lal Ram Singh and his twin brother Shri Ram Singh. And they had kept her imprisoned in this village for several weeks, raping and beating her. She managed to escape and rejoin her gang.' She also suspected that these fellows have been informing the police of her movements. It was revenge, pure and simple.'

～

'For every man this girl has killed she has slept with two,' said the superintendent of police in charge of 'Operation Phoolan Devi'. The police estimate the number of men slain by her or one of her gang in the last year-and-a-half to be over thirty. If that is so, Phoolan Devi could claim mention in the *Guinness Book of World Records* for sex without payment. There is no way of finding out the exact number of men she murdered or she was laid by. But it is certain that not all the killings nor the copulations were entirely of her choosing. On many occasions she happened to be with bandits who went trigger happy; and being the only woman in a gang of a dozen or more she was regarded by them as their common property. She accepted the rules of the game and had to give herself to them in turn. It was more being resigned to being raped than itching for sex like a nymphomaniac.

I was able to reconstruct Phoolan Devi's past by talking to her parents, sisters and one of her lovers, and cross-checking what they told me with a statement she made to the police on 6 January 1979, the first and the only time she was arrested. This was in connection with a robbery in the house of her cousin with whom her father had a dispute over land. Some stolen goods were recovered from her. She spent a fortnight in police custody. Her statement is prefaced by a noting made by the officer. He describes her as 'about twenty years old; wheatish complexion, oval face short but sturdily built'. Phoolan Devi stated: 'I am the second daughter of a family of six consisting of five girls. The youngest is a boy, Shiv Narain Singh. We belong to the Mallah caste and live in village Gurh-Ka-Purwa. At the age of twelve I was given away in marriage to a forty-five-year-old widower, Putti Lal.' Then she talks of her second 'marriage' to Kailash in Kanpur. The rest of her life-story was given to me by her mother, Muli. 'Phoolan Devi was too young to consummate her marriage and came back to us after a few days. A year or two later we sent her back to her husband. This time she stayed with him for a few months but was unhappy. She came away without her husband's permission, determined not to go back to him.' It would appear that she had been deflowered. Her mother describes her as being 'filled up'—an Indian expression for a girl whose bosom and behind indicate that she has had sex. It would appear that she had developed an appetite for sex which her ageing husband could not fulfil. Her parents were distraught: a girl leaving her husband brought disgrace on the family. 'I told her to drop dead,' said her mother. 'I told her to jump in a well or drown herself in the Jamuna; we would not have a married daughter living with us. Putti Lal came and took away the silver ornaments he had given her and married another woman. What were we to do? We started looking for another husband for her;

but it is not easy to find a husband for a discarded girl, is it?' she asked me. Phoolan Devi kept out of her parents' way as much as she could by taking the family's buffaloes out for grazing. She picked up a liaison with the son of the village headman. (In rural India such affairs are consummated in lentil or sugarcane fields.) The headman's son invited his friends to partake of the feast. Phoolan Devi had no choice but to give in. The village gossip-mill ground out stories of Phoolan Devi being available to anyone who wanted to lay her. Her mother admitted: 'The family's *pojeesun* (position) was compromised; our noses were cut. We decided to send her away to her sister, Ramkali, who lives in village Teonga across the river.'

It did not take long for Phoolan Devi to find another lover in Teonga. This was a distant cousin, Kailash, married and with four children. Kailash had contacts with a dacoit gang. He gives a vivid account of how he was seduced by Phoolan Devi: 'One day I was washing my clothes on the banks of the Jamuna. This girl brought her sister's buffaloes to wallow in the shallows of the river. We got talking. She asked me to lend her my cake of soap so that she could bathe herself. I gave her what remained of the soap. She stripped herself before my eyes. While she splashed water on herself and soaped her bosom and buttocks she kept talking to me. I got very excited watching her. After she was dressed, I followed her into the lentil fields. I threw her on the ground and mounted her. I was too worked up and was finished in no time. I begged her to meet me again. She agreed to come the next day at the same time and at the same place.

'We made love many times. But it was never enough. She started playing difficult to get. "If you want me, you must marry me. Then I'll give you all you want," she said. I told her I had a wife and children and could only keep her as my mistress. She would not let me touch her unless I agreed to marry her. I became desperate. I took her with me to Kanpur. A lawyer took fifty rupees from me, wrote something on a piece of paper and told us that we were man and wife. We spent two days in Kanpur.

In the day time we went to the movies; at night we made love and slept in each other's arms. When we returned to Teonga, my parents refused to take us in. We spent a night out in the fields. The next day I told Phoolan Devi to go back to her parents as I had decided to return to my wife and children. She swore she would kill me. I have not seen her since then. But I am afraid one of these days she will get me.'

'What does your Phoolania look like?' I asked Kailash. 'I am told her sister Ramkali resembles her.'

'Phoolan is slightly shorter, lighter skinned and has a nicer figure. She is much better looking than Ramkali.'

'I am told she uses very bad language.'

'She never spoke harshly to me; to me she spoke only the language of love.'

Phoolan Devi had more coming to her. A few days after she had been turned out by Kailash, at a village fair she ran into Kailash's wife, Shanti. Shanti pounced on Phoolan, tore her hair, clawed her face and in front of the crowd that had collected abused her: 'Whore! Bitch! Home-breaker!' What was known only to a few hamlets now became common knowledge: Phoolan was a slut. As if this were not enough, the village headman's son who was under the impression that Phoolan was exclusively at his beck and call heard of her escapade with Kailash. He summoned her to his house and thrashed her with his shoes. Thus at the age of eighteen Phoolan found herself discarded by everyone: her parents did not want her, her old husband had divorced her, her second 'marriage' had come to naught, she had been laid by men none of whom was willing to take her as a wife. It seemed to her that no one in the world wanted to have anything to do with her. She had only two choices before her: to go to some distant city and become a prostitute, or kill herself. There were times she considered throwing herself into the well.

Unknown to her there was someone who had taken a fancy to her. This was young Bikram Singh, a friend of Kailash and member of a gang of dacoits led by a man called Babu Gujjar.

Bikram Singh had seen Phoolan about the village and heard stories of her performance in the lentil fields. One afternoon he came to Gurh-Ka-Purwa with some of his gang and bluntly told Phoolan's parents that he had come to take away their daughter. Phoolan was adamant. 'I will talk to you with my sandals,' she said spitting on the ground. Bikram hit her with a whip he was carrying, Phoolan Devi fled from the village and went to stay with her other sister, Rukmini, in village Orai. It is there that she heard that there was a warrant of arrest against her and Kailash for the dacoity in the house of her cousin. The man who took her to the police station raped her before handing her over. She spent a fortnight in gaol. When she returned home, Bikram came to see her again. He threatened her: 'Either you come with me or I take your brother Shiv Narain with me.' Phoolan was very attached to her only brother, he was just eleven years old and studying in the village school. After some wrangling, she agreed to go with Bikram.

Kailash describes Bikram Singh as fair, tall and wiry. Bikram was obviously very taken by Phoolan. He had her long hair cropped. He gave her a transistor radio and cassette recorder as she was inordinately fond of listening to film music. He bought her a khaki shirt and jeans. He taught her how to handle a gun. She proved a very adept disciple and became a crack-shot.

For the first time in her life Phoolan felt wanted by someone. She responded to Bikram's affection and began to describe herself as his beloved. She had a rubber stamp made for herself which she used as letterhead in the letters she had written for her. It reads: 'Dasyu (dacoit) Sundari (beauty), Dasyu Samrat Bikram Singh Ki Premika' (Beloved of Bikram Singh, emperor of dacoits).

Being 'the beloved of Bikram' did not confer any special privileges on Phoolan. Whether she liked it or not, she had to service the rest of the gang. At the time the leader happened to be Babu Gujjar, a singularly rough customer. He had his own way of expressing his superiority over his gang. He liked to have sex in broad daylight and in front of the others. So Phoolan Devi had to submit to being ravished and brutalized by Babu Gujjar in public. When her turn came to be made love to by Bikram, she complained to him about the indignity. By then Bikram had developed a strong sense of possession over Phoolan Devi. He did not have the courage to admit it, but one night while Babu Gujjar was asleep, he shot him in the head. Bikram Singh became the leader of the gang and at Phoolan's insistence forbade others from touching her. There wasn't much resentment because the gang soon acquired another woman, Kusum Nain, who happened to be better-looking than Phoolan Devi. Kusum, a Thakur, attached herself to the Thakur brothers, Lal Ram Singh and Shri Ram Singh. The two women became jealous of each other.

Despite her many unpleasant experiences with men, Phoolan Devi did not give up her habit of cock-teasing. She sensed that her full bosom and rounded buttocks set men's minds aflame with lust. Nevertheless she persisted in bathing in the presence of the men of her gang. One gangster, now in police custody, who had known her as well as Kusum Nain and Meera Thakur (other female dacoits since then slain) vouches for this: 'The other girls were as tough as Phoolan but they observed certain proprieties in the company of men. They would go behind a tree or bushes to take a bath; not Phoolan; she took off her clothes in front of us as if we did not exist. The other girls used language becoming to women; Phoolan is the most foul-mouthed wench I have ever met. Every time she opens her mouth she uses the foulest of abuse: bhosreekey, *gaandu* (bugger), madarchod, *betichod* (daughter-fucker).'

The inspector of police has in his files a sheaf of letters written to him on behalf of Phoolan Devi. They are a delightful mixture of the sacred and the profane, of high falutin Hindi and sheer obscenity. The one he read out to me began with salutations to the Mother Goddess, under her printed letterhead: 'Jai Durga Mata. Dacoit Beauty, Beloved of the Dacoit Emperor Bikram Singh.' The text ran somewhat as follows:

Honourable & Respected Inspector General Sahib, I learn from several Hindi journals that you have been making speeches saying that you will have us dacoits shot like pye-dogs. I hereby give you notice that if you do not stop bakwas (nonsense) of this kind, I will have your revered mother abducted and so thoroughly fucked by my men that she will need medical attention. So take heed.

It is more than likely that Bikram Singh, besides keeping Phoolan Devi exclusively for himself, also claimed his right as the leader to enjoy the company of Kusum Nain as well. This irked the Thakur brothers. They left Bikram's gang and looked out for an opportunity to kill him. On the night of 13 August 1980, they trapped and slew Bikram Singh. It is believed that the murder was committed in Behmai and the Thakurs unceremoniously kicked Bikram's corpse before it was thrown into the river.

Lal Ram Singh and Shri Ram Singh kept Phoolan Devi in Behmai. They brutalized and humiliated her in front of the entire village. One night, on the excuse of wanting to relieve herself, Phoolan Devi managed to vanish in the darkness. She crossed the Jamuna to the Mallah village, Pal. From there she got in touch with the Muslim gangster Baba Mustaqeem and pleaded with him to help her avenge the murder of Bikram Singh. Mustaqeem agreed. This is how she came to Behmai on the afternoon of 14 February 1981.

~

Gurh-Ka-Purwa is idyllically situated on hill slopes that dip into the None river on one side and level out on the sands of the Jamuna on the other. The headman's double-storeyed house overlooks the None. Alongside it are rows of mud huts with brick-tiled roofs which face the Jamuna. One of the meanest looking is that of Devi Deen and Muli—Phoolan Devi's parents. Apart from cooking utensils and charpoys, all they have is a pet partridge in a wicker cage. At the time I went to see them they had their younger married daughter, Ramkali, visiting them and two unmarried girls with them. Their only son Shiv Narain was at school. The family have got used to the limelight that Phoolan Devi's exploits have focussed on them. 'One crowded hour of glorious life', is to them 'worth an age without a name'. They have been visited by pressmen, photographers and many others who come to whet their curiosity. Old Muli now varnishes her nails and when a visitor comes wears whatever silver jewellery she owns. Ramkali wears lipstick and rouge and knows how to strike poses like a film star. She is an uncommonly attractive young woman with large almond-shaped eyes which she uses like side-winder missiles, a full bosom and slender waist. If Phoolan Devi is anything like her—and most of those who have seen both the sisters are of the opinion that she is better-looking then Ramkali—she must be something.

I could not take my eyes off Ramkali during the hour I spent in their hut. She was aware of the admiring glances she received from our party. 'Everyone who comes wants my photo,' she said saucily to our photographer. He turned to me and asked: 'Isn't she worth a crime? If Phoolan looks anything like her, I am willing to join her gang.'

When we left Gurh-Ka-Purwa, it was high noon. We went through its narrow lanes, stepping gingerly, avoiding the slimy ooze that ran in the middle and the blobs of cowdung strewn everywhere. A large black cobra slithered out of a hole and went along the base of the wall. A herd of buffaloes coming down the lane came to an abrupt halt. The cobra raised its hood and looked angrily around. Seeing that neither the buffaloes nor we meant any harm, it continued its journey and disappeared into a mound of drying cowdung cakes.

～

The police net is closing round Phoolan Devi and her current lover, Man Singh Yadav. They are believed to be hiding in an area of some fourteen square miles along the Jamuna. The police have grounded all fishing and ferry boats to prevent her crossing over. They have announced a Rs 10,000 prize on her head for anyone who gets her dead or alive. She is reported to be ill and in need of hospitalization. The police have arrested some villagers suspected of having taken medicines for her. They keep a watch on the movements of her brother Shiv Narain whom she is reported to have visited last 'sisters' day, to tie a string bracelet on his wrist. She has narrowly escaped capture. Once on 31 March 1981, only a few weeks after Behmai, she almost walked into a police trap and had to shoot her way out. It was a close shave which she herself ascribed to providence. Since then she always carries a silver figurine of her patron goddess Durga on her person. How long Durga will protect her is anyone's guess.

'The average life of our Indian dacoit is about thirty years,' said a police officer to me. 'They usually join these gangs when they are seventeen or eighteen years old. Most of them are captured or shot within ten or twelve years. Phoolan is now thirty. Her career of crime is about to come to an end.'

'It is you press people who have made a common criminal who has the blood of innocent men on her hands into a heroine,' said S.K. Datta, DIG, Police. He gave me many examples of how journals (mainly Hindi) had cooked up all kinds of romantic stories about Phoolan Devi's favourite film songs and her dare-devil escapades. His superintendent, Vijay Shankar, who is in charge of the district in which Phoolan has been operating, added: 'All our normal police work has come to a standstill because of these dacoit gangs. We must clear them out of the countryside before we can attend to other duties. The longer we take in nabbing them, the more acute other tensions become. And how is it that the press has seldom anything to say of the heroism of the policemen who give their lives fighting these gangsters or of the widows and orphans of men slain by these thugs?'

I had no answers. Besides, the atmosphere was Phoolan-charged. We were sitting on a balcony overlooking the Jamuna. Soft breezes, the river shimmering like quicksilver under a full moon, fireflies flitting about among frangipani: 'A savage place! As holy and enchanted as ever beneath a waning moon was haunted by a woman wailing for her demon lover.' One could almost hear Phoolan wailing for Bikram. My reply to the charge against the press was very tame: 'It is human nature: Phoolan Devi has such a beautiful name—Flora, Goddess of flowers. And she may soon be dead.'

'I don't want to kill her,' said Vijay Shankar. 'I don't look upon her as a dacoit but as a child that has lost her way. We will find her and put her on the right path.'

I don't know what that 'right path' can be for one who has taken so many lives except one that leads to the gallows.

NIRAD C. CHAUDHURI, SCHOLAR EXTRAORDINARY

This piece combines two articles that Khushwant Singh wrote on Nirad Chaudhuri, the first soon after the publication of *A Passage to England* in 1959, and the second in 1988, to mark Nirad Chaudhuri's ninetieth birthday.

'There is nothing more dreadful to an author than neglect, compared with which reproach, hatred and opposition are names of happiness.' These words of Dr Johnson were inscribed by Nirad Chaudhuri on my copy of his book *A Passage to England*. These words hold the key to Nirad's past life and present personality. They explain the years of neglect of one who must have at all times been a most remarkable man; his attempt to attract attention by cocking a snook at people who had neglected him; and the 'reproach, hatred and opposition' that he succeeded in arousing as a result of his rudeness.

Nirad had been writing in Bengali for many years. But it was not until the publication of his first book in English, *The Autobiography of an Unknown Indian*, that he really aroused the interest of the class to which he belonged and which, because of the years of indifference to him, he had come heartily to loathe—the Anglicized upper-middle class of India. He did this with calculated contempt. He knew that the wogs were more English than Indian but were fond of proclaiming their patriotism at the expense of the British. That having lost their own traditions and not having fully imbibed those of England, they were a bastard breed with pretensions to intellectualism that seldom went beyond reading blurbs and reviews of books. He therefore decided to dedicate the work 'To the British Empire . . .' The wogs took the bait and having only read the dedication sent up a howl of protest. Many people who would not have otherwise read the autobiography, discovered to their surprise that there was nothing anti-Indian in its pages. On the contrary, it was the most beautiful picture of Eastern Bengal that anyone had ever painted. And at last India had produced a writer who did not cash in on naive Indianisms but could write the English language as it should be written––and as few, if any, living Englishmen could write.

Nirad is not neglected any more. He has become a celebrity and the most sought-after man in the social circles of Delhi. For the last many years, he and his family consisting of his charming wife and three equally remarkable sons have been living continuously under the blaze of arc lamps. Anecdotes of their incredible fund of knowledge are favourite topics at dinner parties.

The first story I heard of the Chaudhuri family was of a cocktail party given by the late director-general of All India Radio, Colonel Lakshmanan. Nirad had brought his wife and sons (in shorts and full boots) to the function. After the introductions, the host asked what Nirad would like to drink: he had some excellent sherry.

'What kind of sherry?' asked the chief guest. Colonel Lakshmanan had, like most people, heard of only two kinds. 'Both kinds,' he replied. 'Do you like dry or sweet?' This wasn't good enough for Nirad so he asked one of his sons to taste it and tell him. The thirteen-year-old lad took a sip, rolled it about his tongue and after a thoughtful pause replied, 'Must be an Oloroso 1947.' I do not know if the story is true. The Chaudhuris' encyclopaedic knowledge has created a lot of anecdotes like those which grew round Professor Spooner, some true, others made up to confirm the truth.

There is little doubt that Nirad can talk on any subject under the sun. There is not a bird, tree, butterfly or insect whose name he does not know in Latin, Hindi, Sanskrit and Bengali. Long before he went to London, he not only knew where the important monuments and museums were, but also the location of many famous restaurants. I heard him contradict a lady who had lived six years in Rome about the name of a street leading off from the Coliseum—and prove his contention. I've heard him discuss stars with astronomers, recite lines from an obscure fifteenth-century French poet to a professor of French literature, advise a wine dealer on the best vintages from Burgundy. At a small function in honour of Laxness, the Icelandic winner of the Nobel Prize for literature, I heard Nirad lecture him on Icelandic literature.

This fantastic accumulation of the bric-a-brac of knowledge has been acquired over years of study aided by a phenomenal memory. His small flat in one of the old bazars of Delhi is crammed with books on all subjects in many languages. He spends a good twelve hours of the day in reading and making notes.

Nirad is a small, frail man a little over five feet tall. He leads a double life—one at home where he is his real self, a conventional Bengali intellectual dressed in kurta and dhoti (in summer only a dhoti), doing his work sitting cross-legged on the floor. He is a devoted husband and a fond father who has taught all his sons himself. As soon as he steps outside the house he dons a different dress and personality. He always wears a suit with a tie and carries a monstrously large khaki solar topee on his head. He is then at war with the new India of Gandhi caps and khadi. He expects everyone to misunderstand him and succeeds in his attempt. For the many years he walked through the bazars to Broadcasting House, the street urchins greeted him with cries of 'Johnny Walker, Johnny Walker' and chanted 'Left, right, left, right', in time with his steps. To Indians outside his home he wants to be, and is, a *kala sahib*. That is the incarnation in which he is known to people who do not really know him; it is the Nirad Chaudhuri of the offensive dedications and not the 500 pages that follow. Nirad is quite emphatically not a kala sahib. He is as Bengali as his Bengali accent and he is more Indian than most Indians of his class because he knows more about his country, its history, literature, flora and fauna than almost any of his compatriots. What is more, in his own way, he has won more friends for India than those who wear their patriotism on their sleeves.

Nirad Chaudhuri is not a modest man: he has much to be immodest about. No Indian, living or dead, has written the English language as well as Nirad Chaudhuri (the only other I can think of as a peer is the neglected writer, Govind Desani.) As a matter of fact there are few English writers who have the same mastery over their mother tongue shown by this Bengali *bhadralok* in the books he has written. (Even if he were not to write another word, he has an assured place in the English world of letters.) The English have been gracious enough to acknowledge his greatness. It is only in his own country that he has been denied the honour he richly deserves. The Government of India issued a fiat to its various publicity organizations not to publish anything by him; and he has been vilified by soured critics in most Indian journals. There is little doubt that the civil servant who initiated the ban never read beyond the dedication of *The Autobiography of an Unknown Indian*.

Nirad is an angry man; and he has much to be angry about. But the combination of pride and anger has made life somewhat difficult for him and his family. Success has not mellowed him. *The Autobiography*, despite its greatness as a work of art, was not a best-seller. With the job gone and three growing sons on his hands, life became hard for the Chaudhuri family. Many jobs were open to him—commissions for articles and broadcasts (from foreign countries) could have come to him for the asking. But what Nirad has never done is to sell himself for money.

An incident illustrates the man's unbending adherence to his principles. Two years ago, the then finance minister, T.T. Krishnamachari, summoned me to his office and asked me to persuade Nirad to write a series of articles on the plight of the Bengal refugees on any terms he liked. I told the minister of the official ban on Nirad. Armed with the assurance that it would be raised, I asked Nirad over to break the good news to him personally. When he came, I told him of the enthusiasm with which Krishnamachari (and H.M. Patel) had referred to his writing and how they were willing to give him a blank cheque and clear official objections.

He sat back in the chair for a couple of minutes without saying a word and then asked me in a slow, gentle voice, 'So the Government of India has decided to raise its ban on me?'

'Yes, it has.'

'But I haven't decided to raise my ban on the Government of India.' Without another word, he picked up his solar topee and walked out of the office.

Nirad cannot suffer criticism. He first tries to ignore it but his pugnacity soon gets the better of his resolve. *The Autobiography,* which has been acclaimed by most English critics was, due to the dedication, adversely criticized by the Indian papers. Nirad tried to take the Indian reaction in his stride. 'A hound of a good breed never pays any heed to the barking of pye-dogs,' he said somewhat disdainfully. But as soon as a leading English literary magazine came out with a mildly critical review, Nirad's dander was up. 'I will teach the . . . a lesson,' he roared shaking his fist in anger. 'Wait and see what I do to them in my next book.'

A Passage to England received the most glorious reviews in the English press. Three editions were rapidly sold out and it had the distinction of becoming the first book by an Indian author to have become a best-seller in England. The bay windows of London's famous bookshop, Foyle's, were decorated with large-sized photographs of Nirad. Some Indian critics were, as in the past, extremely hostile. Nirad's reaction followed the same pattern. At first he tried not to be bothered by people 'who didn't know better'; then burst out with invective against the 'yapping curs'. I asked him how he reconciled these two attitudes. After a pause he replied, 'When people say nasty things about my books without really understanding what I have written, I feel like a father who sees a drunkard make an obscene pass at his daughter. I want to chastise him.' Then, with a typically Bengali gesture demonstrating the form of chastisement, 'I want to give them a shoe-beating with my *chappal*.'

~

On 23 November 1988, Nirad Chaudhuri was ninety. For over fifteen years he has lived in Oxford where he evidently intends to stay till the end—as did the man after whom he patterned his life, Max Mueller. His biography of Max Mueller is sub-titled *Scholar Extraordinary.*

Nirad C. Chaudhuri has good reasons to stay away from India. For some years he was persecuted by the government; then he received only grudging recognition for his scholarship. There were a handful of people (amongst whom I am privileged to count myself) who stood by him in his dark days and gave him the homage due to a man of genius. For a genius he certainly is. Nirad Babu has just completed the second volume of his autobiography. It should be the great literary event of 1988.

The period after the publication of *The Autobiography of An Unknown Indian* brought out the best and the worst in Nirad C. Chaudhuri. His second book, *A Passage to England*—the title being a take-off from E.M. Forster's *A Passage to India*—was largely an eminently readable travelogue though lacking in the acerbic quality of the earlier work. He had become a celebrity but being one did not increase his bank balance. He had dark moods of despair and became edgier than before. His small circle of friends which comprised the Jhabvalas, Mehra Masani and myself made it a point to celebrate Nirad's birthday by rotation in our homes. When John Freeman became Britain's High Commissioner in New Delhi, his wife Catherine took on the annual celebration in her home. An invitation to Nirad's birthday party at King George's Avenue became the hallmark of acceptance by Delhi's literary elite. None of this made much difference to Nirad's touchiness on some subjects, chiefly the chronic shortage of cash. I, who regarded it as a privilege to be able to help him out burnt my fingers doing so. I will let Nirad narrate the episode in his own words. His preface to *The Continent of Circe* entitled 'In gratitude' puts it as follows:

My thanks are due first and foremost to my friend, Khushwant Singh, the well-known Sikh writer, good companion, and man-about-town, for the loan of his portable typewriter. Though it may be said that my mind is feudal, my hands at least are of the machine age. I can write only on a typewriter, and mine was worn out. As soon as Khushwant Singh heard that my project of writing this series of works was held up because I could not immediately replace my broken machine, he lent me his own; afterwards he presented me with a brand new portable. He is also the only fellow-Indian (significantly a Sikh, and not a Hindu) who has put in good words for me in print in India. This needed courage.

But living where I live, even in feeling gratitude I cannot get away from *return indicarum natura,* one aspect of a duality in a great Zoroastrian manner, a secular conflict between Ahriman and Ahura Mazda in which light was bound to triumph over darkness. But the duality of the Hindu existence is like the cat-and-dog life of a maladjusted married couple who can neither separate nor live together. So just when, with the near-completion of one of the essays, my gratitude to Khushwant Singh was at its highest I read an account of the loan of the typewriter in public print. It was contained in an article entitled *An Interview with Khushwant Singh* by an American woman in a magazine which described itself as 'the official publication of the American Women's Club of Delhi'—and in it I read:

Interviewer: 'Who is the best Indian writer today?'

Khushwant Singh (as reported): 'In non-fiction? Without a doubt Nirad Chaudhuri . . . A bitter man, a poor man. He doesn't even own a typewriter. He borrows mine a week at a time.'

I was struck all of a heap. My poverty is, of course, well-known in New Delhi and much further afield, and therefore I was not prepared to see it bruited about by so august a body as the American Women's Club of Delhi. Why did the impressive board of twelve American women who were jointly looking after the magazine think it necessary to publish such small talk about a man who was even smaller by their standards, who had neither of the two things they understood and respected, namely money and official position? Was it because I was a writer? When I would only lament:

Why did I write? What sin to me unknown
Dip't me in ink, my parents' or my own?

Khushwant Singh told me that he had never made the statement in the form and spirit in which it was reproduced, and that he was not even aware of the real intention of the women he was entertaining at tea. Of course, I took his word for it. But even if in the course of a private conversation he had said all that was reported, that would not have made any difference to my affection for him. I tried to show that I bore no grudge by again borrowing the machine after the publication of the article and by most gratefully accepting the present of the new typewriter.

The conduct of the American women, however, I cannot even now understand unless I attribute it to the sad but inexorable law of the American impingement on Asia that the United States will never export any of its products to the East except those of which every decent American is ashamed, taken with its compliment that in retaliation, the East will set its lowest adventurers on the distributors of American money. The arrogance of the almsgiver is fitly matched by the impudence of the beggar.

The Continent of Circe won Nirad the Duff Cooper literary award. Circe, it may be recalled, was a sorceress in Greek mythology. Anyone who drank from her cup was turned into a pig. Nirad Babu's choice of titles leaves one in no doubt of the thesis he meant to expound: India is the sorceress; people who make it their home in the course of time, become dehumanized and turn into swine.

He starts off by asserting that foreigners and Anglicized Indians have never been able to understand India or Indians.

'A man who cannot endure dirt, dust, stench, noise, ugliness, disorder, heat and cold has no right to live in India,' proclaims Nirad Babu. He proceeds to describe his own habitat:

I live just inside the old wall built originally by the Moghul Emperor Shah Jahan, overlooking a fine part and commanding a magnificent view of the famous Ridge, the Jamuna, and the Jama Masjid. It is probably the finest aspect to be seen anywhere in Delhi. My western friends say that it reminds them of the view of the Borghese Gardens from the Pincio. But after independence, for four years, I saw people easing themselves in this park in the morning, sitting in rows. During this time the stench was so foul that after inhaling it for a year I fell ill and came very near death. Within the city I have seen streets running with sewage water and faeces floating on it while, undisturbed by this, vendors of vegetables and other foodstuffs were selling their produce on the adjacent pavements. I have never objected to or minded all this, and I will say that if I have any living knowledge of my country it is a reward for this unflinching realism. So, when Anglicised Indians come to argue with me, I expect them to possess at least a fragment of my knowledge and toleration of these conditions.

He quotes a story, *The Arabian Nights*, in which Prince Diamond wanted to go to the fabulous city of Wakak despite the deadly dangers that lay *en route*. Ultimately, armed with a magic weapon which would protect him from harm, he approached a sleeping giant, Simurg, who was to fly him to Wakak. To test Prince Diamond's ability to stand the ordeal, Simurg let out a stinking fart which lasted for over an hour, filling the atmosphere with a lethal stench. The Prince survived his ordeal because of his magic weapon and was able to visit Wakak. That is the kind of weapon people must arm themselves with if they want to get to terms with India and Indians.

The word Indian is a misnomer; it should be Hindu, meaning the people who live beyond the river Indus or Sindhu. Hinduism is not a religion: the concept of religion is alien to the people who subscribe to *sanatana dharma*, the eternal way. Nirad Babu divides the inhabitants into three ethnic groups: aboriginals, Mongols and those who came later—black, yellow and brown. What gave society its firm base was its caste system which remained mobile till the arrival of the Muslims. It was fossilized by the British.

British contempt for the Hindus as 'degraded, perverse, untruthful, shifty and effeminate' was far off the mark. Alberuni was closer to understanding these complex people and the contradiction in their character: renunciation and avarice, chastity with sex obsessions, morbid respect for animals with beastly cruelty, great learning with unbelievable stupidity.

'Therefore,' he went on to say, 'the scientific theories of the Hindus were in a state of utter confusion, devoid of order, and in the last resort, always mixed up with the silly notions of the crowd.' Alberuni compared their mathematics and astronomy to 'a mixture of pearls and sour dates or dung', and observed 'that both kinds of things were equal in their eyes because they could not raise themselves to the methods of a strictly scientific deduction'.

As might have been predicted, *The Continent of Circe* did not go down well with Indians. They read it and abused Nirad in the strongest language. Nothing pleased Nirad more than being abused for the wrong reasons. He seemed to enjoy provoking people into losing their tempers. I recall one evening at the Jhabvala home when Jhab's mother was visiting them. This Parsi dowager had seen difficult days under British rule. Her husband had been a labour leader and was one of the accused in the famous Meerut conspiracy case. She was an ardent nationalist and proud of her husband's role in the freedom movement. Apropos nothing, Nirad tossed in a wounding remark: 'Parsis are not Indians; no Indian looks upon them as fellow countrymen.'

Mrs Jhabvala tried to keep her cool. But when Nirad repeated the remark, she exploded, 'How dare you insult Parsis! When you were licking the boots of the British, Parsis like my husband were in British jails.'

'That makes no difference whatsoever,' answered Nirad coolly. 'I don't care how many Parsis went to jail; Indians do not look upon them as Indians.'

Mrs Jhabvala promptly retired to her bedroom.

The trouble with Nirad was that he was always right. In my home he had a hot argument with Kingsley Martin famous editor of the *New Statesman and Nation*. It was on some point of English history. Kingsley was a bad loser. When he found that he had lost the argument, he hit below the belt. 'Forgive my drawing attention to your elegant dinner jacket, Mr Chaudhuri, but your flies are open.' The very embarrassed Nirad ran into the bathroom to button up his trousers.

At times he lost patience with my ignorance and loudly called me a fool. His wife protested that by using that kind of language he would lose the few friends he had. 'But he is a fool,' retorted Nirad, 'if he doesn't know these little things, what else can I call him!'

He could be equally unkind to his wife. She was a dark, matronly lady of ample girth. Once, when he got into the car and ordered the driver to take him home, his wife was still busy saying goodbye to her hosts. Suddenly Nirad Babu beamed: 'I must not forget the big black boiler which keeps this little engine going.'

Nirad Chaudhuri's most serious book is *Hinduism*. It is not the platitudinous repetition of what one sees in other books on the subject: Vedas, Upanishads, Puranas, etc. but an altogether novel and refreshing approach to Hinduism as it is practised and what it means to the average Hindu. He fires his first salvo in the introduction:

> Salvation is never the object of the religious observances and worship of the Hindus. The main object is wordly prosperity, and this absorption in the world has made the doctrine of rebirth in it the most appealing and strongly held belief among all the nations put forward by them about existence after deaths They so loved the world that they made the possibility of leaving it for good even after many cycles of birth as remote and difficult as possible.

Just about everything Nirad has to say on Hinduism will raise the hackles of orthodox Hindus but none will be able to fault him on his facts.

Perhaps the only books that did not come up to the high mark Nirad set for himself by his earlier works are *Culture in a Vanity Bag* and *Clive of India*. The first is trivial and perhaps the product of a short phase of obsession with erotica in an otherwise sedate man. The second is a too-laboured attempt to defend a character who most Indians regard as indefensible. However, they do not reduce Nirad's stature. This very small man who, when he strode down Nicholson Road in his solar topee, was jeered by street urchins with cries of 'Johnny Walker, Johnny Walker' towers above his contemporaries as one of the intellectual giants India has produced in recent years.

My Days with Krishna Menon

I had met him before I joined his staff as information officer in the Indian High Commission. During my days in London University, I had heard his name mentioned in student circles. His India League was one of the many organizations agitating for Indian freedom. But it was the only one affiliated to the Indian National Congress and had hitched its wagon to Nehru's rising star in preference (and at times in opposition) to many other Indian leaders who were at that time competing for political pre-eminence. Menon organized receptions for Nehru whenever he came to England. He had him address public meetings and introduced him to prominent socialists, many of whom he had persuaded to join the India League. His appointment as the first high commissioner for India in London which came as a surprise to so many was assumed by those who knew this background. The only person who took several months to believe the incredible windfall in his fortunes was Menon himself. He suspected disloyalty where there was none; he confused candour with cheek and constantly reminded his staff and himself: 'I am the high commissioner, you know!' He surrounded himself with a bunch of sycophants whose chief occupation was to hang round him at all hours and inform on their colleagues. The chief amongst them was a not unattractive girl on the clerical staff (she was later promoted by Menon and then selected to the Indian Foreign Service by a three-man board of which Menon and his friend, Harold Laski, were members) This girl set the pattern of address. Menon was 'H.E.'—His Excellency. She also became the First Lady of India

House and, to the puckish delight of Menon, cocked a snook at the wives of the senior officials. At India House receptions, she received the Churchills, the Edens and the Attlees; she rode in the high commissioner's Rolls-Royce flying the Indian tricolour.

As I said before, I had met Menon during my days at the University. He and Rajni Patel, an ardent communist, were going to attend some sort of international conference in Paris. I was going for a holiday. In those days Paris was the recognized 'fatigue station' for those fagged out by examinations and continence. Menon and Patel had the load of the world on their shoulders: I was preoccupied with visions of Place Pigalle. All of us were equally eager to get to Paris. Few words passed between us in the railway compartment in which we found ourselves. Menon sat hunched in his overcoat shivering with cold. Both he and Patel were representing some august body or the other and kept discussing resolutions they were going to move. They did not react very favourably to my cheerful talk and obscene jokes (of which I have always had a large repertoire).

At Dover we had to get off the train and into the Channel steamer. There was a long queue. Menon became very impatient and decided to go ahead. Patel and I trailed behind him. The ticket collector reminded us somewhat sharply that we had to take our turn. Menon reacted equally sharply. 'You treat us like this because we are coloured. We won't stand for it very long, you know!' The collector was taken aback—so were those waiting their turn in the queue. But it worked. The collector muttered an oath and let us pass.

The reception Menon gave me when I joined his staff still rankles in my mind. I was only an information officer. Between me and Menon was my immediate superior, Sudhir Ghosh, the PRO who, unknown to me at the time, was on very bad terms with Menon. Sudhir had worked for a time with Mahatma Gandhi and had been entrusted by the Mahatma to deliver personal messages to Attlee and Cripps. His pockets used to bulge with letters written by some leader to another. He was adept at veering conversation in a way which gave him the opportunity to quote from these epistles. His office was a veritable picture gallery of important politicians whose autographed photographs hung on the walls. Beneath the large glass slab on his working table was a letter from the Mahatma to him with words to the effect that India needed young, dedicated men like him. It wasn't much wonder that when Sudhir was appointed PRO he looked upon himself as the principal liaison between India's millions and the people of England. The chief instruments of his goodwill were a group of well-meaning but utterly naive Quakers. Sudhir was willing to let Menon do his job if Menon would let him get on with his. Menon was not so accommodating. He refused to allow an 'embassy within an embassy' as he described the PRO's department. Sudhir pleaded with the deputy Prime Minister, Sardar Patel, who was then minister-in-charge of information and broadcasting (including public relations' offices in foreign countries). Menon denounced Sudhir as an intriguer and a 'Patellite'. None of this was known to me when I signed the High Commissioner's visitors' book and rang up his personal secretary for an appointment. I was told that the appointment would have to be asked for by the PRO who would introduce me.

In some respects Menon was a great stickler for protocol. But there was more than protocol behind the snub. Four days later an agitated Sudhir Ghosh hauled me from my room to present me to Menon, who, according to him, was 'furious with him'. He was. My jovial greeting and broad-smiled reference to our having met before was received with a quick shake by his claw-like hand. He had a scowl on his face and turned the full fire of the assault on me. 'Did they teach you any manners in India? I know you have been in the office for nearly a week and you haven't had the courtesy to come and see me. If this is the way you are going to behave I will have to ask for your replacement. I can do that; I am the high commissioner, you know!'

I did not know whether he was pulling my leg or really angry. Nevertheless the grin on my face vanished and I began to stutter explanations, 'I asked for an appointment the first day. I signed the book. I . . . I . . .'

Sudhir Ghosh tried to come to my rescue. 'Sir, it is my fault, I . . .'

'I was not speaking to you, Mr Ghosh,' snapped Menon. 'I will ask for your explanation later. Yes, what have you to say?' he demanded turning to me.

'I am sorry, I have never been a government servant and I don't know the rules. I did the best I knew. Mr Lall knows I have been waiting for the interview and instructions since the day I arrived.'

Arthur Lall of the ICS had already become a great favourite of Menon's. He noticed the scowl on Menon's face lift and ventured to put in a word in my defence. 'That is true, sir. Khushwant Singh did ask me about seeing you and I told him that it would be arranged by Sudhir.'

The scowl re-appeared on Menon's face. 'I will send for you later,' he said, dismissing me. Before I shut the door I heard the storm break loose on Sudhir.

I was very shaken by this experience. Few people had ever spoken to me like that and the only one whom I had forgiven was my father. It took me a long time to soothe my nerves of the humiliation and anger. I thought of resigning from the service. It seemed too much of a defeat—and I did not want to return to India. I took myself for a walk along the Embankment.

I came back a couple of hours later to the office and found a note on my table. It was from Krishna Menon asking me to join him for tea. My first impulse was to tear up the invitation. Then I decided to go and convey my resentment by being aloof and cold.

I didn't have a chance. As soon as I entered the reception room, Menon extricated himself from the ring of admirers and came to greet me. He put his arms round my shoulder and drew me aside. 'I am sorry I spoke to you harshly this morning; I trust you had the intelligence to know it wasn't meant for you. If you haven't, I'll send you back by the next boat.' His face lit up with a smile. It was too much for my humiliated ego. I almost burst into tears. 'I . . . I suspected as much,' I replied.

'Come along and have some tea.' He plied me with cups of tea, *papadams* and *pakoras*. He ordered me to eat. 'I am the high commissioner, you know! You have to obey my orders. Eat this! . . . and this!'

From the very first day a love–hate relationship grew up between Menon and myself. Within the week I found myself an ardent member of the sycophantic group which consisted of Arthur Lall, a Captain Srinivasan of the Indian Navy, Prithi Singh (now in the foreign service) and the girl, 'Miss Singh'. We were the 'inner cabinet'. The rest of the India House staff divided into two: those proven to be pro-Krishna Menon and the rest who not being pro-Menon were therefore traitors to India.

My first act as a member of Menon's inner group was to be instrumental in his designs of getting rid of Sudhir Ghosh. In his resolve to run an autonomous PRO department, Sudhir tripped up badly and in his attempt to retrieve his position he was unworthy of his profession as a Gandhian. The incident as I recall it after many years was somewhat as follows.

It was the autumn of 1947 when Kashmir was overrun by tribesmen coming across Pakistan's frontiers with Pakistani connivance. The Hindu Maharaja belatedly turned for help to India; Indian troops were rushed to stem the tribal onslaught. The Mahatma made a statement exonerating the Indian government's action. This statement, repeated by Reuters, was given prominence in many English newspapers including the *Times*. Sudhir, without consulting anyone, sent off a telegram to Bapu (as he was wont to address the Mahatma) asking him to deny his (Gandhi's) departure from pacifism. This the Mahatma did. Sudhir sent a letter to the *Times* quoting the Mahatma's letter and accusing Reuters of anti-Gandhian bias. Unfortunately, a day earlier I had received the official version of Gandhiji's speech which I had released to the British press through the India House news-sheet *Indiagram*.

This release was worded in exactly the same way as Reuters's. Christopher Chancellor, then head of Reuters, triumphantly quoted *Indiagram* to refute Sudhir Ghosh's allegations. Next morning the *Times* published Sudhir's and Chancellor's letters side by side.

I was in the habit of coming to the office very early. I found a note on my table asking me to see the high commissioner at once.

Menon was in a dark mood. But he kept his temper with me. His quarry had walked into his trap and he wasn't going to leave any loopholes. 'Did you know of Sudhir Ghosh's telegram to Gandhi?'

'No, sir.'

'Did you see Gandhi's reply?'

'No, sir.'

'Does Ghosh see what you put out in your *Indiagram*?'

'He leaves the office early. We reckon to send out press releases by 5 p.m. He usually sees them next morning.'

This last bit seemed like a possible loophole. Menon plugged it at once. 'I want to know the precise minute in which you sent out this press release, the time a copy was delivered to Ghosh, and the time he left the office. There will be no mistakes. I rely on you. This is most serious. Report to me within half an hour.'

I checked the timings. The *Indiagram* had been sent out as usual sometime between 4 and 5 p.m. A file had been left on Sudhir Ghosh's table. I found it on a mound of *Indiagrams* in the 'In' tray. I peeped into Ghosh's engagement diary lying on his desk and saw that on the day in question he had no afternoon engagement. I made my report to Menon. 'Tell Ghosh to see me the moment he comes in. Leave a note on his table.'

I wrote a note and placed it under a glass paperweight on Sudhir's table. This note became an important weapon in Menon's hands.

Ghosh sauntered into the office at 11 a.m. and leisurely began to peruse the daily papers, starting with the *Times*. He summoned me to his office. 'Why was this *Indiagram* sent out without my approval?' he demanded somewhat haughtily.

I could afford to be cheeky. 'It is always sent out between 4 and 5 p.m. You are seldom in the office at the time. If you like, we will dispatch it a day later. Only, the high commissioner is anxious that it should get to the papers that very day. Incidentally, he is most anxious to see you at once!'

'Yes, yes, I will see him when I am free. There is no urgency. In future nothing should leave this office without my approval. These are my orders. I will circulate them in writing. I will see you later.'

I refused to be snubbed and played the double game as adroitly as I could. 'I wish you could settle these matters with the high commissioner. I get one set of orders from him, another from you. And rudeness from both. I will just throw in the sponge.' I marched out triumphantly.

At midday, the high commissioner's phone rang again summoning me up to his room. 'What time did Ghosh come in?'

'About 11 a.m., sir.'

'Did you tell him I wanted him urgently?'

'I did, sir. I had left a note to that effect earlier.'

Menon sent his personal messenger to fetch Ghosh. A very pale and ruffled Sudhir entered the High Commissioner's room. Menon thundered at him, accusing him of deliberate disregard of orders. Sudhir replied blandly that he had come in a few minutes ago and had just then been told by me that he was wanted by the high commissioner. He said that he had seen no note on his table. Menon knew that Sudhir was lying and took the chance of my finding the note. He asked me to leave so that he could deal with Ghosh, by himself. I went straight to Ghosh's office and picked up my (now crumpled) note from his wastepaper basket. Without ceremony, I re-entered Menon's room where the two were having it out and placed the note on the table. Sudhir persisted in his denial. He insisted that he did not see the note.

Menon took it upon himself to suspend Ghosh and ordered me to take over till a new PRO was appointed. He sent a detailed report of the incident to the government, backed by a written statement by me. A personal letter was addressed to Nehru, mentioning amongst other things, Ghosh being a Patellite. Ghosh sent his own version of the affair to Sardar Patel and a personal explanation to Mahatma Gandhi. A week later both men flew to New Delhi to fight the last round of their battle. We were left in peace. India House became, as Menon liked to describe it in his absence, 'a mausoleum'.

There is little doubt that Menon was in the right. And Menon knew how to press his advantage to the full. Neither Gandhi nor Patel could save Sudhir. Patel did, however, wreak his vengeance. By then I had come to be known as a 'Menon favourite'. While Menon was on his way back from Delhi to London, Patel sent telegraphic orders transferring me to Ottawa.

Ghosh was crestfallen. When I went to see him in his office, he was sitting hunched with his elbows on the table and his head between his hands. 'I have no malice against Menon,' he said looking straight at me. 'I have no hatred against anyone. I have been with the Mahatma.'

He told me of all that had taken place in Delhi between Gandhi, the Prime Minister, Sardar Patel and other senior officials. He told me of the 'lying and trickery' Menon had employed to get rid of him. 'But I have no malice against Menon or anyone else in the world; I have been with the Mahatma.' He shut his eyes and meditated for a few moments. He smiled and continued his narrative. Menon, he said, would stoop to anything to gain his ends. He was an intriguer, he had poisoned Nehru's ears against him (Sudhir) and spread stories that Sudhir had become too big for his shoes. Menon was envious because Sudhir was a friend of all the people that mattered: Cripps, Attlee, Sorensen, etc. 'But I have no malice against Menon or anyone else in the world. I have been with Bapu.'[1]

Menon stood by people who stood by him. He refused to give my replacement, P.L. Bhandari (now our Ambassador in some country), who knew the PRO's job far better than I, a chance.

He 'talked' Nehru into taking over external publicity from the information and broadcasting ministry. And as soon as that was accomplished he manoeuvred my transfer to London.

Five months later I was back in England. So began my second tenure with Menon.

~

I was drawn closer into Menon's circle. I rented one floor of the house in which Arthur Lall was living. Lall had become Menon's chief confidant. Menon used to often drop in at the house at Walton Place (behind Harrod's) and after a while began to summon me down into the sitting-room.

Arthur Lall was hypnotized by Menon's personality. He could indulge in the most outrageous flattery. 'You are the greatest speaker of the English language in the world. If I may be permitted to say so to your face, you have a far greater mind than Stalin's or anyone else's. I should know because I work with you.' He would ring up Menon long after midnight and often the two conversed like lovers.[2] I shared a part of the confidence reposed in Lall and though I could not match his words, I did the best I could to give currency to the legends of Menon's great intellect, his brilliant oratory, his contempt for worldly goods and his celibacy.

It was not easy for outsiders to enter Menon's circle. Most tried; few, a very few, succeeded. Menon reacted violently to people's looks and gave them short shrift simply because he did not like their noses or the colour of their skin. He had ways of making them feel small. An excellent information officer working under me, called Pendsay, he always addressed as Bhonsley. An officer who spoke indistinctly was 'Mr Baw Baw'. Two brigadiers of the Indian Army were made to share a tiny cubicle meant for the PRO's stenographer. Some, however, broke through his resistance by sheer persistence.

During my stay in India House there were two notable examples of people who made Menon's charmed circle.

Shri K. was a junior officer in the education department. His sycophancy had been of little avail because Menon simply did not like him. I was present on one occasion when he was particularly savage with K. He was looking through some files when I noticed his eyebrows twitch and his face go pale with anger. He pressed his bell and barked at the messenger. 'Get that ass K.'

He began to mutter. I caught some disjointed words: 'No brains—really the worst of fellows the government sends me!'

Five minutes later K. entered the room rubbing his hands with invisible soap and a nervous, fawning smile hovering on his face. 'Sir, you sent for me.'

The storm broke. 'Have you any brains?' roared Menon, flourishing a file in front of him. 'Did you read my instructions? Do you ever apply your mind to your work?'

'I am sorry, sir, I . . .'

'Get out!' thundered Menon. He flung the file at him. K. collected the papers strewn on the floor and quietly walked out.

Menon clutched his head between his hands. He remained in that position for a long time till the temper was drained out of his system. He looked up and asked me, 'I was very rude to him, wasn't I?'

'Yes, sir, you were a little rough.'

He dialled the internal telephone. His voice was now soft and heavy. 'K., will you come up!'

A minute later a very pale K. re-entered Menon's bureau. 'I am sorry, K., I lost my temper with you. I apologize.'

'Not at all, sir,' replied K. 'It's a privilege to be ticked off by you. It's only then we know we are in the wrong and can rectify our mistakes.'

K.'s promotion was rapid. He was seconded to the Foreign Service by the same board that selected 'Miss Singh'. He served with considerable distinction as India's ambassador in many countries.

Equally successful in gaining Menon's affection (though not respect) was the new military attache, a Sikh Brigadier. The

Brigadier belonged to a landed family of the Punjab and was adept in *durbardari*—courtcraft. His wife was the daughter of a wealthy man listed in Griffin's *Chiefs and Ruling Families of the Punjab* (a sort of *Debrett's Peerage* of the Punjab.) Although her father was neither a chief nor had any ruling powers, the daughter made up for these shortcomings by acquiring the maiden name 'Queenie'.

Menon took an instant dislike to the Singhs. The Brigadier's obsequious manner and nasal tone irritated him. He was calculatedly rude to the couple, referring to him as a moron or the Chief of the Morons. The Brigadier's reaction was charming in its naivete: 'Sir, who cares about such things these days; we are a democracy now.' Menon rightly suspected that 'Queenie' was a gossip. He ignored her at official functions and within the hearing of many people described her in the most uncomplimentary terms. His vocabulary was enriched by years among English working classes. 'Bitch' and 'slut' came easily on his tongue.

The Singhs set about winning over Menon in classic oriental style. They discovered who Menon liked and proceeded to cultivate them. I being a Sikh and therefore a natural rival, was left out. Other favourites were entertained lavishly. 'Queenie' paid special attention to 'Miss Singh' and the secretary of the India League. 'Miss Singh' was courted with flowers and flattery. The secretary had an insatiable thirst which she was willing to slake at anyone's expense. When all seemed to be going well, 'Queenie' slipped up by being indiscreet about 'Miss Singh's' relations with Menon. She was subjected to a terrible tongue-lashing; Menon said to her face what he had been saying in public behind her back. A few days later, the couple called on Menon to crave forgiveness. 'Queenie' made an abject and tearful apology to all parties concerned. Menon stopped referring to the Brigadier as a moron. 'Not a bad chap at heart,' he admitted grudgingly. A few months later the Brigadier claimed with pride that Menon was not only a boss he was proud to serve but also a close friend of the family.

Most people who joined the high commission staff started by being extra loyal to Menon. They denounced his critics and informed Menon of them; they tried to cultivate members of the 'inner cabinet'. Some were soured by their experience, particularly Menon's habit of taking subordinates into confidence and encouraging them to defy their seniors. Some took the discourtesy and mauling they received from Menon as 'all in a day's work'. Outstanding of this class was the late R.S. Mani who was the first deputy high commissioner when I joined office. Seldom have I seen a senior official treated more like a doormat—and like a doormat keep the 'Welcome' sign on his face. Most seniors boasted that they brooked no nonsense and spoke their minds to Menon. I never heard anyone do that in my presence. In my time very few had the courage to hit back. Those who did like Ashok Chanda, for a short while Menon's deputy, or Subimal Dutt, later secretary-general who investigated India House affairs and described them officially as 'chaotic', soon learnt that nothing they said or wrote about Menon made the slightest difference in the esteem in which Prime Minister Nehru held him. In any case most of Chanda's battles with Menon were fought on paper. '*Hum shala ko aisa* file *men mara*'—I gave the bounder such a hiding on the file—was a Chanda favourite. Others learned from the experience of these men and simply bided their time. M.J. Desai, who succeeded Chanda as Menon's deputy, would shrug his shoulders and say, '*Sab chalta hai*'—everything goes. Sir Dhiren Mitra, legal adviser, remained behind a screen of pipe smoke and muttered philosophically, '*Pagul hai*' (He is mad). He was however the first man to draw Nehru's attention to financial irregularities committed by Menon. Some threw caution to the winds. The air attache, Shivdev Singh (now air-marshal) ordered his staff to keep away from Menon's receptions. A telephone operator told him to 'go to hell'. It was to Menon's credit that he went up to apologize to her.

There were aspects about Menon which were akin to madness. He was a demon for work. But a more disorganized worker I have never met. He would waste hours checking menus of the house cafeterias and the mileage and petrol consumption of the fleet of motor cars he had bought for India House, while contracts for supply of jeeps and aircraft involving millions of pounds were bungled. He would spend many hours at conferences where nothing was ever done and then punish himself by keeping awake, till the early hours of the morning—and punish others close to him by summoning them at odd times. (For many days I had to sleep in my office.) I suspected he took drugs or sleeping tablets because I often found him half asleep at his desk. Dozing off at a formal lunch or dinner was a favourite pastime. (A curious trait he shared with Nehru. At a lunch I gave to editors of English papers, both men slept through most of the meal.) Like many men, he was very ill-tempered in the mornings. By noon his bile juices would begin to flow and a more affable Menon would emerge. He could be most cheerful about midnight. I imagined there was something symbolic in the fizzy lemonade he drank before retiring to bed and his own late night effervescence.

Menon was a poor judge of men. He disliked the well-bred and warmed towards the vulgar. Snobs and the old-school *koi hais* he insulted in and out of season. This trait often landed him in trouble—as it did when he got the dubious Mr Potter to handle contracts for the supply of defence equipment for the Indian Army. Potter was Menon's friend. So also were a film producer and his sculptress wife. The former was a Cockney and as poor a film producer as he was a translator of Russian poetry. The latter was a talented artist but also a shameless grabber. The two together made an impossible pair. But with these types Menon was most at ease. And he stood by them in times of trouble. He sheltered them against charges of corruption. If they sired bastards (some did in office) he protected them. If they were down and out, he found them jobs and money. But he also expected lifelong gratitude. He seldom got it.

It was hard to judge the sort of people Menon would like or dislike. As a rule he was suspicious of journalists; for Indians of that fraternity he had a positive aversion. Sundar Kabadi, who was then president of the Indian Journalists' Association, was a thorn in Menon's side. He addressed Menon without any honorifics and could be as rude to Menon as Menon was to him. Alec Reid, a Scotsman with the *Hindustan Times* and his wife Ela Sen;[3] K.P. Ghosh of United Press International (UPI) and his wife Paula Wiking of *Blitz;* and Taussig of *Eastern World* were absolute anathema to him. Amongst the few he liked were Shelvankar of *The Hindu* and Parthasarathy of the PTA, whom he was instrumental in having taken into the Indian Foreign Service. Of the English journalists he often expressed regard for David Astor of the *Observer*. Nevertheless, in my presence he savaged Astor and his colleagues William Clarke and Sebastian Haffner. 'You English are a race of brigands,' Menon exploded apropos nothing before dismissing them. I recall Astor's remark as I was taking him down the lift. 'Public relations for Krishna must be quite a job!' It was.

I tried to discover what exactly it was that Menon liked or disliked about the men and women he met. He had a sense of beauty and the one thing that his favourites had in common were good looks. Lall and Prithi Singh were handsome men. 'Miss Singh' attracted him as a symbol of modern India. He had left Malabar thirty years earlier when Indian women were inhibited. Her chi-chi convent accent and coquettishness completely captivated him. Of the officers' wives, Arthur Lall's wife, Sheila, and mine were favourites for the same reason. They also shared the distinction of being 'misunderstood' by their husbands. And Menon had great understanding of misunderstood wives. In those four years, the only two whom he liked and trusted who could not lay claims to looks were the League Secretary Bridgitte Tunnards (she was in her late fifties and had goitre) and myself. Menon liked tidiness. He liked people to be well dressed. He was himself always immaculately clad in expensive suits. My creaseless grey flannel trousers and tweed coat irritated him to the point of distraction. One morning when I went to show him the press clippings he looked me up and down with a sense of disgust. He rang 'Miss Singh', asked her to cancel his morning's appointments and sent for his Rolls-Royce. A few minutes later he came into my room and literally dragged me by the sleeve into his car. He did not tell me what it was all about. We drove across London to High Street, Kensington. I found myself in a tailor's establishment. Menon ignored my suggestions, chose two of the most expensive pieces in the shop and then asked the tailor to take my measurements. I submitted with embarrassment. On the way back I thanked him profusely as I believed he intended making these a present to me. They were worth more than fifty guineas each. They were not a present—Menon was very close-fisted with his money: the only generosity he ever showed was in sending flowers to ladies he was courting or buying toys for children—whom oddly enough he also courted. Nevertheless, the suits were an excellent buy; I wear them to this day.

Menon disliked most people and made no secret of this. It was not unusual for him to start a conversation with a senior officer with the words, 'Mr So and so, I do not like you . . .' I was often put in situations of extreme embarrassment by his outbursts. One which stands out in my memory was an encounter with the philosopher Dr C.E.M. Joad, who was celebrated for his quick wit and repartee. I had thrown a party for my friend Govind Desani on the publication of his novel *All About H. Hatter* and had persuaded Menon to come. By coincidence Menon and Joad arrived one after the other. I was helping Menon take off his overcoat when he rasped loud enough for Joad to hear, 'If I had known you were going to have that bounder, I would never have come.' I hurried Menon up the stairs and turned with a fawning smile to help Dr Joad take off his leather jacket. He was smoking his pipe unperturbed. He took it out and asked me in his loud, squeaky voice, 'Isn't that fellow called Menon?'

'Yes, sir.'

'What's he doing here?'

'He is high commissioner for India.'

'Yes, of course I know he is high commissioner and all that. But I thought this party was for literate people—writers and critics and that sort—people who read books—not just anybody.' This too was loud enough to catch Menon's ears.

Wherever Krishna Menon went he took good care that he was the centre of attraction. His unusual appearance put him at an advantage. And if there was any danger of anyone stealing the show, he had many tricks to efface his rivals. At the annual banquet of the Royal Society of Cutlers in Sheffield he did this with consummate skill. This was in the first year of independence when the British were still very nostalgic about India. Menon was the guest of honour amongst a crowd of sentimental Englishmen who believed that Indians loved them as much as they loved the Indians—and were grateful to the English for granting them independence. Menon was quick to sense the atmosphere of patronage. He sat through the meal without touching any food or talking to the people near him. When he was asked to speak, he made a bitingly witty oration. He made fun of his hosts. They laughed politely. But it was obvious that they did not like what he was saying and considered it extremely bad form. Menon sat down feeling he had knifed the Cutlers forever. But to everyone's surprise the Cutler chosen to thank the chief guest happened to be a better speaker than Menon. He had the presence of mind to give up the formal speech he had intended to deliver and answer Menon's witticisms about the British with some pungent anecdotes about the Indians. Menon was very discomfited. He began to look ill: he could do that without much difficulty. I saw him turn to a waiter standing behind him and whisper in his ear. I knew he had asked for a cup of tea.

The speaker went on with his oration. After having roused applause with his experiences in India, he turned to his earlier encounters with Krishna Menon. He started narrating what promised to be a highly amusing anecdote about Menon. Just then a cup of tea was placed before Menon. The speaker built his story towards a climax. I saw Menon raise his cup in his shaking hand. As the speaker paused to deliver his punch line, Menon dropped his cup on the table. There was a loud clatter of breaking china. Waiters rushed to clear the debris and mop the table. Everyone was apologizing to everyone else. The speech came to an abrupt end—the anecdote remained untold. Menon's speech, though in bad taste, remained the *piece de resistance* of the evening.

~

As high commissioner Menon was king of India House and the most important Indian in Great Britain. Although this was a great booster of his morale, his vanity was often hurt now that he had also to meet many people more important than he. He devised ways to hold the centre of the stage.

The first Commonwealth Prime Ministers' Conference was much publicized in the British press. Menon, despite his closeness to Nehru, was not taken much notice of. He disliked being, as he himself described, 'a shadow of Nehru'. He called conferences at India House at odd hours. One Sunday, twenty or more of us were summoned on 'urgent' business. We were plied with cups of tea but none of us discovered the nature of the business for which we had been assembled. Every fifteen minutes Menon's brows would pucker with irritation and he would announce, 'It's a damned nuisance, lunch! There is so much work to do and I have to motor fifty miles to look at food I can't eat.' The lunch he referred to was given by the Mountbattens to Nehru and the Attlees in their country home at Romney. So it went on till it was nearly one o'clock and his staff was in a high state of agitation. Menon went. He was almost an hour late. But he did keep Nehru, the Attlees and the Mountbattens waiting for him. Menon made unpunctuality a rule of his life. Being late always attracts more attention than being punctual.

A somewhat different episode was a lunch with Sir Arthur Rank. Rank's organization was planning to make a film on the

Taj Mahal; their PRO, Finney had given me several excellent lunches and wanted his boss to meet Menon to broach the question of facilities the Indian government would provide for shooting the film.

There was considerable excitement in the office, particularly among the bevy of stenographers, when Sir Arthur Rank's heavily embossed invitation card was received. It was assumed that Menon would be delighted to go. But Menon was unpredictable. He announced the invitation at a staff meeting and added that he could not afford to waste his time on film makers, film stars and their ilk. Everyone protested; with great difficulty we prevailed upon Menon to accept. He gave us to understand that it was only for our sakes that he had accepted what would inevitably be a very boring lunch. For the next few days the subject of Rank's lunch was brought up by some device or the other and how the reluctant 'H.E.' had been made to accept—'You see, he's not one bit interested in meeting beautiful film stars. He's only going as a part of his duty.'

The day arrived. Three other members of the staff to whom the invitation had been extended accompanied Menon in his Rolls-Royce to the Dorchester Hotel where Sir Arthur Rank had a suite of rooms. We were received by Finney, taken up to the suite and introduced to some producers and script-writers. There were no glamorous stars; it was a stag lunch. We looked around for Sir Arthur Rank. Finney saw our questioning looks. 'Sir Arthur will be in any moment. Won't you have a drink in the other room?' He herded us into a large octagonal room where the lunch table was laid out and a waiter handed round drinks. Finney went back to the other room and knocked at the door on the side. I followed Finney to tell him that Menon was an impatient, touchy sort of person and should not be kept waiting. Before I could get to Finney, the door on which he had knocked opened and an officious voice demanded, 'Yes?'

'Sir, the high commissioner is here.'

'Who?'

'The high commissioner for India, Mr Menon.'

'What the devil is he doing here?'

'We've invited him for lunch.'

'What on earth for?'

'Sir,' whispered Finney fiercely, 'it's about that film on the Taj Mahal; we thought . . .'

'Oh yes, that Indian film business. Okey-doke. I'll join you in a second.'

A much-relieved Finney announced to us that Sir Arthur was on his way. A minute later the great film magnate made his appearance. He was wreathed in smiles and welcomed Menon. 'Mr High Commissioner, it's a great pleasure and a privilege to have you here.'

Menon extended his paw for a brief shake and then relapsed into a sullen silence. It was obvious the two great men were utterly bored with each other. The lunch was kept going by Finney and I cracking meaningless jokes at the top of our voices. (The modern PRO is a reincarnation of the court jester of medieval times.) As soon as the coffee was finished Menon got up. 'I must get back to my work. Thank you, Mr Rank. (He did not use titles on principle.) If you need any assistance, my PRO will look after you.' Sir Arthur was as keen to speed the parting guest as the guest was to take his leave. 'Thanks for coming. My PRO and yours are friends. They can settle the business between themselves.'

The film on the Taj was never made.

One of the memorable Menon episodes was at Dublin when he went to present his credentials as the Indian ambassador to the Irish Republic. He took with him his three defence service advisors and myself. My wife was asked to be in the party to look after the social engagements.

India was the first country to open a full-fledged embassy in Ireland; the Irish government had consequently planned quite an elaborate tamasha. We did not know the details except for the luncheons and dinners we had agreed to inflict on each other.

On the morning in question, my telephone rang. It was

Menon. His voice was barely audible; he asked me to come to his room at once. I found him in a state of collapse. 'I am very sick,' he groaned. 'You'll have to cancel the arrangements for the presentation of credentials.'

I was aghast. Before I could protest he spoke more fiercely. 'Don't you see I am very ill? I can't go through with it! Ring up the chief of protocol. Give me those pills and a tumbler of water.'

I handed him his pills and the water. He swallowed a couple and fell into a sort of stupor. I thought I'd wait a while to see if he were really ill before I sent for a doctor or rang up the protocol people.

I looked out of the window onto the square. A squad of motor-cycle police drew up noisily outside the hotel. I opened the window to get a better look. The roar of the motor-cycle engines fell on Menon's ears. He opened one eye and asked, 'What is that racket?'

'A motor-cycle squad. I suppose to escort your car to the President's palace,' I replied.

Menon shut his eyes. His face was a little more mobile than it had been five minutes before.

I saw a troop of Irish Guards turn the corner and march towards the hotel. Menon also heard the tramp of marching feet come to a halt beneath the window and the words of command to stand at ease. He opened both his eyes this time and enquired what the new noise was about. 'Regiment of Irish Guards,' I replied. 'They will probably form a procession.'

Menon was positively interested and sat up in bed.

'Shall I ring up the chief of protocol?' I asked.

'Give me another five minutes,' he replied. 'If I don't feel any better, we'll have to call it off.'

The sound of bagpipes assailed our ears. I looked out of the window. 'What is that now?' demanded Menon.

'Irish Highlanders.'

The bagpipes fell silent. A brass band took its place and came to a crashing halt beneath the window. Menon leaped out of his bed with the agility of a panther and took a long look at the motorcyclists, the Guards and the Highlanders. He limped back to bed. 'I suppose it is my duty to go. I'll feel better after a bath. Go and see if the others are ready.'

Half an hour later Menon emerged from his room looking very spruce in his black sherwani, white chooridars and his ivory-handled cane. We lined ourselves beside him.

It was 'Roses, roses all the way' through the streets of Dublin with Menon waving from the open car to the cheering crowds that thronged the pavements.

In the morning Menon presented his credentials to the President. The ceremony was followed by an official reception Where the diplomatic corps and members of Parliament including Eamon de Valera, then leader of the Opposition, were present. In the afternoon Dr Douglas (the President) invited Menon to a quiet cup of tea. This time only my wife and I accompanied him.

We were received by the President in his study. It was a dark, oak-panelled room lined with books. The chairs and sofas were upholstered in leather; a peat fire smouldered in the chimney. The room had a sombre, peaceful atmosphere in which Dr Douglas's pipe seemed to be most appropriate. Menon was ill-at-ease in this old world atmosphere of sedate sophistry. Over a cup of tea and scones—it had to be scones—Dr Douglas asked Menon how India was doing since its independence. Menon launched on a breathless narration of India's mineral wealth, her enormous potential, the first Five Year Plan, naming the hydro-electric projects in various parts of the country, and the millions and millions of kilowatts of electricity they would be producing. He gave figures of export of raw material in precise tons and prices of half-finished manufactures in sterling and dollars. This went on at a rapid pace for a good ten minutes with the President listening patiently and smoking his pipe. Menon realized that he had been somewhat inept in utilizing a polite enquiry to lecture on Indian economics. To make up for the error he asked Dr Douglas, 'And Mr President, how is Ireland's economy doing? How are the exports? Do you have a favourable balance of trade?'

Dr Douglas got his opening and he slipped his rapier in with the deftness which only an Irishman could have deployed. 'Mr Ambassador, we never have a favourable balance of trade,' he drawled as he put his pipe away. 'You see, we don't have very much to sell. Our exports, if you can call them by the name, are invisible exports—dramatists, poets, writers and that sort of thing. Nothing you can calculate precisely in terms of money.'

There were lighter moments in life at India House. Menon's puckish sense of humour contributed to some. I particularly recall the 'reception' we arranged for Vijayalakshmi Pandit, who was then Indian ambassador in Washington. It was common knowledge that she and Menon did not get along. Vijayalakshmi Pandit was due to stop in London for twenty-four hours on her way to India. Menon was anxious to prevent her meeting Indians hostile to him and letting her gather anti-Menon material to transmit to her brother the Prime Minister. Many Indian organizations hostile to Menon had written to her (some unwittingly through India House) asking for an opportunity to meet her. Vijayalakshmi Pandit had forwarded these letters to us so that we would arrange the interviews. We replied to them politely, stating that we would do our best to fit them into her busy programme. A week before her arrival, there was a meeting of the 'inner cabinet' in Menon's room and we decided to arrange a 'busy programme' for her. We rang up British Cabinet ministers saying that Vijayalakshmi Pandit was most anxious to see them before she returned to Delhi to discuss matters with her brother the Prime Minister. So we arranged lunch, tea, cocktail and dinner parties followed by late-night theatre.

Vijayalakshmi Pandit's plane landed at Heathrow in the morning. A crowd of Indians hostile to Menon were present at the airport. We secured permission from the authorities to take the car up to the plane. The High Commissioner's Rolls-Royce flying the tricolour drew up alongside the aircraft. Vijayalakshmi Pandit was delighted at the distinction. She was whisked away from the airport without even seeing the demonstrators. By the time they chased her down to Claridges Hotel we had taken her away to fulfil her first engagement. We told her how anxious many British statesmen were to meet her. So it went on till after midnight. Next morning she was hauled out of bed and deposited in her seat on the plane bound for India. She did not meet anyone we did not want her to meet.

Letters of protest followed her to India. She realized that she had been tricked. Her mood was dark. On her way back to Washington, she refused to allow India House to arrange any appointments for her. She accepted an invitation of the Indian Journalists' Association which arranged a press conference in her room in Claridges. Once more Menon outwitted her. He told her bluntly that she had no business to meet the press in London without consulting him. England was his domain. Vijayalakshmi Pandit gave in. She had to suffer meeting the journalists under my auspices and the best she could do was to vent her spleen on me.

I was often asked whether Menon was a communist. At first I used to react angrily. 'So what! Many of the great freedom fighters of our country were communists.' When I became disillusioned with the creed, I discovered the Party had also become a sort of freemasonry which helped its members irrespective of merit. Menon may or may not have been a card-bearing member of the Party, but his partiality towards those who were assumed scandalous proportions.

A large number of his English friends were communists. That did not surprise me because the communists had been more outspokenly sympathetic towards Indian aspirations than any other political group. Many had worked for the India League. Some expected to be rewarded—and were.

During Menon's tenure as high commissioner quite a few communists, both British and Indian, were given employment in India House. In the PRO department, of which I was in charge for a number of years, there were quite a few communists. Menon's bias in their favour can be gauged from the following episode.

One part of my job as head of department was to write confidential reports on my staff every year. To the best of my recollection in the three or four annual reports I made I gave only two clerks, an Englishwoman and an Indian, adverse reports and recommended their dismissal. The Englishwoman was in the habit of coming an hour late, spending an inordinate time at coffee, lunch and tea breaks and left the office early to 'avoid the rush hour'. I had many occasions to pull her up and tell her that on many days she did no more than half-an-hour's work. She took no notice and was often cheeky. The Indian woman, who was a friend of the other, followed her example except that instead of cheeky she became abjectly humble and shed tears.

Menon had no direct contact with these women; he hardly knew their names. He had no basis whatsoever of knowing how they worked or behaved in office. But every year Menon accepted my staff report, save in the case of these two women. When I left, he promoted them over the heads of others. Both these women were members of the communist party. Other heads of department told me that they had similar experiences.

Was Menon corrupt? Personally never. But many of his friends to whom he entrusted the government's money were manifestly so. And he did not hesitate to take money from dubious characters for the India League and its many satellite organizations. During Menon's tenure as high commissioner the League and its offsprings acquired valuable real estate in the heart of London.

Standing by old friends was a strong trait in Menon's character. Thus he had befriended a humble cook from Malabar who bore the same name. Despite adverse reports against him, he was put in charge of India House cooking with the high sounding title, 'Canteen Officer'. This Menon was given to the bottle—and the number of bottles he consumed kept him chronically in the red. He played ducks and drakes with the canteen money and on more than one occasion staggered into office in a state of intoxication. (At a cocktail party given to a visiting ambassador, Menon the cook gave the ambassador's wife a friendly pinch on her bottom.)

He was often reprimanded, but not fired till after Menon ceased to be high commissioner.

The affairs of the India League and its branch organizations could very well do with some scrutiny. Many a visiting maharaja and industrialist was entertained at India House and then asked to donate money for a students' hostel or a club. In one case—that of a crook of the name of K.S.B. Ahluwalia who at different times passed off as a naval officer, a brigadier, a prince and had done his stint in Indian and British jails—Menon's own role was not above board. He accepted a donation for India League from Ahluwalia in full knowledge of his past and that the money being given was not his and in return recommended him to the Liberal Party of Great Britain as a candidate for Parliament: the Liberals were anxious to put up a coloured man. When details of Ahluwalia's criminal career came to light, it embarrassed everyone concerned save Menon. 'We do not have to know his past, do we?' he said to me nonchalantly when I brought him a sheaf of press clippings on the subject.

Menon did not set any store by truth: he considered truth to be the monopoly of fools who did not have the wits to tell a convincing falsehood. I rarely heard him give a straight answer to a straight question. His instinctive reaction to any question was to question the motive of the questioner and then tailor his reply in such a way as to impugn the motive and also serve his own ends. This exercise called for a certain amount of skill and cunning. Most people confused this skill and cunning with ability. There never was any creative ability in Menon.

My own career as Menon's PRO came to a swift and deserved end. He never thought very highly of my ability: he never thought of anyone having any brains except himself. To any statement made by anyone Menon's first reaction used to be, 'You do not understand.' In my own case he did to me what he had made me do to others.

Kashmir was very much in the news and Menon decided that the Indian point of view should be put across in the form of letters in the press. Issue was taken on an editorial in the *Manchester Guardian*. A letter was drafted by the first secretary, P.N. Haksar, to be sent to the paper under my name. I acquiesced and signed it without demur. The Pakistani PRO, replied. In this process three or four letters appeared under my name—none of which I had written. There was nothing in them which I or anyone of my assistants could not have put across—and perhaps in better language; nevertheless, I had to suffer the indignity of being told that I did not know my job.

The next step was to have press conferences where I was invited as a spectator. The third was to send for my assistants, and communicate orders to me through them. I was familiar with the pattern and knew that my days were numbered. I waited for the opportunity to bring matters to a head. I did not have to waft long. I do not recall the precise details but it had something to do with 'Miss Singh' conveying 'H.E.'s' instructions to my assistant, Jamal Kidwai, destined to be my successor. I pulled her up. She complained to Menon. I was summoned by Menon and asked to apologize to 'Miss Singh'. My response surprised Menon. I was rude to both, slapped my resignation on his table and marched out of the office.

Menon could not believe anyone could resign government service: that was why he took the liberty of being rude to the seniormost of the ICS and other services. I was re-summoned to the office and told that he would ignore my notice. I told him that I had already posted a copy to the ministry and asked for the three months' leave due to me; and that I did not propose to come to the office from the next day and did not give a damn either for him or the Government of India.

This time Menon believed that I meant what I said. His tone changed from bullying to whining. He recounted all that he had done for me; he described me as one of his friends. But my cup of bitterness was full to the brim. 'You have no friends,' I told him.

Those were the last words I spoke to him.

Notes

1   Some years later I met Sudhir Ghosh at the Friends Meeting House in Delhi. He was then member of the Rajya Sabha. His pockets still bulged with letters. He read out one he had received from President John F. Kennedy—and his reply ending with 'love for Jacqueline'.

2   Lall, like Sudhir Ghosh, was a bit of a 'name dropper'. Years later as a professor at Columbia he still referred to his eminent friends by their first names: 'Hubert' (Humphrey); 'Averill' (Harriman); 'Cy' (Vana); 'Nan' (Vijayalakshmi Pandit).

3   After the death of her husband, Ela Sen, despite all she knew Menon had said about her, sought his assistance to get a job. When I expressed surprise she answered, 'One has to live.'

SHRADDHA MATA: THE MAKING OF A HOLY MOTHER

Four funeral pyres ablaze, a fifth corpse in a white shroud surrounded by women wailing and beating their breasts. The acrid smell of burning flesh. And in the midst of this macabre setting, Shraddha Mata reclining on a wood *takhtposh* calmly telling the beads of her rosary. This was in Delhi's Nigambodh Ghat. She, a tantric sannyasin was performing a Maha Kal *yagna*. Graveyards and cremation grounds are regarded as particularly suitable for such rites.

Shraddha Mata is a short, somewhat corpulent lady in her mid-sixties (b.1917). She wears thick-lensed glasses to read; when she takes them off you can see that she is a handsome woman who must have been quite a beauty in her younger days. As they say: ruins proclaim the glory of the monument that it once was. Even today, her fair skin is unwrinkled, her bosom full, her talk animated and her speech blunt: it is always *too* not *aap*—and yet her words exude affection.

'*Kaun?*' she demanded as I turned the flap of the gunny-sack curtain she had put around her little temporary ashram in the cremation ground. 'It is me. I have come for your darshan,' I replied.

'You must have a name, or don't you?'

I announced my name. '*Baithja*,' she said pointing to the bare floor beside her wooden couch. As I lowered myself my feet touched a pair of pink, plastic slippers. '*Arey kaisa admi*

115

hai too!—what kind of man are you? You put your feet on a sannyasin's sandals!'

I apologized. She peered into my face and asked : 'Are you the same fellow who was editor of the *Illustrated Weekly*?' I admitted I was. 'Why did they sack you?' I explained as best as I could.

'Why have you come to see me?'

'Darshan'—and since I could not think of the correct Hindi word, used the English, *'aur thori* curiosity.'

'Arey chhod curiosity-phuriosity!' she snorted with a kindly laugh. 'You must have read what that fellow Mathai has written about me and Pandit Nehru. You want to write the same kind of *bakwas*—rubbish.'

I gave her my word of honour that I would not write anything she did not approve of; and not even bring up the topic of her association with Panditji if she did not want me to do so. But I would like to know more about her, why she had renounced the world and become a sannyasin; what had she got out of it?

She listened quietly as she told the beads of her rosary. After a while she spoke: 'I have read some of your writings. Are you a *nastik*?'

I admitted I was an agnostic.

'You do not believe in *Ishwara*?'

'No, Mataji I do not believe in anything I know nothing about.'

'You seem to be an arrogant man—*ghamandi*.' I protested, 'No Mataji, I have no *ghamand*. I only plead ignorance of what I do not know. May be you have seen Ishwara and can tell me something about Him.'

She promptly cut me down to size: 'Arey ja! You have still to learn the alphabet, *aa, ee, uu,* and you want me to teach you the Vedas! Get rid of your coat-*patloon*, get into a loincloth, sit at my feet for a few years and I will teach you about god. You have a little twig before your eyes which prevents you from seeing the sun. I will remove that twig and you will see this entire *drishti*—cosmos—is Ishwara.'

Thus ended the first seance. 'Come again if you wish,' were her parting words. Something, I do not know what, compelled me to return to Nigambodh Ghat the next evening. The 'welcome' was as blunt as the first. *'Too phir aa gaya'*—you have come again? she demanded. 'You asked me to do so,' I replied. *'Baith.'* I took my seat beside her takhtposh. 'I believe that Mathai has again written something about me in his second book. What has he said?'

I told her that he had written about her association with Pandit Nehru some time in 1948–49, the birth of a son in a Catholic institution in Bangalore, her abandoning the child after a few days, the recovery and destruction of the letters Panditji is said to have written her. She heard my narrative without interrupting me and made a noncommittal comment. 'I warned Panditji then that he should not trust Mathai; he was the kind of viper who would bite him after his death.'

The second seance was followed by a third and a fourth. The Delhi Municipal Corporation ousted her from Nigambodh Ghat. She moved twenty miles away to Shiv Shambhu Dayal Mandir in the Okhla Industrial Estate. I sought her out in her new abode, this time determined to ask her life-story. After some hesitation, she complied.

HER LIFE-STORY

'I am not sure of my date of birth, nor the name of the village in which I was born except that it was in Sultanpur district (U.P.). I was the only child of my mother. My father had taken a second wife and died a couple of months before I was born. I was given in adoption to my father's sister who was Rani of Singhpur-Panhauna, a state near Ayodhya. This was done as the Rani had no child and my father had managed her estates.'

'What caste are you?'

'Brahma-Kshatriya—half-way between the two upper castes.'

'How did you get mixed up with religion—and sannyas?'

Shraddha Mata reclined on a bolster and after pondering for a while replied: 'I'll tell you all. My conversion to the sannyasi's way of life came in three successive stages. I was perhaps born with the desire because even as a child of five I was fascinated by sadhus and sannyasis. I began wearing *gerooa* (saffron) and refused to wear any other colours. Then I came across a statue of the Buddha in the meditation *(dhyan mudra)* pose. I was captivated. I got a small figurine of the same and instead of playing with dolls as other girls of my age did, I always carried my Buddha on me. The third incident that made me finally decide to abandon the world I lived in came two years later when I was only seven years old. As in many landed families, I spent more time with the servants than with my adoptive mother. I was particularly close to the woman who had been my *dhaya* (wet-nurse) who I came to address as *booa*—auntie. One evening she was taken ill and did not come to the house. The next morning I went to the servants' quarters. There she was laid on the ground wrapped up in a shroud. I asked someone "Where is my booa?" They replied "She has gone to Rama." This created a veritable storm in my breast. I wanted to know who that Rama that my booa had gone to was and where he lived. As is customary in our part of India poor Hindus bury their dead and place a charpoy upside down on the grave. I used to visit booa's grave everyday, through sun and rain, winter and summer till the charpoy had crumbled to bits and the grave was hardly recognizable. And every time I asked myself "Where is Rama that my booa has gone to?" It was perhaps a year later when I was eight that I persuaded an old woman who was going on pilgrimage to Badrinath to take me along with her. I slipped out of the house unnoticed at midnight. Instead of going to the railway station where they were sure to look for me, we went along the Ganga and took the train from the next station.

The party of pilgrims returned to the village but I stayed in Badrinath for another six months. Ultimately my adoptive mother Rani Ragho Nath Koer bullied the old woman into telling her where I was and sent a party of men to fetch me. The Rani decided that the one way out for her was to marry me off to someone. I was only nine when she arranged my betrothal. Then real trouble began. My husband-to-be and I quarrelled all the time; we had bitter fights. This went on for over two years till that engagement was called off. I was then twelve or thirteen. Now my quarrels began with my Rani mother. Many times we went into sulks, refused to eat or talk to each other. I got so fed up that I decided to agree to anything that would get me out of the situation. There were lots of distant cousins who wanted to marry me: there was the property that I would inherit and I was regarded as good-looking. Another marriage was quickly arranged. This was with another distant relative called Phanindra Pal Singh. I don't remember exactly whether he had done his Bar or was going to do it. But he was considered quite a catch. Even this marriage did not work out. My husband and his parents kept me under surveillance as if I was a prisoner. I wasn't even allowed to go to the toilet without a couple of maidservants watching me and an armed guard close by. It was not a marriage but a kind of death. Ultimately I wrote a letter to Gandhiji telling him that I belonged to a taluqdar family and had been forced into a marriage against my will. And that I wanted to become a sannyasin, and join him to serve my country. I sent this letter through a cousin who was going to Gandhiji. A few days later I got a reply from Mahadev Desai, saying that Gandhiji had agreed to my joining him and I should come at once. Altogether I had spent no more than five–six weeks with my husband. Then I slipped away.'

'You seem uncommonly well-educated. But you have said nothing about your schooling.'

'Oh that! I had dozens of tutors at home. I was taught Sanskrit, Hindi, English, everything. I did not take any degrees because women in families like ours did not go to school or college or sit for exams.'

Shraddha Mata resumed her narrative. 'I was with Gandhiji for forty days. My husband turned up to claim me and even showed

Bapu our wedding picture. Gandhiji was very firm in his reply. He said: "I know of no taluqdar's daughter; I only know this girl who has come to me. She is like a wave of the Ganges (Ganga *ki dhara*) and you cannot lock her up in a cage. Let her go." I stayed with Gandhiji till I was taken very ill. But by then I had become a free person.'

'How did you come by the name Shraddha Mata? Surely it was not the name given to you by your family?'

'I have had a variety of names. In my horoscope I am Parvati. My real name which was never used is Shyam Kala. At home everyone called me Bacchi Sahib. When I took sannyas I was given yet another name Sushriyananda Saraswati. But somehow it was Shraddha that stuck. I think I gave it to myself at Gandhiji's ashram. Shraddha is an abbreviation of *Sat Ko Dharan*—one who clasps the truth. Mata—mother—came to be appended to it in later life.'

LADY OF THE FORT

This is all that I was able to elicit in the five evenings I spent with Shraddha Mata in Delhi. She invited me to visit her in Jaipur where she would give me whatever she had in the way of photographs of her earlier days and articles written on her. She promised, 'I will tell you what I have told no one else.' That was too tempting an invitation to let go. Ten days later photographer Raghu Rai and I flew into Jaipur.

Hathroi Fort, atop a rocky escarpment broods over the city of Jaipur. Its topmost turret gives a spectacular view of the huddle of pink bazars and beyond them to the range of hills crowned with other forts and palaces. Hathroi was designed to block an invader's path to Jaipur and Amber. It fell into disuse and became the haunt of flying foxes, rock pigeons and sand lizards. In 1953 Maharaja Sawai Man Singh turned it over to Shraddha Mata. She converted the citadel into the headquarters of the

Mahashakti Peeth. The look-out turret from which Rajput warriors had scanned the horizons to sight an approaching enemy is now occupied by a life-sized marble statue of a goddess. When the city of Jaipur sleeps, the goddess and her worshipper keep vigil. Shraddha Mata prays and meditates through the night into the early hours of the dawn.

We stride uphill to a massive gate and let ourselves in through a small aperture. An obese mongrel welcomes us with a happy bark and vigorous wagging of its tail. This is Bhairon; he is a brahmachari dog who has been kept away from the temptations of sex by never being let out of the fortress. While Surendra Singh, Shraddha Mata's young secretary and acolyte, goes to announce our arrival, we take a look at the courtyard. It has a well in the centre; pigeons rest deep down its sides and fly out like bees from a hive. On one side is a pumpkin patch smelling of green leaves; against another wall is a marble statue of Shiva; a woman squats in front reciting *jap* out of a hymnal. Rising above the parapet of the well are the priests' quarters; their women-folk are busy cooking the morning meal. Through a turning, twisting, perpetually shaded passageway a flight of broad stone stairs mounts skywards to the turret temple. Along the parapets on either side are Shraddha Mata's *gufa* (cave) and her 'reception rooms'. We take off our shoes and go up to greet her. 'First go and pay homage to the goddess; she will rid you of your *nastikta* (agnosticism) and give shakti to your pen. Then come back to me.'

Shraddha Mata has a lot to say and drops broad hints that she may not have too long a time at her disposal to say it. Mathai's insinuations about the nature of her relationship continue to bother her. She denounces him as one of the 'anti-Hindu' group who conspired to create misunderstandings between her and the late Prime Minister. 'A good man continues to reform and become better till his last breath; an evil man remains evil till he dies,' she remarks. 'And what was it that I tried to instil into Nehru's mind? Only that India had a great spiritual tradition which must not be thrown away in the name of secularism. I believe in democracy: it liberates people from fear. But if you wish to preserve democracy you must replace the void created by the absence of fear by something positive, something spiritual which gives you a sense of responsibility and discipline. I call this *Adhyatmik Samajvad,* the nearest English equivalent is spiritual policy. Otherwise the only alternative is the *dandebazi* (rule by force) of the MISA.'

I looked up my notes and asked her to resume the narrative of her life from the time she left Gandhiji's ashram. 'For the next three years or more I worked with the Harijan Sewak Sangha, organizing night schools in villages round Agra and in the Avadh region. My chief contacts were Thakkar Bappa and Acharya Jugal Kishore. This must have been between the sixteenth and nineteenth years of my life. Then I threw it all up and retired to the Himalayas. I lived in a cave above Gangotri from where the holy Ganga begins its course.' She observed the strictest vow of silence (*kashta maun*) and lived off whatever wild berries were available at the height (21,000 feet), sucking icicles to slake her thirst.

Apparently she was back in the plains in the early 1940s—and politically active. There was a warrant for her arrest during the 1942 'Quit India' movement. She evaded it by remaining underground. She was taken very ill and for a while was treated by sadhus in the jungles of Koil Ghati.

It was early in 1943 that she decided to be formally initiated into a sannyasi order. As required by tradition she first sought the permission of her adoptive mother. By now Mateshwari, as she called her, had reconciled herself to her daughter's waywardness and gave her consent. At Ayodhya she was accepted as a *dandiswami* sannyasin by Sri Karpatriji, and given another name, Sushriyananda Saraswati. Before the initiation there was considerable debate on the issue as neither a woman nor anyone who was not a Brahmin had been admitted by the Sankarapeeth. The Arya Samaj supported her against the orthodox elements. For sometime after the initiation ceremony she stayed in the village temple built by her mother. Then suddenly one morning, clad in her deer skin and with *kamandal* (bowl) in her hand she disappeared from her village to return to her cave in the Himalayan vastness.

KALI REINCARNATED

How and when she returned to civilization is shrouded in mystery. According to her sometime in the year 1946 she found herself in the Kali Temple in Calcutta. The 'transport' had been preceded by a mystic experience during Navratri when she had a clear vision of Kali enthroned in Kalighat. It was accompanied by ecstatic vibrations ('spirit of pure joy' is how she described it) and a subtle emanation of the fragrance of sandalwood. She felt that the goddess had sent for her to make her an instrument of some divine design. She describes the mystic journey, analogous to the holy Ganga's descent from Gangotri to the Bay of Bengal. She spent the day amongst the throng of worshippers. Apparently her presence did not attract any attention. When the evening service was over she hid herself behind the goddess. The priests locked the sanctum without noticing her. She spent the night in prayer and meditation. Next morning when the head priest, Haripada Bandopadhyaya, opened the temple door he saw standing beside the statue of the Goddess a young woman who looked every inch a fair reincarnation of Kali; long tresses (*jata*) falling down her shoulder, torso covered with leopard skin, trident in one hand, kamandal in the other. He prostrated himself before her.

The news spread like wild-fire through the metropolis. Pilgrims in their thousands came to pay her homage. Offerings of fruit, flowers, coconuts, silver and gold jewellery were heaped at her feet. Amongst her visitors was Justice Rama Prasad Mookerjee of the high court of Calcutta who was the elder brother of Shyama Prasad Mookerjee, minister in Nehru's cabinet.

Shraddha Mata was persuaded to give up her vow of silence to give her message to the people. For several weeks following she was housed in the palace of Rani Rasmoni in Dakshineshwar (where before her Swami Vivekananda and Sister Nivedita had stayed). She was invited to expound on the Gita. She did so to large audiences, sometimes addressing four meetings in a day. But she never failed to spend some time of the day or night at the Kali temple. Her chief achievement was to persuade the priests and worshippers to give up sacrificing animals to the goddess and instead make offerings of corn, grain and vegetables.

THE NEHRU CONNECTION

Shraddha Mata was not very anxious to discuss her relationship with Nehru; I did not press her on the subject. But in the course of our dialogue Mathai's insinuations in his two books on Nehru and the conjectures made by the press surfaced. In several interviews given to a variety of journals, she has said that it was Shyama Prasad Mookerjee who brought her to Delhi and fixed the interview with the Prime Minister. She was given fifteen minutes to have her say; she was with him for an hour-and-a-half. What she said to Nehru in the first meeting can be briefly summed up as follows: Nehru's secularism ignored the religious and cultural traditions of India and had therefore little support of the sadhus and sannyasis who were guardians of these traditions. Nehru did not give Sanskrit the place it deserved as the mother of all languages. He had toyed with the idea of introducing the Roman script to replace Devanagari and other vernacular scripts. He wanted the wording in the Constitution to be 'India that is Bharat' instead of what it finally emerged under her insistence as 'Bharat that is India'. And so on.

I told her that I had gathered from some members of Nehru's household that she had met Nehru no more than three or four times. She smiled and replied: 'That's all they know about. I will tell you what I have not told anyone before. At the very first meeting that took place in the house on Aurangzeb Road we established a rapport which seemed to indicate that we had known each other in our previous lives. I could see Panditji was attracted to me (*prabhavit huey*). He was impressed with what I had to say. And I do not deny that he was attracted towards this,' she said pointing to her face and features. 'I met him many times and for many hours at a stretch. I sensed his growing attachment to me. He asked me many times about my marriage and my husband. I can say that had I been free and not taken the vows of a sannyasin, it would have been me and not any of the other women whose names have been linked with him (Lady Mountbatten, Padmaja Naidu, Mridula Sarabhai) that he would have wanted to marry. But it never came to it. I told him quite firmly that I was a sannyasin and that he, as a Brahmin, was expected to honour Hindu tradition. At one time he addressed me in his letter to me as Priya (Dear) rather than Mata as others did and I told him that was not proper. He did not repeat it.' With some hesitation I asked her if the relationship, as stated by Mathai, had gone beyond the platonic. She replied in two words spoken with considerable feeling: '*Asat hai*—it is not true.'

Like other relationships, the Nehru–Shraddha Mata association became the victim of misunderstandings—some of them deliberately planted in Nehru's mind by people like Mathai, whom she describes as a member of the anti-Hindu lobby. There is little doubt that Shraddha Mata spoke the language of Hindu obscurantists like that of the leaders of the Rashtriya Swayamsevak Sangh (RSS). She admits that at one time Nehru told her that she saw everything from the Hindu point of view (*Hinduon ki drishti sey*). The meetings became less frequent and then ceased altogether.

For a while Shraddha Mata lived in the Harijan basti in Delhi, then at the invitation of Raja Jugal Kishore Birla moved to Birla House, then to Birla Mandir and finally to a hut constructed for her on the ridge behind the temple. She was in Faridabad the day Gandhiji was assassinated. She spent the following fortnight chanting hymns from the Gita.

Sometime in 1952 Shraddha went abroad. She toured Europe, the United States, East Africa—and everywhere she went she gave discourses on the Gita, which were heard by large crowds. When she returned to India she did not bother to contact Nehru. The Maharaja of Jaipur, Sawai Man Singh, and his wife, the luscious Gayatri Devi had become her disciples. He gifted the Hathroi castle to Shraddha Mata. She moved to Jaipur and set up her 'world peace army'. Panditji misunderstood her intentions and regarded her venture as an attempt to revive feudal traditions among erstwhile Rajput princes. 'Sukhadia created mischief,' she says (M.L. Sukhadia was then chief minister of Rajasthan.) 'When Nehru visited Jaipur, a *mehfil* was arranged by Hari Bhan Upadhyaya. I was cordial. But distant.' When Nehru had his first stroke, Shraddha Mata wrote to him expressing her concern. He replied asking her to forget her past bitterness. That was the last communication between them. 'When I was close to him I could transmit some of my shakti to him,' she says. 'Once distance had been created, I was no longer able to do so. I could not help him in his affliction.'

Her reference to Panditji's death gave me the opportunity to ask her what she made of death and dying. Her views are traditionally Hindu. According to her one lot of human beings evolve from human birth to human rebirth, getting closer and closer to the light eternal. The other lot who have evil within go through all eighty-four lakh *yonis* till they are purged of their evil. I protested. 'Mataji, you are only making statements; there is no evidence to substantiate any of this eighty-four lakh yoni business.' She replied in excellent English. 'There can be no empirical evidence for this kind of thing. You can only realize the truth through insight brought about during samadhi. No one can provide physical proof of such phenomena because cosmic truth is reflected when man goes beyond sensory perceptions.' I asked her to explain why if there was a god there was so much injustice in the world? Why good men suffered and evil men prospered? Once again she explained in the traditional—'*Pichley janmon key karm:* paying for deeds done in past lives.' All this was beyond me. So also her reasoning about why there ought to be nine Durga Pujas and not eight or ten. 'Because,' she maintained, 'ultimately energy is in nine stages of radiation, one layer after the other—that is the tantric belief.'

The next morning I was made more aware of the great gulf that divides the agnostic from the believer. We were seated on the parapet of the fort. It was very warm. A cord connecting the table fan to the switch came loose. Surendra Singh who had just come down from the temple after a session of prayer and meditation put the cord back in the switch hole. Then he pointed to a bare patch on the cord and said, 'You see by mistake I touched the naked wire but it did not give me any shock! That is because the shakti generated by prayer and meditation is still in me.' Shraddha Mata endorsed this by adding: 'And also because I am here beside you.' I was sorely tempted to ask Surendra Singh to touch the live wire again and let me see the power of spiritual shakti pitted against the electrical, but I did not want to be thrown out.

MATHAI: HE IS A LIAR

I had planned to put off the questions about her association with Pandit Nehru to the last so that I could get the rest of her life-story before running the risk of an abrupt dismissal. But she had brought up the subject herself so many times that I was sure she would not be upset by my asking her for further elucidation. 'Mathai in his first book has written that after returning from Bangalore you had settled in Jaipur as a mod young lady with short-cropped hair, using lipstick and wearing jeans . . . Is that so?'

Shraddha Mata exploded in a string of expletives: '*Ullu ka pattha!* (son of an owl) *moorakh!* (stupid) *agyani!* (devoid of knowledge). His skull needs examining. See all these letters.' She unwrapped a bundle of letters and handed me one from the late

Sawai Man Singh, Maharaja of Jaipur, donating Hathroi Fort to her. It began with 'Respected Mataji' and ended with 'your devoted S. Man Singh'. Shraddha Mata asked me: 'You think the Maharaja would have addressed me in this way and given me property worth over two crores if I was wearing lipstick and slacks?'

ARTICLES, ESSAYS AND
NON-FICTION BOOK EXCERPTS

DOOMSDAY IN YOGILAND

On the evening of 3 February 1962—to be exact, at 5.35 p.m.—
eight planets joined forces in the Capricorn and declared war on
the world. Precisely at that time thousands of sacrificial fires were
lit all over India. Yogis in loincloth and ashes, sadhus with matted
hair, pandits with their foreheads smeared with sandalwood paste
began to chant litanies from the sacred texts. The battle was on.
Wicked planets versus the holy men of Hindustan.

The astrologers had forecast the end of the world unless the
gods were adequately propitiated. In Delhi, the chief priest, Swami
Narsingh Giriji Maharaj, distributed printed copies of his prophecy
that 'terrible things' would follow the conjunction of the planets.
'The earth will be bathed in blood of a thousand kings,' it stated.
Rich businessmen gave large sums of money to the Swami; women
prostrated themselves at his feet. He promised to intercede on
their behalf and expressed the hope that the sacrificial prayers
might save India. But, he added with a sardonic smile, he could
not say what would befall other lands.

A week before the fateful forty-eight hours, buses, trains and
aeroplanes were packed with people going to join their families. The
stock market declined; the bullion exchange announced it would
close in time to let people get home; attendance in offices and
schools fell; many shops were shut with notices bearing the legend:
'May open on the 6th February.' A new Sanskrit word came into
the people's vocabulary—*ashtagrah*—eight—a star conjunction.
Cynics described it as an outbreak of 'conjunctionitis'.

Indian cities presented a strangely deserted appearance for two nights and days. There were innumerable encampments where large congregations listened to the chanting of hymns and saw the sacred flames fed with ghee, rice and sliced coconut. In Delhi alone, the priests intoned the name of the warrior goddess, as many as 4,810,000 times. Equally popular was the hymn, *Gayatri*, from the Rig Veda, which runs:

O, most splendrous Sun, this prayer is offered to thee. Receive this craven worshipper as a loving man seeks a woman. May thou in the contemplation and wisdom be our Protector . . .

All through the night the loudspeakers blared monotonously: 'O, most splendorous Sun . . .' Those who could not chant the Sanskrit hymn themselves, hired pandits to do it for them at a standard fee of fifty-one rupees—not too heavy a premium for insurance against injury during life and against fire in the hell hereafter.

The issue between the priests and the planets was fiercely contested. On the evening of 5 February, the moon deserted the conjunction in the Capricorn and the enemy were in full retreat. The battle was won.

In these forty-eight hours and twelve minutes India literally burnt hundreds of tons of precious clarified butter, rice, coconut and other edibles. At least a million dollars passed from the pockets of the credulous to obese Brahmins who maintain a tight monopoly on the right to perform sacred ritual. A senior member of the government's Planning Commission stated that the loss to the nation owing to the stoppage of work during the 'crisis' totalled thirty-five crores of rupees (then about seventy million dollars).

Sacred Hindu texts, the Vedas, compiled more than a thousand years before the birth of Christ, accept astronomy and astrology (*jyotish*) as two branches of one science. Many treatises dealing with the forecasting of events were written by Hindu astrologers, of which the most famous is the *Brihat Samhita* by Varaha Mihira who lived some time about the middle of the sixth century AD. A commentary on Varaha Mihira written by one Bhattotpala in the ninth century AD is used extensively in present-day India. Long before these eminent scholars, the astral diviner had been given a place of honour in the councils of princes. The sage Garga, who preceded Varaha Mihira by over two centuries had proclaimed:

> The king who does not honour a scholar accomplished in horoscopy and astronomy, clever in all branches and accessories, comes to grief . . . As the night without a light, as the sky without the sun, so is a king without an astrologer: like a blind man he erreth on the road.

Garga's warning was heeded by the Hindu princes. As the courts of Europe had their clowns, the courts of Hindustan had their astrologers whose duty was to cast horoscopes of the royal progeny, select days which were auspicious for marriages or martial enterprises. If their prognostications went wrong, they paid the penalty at the block. Many astrologers perished; but astrology persisted. Even reverses at the hands of Muslim, and later, English invaders did not shake the Hindu's faith in the stars. In AD 1761 on the famous battlefield of Panipat, the Marathas, who out numbered the Afghans by two to one, waited for several months till the chief astrologer assured them victory if the battle were commenced before dawn on 14 January. It was. Six hours later, the Maratha host had bitten the dust, having lost 30,000 men. Hindus lost their power in northern India—but not their belief in the prognostications of astrologers. Each time they fought the English, they did so only after their astrologers had predicted victory over the foreigners. By 1849 the British had annexed the whole of India. And now that British and Muslim domination is over, the astrologer (*jyotishi*) has come back into his own. No attempt has ever been made to enumerate them but 25,000 is likely to be a conservative estimate. In addition there are innumerable others in all walks of life who practise astrology as a hobby.

There are many schools of astrology based on the different commentaries on Varaha Mihira; they can however be divided into two broad categories, the northern and the southern.

Some educated Hindus are sceptical about the claims made by astrology but they bow to astrological predictions in some form or the other. The exact time of birth of every Hindu child is carefully noted down and communicated to the family priest to enable him to draw up a horoscope. The horoscope becomes a Hindu's constant guide. It determines when his head is to be shaved, the day he will wear his sacred thread and the term when he will join school. Even amongst the most Anglicized who dismiss horoscopy as so much hocus-pocus, the document is consulted when a marriage is arranged: Hindus interpret the saying that marriages are made in heaven absolutely literally. Parents who advertise their marriageable sons and daughters in the newspapers invite interested parties to 'please correspond with horoscope'. Asking for photographs is considered bad form and contrary to the oft-proven truth that beauty is skin deep. The date of marriage is chosen after a careful check of the horoscopes of the bridal pair and must be within the days prescribed by the astrologers as auspicious. In India there are 'marriage seasons'; only atheists and the utterly impatient dare to have off-season nuptials. Between the 3rd and the 5th of February there was not a single Hindu marriage performed in India. What greater homage could 500 million people pay to the 'science' of astrology?

Indian Muslims have their own methods of divination but astrology is not one of them. They have no horoscopes made nor believe in 'auspicious' days. But all other communities of India—Christians, Sikhs, Jains and Parsees—acknowledge the influence of the stars in some form or the other. The case of the Sikhs is particularly interesting. The founder Gurus (fifteenth–seventeenth centuries) strongly disapproved of soothsaying. Nevertheless, the first Sikh to be ruler of the Punjab, Maharaja Ranjit Singh

(1780–1839) became an ardent believer in astrology. He never launched on a campaign without first consulting astrologers. His faith in the stars increased as he won most of his battles. When he was stricken with paralysis, an English doctor attending on him tried his best to get him to move from his tent pitched alongside a rice-field, to the palace in the fort where the air was fresher. The royal astrologer was, however, of the opinion that changing location until a particular combination of stars had changed would be fatal. The Maharaja had more faith in the stars than in English medicine and continued to lie in the damp and unsalubrious atmosphere till the astrologer gave him the 'all clear' sign. In his palace he again consulted the leading astrologers of the country and asked them how long he could expect to live. They consulted the Maharaja's horoscope, put their heads together and assured him he had at least another ten to fifteen years to go. Four days later, the Maharaja was dead.

The fate of Ranjit Singh did not adversely affect the Sikhs' un-Sikh faith in astral prophecies. New versions of a book known as the *Sau Sakhi* (Hundred Fables) ascribed to the last of their Gurus, Gobind Singh (1666–1708) have a habit of being discovered in cave libraries of hermits. One version prophesied a Sikh empire all over India. A year after its appearance, the Sikhs suffered a series of crushing defeats at the hands of the British and even lost their own kingdom. On the outbreak of the Mutiny in 1857 the British themselves published an edition prophesying an alliance between themselves and the Sikhs in which the allies would recapture Delhi from the mutineers and crush the revolt. This 'prophecy' paid handsome dividends as the Sikhs were in the vanguard of the British assault on the capital. Thereafter several other versions of the *Sau Sakhi* appeared, prophesying an invasion from Russia and the downfall of the British Empire. These were often corroborated by prophecies in an equally mysterious book, the *Bhrigu Samhita* which has been in great vogue in the Punjab. Neither of these books nor any astrologers prophesied the going of the British when they actually went in 1947, nor of the terrible riots which displaced ten million people and took a toll of over 100,000 lives in northern India.

During the 1962 astral crisis, the High Priest of the Golden Temple of Amritsar issued a manifesto reminding the Sikhs that belief in astrology was forbidden by their faith. Few Sikhs participated in the rounds of prayers or slept out in the open for fear of earthquakes; they flocked instead to the bars and restaurants for a hearty final meal. Typical of their race was the reaction of a taxi-driver who cocked a snook at the law by drinking a bottle of country liquor in the centre of the road. 'Don't give a damn,' he yelled to his more cautious mates, 'tomorrow there will be no police, no law courts, no prohibition—no nothing.'

Faith in astrology is common to all strata of present-day Hindu society. The late President, Dr Rajendra Prasad, was a firm believer and consulted astrologers on the future of the country through the horoscopes of its many leaders. Most members of Nehru's Cabinet had their favourite astrologers who often travelled across the continent to tender advice on state affairs. The first chief minister of the Punjab had a resident astrologer to help him make up his mind. Another prominent politician also, the chief minister of one of the states of the republic, used to issue prophecies made by him along with the official calendar. He was convinced that Tuesdays were inauspicious for him and would refuse to make important decisions on that day. He was proved right. The Opposition moved a vote of no-confidence on a Tuesday. The chief minister gave up without a fight; it was written in his kismet. A considerable section of even the Anglicized or Americanized intelligentsia succumb to astrological superstition. Between the 3rd and the 5th February, many senior officers of the armed forces and the Indian Civil Service—the elite of India's bureaucracy—rejoined their families. At any committee meeting in the Secretariat one will see a number of officers wearing rings with ruby, amethyst, opal, topaz or amber, etc. These are not chosen personally; they are 'good luck' stones prescribed by astrologers.

The one great exception to the general rule of acceptance of astrology (and all other forms of soothsaying) was the Prime Minister, Jawaharlal Nehru. He ridiculed the people who went to bathe in the sacred rivers during solar and lunar eclipses in the belief that thereby they were helping the heavenly bodies from being devoured by a demon. He made scathing references to the hysteria which was sweeping over the country. He was promptly rapped on the knuckles by Dr Sampurnanand, ex-chief minister of Uttar Pradesh. Astrology, he stated, was as perfect or imperfect as any other science and that the head of the government had no business to deny it without fully investigating its claims. An astrologer may err but astrology was infallible, he said. He also warned the Prime Minister to be more careful in his movements while the planets were in Capricorn.

The Prime Minister survived; so has the rest of the country. Do Indians feel a little silly at the end of it all? Or do they believe that it was the chanting of the Vedic mantras which turned back the tide of malevolent waves sent down by the planets? In some areas angry young men smashed the loudspeakers and deprived the priests of their ill-gotten gains. In tea and coffee bars college students argued heatedly why the government had not been more firm with these charlatans who had made India a laughing stock of the world. There were also letters in the newspapers claiming that the Sanskrit *Om* contained in it the seed of salvation and if it was intoned in the prescribed manner, it set up vibrations which had the power to repel evil influences; and it was by the chanting of millions of Oms that the Hindus had saved India and the rest of the world. The debate goes on.

Holy Men and Holy Cows

The Jamuna, which flows past the eastern wall of the old city of Delhi, is a sacred river. In sanctity, it ranks after the Ganga, into which it runs a couple of hundred miles farther down its course, and the Godavari, which cuts across central India. On the Jamuna, the most sacred spot is Nigambodh Ghat, where, according to legend, sacred Hindu texts were washed up. To Nigambodh Ghat come pilgrims from distant parts of India. From the early hours of the dawn, thousands of men and women bathe in the stream, throw palmfuls of water to the rising sun and to their ancestors in heaven.

Delhi's biggest cremation ground is also at Nigambodh Ghat. Strapped in shrouds (white for males, red for females), the dead are brought to the ghat, dunked in the sacred water, then consigned to the flames. In a rectangular space no larger than a football field, at least a dozen pyres can be seen burning fiercely at any time.

After dark, when the mourners have departed, Nigambodh Ghat is an eerie sight. Two attendants are on duty to supply wood and otherwise help in disposing off corpses brought in at night. (Many Hindus cremate their dead within a few hours of death.) The only other people present are ill-clad beggars, who in wintertime warm themselves by the funeral fires, and, winter or summer, groups of sadhus.

For the sadhus, a cremation ground is hallowed ground. It is a burning reminder that the world we live in is an illusion (maya) and that death is the real awakening into an after-life (or if a person has been evil, into a continuous circle of after-lives). Some sadhus smear their bodies with the ashes of the dead. Some require the ceremony of initiation to be performed in the flaming light of a circle of funeral pyres. One sect, the Aghorins, requires a neophyte to eat a bit of a corpse in order to overcome the feeling of disgust.

'Can I see a ceremony of sadhus' initiation here?' I asked one of the cremation ground staff when I went there one night.

The man was armed with a sharp-pointed bamboo pole. His chief function was to puncture skulls to prevent them from exploding with the heat. He wiped the sweat off his brow. 'I haven't seen one for more than five years. We don't like too many sadhus here. If relatives find the ashes of their dead missing, they create trouble.'

'Who are those people?' I asked, pointing to three men naked save for their loincloths. They were smoking a chillum (small clay pipe).

'Those!' exclaimed the skull-smasher contemptuously. They are common beggars pretending to be sadhus. They do not like to work and they like ganja (hemp). So they smear ashes on their bodies, extract alms from women and have a merry time. There are few genuine sadhus left these days. If you want to meet them you should go to Hardwar or Rishikesh or even farther up the mountains from where the holy Ganga mai (mother Ganges) comes. You will find them in jungles and caves doing penance.'

He picked up a faggot that had fallen off, put it back on the pyre and wandered away to see how things were going with the other pyres. I wandered toward the chillum-smoking trio.

'*Om Namo Shivaya*,' (the greeting used by sadhus who worship Shiva) exclaimed one loudly.

'*Jeevit raho!*' (may you live a long life) chimed in another.

'Give the sadhus something. Ishwara will reward you in this world and the next.'

I walked past them. I heard one of them mutter: 'One of those coat-and-pantaloon black sahibs!'

The skull-smasher was right; genuine sadhus are hard to find. Charlatans outnumber the seekers of truth. No one knows exactly what entitles a man to call himself a sadhu. And sadhus seldom stay in one place for any length of time. Many live in mountain fastnesses or in dense jungles far removed from the reach of census inspectors. The earlier census reports put their number at five million. The present figure is under half-a-million. The British were eager to swell the figure in order to prove the Indians' reluctance to work. Free India's rulers are equally eager to destroy the image of India as yogiland.

'The word sadhu derives from the Sanskrit *sadhana*—to meditate. A variety of holy men go under the name sadhu. There are scholars (*acharyas*) immersed in the study of sacred texts who often become teachers (or gurus). There are men who join hermitages (ashrams or maths) where they live with a community of monks under the guidance of a swami. There are sannyasis (renouncers), who attach themselves to one or the other order of ascetics and spend their time in prayer or meditation at one of the many holy places of the Hindus. There are yogis (from yoga—union) who seek communion with god through a system of physical and spiritual discipline.

In this last category are some whose powers have defied scientific explanation: yogis who can remain alive buried six feet under the earth for as long as a week or drink a pint of nitric acid and munch the glass container without any ill-effect. Some are said to have powers of levitation; some are known to be able to stop the beating of their hearts for a few minutes. At lower levels are yogis who exhibit their conquest of pain by devious forms of physical torture—lying on beds of nails, standing on one leg for many years, keeping a hand raised until it shrivels, holding a hand clenched until the nails pierce the palm. At the extreme end are the Aghorin cannibals who indulge in human sacrifice (when caught, they hang) and conquer disgust by eating carrion and excreta.

Sadhus have many sects and differ in their dress and accoutrements. The *nirmalas* (unsullied) wear pure white. Most orders wear salmon, ochre or saffron, or, if they are Buddhists, yellow. Many wear only a loincloth and smear their bodies with ashes. Ash symbolizes death; it also keeps away flies and mosquitoes.

The *nangas* are 'clad in the sky'. Their hair-styles range from the close-shaven eggshell, to a tuft or a yard-long pigtail, to a matted mound of uncut hair coiled on top of the head or hung loose about the shoulders. Some orders shave their beards; most let them grow. Almost all carry begging bowls, staffs and rosaries made of holy basil, lotus seed or human teeth.

Most sadhu orders enjoin strict vegetarianism and celibacy. The chief exceptions are tantric sects (worshippers of Shakti, goddess of strength, consort of Shiva), who believe in the use of intoxicant and sexual intercourse as a means of achieving mystical experiences. Women are seldom admitted to sadhu hermitages as full members, but it is not unusual to find a woman donning an ochre robe and describing herself as a *sadhvi* or a *yogin*.

Sadhuism in all its tortuous forms has been known from the earliest times. It is based on the conviction that self-denial and penance purge the body of sin and so aid a person to break out of *samsara*—the cycle of birth, death and rebirth. Penance is *tapas*—the heat which burns out impurities from the soul and the body. The law-giver Manu (third century BC) stated the rules categorically:

> Let a sadhu go forth from the village into the forest and reside there, duly controlling his senses. Let him offer those five great sacrifices according to the rule, with various kinds of pure food fit for ascetics, or with herbs, roots and fruit. Let him wear a skin of tattered garment; let him bathe in the evening or in the morning; and let him always wear his hair in braids, the hair on his body, his beard, and his nails being unclipped . . . Let him

be always industrious in privately reciting the Veda; let him be patient of hardships . . . ever liberal . . . and compassionate toward all living creatures . . . in summer let him expose himself to the heat of five fires, during the rainy season live under the open sky, and in winter be dressed in wet clothes, gradually increasing his austerities . . . departing from his house . . . let him wander about absolutely silent, and caring nothing for enjoyments that may be offered. Let him always wander alone without any companion, in order to attain final liberation . . . let him not desire to die, let him not desire to live, let him wait for his time, as a servant for the payment of his wages.

The patron god of sadhus is Shiva, the destroyer aspect of the Hindu trinity consisting, besides him, of Brahma the creator and Vishnu the preserver. There are seven orders of Shaivite sadhus of whom the *dasnami* (ten-named—from the ten disciples of Shankara, the eighth-century monist philosopher) are the most numerous. Worshippers of Vishnu also have some sadhu orders. Indeed, sadhuism seems to be contagious. There are Sikh sadhus and Muslim fakirs and even Christian sadhus. Most of them adopt the paraphernalia of the Hindu sadhu, however: ochre robe, begging bowl, pilgrim staff, long hair and beards.

One does not have to go very far to meet some kind of sadhu. Sadhus are found in the marketplaces of every city and town. And every village has its *babaji* (old man) who has let his hair grow wild, wears saffron and lives in a hut some distance away from habitation. He does no work; he expects people to feed him. And whether he likes it or not, he is assumed to have powers of healing and prophecy. He is medicine man, soothsayer, psychiatrist and philosopher all rolled into one. Women touch his feet and invoke his blessings for their children. The men are less enthusiastic about sadhus—particularly if they happen to be young and handsome—but even the men do not dare to cross a sadhu's path or speak lightly of him. A sadhu's curse is dreaded by everyone.

What angers the educated, Westernized Indian is that sadhus not only live off others, they do no work at all. As a people, Indians are not known for their eagerness for social work, but sadhus go to the extreme of concerning themselves solely with achieving peace of mind.

The floods, epidemics, earthquakes, droughts and famines which visit this unfortunate country with tragic regularity are not allowed to disturb the tranquil atmosphere of the sadhu hermitage or ruffle the serenity of the holy man in his samadhi (meditation). Rarely does one see a saffron-clad volunteer in any relief camp. The privilege of service is left to Christian organizations.

Only in recent years has hostile criticism stirred the sadhus conscience and forced them out of their sanctum. But to this day, social service is largely the monopoly of one mission, the Ramakrishna (so named after the Bengali divine, Ramakrishna, 1836–86). Even the officially inspired Bharat Sadhu Samaj, founded in 1956, restricts its activities to 'the promotion of religious and social progress, building of national character, development of virtue and renunciation of vice, safeguarding religious institutions and sanitary conditions at places of pilgrimage'. It has not responded to the appeal for volunteers made by the Famine Relief Committee.

The sadhus' professed renunciation of worldly affairs, however, does not inhibit some of them from taking an interest in politics. The politician-sadhu's excuse is invariably that he is there to protect the interests of dharma (religion). Since Independence, sadhus have been demanding protection for the cow (so strong was Hindu feeling on the subject that cow protection was inserted as a directive clause in the Constitution).

It was left to the states to implement this provision and all but four of the seventeen states have duly made cow-slaughter an offence. But this is not considered good enough and a mass agitation has been launched to force Parliament to pass legislation for the whole of India. In this, Hindu religious and political parties have come together. It has provided the sadhus an opportunity to reassert themselves as defenders of the faith. It has given the sadhu-politician something to say.

There are four sadhu members of Parliament.[1] Two belong to the Ramakrishna order; one is a priest of a well-endowed temple. In Parliament, these have certainly observed *maun-vrat* (the vow of silence) as becomes good sadhus. The fourth, Swami Rameshwaranand, has more than made up for the reticence of his colleagues. He has been named many times by the Speaker for disorderly conduct. He was the chief rabble-rouser on 7 November 1966, when, at his exhortation, sadhus laid siege to the Parliament House, set fire to government buildings, motor cars and buses. According to the government, seven people were killed in this riot. (The number given by the Hindu right-wing journal *Organizer* was seventy-four. Pakistan Radio put it at 475). Swami Rameshwaranand is on bail awaiting trial.

It was with my now-obvious anti-sadhu bias that I went to see the secretary of the Bharat Sadhu Samaj. The organization has a spacious double-storeyed building in Delhi's most select residential area, the Diplomatic Enclave, where all the embassies are and where the local millionaires reside. I had made no appointment but was welcomed and asked to wait. It was a large, cold room divided by a six-foot high wooden partition. On the partition was a calendar with a picture of Pandit Nehru wearing a caste mark (he never wore one in his life). There were also three large posters in Hindi announcing the cow-protection rally of 7 November. Alongside one of the posters was a map of Delhi with the route of procession marked in red ink.

I heard the clip-clop of sandalled feet come down the stairs and enter the room. 'Did you want to see me?' the man asked in impeccable English.

'Yes, sir. You are Swami Ananda, secretary of the Samaj?' (I answered the question myself by touching his feet.)

Swami Ananda (Lord of Bliss) is a handsome man in his fifties—long grey hair curling about the ears, large bright eyes and a wispy beard covering his Adam's apple. He led me to the other side of the partition. This was his office. Files were stacked against the walls. Even his table was cluttered with papers.

He sat down on his swivel chair and brushed his beard. Sadhus are reluctant to talk about themselves, but I took the chance and boldly asked him: 'Swamiji, why did you become a sadhu? You are obviously well-educated. You speak excellent English. You could have got a good job anywhere.'

Swamiji graciously accepted my compliments. He ran his slender fingers over his locks and replied, 'English literature was my favourite subject at the university. I used to stand first in my class.'

'You are from Bengal?'

He did not like the innuendo about his accent. 'I am from India . . . from the world. Hinduism is not like Christianity or Islam, restricted to followers of Jesus Christ or Mohammed. Hinduism is a universal religion.' He opened his arms wide as if he was taking the universe in his embrace. 'It is the religion of love.' He closed his arms and clasped the universe to his bosom. 'Hinduism is love for everyone, everything.' He closed his eyes and rocked in his chair.

'Why did you become a sadhu?'

He opened his large eyes. 'Why? That is an interesting question.' After a short pause he continued. 'Because I wanted to realize the truth about myself. All our holy books tell us that the aim of life should be self-realization.'

'How did you get started?'

'My English teacher, he was an American. I forget his name. Reverend Tucker or something like that. He was a Christian sannyasi. He taught me to adore Jesus Christ. I began to love Christ so much that whenever I thought of His crucifixion, I used to weep like anything. Well, it was this American missionary who said to me, 'Go and serve the people.'

'I first joined the Ramakrishna Mission. I was not very happy there because they worship Ramakrishna as god. Then I wandered about from one holy place to another: Jagannath Puri, Benares,

Hardwar, Rishikesh. I bathed in all our holy rivers. I spent many years in the Himalayas fasting, praying, meditating. Then I felt I was ready to become a full-fledged sadhu I went to Hardwar for my initiation.'

'How exactly is a sadhu initiated?'

Swamiji looked alarmed. 'That is a secret. No sadhu will tell you of his initiation or the *gut mantra* (the mystic formula whispered by a guru in the ears of the disciple).'

I told him I had read an excellent account of it in Swami Agehananda Bharati's classic, *The Ochre Robe*. (This book is proscribed by the Indian government. Bharati, an Austrian convert to Hinduism, is professor of sociology at Syracuse University.)

Swamiji, despite his religion of love, made uncharitable comments about Bharati. Then he proceeded to tell me of his own initiation. 'I was initiated into the *Dashnami* order (the same as Bharati's). I studied the philosophy of Shankara. I was filled with light and love.'

'Swamiji, what are your views on cow-protection?'

'The cow is sacred. Its milk is essential for anyone who wants to lead a spiritual life. Cow's milk, curds, butter and buttermilk keep a man's body healthy without exciting his sex.'

'Sex?'

'Yes, sex. A black cow's milk is better than that of a white one,' he assured me. He saw the bewilderment on my face and explained: 'Self-preservation is as important as self-realization. In order to preserve oneself, one must preserve one's semen—*bindu*. A real sadhu does not waste one drop of his bindu. He draws it up his spinal cord and lets the life force spread in his frame.' Swamiji inhaled deeply, expanded his chest and slapped it to illustrate the tonic qualities of retained bindu.

I recalled reading about it in Arthur Koestler's *The Lotus and the Robot* (also proscribed by the Indian government). Swamiji, too, had read the book. And once again he expressed himself strongly.

'What about the economic aspects of cow-protection?' I asked, trotting out the data: 235 million cows; cows dying of hunger; people dying of hunger.

Swamiji had heard all this before: 'If the government can spend ten crore (100 million) rupees on an abattoir, it can spend ten lakhs (one million) on *gau shalas* (cattle-pens). If we feed them better, they will yield more milk. We need their dung to fertilize our land. Unless chemical fertilizers have a little natural manure mixed in them, they can turn fertile land into a desert. And cows' urine is full of medicinal properties. It is used in many Ayurvedic medicines. My friend, economics are in favour of cow-protection.'

'Only the Hindus want cow-protection. How can we call ourselves secular if we give in to the demands of one religious community?'

'My friend,' replied Swamiji in a very condescending voice, 'it seems you have lived abroad too long. Does secularism mean we should deliberately hurt the religious feelings of the Hindus, who form 85 per cent of the population of the country? And you take it from me, hundreds of thousands of Muslims, Christians and Sikhs are with us on this issue. And don't you realize how bad it is to consume the flesh of an animal whose milk you drink? It is like eating your mother. That's what makes beef-eaters stupid.' He quoted Shakespeare: 'I am a great eater of beef and I believe that does harm to my wit. That's from *Twelfth Night*.'

Swamiji then told me how, in 1956, Gulzari Lal Nanda, then minister of planning, had persuaded him to become secretary of the Sadhu Samaj. 'We have 10,000 members drawn from all sects. One day, all sadhus will join this organization and help to raise the moral standards of the world.'

I asked his opinion of another well-known sadhu leader. Swamiji's brow wrinkled. 'He is no sadhu! He drinks wine, eats flesh, fornicates with virgins. He bloody bugger.'

I was alarmed at the language. Swamiji reassured-me: 'Ours is a religion of purity and love. We can't have frauds among us.'

I mentioned yet another name, a sadhu who had gone on a lecture tour of the United States. 'Absolute fraud,' Swamiji assured me. 'He also bloody bugger.'

It became a game. The score for loving everyone was five; 'bloody buggers' won by a margin of seven.

I touched Swami Ananda's sandals and took my leave.

Later in the day I went back to Nigambodh Ghat. Half-a-mile north of the cremation ground was a sadhus' encampment organized by Hindu religious and political groups: Arya Samaj, Sanatan Dharma Sabha, Bharatiya Jan Sangh and the militant Rashtriya Swayamsevak Sangh (RSS). The encampment was on a stretch of sand between the river and a dual highway which encircles the city. The police were present in strength. There were nearly a hundred constables armed with metal-tipped bamboo staves and handcuffs. A fleet of paddy wagons lined the road.

I left the tarmac of the twentieth century and trod the ancient sands of time. First were the nangas squatting on the ground in rows listening to their guru. Not one of them wore a stitch of clothing. The next lot were an order from Central India, dressed in ochre robes. They sat around a pit in which burned a sacrificial fire, chanting hymns and throwing in palmfuls of rice and clarified butter.

Near the river were the tents of yet another order from somewhere in Bihar. They looked prosperous. They had brought their elephant with them (an elephant costs more than a Cadillac and consumes more rupees' worth of fodder than two motor cars consume gas). The animal was spraying itself, and anyone who came within range, with sand.

I gave it a wide berth and came to the *akhada* (open air gymnasium). Here, under a banner with the legend 'Young Men's Hindu Athletic Club' topped with the figure of a cow, were a band of youths wrestling. Then at last I came to the group which was due to march into the city to coerce tradesmen into shutting their shops as a protest against the government's reluctance to ban cow-slaughter.

There were several hundred people there, sadhus and others, squatting on the sand. A sadhu in saffron robes sat on a dais addressing them through a loudspeaker. My arrival—I was wearing European clothes—attracted attention. The speaker quickly tailored his speech to suit the occasion. His barbed shafts were now aimed at Indians who aped the West.

'Our ancients used to begin their day by taking the name of god. Indian gentlemen of today, educated in England and America, do not believe in god. Do you know how they begin their day? I will tell you. They start by eating a biscuit.' He pronounced it as *bis* (poison) *coot* (powdered).

The audience burst into laughter. Many people turned around to look at me. The speaker warmed to his theme of how the West had corrupted Hinduism. He related a story of an Anglicized Indian sahib who wanted to cross a river and called out to the boatman in English: 'Hey you, black man, come here!'

The boatman, who did not understand English, naturally took no notice.

The Indian sahib yelled in rage, 'Come at once you *biladee* (bloody).' No result. Then he spoke more politely in Hindi: 'Brother, please take me to the other side.'

The boatman brought his vessel to the bank and began to row across. He asked the Indian sahib what he had learned in foreign lands. The Indian sahib told him of the sciences and philosophy he had learned at Oxford. When they were in midstream the boat sprang a leak and began to sink. The sahib screamed with terror. And as the boatman swam away to safety, he asked: 'And didn't they teach you how to swim across an Indian river when you went to this Oxford or *phoxford* or whatever you call it?'

The lesson went home. The crowd raised peals of laughter. They turned back to look at me and renew their mirth. The speaker was happy. His tone became soothing: 'And so, my dear friends, my beloved Indian brothers, do not forget your great past, your religion and your gods. Veneration of the cow mother is an essential part of the Hindu dharma. We will shed the last drop of our blood to protect our *gau mata* (mother cow).'

Someone in the audience shouted. *'Dharma desh ka nata hai.* (Religion and nation are related, one to the other.)

The crowd yelled back: *'Gau hamari mata hai.'* (The cow is our mother.)

The meeting ended. The crowd formed itself into a procession with the nanga sadhus in the van. They trudged across the sand towards the highway proclaiming their bovine birth at the top of their voices.

A phalanx of khaki-and-red-uniformed policemen barred their way. The inspector stepped in front, dropped the swagger stick he had under his arm on the sand and touched the feet of one of the nangas in the middle of the front row. With the palms of his hands joined as in prayer, he pleaded: 'Maharaj (your holiness), this far but no farther.'

He bent down and touched the nanga's feet a second time. 'Maharaj, we are your children, forgive us. But no farther.'

It was obvious that neither the inspector nor any of his constables would lay hands on any of the sadhus.

'Why don't you put an end to this wickedness?' demanded the nanga.

'Maharaj,' whined the inspector, 'we revere the gau mata. But we are servants of the government. Once you persuade the government to forbid cow-killing, we will flay alive anyone who touches a cow. Maharaj, our bread and our honour are in your hands.' The inspector touched the feet of the nanga for the third time.

The sadhus' feelings were assuaged. The memory of the bloody Monday of 7 November was still fresh. The procession turned back to the encampment triumphantly shouting its slogans.

I left the sands of the Jamuna and drove to the home of my friend Cyrus Jhabvala, a Parsee architect, and his novelist wife Ruth, who is Jewish. There were other friends present. I was among my own type—Anglicized Indian sahibs.

I narrated my experiences of the day. It was our turn to laugh. We defied our traditions. We drank Scotch. We ate beef sandwiches. ('Not-so-holy cow—imported beef,' explained my host. Someone stretched his hand across the table: 'Ruth, can I have one of your kosher pork sausages, please?')

And so it went on until we felt we had liquidated all the sadhus and freed our countrymen of the Hindus' silly food fads. Then our host spoiled it all with a short speech: 'Listen, chaps! When the chips are down, you know very well that however Westernized the Indian and whatever religion he may have or not have, whenever he eats beef he has a sense of guilt—a teeny-weeny bit of a bad conscience. And not one Indian will bandy words with a sadhu for fear of arousing his wrath. It is like our attitude towards sati (immolation of a widow on the pyre of her dead husband). We condemn it but we cannot help admiring a woman who becomes a sati. These things have been with us for over 4,000 years. They are in our blood and in our bones. We cannot fight them with reason. They are stronger than reason.'

Notes

1. This article was written in the year 1967.

GOING GAGA OVER YOGA

The name of Swami Dhirendra Brahmachari rouses different kinds of reactions in different people. Although everyone respects his knowledge of the ancient science of yoga, not everyone approves of the way he uses that knowledge. A yogi should not have any worldly interests, Dhirendra Brahmachari is very much a man of the world. He is a kind of court yogi having taught yoga to the late Prime Minister Jawaharlal Nehru, his daughter Indira Gandhi, the present Prime Minister, her two sons, many ministers of the Cabinet and hosts of senior government officials. Although everyone will admit that he looks every inch the picture of a sage of ancient times, many disapprove of his frequent appearances on television. He is most photogenic. He is over six feet tall and beautifully proportioned. He wears his jet black hair down to his shoulders and sports a Christ-like beard. His skin is clear, his eyes sparkle, his features are like those of Grecian gods. He is always draped in very fine muslin and wears nothing except sandals on his feet. Although he is, as his name signifies, a brahmachari (celibate), he has a bevy of young, attractive lady secretaries and instructors on his staff. Other yogis, envious of his success, call him the Rasputin of New Delhi.

Dhirendra Brahmachari has published two books on yoga and is currently director of Vishvayatan Yoga Ashram occupying about 12,000 square metres of land in the heart of the capital. The ashram has a thirty-bed hospital, a laboratory, reception rooms, offices and the director's residence. He was once chairman and is today a very influential member of the Central Council of

Indian Medicines set up by the government to sponsor research in Ayurveda, homoeopathy and yoga. In the current Fifth Five Year Plan a grant of forty-six lakh rupees has been earmarked for promotion and research on the medical benefits of yoga.

It was a very cold New Year's morning that I called on Swami Dhirendra Brahmachari. A young lady ushered me into his office. He was seated in a swivel chair behind a large glass-topped desk with the usual paraphernalia of pens and writing pads. There were three telephones on a side-table. From underneath the table emerged three white Pomeranians to scrutinize me. Swamiji ordered them back to their place, waved me to a chair and continued to exchange New Year's greetings over the phone. It was some time before he buzzed the operator and told her not to put in any more calls till he had finished with me.

I re-introduced myself and asked him how he could sit in the cold room draped only in thin muslin. 'What cold? I do not feel any cold,' he replied with a smile. He fished out a pack of photographs from his drawer. 'This is a new laboratory I am setting up in the mountains to study the effects of yoga at high altitudes in sub-zero temperatures.' The photographs were of a kind of watchtower standing on a hilltop with snow on the ground. In the forefront was Swami Dhirendra Brahmachari in his scanty drapery with one arm resting on a young girl in a fur coat and snow shoes. 'She is one of my German disciples,' he explained.

I had met him twenty years ago. It was at the height of summer with the temperature well over thirty-eight degrees celsius. I was hot and perspiring. He did not have a bead of sweat on his body and looked as fresh as after a bath. Except for a very slight recession of the hairline on his forehead, he did not look any older. I had heard his admirers say that although he was born over seventy years ago, yoga had made him ageless. He looks a very well-preserved man of fifty.

'Swamiji, how old are you?' I asked him. 'Two questions I will not answer,' he replied quite firmly. 'One is about my age,

the other is about my family background. I am a yogi—the past
is dead.'

Swami Dhirendra Brahmachari is a Brahmin from Bihar. He
founded his first yoga centre at Lucknow thirty-five years ago, the
second a few years later near Jammu and, with a grant from the
government, the third one in Delhi in 1969. 'Suddenly everyone
is interested in yoga,' he said. 'Indians, Americans, Europeans,
Australians, everyone. It is like a flood.'

Swamiji is right. In recent years there has been a veritable
explosion of yoga institutes all over the world. In India it is a
part of the renaissance of everything indigenous and Hindu.
Enthusiasm for yoga is more noticeable amongst the Hindus who
form 85 per cent of the population of the country than amongst
Muslims, Christians, Sikhs or other smaller communities. Its
acceptance in the West, chiefly in the United States, has added
to its prestige in India. It has also become a valuable earner of
foreign exchange. Yogis fly round the world setting up institutes
wherever they go. The stream of foreign enthusiasts coming to
India for at-source inspiration has increased steadily and, as the
Swamiji says, the stream of yoga has come into spate.

Research on the medical benefits of yoga is a phenomenon
of recent years—once again stimulated by pronouncements of
foreign, mainly American, doctors. One that attracted worldwide
publicity was an experiment on rats carried out by the Institute
of Medicine of the Benaras Hindu University (BHU).

I asked Swami Dhirendra about the rat experiments. He
exploded in a guffaw of angry laughter, 'You mean that Udupa
fellow making rats do *shirshasana* (headstand)! Absolute nonsense!
I am going to put an end to that kind of humbug by stopping
the grant to his institution.'

Swami Dhirendra Brahmachari has no doubt that yoga cures all
kinds of diseases. His method of diagnosis is however somewhat
unorthodox and the subject of lively comment among his critics.
He makes his patient lie on his or her back, takes a string, places
one end on the navel and measures the distance between the navel

and the right and left nipple. 'Since ladies' breasts vary in shape and size and some are firm and others drooping, I measure the distance between the navel and the left toe and the navel and the right toe,' he explained. And continued, 'The navel is the centre of the 72,000 nerves in the human body. Every malaise manifests itself by shifting the navel upwards, downwards or sideways. If it goes upwards, you can be sure the person suffers from flatulence or some other stomach ailment. If it is lower than its seat, the person has loose motions. If it is either to the left or the right, he or she suffers from belly-ache. The navel is like the pulse. When I feel the navel, I can tell blindfolded what is wrong with the person.'

We were interrupted by Swamiji's lady secretary with a pack of visiting cards and messages from VIPs. 'You go and look around the clinic,' he said dismissing me. 'If you have any more questions, you can come back.'

Dr R.N. Sinha who has been chief medical supervisor of the ashram for the last six years took charge of me. On the lawn a group of beginners was being put through the initial cleansing (*kunjal*). They were given tumblerfuls of tepid water and then put through gyrations to loosen their bowels. One after another they hurried into a line of lavatories behind the lawn.

'They will expel everything in their stomachs till the water coming out of the rectum is as clear as the water that went in the mouth,' explained Dr Sinha. 'There are other techniques of stomach-cleansing; one is to eat a full meal or drink a bellyful of water, stick a finger at the back of the tongue and vomit it all out. This cleansing must be done at least once in seven days.'

'How does it differ from an enema or a colonic irrigation?' I asked.

'Enemas only cleanse the lower bowels; yogic cleansing evacuates everything there is in the body. It has to be followed by cleansing the nasal passage by sucking water up the nostrils and bringing it out of the mouth. We also teach them to pass a string through the nostrils into the gorge. Likewise we train patients to swallow a twenty-foot-long (6.15 metres) muslin bandage and pull it out. It brings out all remains of food, phlegm, sinuses, mucus—everything. Most patients begin to feel better after this kind of purging. Would you like to see it done?'

'No, thank you.'

The Vishvayatan Yoga Ashram specializes in treating four ailments: asthma, diabetes, gastro-intestinal disorders and arthritis. Dr Sinha maintains that of these ailments they have obtained the best results in treating stomach disorders. 'Ninety-nine per cent of Indians suffer from some stomach trouble or other; the remaining one per cent do not know that they suffer from it,' he remarked with a wry smile. 'Most Indians have dysentery or constipation, hyper-acidity or flatulence which often affects their hearts. All this disappears with internal washing.'

Amongst the people who come for treatment at the ashram a fair proportion are men suffering from impotence. 'Our treatment cures a lot of them,' maintained Dr Sinha. Yoga tones up the system. And if you throw in the notion of virility, the chances of success are very good. All said and done, impotence is in the mind and not in the sexual organs.

At the time I visited the ashram hospital there were only eight male and two female patients. Three men were there for the cure of asthma. Two said yoga had done them some good; the third had not benefited at all. One patient suffering from chronic constipation said yoga had helped him move his bowels. A young girl suffering from TB of the hip-joint had not responded to the treatment.

The ashram laboratory where blood, sputum, urine and faeces of patients are examined is a shoddy collection of microscopes, test-tubes, heaters and other equipment all cluttered up in a shed. It was apparent that few of the instruments had been used or records kept. Nevertheless, Dr Jain, the pathologist, maintained that the results were 'definitely encouraging'.

I returned to Swami Dhirendra Brahmachari's office. His table was strewn with bouquets of flowers and he was still busy on the phone wishing somebody or the other a very happy and prosperous New Year. He put his hand on the mouthpiece and said, 'There is a lot of misunderstanding about yoga in foreign countries, too many charlatans who go about in America-*Shamerica* lecturing on yoga without knowing anything about it. You must put them right.' Then he resumed talking into the instrument.

WHAT IS YOGA

There is indeed a lot of misunderstanding about yoga. The main culprits are Indians who make tall claims for it and the gullible foreigners, chiefly the gullible Americans.

Yoga means much the same as the English word yoke—a system designed to yoke the human with the divine. There are many paths prescribed to achieve this goal of union with god. The Bhagavad Gita recommends three; the path of knowledge, the path of devotion and the path of good deeds. All the three paths assume that the human mind cannot comprehend the Divine if the body in which it is encased is imperfect. Hence the system of yoga exercises to make the body a fit receptacle of Divine Wisdom; *mens sana* can only exist *in compore sano*.

The system of yoga exercises was evolved 4,000 years ago. Among the relics found in the ruins of cities of the Indus Valley are figurines showing ascetics in yogic postures. The Aryans who invaded India (circa 2000 BC) adapted and systematized yoga. The most important treatise on the yoga of the body are the aphorisms of Patanjali who lived some time during 1200 BC.

Yoga of the body can be divided into three broad groups of exercises. The first consists of a variety of *asanas*. The second consists of regulating the rhythm of breathing *(pranayama)* accompanied by silent repetition of the mystic syllable Om or some other sacred mantra. This enables the practitioner to go on to the third stage, viz., to control his senses, to enable him to meditate and attain samadhi—the state of superconscious stillness during which he has communion with the Divine.

An extreme form of the culture of the body known as Hatha yoga is said to give supernatural control over bodily organs and develop occult powers. The goal of the Hatha yogi is to activate latent forces in his body. This is based on the notion that the base of the spine is a she-serpent *(kundalini)* curled three-and-a-half times in a state of hibernation. She can be roused from her slumber by assiduous yogic practice. When this happens she climbs upwards along the spine and passes through six chakras located at definite points (attended by progressively increasing powers) until she reaches the seventh and last chakra located in the apex of the skull where she is united with Shiva. In ancient tantric texts these circles are depicted as lotuses of different colours with specified numbers of petals.

The sexual implications of this serpentine theory are all too apparent. The seat of the dormant she-snake is between the genitals and the anus. The practitioner is enjoined to become like the gods, an *urddhvaretas,* one in whom the semen flows upwards. The semen (or bindu) is regarded as the life-substance and must never be dissipated. It follows that only the celibate can rouse the serpent within him. Hatha yoga is said to give the practitioner power to indulge in coitus without losing his bindu—he can even recover it after he has discharged it.

Many remarkable feats performed by Hatha yogis have been recorded. In 1837 Yogi Hari Das was buried alive at Lahore in the presence of the Sikh Maharaja Ranjit Singh and a visiting delegation of British officers. Relays of sentries mounted guard on his grave. After forty days he was dug out and revived by a massage. Yogis walking over beds of live coals, lying on beds of nails for long hours, drinking acids, chewing up electric bulbs have been witnessed by thousands of people. However not all Hatha yogis succeed in their endeavours. In 1961 a yogi of Trivandrum claiming to have acquired the power to fly, climbed up a palm tree to await the right kind of cloud which would bear him aloft. The cloud never arrived. The most celebrated debacle in the history of Hatha yoga took place on 13 June 1966 in Bombay. Yogi Lakshman Sundara Srikant Rao appeared before a vast crowd to demonstrate his ability to walk over water. He went down like a stone.

I asked Swami Dhirendra Brahmachari about serpent power. 'Is there anyone today who has been able to rouse the kundalini within him?' The Swamiji's reply, though somewhat obscure, implied that such a person does indeed exist. 'Rousing the kundalini is the ultimate goal of a yogi,' he said. 'The experience cannot be described. Only he knows who knows.' Then he proceeded to list signs by which one who had roused the she-serpent within him could be recognized. 'He is slim, his face is radiant, his eyes sparkle, his ears catch all the ten kinds of sounds there are, his body is free from sickness, his digestion is perfect, his urine and faeces do not emit unpleasant odours, he has no nervous tension, his semen instead of running downwards, as in most mortals, runs upwards.' To help me further in identifying the person who had roused his kundalini, Swamiji casually mentioned that many years ago his personal servant had remarked that, although his master used the same spot every day in the field to urinate and defecate, a strange fragrance came from the spot, instead of a bad odour.

I asked him about Yogi Bhajan who teaches *kundaliniyoga* and has a sizeable following in the United States.

'That fellow is no *yogi-shogi*,' scoffed Swami Dhirendra Brahmachari. 'I warned him that he was doing wrong. I told him that the only thing that would save him from hell would be the accumulated goodness of his American disciples. It is people like this Bhajan Yogi and that Udupa chap with his rats who are giving people wrong ideas about yoga.'

One of the benefits claimed by yoga is an equable temper and a sweet tongue which does not lend itself to speaking ill of anyone.

~

Katil Narasimha Udupa (fifty-five) is an FRCS of Canada, a Fellow of the College of Surgeons from Michigan and has worked in the Peter Bent Brigham Hospital in Boston. For the last seventeen years he has been professor of surgery and director of the Institute of Medicine of the Benaras Hindu University. Testing the effects of yoga on rats was his idea. He has a grant of Rs 60,000 to try out his experiments.

Dr Udupa handed me a sheaf of reports on which he had based an article he sent to the *Journal of the American Medical Association* (JAMA) on the results of his experiments. The article roused a lot of interest in America.

Dr Udupa's 'guinea-pigs' are students from the university. Modern equipment including a polygraph which records the heart, respiration, blood pressure and 'a whole-body counter' which records intake of isotopes is already in commission.

A yoga clinic has been given a wing of its own in the new university hospital. Here patients who have not responded to conventional medicines are sent. Dr Udupa mentioned some diseases in the treatment of which yoga has proved its worth; thyroid toxiasis, high blood pressure, diabetes, asthma, arthritis and nervous dyspepsia. It is too early to gauge the results as the experiment is very new and only four patients had registered themselves for treatment. Nevertheless Dr Udupa maintains that in the treatment of arthritis quite remarkable results have been achieved in a short period by the 'unlocking of joints'. When I told him that I had seen similar results at nature cure clinics where all that had been done was to cleanse the patients' bowels by colonic irrigation and keeping them on a fast for a few days, he replied, 'There are many ways of getting to the top of the Everest, yoga is also a kind of naturopathy.'

I asked him about his experiments on rats. He was somewhat embarrassed because of the publicity that it had received. 'I made the mistake of talking to an American journalist. He went and put it in all the papers.' I persisted in my enquiries. The doctor had acquired sixteen albino mice, stuck their heads in test-tubes with open bottoms so that their snouts were in the open. He had kept them in the shirshasana position for an hour and then examined their heart-beats, blood pressure and response to stimuli. 'The effects were exactly the same as in humans. The rats were rejuvenated.'

'Why then were the experiments abandoned?'

'There was a spate of letters of protest from the SPCA including one from Dr Rukmini Arundale of the Thepsophical Society. Despite the fact that there was no cruelty of any kind—on the contrary the rats seemed to benefit from the experience—I was asked to discontinue the experiments.'

The borderline between yoga ot the body emphasizing asanas and yoga of the mind is very thin. Physical yoga includes pranayama with repetitions of sacred formulae. Yoga of the mind, though it obviates the need of asanas, also requires the practitioner to regulate his breathing while he meditates. The most successful teacher of the yoga of meditation is Maharishi Mahesh Yogi. Although his transcendental meditation has few adherents in India and is often criticized as the 'capsule method' or 'instant meditation', its success elsewhere is remarkable. The Maharishi who claims to teach the 'science of creative intelligence' has an estimated 2,000 centres managed by the Maharishi International University with Dr Keith Wallace, professor of philosophy, as president. At one time Mahesh Yogi's disciples included Mia Farrow and the Beatles. In England, Maharishi's institutes charge about Rs 480 for four ninety-minute lessons. This gave the London weekly, the *Observer,* an opportunity to caption an article on the subject as 'Cash Vibration'.

The one country to have categorically rejected yoga is the Soviet Union. Marxists have understandably no time for meditation or mysticism, but their rejection of yoga as a physical cult is difficult to comprehend. An article in the Moscow journal *Health* denounced the head stand as dangerous to health. This brought forth a riposte from an Indian rhymester in the *Times of India.*

The pundits of yoga are wrathful
That their credo has been questioned abroad;
There is wild indignation at the insinuation
That shrishasana is a fraud.
'Are the centuries of practice forgotten?'
They ask with a measure of scorn.
Are Nehru and Menuhin not really being genuine
When they stand on their heads every morn?
Devotees everywhere have joined the issue—
They brandish a rod in their pickle
They won't take it prone, this effrontery shown
By the land of the hammer and sickle.
Viewed calmly, the Soviets may well
Have a point, when all's said and done
To perch on one's neck, in Omsk or Uzbek
May not be their notion of fun.
We may claim that by standing inverted
Our grey matter is cleansed and made new
But Reds in the know, will be able to show
Brainwashing is the best thing for you.

Most educated Indians accept yoga as the best form of nature cure and better than any other system of exercises. It is difficult to make any estimate of those who practice it, but it is a safe guess that it runs into millions. But there are a few who are very sceptical. I.S. Johar, a well-known film-star comedian whose first wife teaches yoga at the health club of the Taj Mahal Hotel in Bombay, denounces it as a dangerous hoax. 'What did our ancients know about blood pressure or the toxins that holding the breath can produce? I can give you innumerable instances of people who lost their sense of balance by standing too long on their heads, of people who have done irreparable injury to their spinal cords by doing some of the asanas and strings that surgeons have taken out of the lungs and bellies of yoga enthusiasts. The Soviets are quite right in putting an end to this hocus-pocus,' he said.

There is little doubt that yoga asanas do for the human body and mind what no other system of exercises either aims to do or achieves. Swami Dhirendra Brahmachari is a splendid example of what it can do for the body. Dr Sinha listed yoga's superiority over other exercises. 'Other exercises consume energy; yoga is designed to preserve it. There is no sweating, no running out of breath, no hardening of the muscles. And yoga asanas are designed to improve the functioning of every organ in the body including the eyes, ears, heart, lungs, liver and the kidneys.' The *shavasana* (corpse pose), claims Dr K.K. Datey, one of India's leading cardiologists, is most beneficial for people with high blood pressure and cardiac disorders. Controlled breathing and meditation soothes the nerves, reduces hypertension and thus releases many people from dependence on tranquillizers and drugs. Auto-suggestion plays an important role in the success of yoga. Emile Coue's formula, 'every day in every way I am getting better and better', is assiduously inculcated. Catechisms are taught to schoolchildren. 'How does yoga help you?' asks Shobha Shirodkar, principal of the Arya Samaj School in Santa Cruz (Bombay). Her class chant the reply in chorus, 'Yoga gives concentration and helps us to go further in life.'

'What does yoga do for our body?'

'It cleanses the body, it slows down our heartbeat and we can live longer.' Another yoga ashram has a banner above its entrance gate proclaiming: 'An Asana a Day Keeps the Doctor Away.'

The findings at Swami Dhirendra Brahmachari's ashram and the Benaras Hindu University were not very convincing. Since 1957 a team of doctors of the All India Institute of Medical Sciences (AIIMS) has, in collaboration with the Indian Council of Medical Research (ICMR) conducted experiments on 500 yogis on a more scientific basis. Dr B.K. Anand, a neuro-physiologist who is the leader of the team, says that they were trying to find answers to three questions. First: can yogis influence their internal activities by meditation? Second: can they live without nutrition in an atmosphere with very little oxygen? And third: what changes take place in their brains when they are so engaged? The institute has constructed a black, soundproof room, a box which can be sealed against air, attached to an electroencephalograph to record the activity of the brain. The doctors found that some yogis achieved incredible degrees of automatic control requiring minimal amount of energy. Whereas a normal human being can lower his metabolic rate by 10–12 per cent, the yogis could lower it by as much as fifty per cent. Heartbeats were slowed down to 'near heart-block'—thirty to thirty-five per minute compared with the usual seventy-two.

The most interesting of the findings of the AIIMS were the changes in brain activity during meditation. The relaxed brain has waves called alpha activity which can be influenced by external stimuli such as the flashing of a light or a thud. In the case of the yogis in trance this alpha activity did not respond to external stimuli. The team came to the conclusion that 'meditation has most definitely done something'.

Two years ago one member of the team, Dr G.S. Chhina, read a paper on his findings at the 26th International Congress of Physiological Sciences in Delhi. He confirmed that yogis could walk over burning coal without blistering their feet, expose their bodies to prolonged dousing in chilled water without any sign of discomfort, stick water into their rectums and even suck radio-opaque fluid into the urinary tract. In some cases, penile erections and ejaculations were performed without anything touching the genitals.

~

Bellur Krishnamachar Sunderaya Iyengar (fifty-seven), a widower with five children, is the best-known teacher of yoga in India. He is a man of modest education but his book *Light on Yoga* (Alien & Unwin) is now in its seventh paperback edition and has been translated into many Indian and foreign languages. When Iyengar's wife died four years ago, his students raised Rs 3.5 lakhs to build in stone and marble the Ramamani Iyengar Memorial Yoga Institute in Pune.

The institute is designed to conform to Patanjali's teachings on yoga. Patanjali had an obsession with the figure eight. The institute has one massive column symbolizing the human spine with eight sections branching out to eight large windows representing the eight lamps of yoga: body, breath, consciousness, mind, will, action, knowledge and surrender to god. It has three storeys representing the quest of the external, the internal and consummation with the Divine. It is seventy-one feet high. 'Seven plus one make eight,' explained Iyengar naively; and it has eighty-eight steps leading to the top of the dome where there is a red ochre idol of the monkey-god Hanuman, son of the wind and Hindu symbol of energy. The institute has figures of Hindu gods and goddesses but in every room the place of honour is reserved for a marble bust or photograph of the late Ramamani. 'She gave me the strength to carry on,' says B.K.S. Iyengar.

Iyengar has taught yoga to over 50,000 men and women all over the world. He showed me a silver Omega alarm wrist-watch presented to him by Yehudi Menuhin with the inscription 'to my best violin teacher'. Among other celebrities taught yoga by him was the late Queen Elizabeth of the Belgians when she was eighty-four, Gina Bachauer, Lily Kraus and Clifford Curzon. Iyengar has made yoga very profitable. His American students pay the equivalent of Rs 900 for a three-week course. Over a hundred Americans come over from the States every year. He conducts yoga lessons in Bombay once every week and is paid handsome fees wherever else he goes. The one thing that distinguishes B.K.S. Iyengar from most other Indian teachers of yoga is that he restricts his instructions to teaching asanas and breathing without overloading it with Sanskrit mumbo-jumbo and mysticism. Although a strict vegetarian and a teetotaller he does not insist that his pupils do the same.

All he wears when conducting the classes is a pair of striped shorts. He has a thin red line running down the middle of his forehead to indicate that he is an Iyengar Brahmin. A dozen men and women yoga teachers from America were taking a refresher course. One lady was as bald as an egg-shell, another had a blood-shot eye, a third one had a knee injury—all three were trying out yoga as the last resort.

My eyes rested on a full-bosomed, broad-hipped woman in the headstand position. Her long hazel-brown hair was strewn over the floor. Although she was upside down she looked altogether too healthy to need more health. She noticed my interest in her and stood on her feet; her hair now hung down to her waist. She joined the palms of her hands and greeted me, 'Namaskar, I am Jyoti Vernon.'

'You are an American. How come you have a Hindu name?' I asked her.

'Yes, I am American. I was born Carol David, but ever since I started on yoga I adopted an Indian name. Everyone including my husband calls me Jyoti.' She introduced me to her husband Eugene Vernon who is a practising attorney in San Francisco. The Vernons have one child of their own and have adopted another. They were in India to find yet another child to adopt and take a refresher course with Iyengar. She has been teaching asanas for some years and is well-acquainted with the yoga movement in California. According to Jyoti, in California alone yoga enthusiasts run into the thousands. Many go in for the spiritual instruction and are disciples of swamis, gurus and other varieties of Indian godmen. But the majority stick to the physical aspect of yoga.

Back in Benaras Hindu University I again met Dr Udupa and his assistants gathered together in the house of Vice-Chancellor Dr K.L. Shrimali, one-time minister of education in the Central government and an ardent believer in yoga. I tried to provoke them. 'I concede that yoga asanas are good for health and perhaps achieve better results than other systems of exercises. I even concede that meditation may do some good to the mentally disturbed, but I cannot comprehend why a healthy man with a healthy mind should waste his time concentrating on some point between his eyes or his navel.'

Dr Shrimali gave a guarded reply: 'It is said to make a healthy mind more creative. Everything anyone does he can do better after a course of meditation.'

'There is no evidence of increased creativity following meditation. Give me one example of a creative yogi.'

They looked at each other. Once again it was Dr Shrimali who replied. 'Sri Aurobindo.' (A Hindu anarchist-turned-philosopher who died in December 1950).

'Yes, Sri Aurobindo. You can't deny he was a philosopher,' added Dr Udupa.

'Can you name any other? After all the number of meditating yogis runs into hundreds of thousands.'

There was complete silence. It gave me the opportunity to have my last fling. 'Anything worthwhile is created by restless minds. World's greatest artists, musicians, scientists, writers, poets had tortured minds. Your mental equipoise only produces mental equipoise. Nothing else.'

'You may have a point there,' conceded Dr Shrimali. 'Our yoga experts should look into the effects of yogic meditation on the creative impulse. Fortunately for us we cannot do this by experimenting on rats,' he said with a smile.

WHY I SUPPORTED THE EMERGENCY

The Emergency has become a synonym for obscenity. Even men and women who were pillars of the Emergency rule and misused their positions to harass innocent people against whom they had personal grudges try to distance themselves from their past in the hope that it will fade out of public memory forever. We must not allow them to get away with it. Because of them many mistakes were made which must be avoided the next time conditions require the suspension of democratic norms for the preservation of law and order.

With some reservations I supported the Emergency proclaimed by Mrs Indira Gandhi on 25 June 1975. Let me explain why. I concede that the right to protest is integral to democracy. You can have public meetings to criticize or condemn government actions. You can take out processions, call for strikes and closure of businesses. But there must not be any coercion or violence. If there is any, it is the duty of the government to suppress it by force, if necessary. By May 1975 public protests against Mrs Gandhi's government had assumed nationwide dimensions and often turned violent. With my own eyes I saw slogan-chanting processions go down Bombay's thoroughfares, smashing cars parked on the roadsides and breaking shop windows as they went along. The local police was unable to contend with them because they were too few, the protesters too many. The leaders of Opposition parties watched the country sliding into chaos as bemused spectators hoping that the mounting chaos would force Mrs Gandhi to resign.

The unquestioned leader of the anti-Mrs Gandhi movement was Jayaprakash Narayan, a man for whom I had enormous respect and admiration. He had become the conscience keeper of the nation. But it was Lok Nayak, as he came to be known, who crossed the Lakshman rekha of democratic protest. His call for 'total revolution' included preventing elected members of state legislatures from entering Vidhan Sabha buildings. He announced his intention to gherao Parliament house and even asked the police and the army to revolt against the government. I wrote to Jayaprakash protesting that what he was advocating was wrong and undemocratic. He wrote back justifying his stand. I published both my letter and his much-longer reply in the *Illustrated Weekly of India* which I then happened to be editing. I believe, and still believe, freedom to speak one's mind is the basic principle of democracy.

Early June I was attending a conference in Mexico City. I arrived back in Bombay the day the Emergency was declared. The night before all the Opposition leaders had been picked up from their homes and put in jails across the country. The *Times of India* offices were in pandemonium. We were told that censorship had been imposed on the press: we had to toe the line or get out. I was determined to resist and thought if editors of other papers published by Bennett, Coleman & Co. would form a united front against censorship we would succeed in making the government change its mind against the press. I expected Sham Lal, editor of the *Times of India*, to become our leader. He bluntly refused to do so. Sham Lal's number two, Girilal Jain, resident editor in Delhi, went one better by lauding the emergence of Sanjay Gandhi as the new leader. Not one other editor was willing to risk his job. Editors of the *Navbharat Times, Maharashtra Times, Dharmyug, Filmfare, Femina, Sarika* decided to stay away from the protest meeting we organized. Inder Malhotra's behaviour was enigmatic. He kept going up and down the floors greeting everyone with 'jai ho' and moving on. He never looked anyone in the eye. To this day I don't know whether he was for or against the Emergency. For three weeks I refused to publish the *Illustrated Weekly*. My friend from my college years in England, Rajni Patel, who became the dominant voice on the board of directors, told me bluntly: 'My friend, if you are looking for martyrdom, we'll give it to you.' The board chairman, Justice (rtd) K.T. Desai, was gentler. 'You don't realize how serious the government is about censorship on the press. If you refuse to publish the journal we will have no option but to find another editor. Why not give it a try to see how it goes?' I agreed to give it a try. After all, I had criticized Jayaprakash Narayan's call for a 'total revolution' as undemocratic. The Allahabad high court judgement declaring Mrs Gandhi's membership of Parliament invalid weakened her position and she was persuaded by her closest advisors to strike out.

The Emergency, when first imposed, was generally welcomed by the people. There were no strikes or hartals, schools and colleges re-opened, business picked up, buses and trains began to run on time. People are under the impression that the Emergency administrators were very efficient. They were not. A few days after it was promulgated I got a call from H.Y. Sharada Prasad asking me to come over to see the Prime Minister. I was not to tell anyone about the appointment. The next day I met her in her South Block office. I pleaded with her to withdraw censorship on the press. 'Editors like me who support you have lost credibility. Nobody will believe that we are doing so of our free will and not being dictated to,' I argued. She remained adamant. 'There cannot be any Emergency without censorship on the press,' she maintained. I returned to Bombay disappointed. Back in the office, I found in my mail a letter reading, 'How did your meeting with Madame Dictator go?' Signed George. George Fernandes had gone underground but someone (obviously in the PMO) had informed him about my meeting. The same afternoon four leading members of the RSS, against whom warrants of arrest had been issued, boldly walked into my office and for half an hour questioned me about what had passed between the PM and me. And then, as boldly, walked out.

The censorship was also selective and eccentric. Some papers like the *Indian Express* were made targets of Mrs Gandhi's ire. Others like the *Times of India* and *Hindustan Times* were left alone. As was the weekly *Blitz*, owned by the most unprincipled editor of our times, Rusi Karanjia, who enthusiastically supported Mrs Gandhi. Kuldip Nayar was arrested. For no reason whatsoever, so was his eighty-two-year-old father-in-law, Bhim Sain Sachar, once chief minister of Punjab. Ramesh Thapar, once very close to Mrs Gandhi, closed down his *Seminar*. His sister, Dr Romila Thapar, who kept her distance from politics, was harassed by income-tax sleuths for many days. Mrs Gandhi could be very vindictive against people she had once been close to.

In Bombay, censorship had its lighter sides. Vinod Mehta, who edited the sleazy girlie magazine *Debonair*, was asked to have his articles and pictures cleared before they were sent to the printer. The censor looked over the pages. 'Porn? Theek hai! Politics no.' Most of it was soft porn. It was quickly cleared. I was not subjected to the indignity of pre-censorship except for a few hours. I happened to be at a luncheon reception given by Governor Ali Yavar Jang in honour of President Fakhruddin Ali Ahmed. Out of the blue the President turned to me and said loudly, 'What is all this you keep publishing in your journal? Don't you know there is an Emergency?' I didn't know what he was referring to. Nor did S.B. Chavan, chief minister of Maharashtra, who overheard the President's remark. When I returned to my office I found a pre-censorship order slapped under the CM's authorization on the *Illustrated Weekly*. The offending article had in fact appeared in *Femina* and not in my journal. I rang up Sharada Prasad. Mrs Gandhi was due to go abroad the next day. Chavan was told to withdraw the censorship order immediately. He did so as tamely as the braggadocio with which he had imposed it.

During the Emergency I was frequently in Delhi to help out Maneka Gandhi and her mother, Amtesh, with their magazine

Surya. I saw something of the caucus which was running the government. Siddhartha Shankar Ray had drafted the regulations; Sanjay was the kingpin. Besides his kitchen cabinet comprising his wife and mother-in-law, there was the old family retainer, Mohammed Yunus (Chacha); civil servant Navin Chawla; Kishan Chand, Lt Governor of Delhi, who later ended his life by jumping into a well; and Jagmohan, who was put in charge of clearing slums which he did with ruthless zeal. There was the Rasputin figure of Dhirendra Brahmachari, swamiji to the royal household; and two pretty women, Ambika Soni and Rukhsana Sultana—Sanjay had an eye for pretty women. He also had an enthusiastic supporter in Bansi Lal who had allotted him land in Haryana where he was CM on the rustic truism '*bachda pakad lo toh ma toh peechey chali ayegee*'—catch the calf and its mother is bound to follow you. He had I.K. Gujral packed off to Moscow and replaced by the more amenable Vidya Charan Shukla as information and broadcast minister.

Because of my frequent visits to Delhi to monitor the progress of *Surya*, I saw quite a bit of the Gandhi family, particularly Sanjay and his in-laws. He was more relaxed with Maneka's family than with his own. He was a man of few words but with enormous zest for work. He was a strict teetotaller and even avoided drinking tea, coffee, aerated drinks and iced water. In some ways he epitomized the slogan he had coined: *Kaam ziyaada, baatein kum*—work more, talk less. He was a young man in a hurry to get things done. He had no patience with tedious democratic processes and red tape, no time for long-winded politicians or bureaucrats. The fact that he had no legitimacy for imposing his fiats on the country, besides being the son of the Prime Minister, was of little consequence to him. Unlike Maneka he never used strong language and was extremely courteous towards elder people like me. In his younger days he was known to have stolen cars—he had a passion for cars. He had been in many brawls: despite his modest size he rippled with muscles. I took to him as a loveable goonda.

For many months this coterie ruled the country. Anyone who crossed their paths was promptly put behind bars. There was not a squeak of protest. Virtually, the only party which kept a passive resistance movement throughout the period were the Akalis. Long before the Emergency was lifted it had lost public support. Arbitrary arrests, the ruthless way Jagmohan bulldozed slums in Delhi made people believe the wildest canards, of the way men were picked up from bus and cinema queues to be forcibly sterilized, as true. Nobody ever verified the facts but most people lent willing ears to stories of Sanjay's excesses. The Emergency, which was well received when it was imposed, and even justified by a sage like Acharya Vinoba Bhave, was distorted into an abominated monster which had to be destroyed for ever. There may be other occasions to impose an Emergency in the country. If we do not make the mistakes of 1975–77 we would be able to keep the country on the right track when it begins to wobble.

THE HANGING OF BHUTTO

Khushwant Singh was in Islamabad—Rawalpindi on 4 April 1979,
the day Zulfikar Ali Bhutto went to the gallows. He had been given
an appointment by President Zia-ul Haq for the same evening
which, understandably, was called off. The first part of this article
describes his experiences in Lahore, Rawalpindi and Karachi during
those fateful days. The second part gives an account of Bhutto's
last hours, and is based on interviews with eye-witnesses, including
two men who actually saw the hanging.

The first thing they did was to confiscate the Scotch I had brought
with me; the second was to take me in their embrace and say
'*Kush amdeed*'—welcome to Pakistan. The customs official who
did so explained with relentless Punjabi logic: 'Law is law and
friendship is friendship.'

The experience at Lahore airport was symbolic of the
atmosphere that prevailed in Pakistan the week preceding the
execution of Bhutto. Whatever he may have done—and that is
fiercely debated—and whatever be the consequences of hanging
him, hang he must because no one is above the law and the law
found him guilty of murder.

There was a third thing about Pakistan that occurred to me even
before I put foot on its soil, viz., the contrast with India. As the
'fasten your seat belts' sign came on and the Fokker Friendship
descended from the azure sky through the dusty haze, and the
landscape became clearer, I realized how little it had changed.
We flew over several villages. They looked exactly as they did in
1947: a shapeless huddle of flat-roofed mud homes with usually

only one building made of brick and plaster and fresh with a new coat of paint, white or green. And this one building was then as it was now invariably a mosque. As the plane touched down, the air-hostess announced the temperature at Lahore and told us to correct our watches. It occurred to me that while Pakistani time was thirty minutes behind ours Pakistan was thirty years behind us in every field of development: agricultural, industrial, educational and social. It did not make sense because they were the same people as we, man to man they were physically fitter than us, and being more united by faith and speaking one language they had fewer problems than us. To start with they had forged ahead of us, and then for some inexplicable reason slowed down and stagnated.

Of course, we were lucky in having long years of stability under Jawaharlal Nehru and Indira Gandhi while they were changing rulers every other year. Nehru put us on the right path, building an industrial base and at the same time developing our villages by linking them with roads, digging tubewells and electrifying them. The Pakistanis concentrated their energies on improving their cities where the rich upper classes live. Lahore is a good example of lopsided priorities. While the villages surrounding remained untouched, the city had its roads widened to provide for chariot-sized limousines of foreign make: Mercedes Benzes, Volvos, Toyotas (one fellow is said to have paid over eight lakhs for a secondhand car of Italian make). More parks for the Brown Sahibs' babalog, big bungalows like those in which the rich and the corrupt Indians of the cities live. The bazars sell much the same kind of junk as ours; only their textiles are fancier than ours. They have many more music shops selling tapes. One book store I visited, Ferozesons, is bigger than any we have in India. Almost everything is more expensive than in India. And despite the harsh penalties imposed by the *Nizam-i-Mustafa*, liquor is easily available but at exorbitant prices. The one item we share in equal measure is corruption; it is as much on the up and up in Pakistan as it is in India.

To me more important than whether or not Zia would hang Bhutto was to find out whether or not the Pakistanis believed that Bhutto deserved to be hanged. From the few people I met in the first four days of my stay in Lahore and Islamabad I gathered that most Pakistanis believed that not only was Bhutto guilty of the murder of Nawab Kasuri, but of many other diabolical crimes for which he had not been brought to book. These included assassination of political opponents, torture, humiliation (buggery of a son in the presence of his father, abduction and raping of unmarried girls etc.). However a large proportion were equally convinced that though he had brought about a reign of terror the prosecution had failed to prove his hand in the murder of Kasuri and if the constitution of the courts had not been what it was, or if Bhutto had been tried under Islamic law, the outcome would have been different. But no sooner was Bhutto executed than opinion swung in Bhutto's favour.

I was at a disadvantage at Lahore as most of my friends had suffered at Bhutto's hands and their families were bitter about it. My closest friend, the late Manzur Qadir, had been put out of President Ayub's Cabinet because Bhutto (himself a gay liver and a hard drinker) had published pamphlets denouncing the teetotaller, god-fearing, Manzur as a non-believer. Manzur was the chief defence counsel in prosecutions launched by Bhutto against his political adversaries. After Manzur died, Mohammed Anwar took over the defence of Bhutto's victims. He organized the Lahore High Court Association to protest against Bhutto's high-handedness. He was beaten up by the police and gaoled for fifteen days. He died soon after. My first call of duty was to pay homage at his grave. I strewed jasmine flowers and read the epitaph from Iqbal's *Shikwa*:

Qaid-i-Mausam se tabeeat rahi azad uskee
Kash! gulshan men samajhta koee faryad uskee

(He remained free of the shackles of the changing seasons
Alas! there was no one in the garden to listen to his pleadings.)

The epitaph was a deserved tribute to Anwar's character. He was not anti-Bhutto but anti-tyrant. Anwar had often told me that Bhutto was not only a wicked man but also bordering on insanity.

The baton passed from Anwar's hands to those of M.A. Rehman who led the prosecution's case against Bhutto and four men of the Federal Security Force (Bhutto's private army) in the murder of Nawab Kasuri on the night of 10–11 November 1974. It was in Rehman's home that I met the murdered Nawab's son, Ahmed Raza the man Bhutto really wanted eliminated. Ahmed Raza has had a charmed life; he escaped as many as eighteen attempts to kill him. Bhutto emphatically denied that he ever wanted Ahmed Raza killed and dismissed him with lofty disdain as 'a mere nobody'. Ahmed Raza is a man of substance; he was a student leader, one of the founder members of Bhutto's Pakistan People's Party (PPP), a member of the Pakistan National Assembly, and the leader of the anti-Bhutto faction of the same party. He was not a nobody but a somebody who had become a thorn (maybe not a big one) in Bhutto's side. Behind his back Ahmed Raza was known as a *bhaunka*—the barker—and also as a chota Bhutto. He was in the witness box for eight days, five hours every day. The defence was unable to break his testimony in the cross-examination.

The pro-Bhutto element which was substantial and as vehement in his defence usually avoided getting into arguments about its leader's involvement in Nawab Kasuri's murder. Instead they emphasized Bhutto's unique status as the only leader of world stature that Pakistan had produced since M.A. Jinnah (he was the *Qaid-i-Azam*, the great leader; Bhutto was the *Qaid-i-Awam*, the leader of the people.) When the anti-Bhuttoists condemned him as the architect of the destruction of Pakistan by forcing East Pakistan to break away and for his inept handling of the Baluchistan and North West Frontier Province (NWFP) dissidents, the pro-Bhuttoists were equally vehement about how he alone had saved whatever remained of Pakistan after the disastrous defeat at the hands of India in December 1971, the man who led a vanquished nation to deal on an equal level with victorious India at the Simla conference, the man who liberated the 93,000 prisoners of war (POWs) from Indian camps, and so on.

Between the two contending points of view there was no meeting ground. To one lot Bhutto was a villain; to the other a hero. The only point everyone agreed upon was that Bhutto was also a playboy: flamboyant in his dress, lavish with the use of public money, lascivious in his relations with women. (He had three wives: the first, Begum Ameer, was a cousin fifteen years older than himself; the second, an Iranian divorcee Nusrat who bore him four children; the third a Bihari sex-bomb who divorced her Bengali husband to share Bhutto's bed and now lives in London.) He was not very discreet in his liaisons. As a cabinet minister he was caught in *flagrante delicto* with the wife of a visiting head of state. General Ayub reprimanded him but like an indulgent father did not throw him out. He had cavise to regret his paternal benignity. It was also common knowledge that Bhutto was a sadist. He beat his wife Nusrat often enough to compel her to wear long-sleeved blouses to hide the marks of injuries and at least once drove her to such despair as to take an overdose of sleeping tablets. He was at once an aristocratic *wadhera* (landlord) and a gentleman in the European mould, and a guttersnipe using language worthy of an urban hoodlum. Many people told me that when he lost his temper, which was often, he used epithets like *haramzada* (bastard), *sooer ka baccha* (son of a pig) and *madarchod* (mother-fucker).

Yet another point on which both the pro- and the anti-Bhutto elements were agreed was that if Bhutto had been released and allowed to contest the elections, he would have swept the polls. How then can an outsider make an assessment?

General Zia had given me an appointment for the evening of 4 April. I arrived in Rawalpindi two days earlier. Our Press Counsellor O.P. Khanna drove me round the Central Gaol where Bhutto was housed. It is a fortress-like square structure situated

between the airport and the President's House once occupied by
Bhutto. The place bristled with barbed wire, soldiers and armed
police. It was cold enough, and the thought of an unshaven Zulfie
squatting on the damp floor of a dark dingy cell awaiting the
hangman sent a shiver down my spine. Hadn't he said that when
he died, the Himalayas would shed tears? And so it seemed. By
the time we got to Islamabad (fifteen kilometres from Rawalpindi)
a fine drizzle was coming down.

There were over a hundred foreign journalists and newsreel
cameramen in the Holiday Inn. They were hunched over cups of
black coffee like so many vultures on the parapet of some abattoir.
The presiding genius was Mark Tully of the British Broadcasting
Corporation (BBC). Where and how he picked up news of what
Zulfie was doing in his cell, who saw him at what time and what
they said to each other, remains a mystery. But the first thing
everyone said after good morning or hello was, 'Did you hear
Mark Tully on the BBC?' General Zia's bureaucrats hated him,
the staff of Holiday Inn loved him; we journalists envied him.

I had nothing much to do. So Khanna and I went off to see
Khak 'ur Khoon a much-lauded film on the Partition theme
produced by a government agency. I was sorely disappointed at
its crudely propagandist approach to the great tragedy. All the
angels were on the side of the god-fearing Muslims; almost all
the devils on the side of the Hindus and Sikhs. It exploited the
stereotype notion of the cunning Hindu Bania with Rashtriya
Swayamsevak Sangh (RSS) sympathies paying the simple-minded
Sikh to murder Muslims. I only saw half the film—but that was bad
enough. I was told the second half was much worse. Apparently,
our Embassy had lodged a protest against this wilful falsification
of history and the harmful effects it would have on the minds
of young Pakistanis. In an otherwise depressing atmosphere, this
film made me even more depressed.

The evening in the house of the Lambahs, a young couple in
the Indian Embassy, roused my spirits. There were lots of Pakistani
journalists with their wives and girlfriends. Warm, friendly and

a good-looking bunch they were too. The topic of conversation was restricted: one question and two answers. Will Zia hang Bhutto? Answers: Yes, he will. Or, no he won't. Most agreed that General Zia need not have put himself in the predicament he found himself in: where there was neither room to move nor to stand—*Na jai raftan, na pai mandan.*

ONE DAY BEFORE THE HANGING

The chill rain and wind blew all morning. In the afternoon I called on Abdul Hafeez Pirzada at Piracha House, once occupied by Nusrat and Benazir Bhutto. Their pictures were on the walls. Pirzada, who was a minister in Bhutto's cabinet, was convinced that Bhutto would not be hanged. Mumtaz Bhutto, Zulfie's cousin, came in looking dishevelled and out of sorts. He had waited half an hour in the rain at the gaol gates and had not been let in.

Shankar Bajpai, the Indian ambassador in Islamabad, returned from briefing Delhi on the situation in Pakistan. I recalled that a year ago he had told me that General Zia would hang Bhutto. He had not changed his opinion. It was heartening to discover that the diplomatic corps in Islamabad regarded Bajpai and his team the best informed on Pakistani affairs. When I told him about my conversation with Pirzada, he brushed it away with a wave of his hand and repeated, 'They will hang him for sure; when I cannot tell . . .' I tried to solicit the views of Lady Vicky Noon and Miandad Aurangzeb, Wali of Swat and his wife Begum Naseem, daughter of the late General Ayub Khan. Like seasoned diplomats they parried my questions.

4 APRIL 1979

I rose at 5 a.m. The sky was an azure blue, the Marghala Hills looked washed and green. 'What a beautiful morning!' I said to myself, 'Allah is in His Heaven and all is right with Pakistan.' Was it? I heard the sputter of motorcycles. Fifty men in air force grey and white spats took their places in front of the hotel. They were followed by jeeps loaded with soldiers. The hotel was surrounded on all sides. I sent for coffee. I asked the waiter if he had any news. He said that he had heard that the gaol and the airport had been cordoned off at night and people were saying that the worst had happened. He added the words '*Bahut ziatee hooee*' (too much) and '*zulum hua*'. Neither the English nor the Urdu papers mentioned anything on the subject. Had Zulfie been taken to Lahore for the final act? I rang up Bajpai. As usual he knew. He had heard over the Voice of America (it had beaten the BBC) that Bhutto had been executed at 2 a.m. in Rawalpindi. But he had no confirmation. I was chilled to the bone.

I went down to the dining-room to join the vultures' club. It was true. Zulfie was dead. His body had been flown to be interred in the family graveyard in village Nau Dero near Larkana. By then a new story was in circulation viz., that the Chinese Air Force had come to plead with General Zia to let them take Zulfie away to be confined for life in China but the General had jumped the gun by hanging him. The men in uniform outside the hotel were to escort the Chinese back to the airport.

Khanna and I drove to Rawalpindi to see if anything was happening. All seemed normal—if you can describe streets bristling with the soldiers and policemen as normal. Most shops were open, people were going about their business. But there was an atmosphere of fear and sullen resentment: supplements of *Jang* announcing the execution were selling fast; people lowered their voices when they talked; not even hawkers cried out their wares. I saw four men being led away in handcuffs: they may have been thieves.

There was some action in the afternoon. As the prayers ended people formed a procession: burqa-clad women in front, the men behind them. They raised slogans: '*Zia kutta! Hai! Hai!*' and 'Zulfikar Ali Bhutto, *zindabad!*' Four policewomen who faced the women protesters were brushed aside. Policemen retreated before the marchers: Pakistani men have an exaggerated respect for the burqa-clad which they do not have for the unveiled. Tear gas bombs exploded, the marchers broke ranks and fled. Some men were apprehended (not Mumtaz Bhutto or Pirzada), offices of *Jang* were put to the flames. An American cameraman had his leg blown off. An army captain riding a motorcycle was knocked down and almost beaten to death by the mob. That was all.

My friend Rehman called me from Lahore. He said nothing had happened in the city. The BBC news reported otherwise. Suneet Aiyar called from Karachi and said nothing had happened in Karachi. The BBC report said otherwise.

My appointment with General Zia scheduled for that evening was cancelled. That was understandable. But the order that no journalists were to leave Islamabad to visit other cities was hard to accept. The pitch had been queered by *Nawa-i-Waqt* stating that the BBC and All India Radio were between them causing all the mischief in Pakistan.

THE DAY AFTER

The next day at a luncheon given for me by the *Pakistan Times* there were over forty journalists present. It was strange that the same people who for months had talked of little besides what Zia would do to Bhutto now talked of the weather. My statement that Zia had committed a political blunder and Bhutto's ghost would haunt Pakistan for many years to come, elicited no response whatsoever.

They did not stop me from leaving Islamabad. The Pak Airways plane was packed. I arrived in Karachi on Friday, 8 April. They expected demonstrations after *jumma* prayers. At my request our consul-general, Mani Shankar Aiyar and his Sikh wife Suneet drove me round the city. All shops were shut because Friday is a public holiday. But we passed many open spaces where boys were playing cricket or hockey. We passed the grand Memon Masjid and the huge single-domed air-conditioned mosque. The congregations had dispersed and everything was peaceful—as peaceful as the grave. I was told that Karachi had never been for Bhutto.

At Karachi I met Sardar Sherbaz Khan Mazari, leader of the PDP in Baluchistan, Khuro who had once been chief minister of Sindh, and Pesh Imam, secretary-general of Air Marshal Asghar Khan's Tehrik-i-Istiqlal party. The fate of poor Zulfie did not exercise their minds very much. Mazari was concerned with the repression of the Baluchis by Bhutto. The Khuros (particularly their Cambridge-educated daughter Hamid) with how the Sindhis had suffered at the hands of the Urdu-speaking *mulhajareen* (refugee settlers) a body pejoratively described as *tiligars* (starlings—because they chitter so much) from Uttar Pradesh and Bihar and the arrogant, bullying Punjabis. Pesh Imam felt that the PPP had disintegrated, the people disenchanted with backward looking mullahs of the numerous *jamat*s and the future beckoned the Tehrik. The few journalists I met in Karachi dismissed the Tehrik as of no consequence.

The breakdown of Pakistan's political parties almost sounded feudal. The PDF, in power in Baluchistan, and the NWFP is dominated by baronial landlords, the jamats by the Muslim clergy and the Tehrik by men in the professions. The only doubtful factor is Bhutto's PPP. Now that Zulfie has become a martyr, his widow Nusrat or daughter Benazir may emerge as leaders invoking the spirit of their dead man.

II

The curtain rose for the final act in the drama of Zulfikar Ali Bhutto's life at 8.30 a.m. on 18 March 1978. The scene was the main courtroom of the high court of Lahore. It is a large hall divided into three by two sets of wooden railings. On the northern end sitting at a higher level were five judges in their wigs and black gowns. Facing them in the main body of the hall were members of the High Court Bar including counsels for the prosecution and the defence likewise attired in black. Behind them separated by another railing were members of the public. And on the western wing, alongside the judges and the lawyers, stood the five accused with armed police escort behind them. Chief amongst them was Zulfikar Ali Bhutto, impeccably dressed in a light Spring suit and sporting a tie.

No prior notice had been given of this day of judgement. The lawyers engaged in the case had been rung up by the registrar in the early hours and asked to be present in the main room. The accused were brought in from Kot Lakhpat gaol in the Black Maria under heavy escort. Word had however got round and the court room was packed.

All eyes were turned on acting chief justice, Mushtaq Hussain. He read a summary of the unanimous verdict of the five judges in the case of the murder of Nawab Mohammed Raza Kasuri on the night of 10–11 November 1974 at Lahore. All the accused had pleaded not guilty. Four had presented their defence. Only one, Zulfikar Ali Bhutto, had refused to take part in the proceedings.

Justice Mushtaq Hussain finished reading the findings of the panel of judges and proceeded to pass the sentence 'to be hanged by the neck till you are dead'.

All eyes turned from the judges to the accused—mainly on Zulfikar Ali Bhutto. He heard the sentence without flinching and simply turned his face away from the judges. He was lost in his own thoughts. 'You could see that he was stunned', said one of the lawyers, 'but he showed no sign of fear or anger, it seemed as if he had not heard the judge. Or believed it was some kind of grim charade he was witnessing.'

There were no slogans of any kind, no expression of approval or disgust. Neither Bhutto's wife Nusrat nor his daughter Benazir was in court. And armed police were all over the place.

Lawyers representing the four other accused went over to them for consultation; Bhutto having boycotted the high court proceedings had no one to talk to him and remained lost in himself for some time.

Back in Kot Lakhpat gaol, six rooms had been reserved for Bhutto. He went straight to his bedroom and flopped on it fully dressed. He had his eyes fixed on the ceiling. 'He lay there for an hour or more without moving,' says a warder. 'Only when I approached him and asked him if he would like to eat something, I noticed he had been crying. He did not answer me.'

At 11 a.m. the lawyer Yahya Bakhtiar came to visit him. The two men embraced each other and broke down: 'Is this the end?' asked Bhutto. 'No,' replied Bakhtiar emphatically. 'We shall appeal against the sentence.' They talked for quite sometime. Bhutto's spirits were revived and he was more himself.

According to gaol rules, prisoners condemned to death have to be lodged in specially designed cells on which constant watch can be maintained to prevent inmates from taking their own lives. Only in the morning and evening are they let out for half-an-hour to take exercise or *tehlaee*.

At 5 p.m. Bhutto was removed to a condemned cell—but at his insistence he was allowed to wear his own clothes, keep his own bed and chair and eat his own food. He was given writing material and got all the magazines and newspapers he desired. The mood of depression descended on him again and according to a jail warder, 'He lay on his bed like a dead rat.' This lasted for a couple of days.

It seems that the appeals of clemency from different heads of state published in the papers revived his sagging spirits. He began to believe that the chorus of protests from all parts of the world would deter the courts and rulers of Pakistan from doing him harm and all the exercise was to break his morale. He resolved to show no sign of cracking under the strain.

Yahya Bakhtiar filed the appeal in the Supreme Court. Since the court was located in Rawalpindi, in mid-May Bhutto and his co-accused were transferred to the gaol in Rawalpindi—ironically alongside the very mansion from which only a few months earlier he had ruled Pakistan. A set of four rooms normally reserved for women convicted of murder were prepared for him. He had a bedroom, a study, a bathroom and a kitchen all—to himself. Once again gaol regulations were overlooked in order to make the distinguished prisoner comfortable. He was given a *niwar* bed instead of a hospital-type steel bed, a rubber-foam mattress, his own blankets, fan and light with the switchboard within his reach. He was also furnished with a table, chair, table-lamp, books and magazines. His food and his Havana cigars came from his home. He wore his own clothes (he had two suitcases full of them) and used his own shaving kit. He was allowed an hour everyday with his counsel and could take his half hour of tehlaee at times of his own choosing. Since winters in Rawalpindi are sharp, he was provided with electric heaters. His wife and daughter joined him for tea in the afternoon. Very often, Benazir lay on the same bed with her father and the two talked in whispers to avoid being overheard by the ever-present warders and to ensure their dialogue was not recorded by bugging devices.

On 6 February 1979 the Supreme Court dismissed Bhutto's appeal. He was not present in court. The news was conveyed by the gaol superintendent. His only comment was: 'This is very sad,' followed by a question, 'Was it unanimous?' The superintendent without checking replied, 'Yes.' Bhutto remarked, 'That is very surprising.'

When the news reached Nusrat Bhutto at Sihala (fifteen miles from Pindi) where she was under house arrest, she got into a car, broke through the police cordon and stormed up to the gaol gates. She was allowed to meet her husband. She collapsed in her husband's arms. When she came to, the first question he asked her was, 'Was it unanimous?' Nusrat told him that of the seven judges of the Supreme Court three had given him the benefit of the doubt. 'Don't worry!' he assured her. 'We will go in for a review.'

Once the death sentence had been confirmed, the gaol authorities decided to treat Bhutto as they treated other convicts under sentence of death. They took away his shaving kit, removed the niwar bed (niwar can be used to hang oneself) and stopped home food. Bhutto refused to eat jail food and refused to lie in the hospital bed. Instead, he spread the rubber foam mattress on the floor: it was to be his bed till the last day. By the afternoon, the government relented and let him have home-cooked food.

LAST HOPE EXTINGUISHED

On 24 March 1979 the Supreme Court rejected the review petition. The last ray of hope was extinguished. Yahya Bakhtiar's role as Bhutto's lawyer was over but he requested the court to let him see Bhutto. The prosecution represented by M.A. Rehman made no objection. Outside the court room Yahya Bakhtiar told waiting pressmen that there were grounds for a second review petition. Meanwhile, the superintendent of the gaol wrote a formal memorandum to Bhutto informing him of the confirmation of the death sentence and telling him that he had seven days to make a petition for mercy. When he took it to Bhutto and asked him to sign on the carbon copy, he refused to do so and dismissed him brusquely, 'Yes, yes I know all about it.'

The next day (25 March 1979) the Lahore High Court issued a 'Black' warrant to the five convicted men specifying that they were liable to be executed after 4 April 1979. The exact date was kept a secret.

Bhutto was allowed to receive as many relatives and friends he wished to receive. His first wife, Begum Ameer, uncles, cousins, including Mumtaz Bhutto, and erstwhile cabinet colleague, Hafeez Pirzada, were amongst the many who came to see him. All visitors were searched and no one was allowed inside the cell, a six-foot wide table was placed in front of the iron grill to prevent physical contact (or passing of cyanide or other poison).

One night Bhutto sent for the deputy superintendent of the gaol and asked him to send for Hafeez Pirzada. Bhutto made no specific request to Pirzada to appeal for mercy but the words he used, '*Marna bahut mushkil hota hai*' (dying is not easy), and the fact that Pirzada did in fact file a petition after his last meeting on 1 April 1979 indicates that Bhutto without relenting from his determination never to beg for his life still hoped that somehow, someone would make General Zia hold his hand. While leaving the jail Pirzada was asked by pressmen whether Bhutto had made an appeal for mercy. He replied, 'No, he has not. But I will do so.'

Pirzada appealed to President Zia to spare Bhutto's life. His appeal was widely published but there was no comment from the President's office.

The decision to execute Bhutto on 4 April was taken two days earlier (2 April). Rules required executions to take place at 5.30 a.m. (or 6 a.m. in winter)—but the hour was fixed at 2 a.m. to avoid demonstrations and give time to have the body flown to Larkana and interred in the family graveyard in village Nau Dero. Meanwhile, the hangman Tara Masih was brought from Bahawalpur to Lahore. There was speculation that the condemned man might be taken to Kot Lakhpat gaol to be executed.

On 3 April 1979 Nusrat and Benazir Bhutto were brought from Sihala to Rawalpindi jail at 11 a.m. They demanded to be told whether or not this was to be their last meeting. They received an evasive reply: '*Ap yeh hee samajh le* (you may take it as so).' When the wife and daughter told Bhutto of it, he sent for the gaol superintendent and received confirmation that as far as *mulakats* (meetings) were concerned this was to be the *akhree* (last). The exact hour when the hanging would take place was not divulged.

Nusrat and Benazir spent three hours with Bhutto talking across the table. For once Bhutto was indiscreet and gave instructions about some papers which he had secreted away behind the walls in his Larkana house. Within four hours the house was searched and the papers recovered.

SHE COULD NOT EMBRACE HER FATHER

There are heart-rending accounts of this last meeting between Bhutto and his wife and daughter. Benazir's request to let her embrace her father or at least touch his feet before going was firmly turned down. A silver salver in which tea was served to Bhutto was handed back to her with the words '*Ab sahib ko iskee zaroorat nahin padegee* (the Sahib will not be needing this anymore).' It was obvious that the hour of doom was near. Nusrat and Benazir left the jail around 2.30 p.m. and demanded to be taken to see President Zia-ul-Haq. The superintendent rang up the President's house and was told to tell the ladies to put whatever they wanted to say on paper.

At 4 p.m. a magistrate arrived with writing material and asked Bhutto to write his last will which he would attest for him. Bhutto spent an hour or more writing out his last message. No one will ever know what he wrote because with his own cigar lighter he burnt the paper to ashes.

At 6 p.m. he asked for hot water and his shaving set, saying, 'I don't want to die looking like a mullah.' And after he had erased the growth on his chin he looked into the mirror and remarked in self-mockery, 'Now, I look like a third world leader.'

A maulvi arrived with a *tasbih* (rosary) and a *musalla* (prayer mat) to assist Bhutto in his last prayers. Bhutto put the rosary round his neck but told the maulvi to remove the prayer mat and himself as he did not need anyone's assistance to meet his Maker. Then the bravado went out of him. He lay down on the mattress and went into a kind of coma. As the time of execution drew near other inmates of the jail were woken up and ordered to chant verses from the holy Quran. Only Bhutto remained impervious to the goings-on. At 1.30 a.m. jail officials accompanied by a magistrate and doctor arrived to take him out on his last journey to the scaffold. The superintendent shook him and said 'Bhutto *sahib, janey ka waqt aa gaya hai* (It is time to go).' There are different versions of what followed. According to one, Bhutto was roused and as soon as he saw the men with handcuffs, he panicked. He tried various ploys to play for time: he wanted to take a bath, write his will, have a cup of tea. But all were firmly but politely denied to him. According to the second version, he refused to be woken up. The superintendent feared that he had taken his own life and sent for the doctor. The doctor felt his pulse, heard his heartbeat through his stethoscope and opened his eye-lids to make sure that he was alive. In either case, he was unable or unwilling to get up and had to be put on a stretcher. Since he was supine his hands were cuffed in front instead of behind him as prescribed for condemned men on their last journey.

Extensive precautions had been taken against possible attempts to storm the gaol: names of the Palestine Liberation Organization and even some foreign governments were whispered as likely to make a desperate bid to save Bhutto. Precautions taken included look-outs for parachutists and hostile helicopters. Consequently, a very large number of defence personnel were present in the gaol at the time. It is estimated that upwards of 250 men saw the execution with their own eyes.

FINISH IT!

The scaffold is quite a distance from the condemned cell. The party with Bhutto on the stretcher arrived at the foot of the gallows at about 1.45 a.m. As the stretcher was put down and the superintendent approached Mr Bhutto, he suddenly sat up. He mumbled some words which were interpreted as, 'Nusrat will be left alone.' When the handcuffs were unlocked and his hands tied behind him, he is reported to have protested that the knot was too tight. Then without assistance he went up the steps to the gallows. Before Tara Masih put the black hood over his face, Bhutto's lips moved. According to one version, he mumbled 'Finish it!' According to another, his lips moved but no sound came from them. The trap was sprung exactly at 2 a.m. and the dapper, flamboyant Zulfi, once President and Prime Minister of Pakistan and next to Jinnah, its most popular leader (Qaid-i-Awam), plunged to his doom.

At the time of his death, Bhutto was dressed in salwar kameez which he had elevated to the status of an *awami* suit. He had a gold Zenith watch on his wrist and a gold ring with three diamonds on his finger. After Hayat Mohammed, a humble servitor in a Pindi mosque, had bathed his corpse and draped it in a shroud, somebody noticed that the diamond-studded ring was missing. The superintendent immediately arrested Tara Masih and Hayat Mohammed and ordered them to be searched. The ring was found in the pocket of the hangman, Tara Masih. Both the watch and the ring were handed over to Benazir Bhutto the next morning.

The body was flown to Larkana and then taken to Nau Dero. Bhutto's first wife, Begam Ameer, fifteen years older than him, his uncles, aunts and other relatives were allowed to see the dead man's face. It was serene and calm as if in deep slumber with no visible marks of injury save a gash in the neck. (There is no truth in the story that men who are hanged have their necks elongated and their eyes and tongues hang out).

Bhutto's execution will wipe out memories of his evil deeds and highlight some of the good he did for his country. He is already being acclaimed as a martyr. There are reports of people going to his grave to offer *fateha* for the peace of his soul. Many are reported to kiss the grave, pick up the dust about the grave and smear it on their foreheads. In every hamlet, village, town and city stretching from the Khyber to Karachi groups gather to offer *ghaibana namaz-i-janaza* (funeral prayers in the absence of the body). Bhutto's ghost has already emerged from its tomb; it will not be long before it turns the illusory dreams of power of the ruling generals into a nightmare.

THE SIKH HOMELAND (FROM *A HISTORY OF THE SIKHS*)

Khushwant Singh's two-volume *History of the Sikhs* is widely regarded as the authoritative work on the subject. Based on meticulous, scholarly research of original documents in Gurmukhi, Persian and English, the two volumes (1469–1839 and 1839–1988) cover the social, religious and political background that led to the formation of the Sikh faith and, spanning 500 years of Sikh history, include events leading upto Operation Bluestar and its tragic aftermath.

The first of the two extracts below is the opening chapter of Volume I, while the second extract is taken from the concluding chapter of Volume II.

Punjab has a geographical unity distinct from the neighbouring countries and the rest of India. It is shaped like a scalene triangle balanced on its sharpest angle. The shortest side is in the north and is composed of the massive Himalayas, which separate it from the Tibetan plateau. The western side is bounded by the river Indus from the point it enters the plains to another point 1,650 miles downstream, where it meets the confluence of the Punjab's rivers at a place appropriately named Panjnad, the five streams. Westwards of the Indus runs a chain of rugged mountains, the Hindu Kush and the Sulaiman, pierced by several passes like the Khyber and the Bolan which have served as inlets for the people of the countries which lie beyond, Afghanistan and Baluchistan. The eastern boundary of Punjab's triangle is not clearly marked, but from a point near Karnal where the Jumna plunges southeastwards a jagged line can be drawn up to Panjnad, which will demarcate the state from the rest of Hindustan and the Sindh desert.

Punjab, except for the salt range in its centre, is an extensive plain sloping gently down from the mountains in the north and the west towards the desert in the south. Across this monotonously flat land flow six large rivers: the Indus, Jhelum, Chenab, Ravi, Beas and the Sutlej. In the intra-fluvial tracts or doabs[1] between these rivers and in the western half of the tract between the Sutlej and the Jamuna live people who speak the Punjabi language and describe themselves as the people of Punjab. The homeland of the vast majority of the Sikhs is in the doabs between the Chenab and the Jamuna.

THE NAME: PUNJAB

When the Aryans came to India there were seven rivers in Punjab, so they named it Sapta Sindhva, the land of the seven seas. The Persians took the name from the Aryans and called it the Hafta Hindva. Sometime later, after the seventh river, the Sarasvati, had dried up, people began to exclude the Indus from the count (since it marked only the western boundary of the province) and renamed it after the remaining five rivers as Pentopotamia or the *panj-ab,* the land of the five waters.[2]

CLIMATE AND LANDSCAPE[3]

The climate of Punjab ranges from bracing cold in the winter to scorching heat in the summer. Extremes of temperature and the two monsoons produce a variety of seasons and a constantly changing landscape.

The spring is traditionally ushered in on Basant Panchami, which falls early in the month of February. It is Punjab's blossom time, when, in the words of Guru Nanak, 'all is seemly; the woodlands are in flower and loud with the humming of bumble bees'. The countryside is an expanse of mustard yellow, broken by solid squares of green sugarcane with its fluffy pampas plumes. If the winter monsoon has been good, a crop of wheat, barley, gram, oil-seeds, arid tobacco will cover the land with lush abundance. Peasants supplement the rain by canal water, or, where there are no canals, by Persian wheels turned by bullocks or camels. Around the wells grow vegetables: carrots, radishes, cabbages and cauliflower. Branches of jujube trees sag under the weight of their berries. In springtime, the sounds that pervade the countryside are the creaking of Persian wheels, the call of partridges, and the monotonous *kooh, kooh,* of flour mills.[4]

The sugarcane is cut, its juice squeezed out, boiled in large cauldrons, and solidified into dark, brown cakes. The canary yellow of the mustard is replaced by newly-sown cotton and the golden-brown of ripening wheat—and we know that spring has given way to summer.

Trees shed their leaves and after a short period of barrenness come into blossom. While the margosa is still strewing the earth with its brittle ochre leaves, the silk cotton, the coral and the flame of the forest burst into flowers of bright crimson, red and orange. Even the thorny acacia, the commonest tree of Punjab, is covered with tiny pale pom-poms. Persian wheels and the partridges are silent: instead there is the screaming of the koels in the mango groves and the crying of barbets.

The wheat is cut and winnowed in the warm breeze. In the words of Guru Nanak: 'The sun scorches . . . the earth burns like an oven. The waters give up their vapours, yet it burns and scorches relentlessly.' The temperature rises to a fever heat. The parched earth becomes an unending stretch of khaki with dust devils spiralling across the wastes. Even the stolid peepal and the tamarisk are shorn of their leaves and the only green that meets the eye are bushes of camel-thorn, prickly cactus and the akcalotropis. The succession of hot days and shimmering mirages is occasionally broken by fierce storms which spread layers of dust and sand over everything. All through the torpid afternoons comes the call of the brain fever bird in a rising crescendo, *peeooh peeooh*. On moonlit nights one can see the wavering arrow-head formations of geese honking their way northwards to the snowy Himalayas.

The blazing inferno lasts from the end of April to the end of June. Then come the rains.

The monsoon makes a spectacular entry. It is heralded by the monsoon bird[5] which fills the dusty plains with its plaintive cries. The colourless grey sky suddenly fills with dense masses of black clouds. There are flashes of lightning and the earth shakes with the rumble of thunder. The first big drops of rain are swallowed by the dust and a heavenly fragrance rises from the earth. Then it comes in torrents, sheet upon sheet, and continues for several hours. Thereafter the skies are frequently overcast; clouds and sunshine contend for dominion; rainbows span the rainwashed landscape; and the setting sun fires the bulbous clouds in hues of red and purple. Two months of incessant downpour turn the land into a vast swamp. Rivers fill up and become a mass of swirling, muddy waters. Punjabis, who have to live through many months of intense heat every year, love the monsoon. It is the time for lovers' trysts and the reunion of families. Life begins afresh. There are new leaves on many trees and grass covers the barren ground. Mangoes ripen. The clamour of the koels and the brain fever bird is drowned in the song and laughter of girls on swings in the mango groves.

By the time the monsoon is over, it is cool again. The dust has settled and the countryside is green once more. If the summer monsoon has been good—neither too spare to create a drought nor too heavy to cause floods—all is well. A new crop of rice, millet, maize, indigo and pulses of many kinds is sown. The peasants wind brightly-coloured and starched turbans round their heads, put on waistcoats covered with mother-of-pearl buttons, tie bells round their ankles, and dance the bhangra to the beat of the drum. From October to the festival of the lamps (Diwali) in November there is a succession of fairs and festivals.

There is little rest for the peasant. Cotton is to be picked and the land ploughed again for sowing wheat and gram. Persian wheels begin to turn. The *kooh, kooh* of the flour mills is heard in every village. Partridges call in the wheat fields. And at night one hears the honking of geese on their way back to Punjab.

Once more it is wintertime. The starlit nights are cold and frosty, the days full of blue skies and sparkling sunshine. The mustard is in flower, the woodlands are loud with the humming of the bumble bees, and all is seemly once again.

Punjab is essentially a rural state made up of innumerable mud and brick villages built on the ruins of older villages. At one time most of them were fortified. Even today one comes across remains of baronial castles and ancient battlements that rise out of the rubble or the village dung heap. Until the fifteenth century Punjab had only two important cities, Lahore, which was the seat of most governments, and Multan in the south, which had a busy market dealing with commerce coming up the rivers from Sindh and caravans from Baluchistan and Persia. There were also several towns like Rawalpindi, Jhelum, Wazirabad, Gujarat, Gujranwala, Sheikhupura, Saidpur now called Eminabad, Pak Pattan, Kasur, Sialkot, Ludhiana and Sirhind, whose various fortunes rose and fell with those of their feudal overlords (or, as in the case of Pak Pattan, with the popularity of the religious order of which it was the centre). Nothing remains of the extensive forests which once covered large parts of Punjab. Up to the sixteenth century there were jungles in the north where rhinoceros[6] (and probably elephants) were found. In central Punjab there was the notorious *lakhi* (the forest of a hundred thousand trees).[7] which gave Sikh outlaws refuge from their oppressors. There were equally dense forests in the Jalandhar Doab and one long belt of woodland stretching from Ludhiana to Karnal. Up to the middle of the nineteenth century these forests teemed with wild life: lions, tigers, leopards, panthers, bears, wolves, hyenas, wild boars, nilgai and many varieties of deer. The flora and fauna survived the incursions of foreign armies but succumbed to the indiscriminate felling of trees and slaughter of game in the nineteenth and the present century. The desert with its camels and goats—the only animals which can thrive on cacti and thorny scrub—are a phenomenon of recent times.

ANTIQUITY

Indologists are not agreed on the age of Indian civilization except that it is among the oldest in the world and that its cradle was in Punjab.

Near Rawalpindi, spears and hatchets made of quartzite have been found which date human habitation in the region to between 300,000 and 500,000 years ago.[8] Agricultural implements made of copper and bronze have been found in mounds of both sides of the river Indus which prove the existence of fairly organized rural communities between 2500 to 2000 BC. Nothing more is known about these communities, nor would it be right to describe them as civilizations. We are, however, on surer ground when we come to the archaeological remains of Mohenjodaro in Sindh and Harappa in southern Punjab, both of which were unearthed in the 1920s. From the sculpture, pottery, jewellery, fabrics and other relics (particularly seals bearing extremely beautiful figures of bulls, rhinoceros and other animals) found among the ruins of baked-brick buildings in these cities (and subsequently in many other places) it can be presumed that the people of the Indus Valley had attained a high degree of civilization. They lived in multi-storeyed houses with marble baths; their craftsmen made goods which were sold as far away as Mesopotamia; and they had evolved some form of religion around the worship of a mother-goddess and her male consort. Neither the hieroglyphics nor the relics found in these cities have yet revealed all their secrets; archaeologists and historians are still disputing the identity of the people who made them. The generally accepted view is that these cities flourished between 2500 and 1500 BC and that they were destroyed by a people known as the Aryans who began to infiltrate into Sindh and Punjab about fifteen centuries before the birth of Christ.[9]

The Aryans, who were tall and fair, drove out the darker-skinned inhabitants and occupied most of Northern Hindustan. The newcomers were a pastoral people with a religion and a language of their own. Both of these were further developed in the land of their domicile. It was in Punjab that Vedic Hinduism was evolved, and many of the great works of Sanskrit literature written.

The Aryans were followed by other races. The Persians under Darius (521–485 BC) conquered Northern Punjab, and for a hundred years his successors ruled over Peshawar, Taxila and Rawalpindi. In 326 BC Greek armies under Alexander the Great crossed the Indus and swept on as far as the Beas. Although the Greeks left behind by Alexander were deprived of power by the Indian Mauryas a few years after his death, they left a permanent impress on the face of Punjab. In Peshawar, Taxila, and perhaps in some other towns as well, Greek artists produced some of the greatest works of sculpture found anywhere in the world.[10]

Mauryan power was extinguished by Bactrian invaders. Menander is believed to have gone across central Punjab and beyond the Beas. The Bactrians were followed by many Scythian tribes. When the dust raised by the invading armies had settled, the Indian Guptas spread their benevolent rule over the country. For some centuries they were able to block the gaps in the mountains and keep out other invaders. By 500 AD, the pressure from Central Asia became too great and once more the sluice gates were forced open to let in the Mongoloid Huns. The Huns were subdued and expelled by Vardhana. His son Harsha was the last great Indian ruler of Punjab. After Harsha's death in 647 AD, Vardhana's empire disintegrated and races living across the Sulaiman and Hindu Kush mountains began to pour into Hindustan. The new conquerors who came belonged to diverse tribes but had one faith: they were Muslims.

In AD 1001 came Mahmud of Ghazni. Thereafter the Afghans came like the waves of an incoming tide, each column advancing further inland into Hindustan. The Ghaznis were followed by other Afghan tribes: the Ghoris, Tughlaks, Surs and Lodhis.

Between the succession of Afghan invasions came the terrible visitation in 1398 of the Mongol, Taimur, an invasion from which northern India did not recover for many decades. A hundred years later Babur, who was one of Taimur's descendants, started dreaming of an empire in India. His opportunity came with the decline of the Lodhi dynasty. After a few unsuccessful attempts, he finally defeated and slew the reigning Afghan, Ibrahim Lodhi, on the field of Panipat in 1526, and set up the most powerful and long-lived dynasty in the history of India.

PEOPLE OF PUNJAB

The ethnic pattern of Punjab has changed with every new conquest. At the time of the birth of Nanak (AD 1469) it was somewhat as follows:

In the north west stretching along both sides of the Indus were Pathans and Baluchis—the former on the upper and the latter on the lower reaches of the river. These people, like their neighbours (Gakkhars, Awans, Janjuas, and others who settled between the Indus and the Jhelum) were divided into innumerable warring tribes, jealously preserving their traditions and way of life but united in their fierce loyalty to the Islamic faith. On the northern fringe of the country in a narrow belt running along the foothills of the Himalayas were the domains of Hindu princes who had fled the plains in front of the Muslim onslaughts. In this sub-montane region intersected by mountain streams and deep ravines, made impassable by entangled bushes of lantana, vasicka and ipomea they built chains of forts which defended them from further inroads of Muslim invaders. Here they burnt incense to their gods and preserved their egalitarian society in which the Brahmin and Kshatriya exploited the lesser castes. In the rest of Punjab, consisting of the vast champaign stretching to the Jamuna and beyond, the countryside was inhabited by Jats and Rajput agricultural tribes, the cities by the trading Banias, Mahajans, Suds and Aroras. In all cities, towns and villages there were the dark and somewhat negroid descendants of the aboriginals who were considered beyond the pale of the caste system, forced to do the dirtiest work and then condemned as untouchables. In addition to all these were nomadic tribes of gypsies wandering across the plains in their donkey caravans, with their hunting dogs and herds of sheep and goats.

BIRTH OF PUNJABI NATIONALISM

The Punjab, being the main gateway into India, was fated to be the perpetual field of battle and the first home of all the conquerors. Few invaders, if any, brought wives with them, and most of those who settled in their conquered domains acquired local women. Thus the blood of many conquering races came to mingle, and many alien languages—Arabic, Persian, Pushto and Turkish—came to be spoken in the land. Thus, too, was the animism of the aboriginal subjected to the Vedantic, Jain and Buddhist religions of the Aryans, and to the Islamic faith of the Arabs, Turks, Mongols, Persians and Afghans. Out of this mixture of blood and speech were born the Punjabi people and their language. There also grew a sense of expectancy that out of the many faiths of their ancestors would be born a new faith for the people of Punjab.

By the end of the fifteenth century, the different races who had come together in Punjab had lost the nostalgic memories of the lands of their birth and begun to develop an attachment to the land of their adoption. The chief factor in the growth of Punjabi consciousness was the evolution of one common tongue from a babel of languages. Although the Punjabis were sharply divided into Muslims and Hindus, attempts had been made to bring about a rapprochement between the two faiths and a certain desire to live and let live had grown among the people. It was left to Guru Nanak and his nine successors to harness the spirit of tolerance and give it a positive content in the shape of Punjabi nationalism.

It is significant that the spirit of Punjabi nationalism first manifested itself in Majha, the heart of Punjab, and among a people who were deeply rooted in the soil. Although the founders and many of the leaders of the movement were not agriculturists, its backbone was the Jat peasantry of the central plains.

There are as many conjectures about the etymology of the word Jat[12] as there are of the origin of the race. It is now generally accepted that the Jats who made the northern plains of India their home were of Aryan stock. They brought with them certain institutions, the most important being the panchayat, an elected body of five elders, to which they pledged their allegiance.[13] Every Jat village was a small republic made up of people of kindred blood who were as conscious of absolute equality between themselves as they were of their livelihood as weavers, potters, cobblers or scavengers. The relationship of a Jat village with the state was that of a semi-autonomous unit paying a fixed sum of revenue. Few governments tried to assert more authority, and those which did soon discovered that sending out armed militia against fortified villages was not very profitable. The Jats' spirit of freedom and equality refused to submit to Brahmanical Hinduism and in its turn drew the censure of the privileged Brahmins of the Gangetic plains who pronounced that 'no Aryan should stay in the Punjab for even two days' because the Punjabis refused to obey the priests.[14] The upper caste Hindus' denigration of the Jat did not in the least lower the Jat in his own eyes nor elevate the Brahmin or the Kshatriya in the Jat's estimation. On the contrary, he assumed a somewhat condescending attitude towards the Brahmin, whom he considered little better than a soothsayer or a beggar, or the Kshatriya, who disdained earning an honest living and was proud of being a mercenary. The Jat was born the worker and the warrior. He tilled his land with his sword girded round his waist. He fought more battles for the defence of his homestead than the Kshatriya, for unlike the martial Kshatriya the Jat seldom fled from his village when the invaders came.

And if the Jat was maltreated or if his women were molested by the conqueror on his way to Hindustan, he settled his score by looting the invaders' caravans on their return journey and freeing the women he was taking back. The Punjabi Jat developed an attitude of indifference to worldly possessions and an instinct for gambling with his life against odds. At the same time he became conscious of his role in the defence of Hindustan. His brand of patriotism was at once hostile towards the foreigner and benign, even contemptuous, towards his own countrymen whose fate depended so much on his courage and fortitude.

SUMMING UP

The five centuries of the history of the Sikhs may be divided into two: the first 300 years are roughly divisible into three periods of one hundred years each; the second one-third into four periods of fifty years each. Guru Nanak proclaimed his mission around the year AD 1500. A little over a hundred years later (in 1604) Guru Arjun completed the compilation of the sacred scripture, the Adi Granth, and gave the Sikhs a holy city of their own, Amritsar. These hundred years saw the evolution of Sikh religious philosophy. In the hundred years that followed, the Sikhs gradually turned from a quietist sect of Nanak Panthis (those who followed the path of Nanak) to a group animated by visions of power. The seal of approval was given by the establishment of the militant fraternity of the Khalsa by the last of the Sikh Gurus, Gobind Singh, in 1699. The century that followed witnessed Sikh ascendancy as a political power, with Banda Bairagi striking a near-fatal blow to Mughal rule in the Punjab, followed by marauding bands of the Dal Khalsa spreading their arms from Attock to the Ganges. Its conquests were consolidated by Ranjit Singh when he captured Lahore in 1799 and proclaimed himself Maharaja of the Punjab.

Maharaja Ranjit Singh's forty years (1799–1839) remain the golden age of Sikh political achievement. With his death began the disintegration of the Sikhs as a political and social force. The two Anglo–Sikh wars ended in the defeat of Sikh armies and the annexation of their kingdom in 1849. Their social decline, though little noticed in the earlier stages, began at the same time. The *kesadhari* Khalsa were threatened with extinction as large numbers began to abandon the external forms (unshorn hair and beards) and became *sahajdhari* Sikhs. The Khalsa tradition was artificially kept alive by the British according kesadhari Sikhs economic and political privileges like preferential recruitment in the army and the civil services, and later, separate electorates and the reservation of seats in the legislatures. This induced the kesadhari Khalsa to distance themselves from the sahajdharis as well as from Hindus who believed in Sikhism. There was a parallel decline in the quality of Sikh political organizations, their leadership and their methods of approach. In the late nineteenth century, up to the end of the First World War, it was the Chief Khalsa Diwan led by aristocrats like Sir Sunder Singh Majithia, Harbans Singh Majithia, Harbans Singh of Attari, and, on the outer periphery, men like Raja Sir Daljit Singh and Sir Jogindra Singh—all well educated, loyal to the British and believing in representations and constitutional methods. After the war, the Chief Khalsa Diwan retreated into the background and was replaced by the Akali Dal. The Akali Dal discovered that confrontation with the administration through non-violent non-cooperation and passive resistance was more productive of results than representations to the rulers or resolutions in legislatures. A new breed of leaders consisting largely of village *jathedars* came to the fore. However, in these early years of agitation, they accepted as their leaders educated men dedicated to their cause: such men were Baba Kharak Singh, Mehtab Singh and Master Tara Singh. They also left the task of political and constitutional negotiations to men of knowledge and experience like Ujjal Singh, Buta Singh and Sampuran Singh, who represented the community at the Round Table Conferences. Nearer the time of the transfer of power, there were shrewd politicians like Gyani Kartar Singh to negotiate on behalf of the Sikhs. At the same time, they benefited from the more-than-willing guidance tendered to them by leaders of the Indian National Congress. This covered up for inexperienced mediocrities like Baldev Singh, who accepted Pandit Nehru as his mentor.

It was after Independence and the partition of Punjab that the quality of Sikh leadership was vulgarized and went into rapid decline. Able men like Swaran Singh, Pratap Singh Kairon and Giani Zail Singh went out and joined the Congress party. The educational and ethical standards of the emerging Akali leadership fell well below the level of their predecessors. Factionalism, switching parties to better prospects of getting ministerships or lucrative posts in state-controlled enterprises, became the chief motivating factors. Corruption became rampant in the gurdwaras. Misuse of gurdwara funds for political purposes and manipulating the enormous patronage of the Shiromani Gurdwara Prabhandak Committee (SGPC) over the appointments of head priests, granthis, ragis, sevadars, the personnel of thousands of educational institutions, hospitals and orphanages were used to consolidate personal political power. The prime example of the degradation in the quality of leadership of the SGPC was Gurcharan Singh Tohra, a leftist of very little education who succeeded in being re-elected president for sixteen successive terms and, at the same time, had two terms as a member of Parliament, which he rarely attended. In secular politics, it saw the emergence of men like Badal. Balwant Singh and Amarinder Singh, whose sole commitment was to themselves. Gentlemen-politicians like Barnala were sidelined. In due course, the clergy, consisting of head priests, ragis and granthis felt that they had been left out in the cold for too long and staked their claim to control gurdwara funds and have their voice heard in community politics. Thus, the elected SGPC yielded power to priests nominated by it. It saw the elevation of the hymn-singer Darshan Singh Ragi[15] to the post of acting head priest of the Akal Takht and, for a very short period, guiding the destinies of the Panth. In their turn, the clerics had power wrenched out of their hands by lads of the All-India Sikh Students' Federation (AISSF) and nominees of the Damdami Taksal reared in the Bhindranwale school of terrorism. It is they who began to call the shots in more senses than one.

The Sikhs' self-image bears little resemblance to reality. The spirit of one-upmanship which had helped them in becoming the most prosperous and go-ahead community of India was replaced by empty bombast. Devotion or religion gave way to a display of religiosity. Religious life declined into meaningless ritual and *Akhand Paths* through hired granthis; worship of the Granth, as if it were an idol, replaced its study as an hymnal of religious philosophy; and kirtans by professional ragis demanding high fees like film playback singers proliferated. Ragis and granthis acquired vested interests in perpetuating these practices. Despite claims of outlawing the caste system, discrimination against lower-caste Sikhs is only a shade less than amongst Hindus. The message of goodwill towards all mankind enshrined in the Granth has been reduced to a litany to be chanted on ceremonial occasions; Guru Gobind Singh's exhortation to draw the sword only after all other means have failed to bring evil-doers to the right path is honoured more in the breach than in observance. Few people dare to condemn gangsters who haul out innocent, unarmed people from buses and kill them, lob grenades in crowded marketplaces and cinemas. The Hindu baiter, Sant Jarnail Singh Bhindranwale, has become a martyred hero of lumpen sections of Sikh society. At times it appears that perhaps the Khalsa have run the course of history prescribed for them and that their Gurus in their inscrutable wisdom have given them leaders who will fulfil their deathwish.

Notes

[1] The intra-fluvial tracts or mesopotamias are known in the Punjab as doabs—two waters. Except for the doabs between the Indus and the Jhelum and the Sutlej and the Jumna, they are known by a combination of the names of the two rivers between which

they lie. These names were coined in the time of Emperor Akbar, presumably by his minister, Todar Mal.

2 Another name by which parts of the Punjab was known in ancient time was *madra desha*, the land of the *madras*. So named after Madri, the mother of the Pandavas.

3 The description of the seasons in this chapter are taken from Guru Nanak's *Barah Mah* (The Twelve Months), carried in full elsewhere in this book.

4 The blasts are produced by an empty pitcher placed on the mouth of the exhaust pipe of the diesel engine.

5 The pied-crested cuckoo *(clamor jacobinus)* takes advantage of the monsoon winds and flies from the East African Coast ahead of the clouds. It usually reaches the coast of India a day or two before the monsoon breaks; hence the name, monsoon bird.

6 In the *Babar Nama* the Mughal conqueror Babar who invaded India in AD 1526 writes of hunting rhinoceros in the Punjab.

7 In the *Khuldsal-ut-Tawdrikh* Sujanj Rai, who lived in the latter part of the seventeenth century, described the *lakhi* in the following words: 'Every year the floods overspread the land far and wide, and when the water subsides so many jungles spring up all over this country owing to the great moisture, that a pedestrian has great difficulty in travelling. How then can they ride?'

8 See, S.M. Ikram and Percival Spear, eds., *The Cultural Heritage of Pakistan*, pp. 20–24, Sir R.E. Mortimer Wheeler, *The Indus Civilization*.

9 A.L. Basham, *The Wonder that Was India*, p. 28.

10 Examples of the Gandhara School can be seen in museums at Peshawar, Taxila, Lahore, Delhi, Mathura, and many other cities.

11 These three flowering bushes are found all over India. The *adhatoda vasicka* is used to make medicinal syrup; the ipomea is grown to reinforce canal banks. Since it blossoms most times of the year it is known in Punjabi as *sadd shudgan* (ever-in-marital-bliss).

12 Cunningham followed Todd and other European scholars in believing that Jats were of Scythian stock.

13 *Panch men parmesvar.* There is god in the five elected men.

14 See Mahabharata, VIII, verses 2063–2068 *(Karna Parva.)*

15 Darshan Singh (born in 1936) in the village of Suranwala (District Sahiwal now in Pakistan) is an Arora Sikh. He has a master's degree in music. He is the most highly paid ragi and preacher. He came into politics after 'Operation Blue Star' and was twice detained in prison for his fiery sermons denouncing the government.

THE MONSOON IN INDIAN LITERATURE AND FOLKLORE

Monsoon is not another word for rain. As its original Arabic name *(mausem)* indicates, it is a season. There is a summer monsoon as well as a winter monsoon, but it is only the nimbus southwest winds of summer that make a *'mausem'*—the season of rains. The winter monsoon is like a quick shower on a cold and frosty morning. It leaves one chilled and shivering. Although it is good for the crops, people pray for it to end. Fortunately, it does not last very long.

The summer monsoon is quite another affair. It is preceded by several months of working up a thirst so that when the waters come they are drunk deep and with relish. From the end of February, the sun starts getting hotter and spring gives way to summer. Garden flowers wither. Wild flowering trees take their place. First comes the silk cotton, the coral and the flame of the forest, all scarlet and bright orange. They are followed by the *firier flamboyant,* known in India as the gulmohur. The last of the hot summer's flowering trees is the laburnum which is a bright, golden yellow. Then the trees lose their flowers as well as their leaves. Their bare branches stretch up to the sky as if begging for water, but there is no water. The sun comes up earlier than before and licks up the drops of dew before the fevered earth can moisten it up. It sears the grass and thorny scrub till they catch fire. The fires spread and dry jungles burn like matchwood.

The sun goes on, day after day, from east to west, scorching relentlessly. The earth cracks and deep fissures open their gaping mouths asking for water, but there is no water—only the shimmering haze at noon making mirage lakes of quicksilver. Poor villagers take their thirsty cattle out to drink; both man and beast are struck down with the heat. The rich wear sunglasses, and hide behind curtains of khas fibre on which their servants pour water.

The sun makes an ally of the breeze. It heats the air until it becomes the loo (India's khamsin) and sends it on its errand. Even in the intense heat, the loo's warm caresses are sensuous and pleasant. It brings up prickly heat. It produces a numbness that makes the head nod and the eyes heavy with sleep. It brings on a stroke which takes its victim as gently as the breeze bears a fluff of thistledown.

Then comes a period of false hope. The temperature drops. The air becomes still. From the southern horizon a black wall begins to advance. Hundreds of kites and crows fly ahead. Can it be . . .? No, it is a dust-storm. A fine powder begins to fall. A solid mass of locusts covers the sun. They devour whatever is left on the trees and in the fields. Then comes the storm itself. In furious sweeps it smacks open doors and windows, banging them forward and backward, smashing their glass panes. Thatched roofs and corrugated iron sheets are borne aloft like bits of paper. Trees are torn up by the roots and fall across power lines. The tangled wires electrocute people and set houses afire. The storm carries the flames to other houses till there is a conflagration. All this happens in a few seconds. Before you can say Chakravarti Rajagopalachari, the gale is gone. The dust hanging in the air settles on books, furniture and food; it gets in the eyes and ears, throat and nose.

Rudyard Kipling has described the pre-monsoon heat of northern India in his story *False Dawn*,[1] in which an ardent suitor caught in a dust-storm proposed marriage to the wrong sister:

> I had felt that the air was growing hotter and hotter, but nobody seemed to notice it until the moon went out and a burning hot wind began lashing the orange trees with a sound like the noise

of the sea. Before we knew where we were the dust-storm was on us, and everything was roaring, whirling darkness.

Again it was Kipling who captured the feeling of listlessness that the months' searing heat produces:[2]

No Hope, no change! The clouds have shut us in,
And through the cloud the sullen Sun strikes down.
Full on the bosom of the tortured town,
Till Night falls heavy as remembered sin
That will not suffer sleep or thought of ease,
And, hour on hour, the dry-eyed Moon in spite
Glares through the haze and mocks with watery light
The torment of the uncomplaining trees.
Fall off, the Thunder bellows her despair
To echoing Earth, thrice parched. The lightnings fly
In vain. No help the heaped-up clouds afford.
But wearier weight of burdened, burning air,
What truce with Dawn? Look, from the aching sky
Day stalks, a tyrant with a flaming sword!

This happens over and over again until the people lose all hope. They are disillusioned, dejected, thirsty and sweating. The prickly heat on the back of their necks is like emery paper. There is another lull. A hot petrified silence prevails. Then comes the* shrill, strange call of a bird. Why has it left its cool bosky shade and come out in the sun? People look up wearily at the lifeless sky. Yes, there it is with its mate! They are like large black-and-white bulbuls with perky crests and long tails. They are pied-crested cuckoos *(Clamator Jacobinus)* who have flown all the way from Africa ahead of the monsoon. Isn't there a gentle breeze blowing? And hasn't it a damp smell? And wasn't the rumble which drowned the bird's anguished cry the sound of thunder? The people hurry to the roofs to see. The same ebony wall is coming up from the east. A flock of herons fly across. There is a flash of lightning that outshines the daylight. The wind fills the black sails of the cloud and they billow out across the sun. A profound shadow

falls on the earth. There is another clap of thunder. Big drops of
rain fall and dry up in the dust. A fragrant smell rises from the
earth. Another flash of lightning and another crack of thunder
like the roar of a hungry tiger. It has come! Sheets of water,
wave after wave. The people lift their faces to the clouds and let
the abundance of water cover them. Schools and offices close.
All work stops. Men, women and children run madly about the
streets, waving their arms and shouting 'Ho, ho'—hosannas to
the miracle of the monsoon.

The monsoon is not like ordinary rain, which comes and
goes. Once it is on, it stays for three to four months. Its advent
is greeted with joy. Parties set out for picnics and litter the
countryside with the skins and stones of mangoes. Women and
children make swings of branches of trees and spend the day in
sport and song. Peacocks spread their tails and strut about with
their mates; the woods echo with their shrill cries.

After a few days the flush of enthusiasm is gone. The earth
becomes a big stretch of swamp and mud. Wells and lakes fill
up and burst their bounds. In towns, gutters get clogged and
streets become turbid streams. In villages, mud-walls of huts
melt in the water and thatched roofs sag and descend on the
inmates. Rivers which keep rising steadily from the time the
summer's heat starts melting the snows, suddenly turn to floods
as the monsoon spends itself on the mountains. Roads, railway
tracks and bridges go under water. Houses near the river banks
are swept down to the sea.

With the monsoon the tempo of life and death increases.
Almost overnight grass begins to grow and leafless trees turn
green. Snakes, centipedes and scorpions are born out of nothing.
At night, myriads of moths flutter around the lamps. They fall in
everybody's food and water. Geckos dart about filling themselves
with insects until they get heavy and fall off ceilings. Inside rooms,
the hum of mosquitoes is maddening. People spray clouds of
insecticide and the floor becomes a layer of wriggling bodies and
wings. Next evening, there are many more fluttering around the

lampshades and burning themselves in the flames. The monsoon has its own music. Apart from thunder, the rumble of storm-clouds and the pitter-patter of rain-drops, there is the constant accompaniment of frogs croaking. Aristophanes[3] captured their sound: *'Brek-ek-ek-ex, Koax, Koax! Brek-ek-ek-ex, Koax Koax!'*

While the monsoon lasts, the showers start and stop without warning. The clouds fly across, dropping their rain on the plains as it pleases them, until they reach the Himalayas. They climb up the mountain sides. Then the cold squeezes the last drops of water out of them. Lightning and thunder never cease. All this happens in late August or early September. Then the season of the rains gives way to autumn.

The monsoon is the most memorable experience in the lives of Indians. Others who wish to know India and her people should also see its impact on the country. It is not enough to read about it in books, or see it on the cinema screen, or hear someone talk about it. It has to be a personal experience because nothing short of living through it can fully convey all it means to a people for whom it is not only the source of life, but also their most exciting contact with nature. What the four seasons of the year mean to the European, the one season of the monsoon means to the Indian. The summer monsoon is preceded by desolation; it brings with it the hopes of spring; it has the fullness of summer and the fulfilment of autumn all in one.

It is not surprising that much of India's art, music and literature is concerned with the summer monsoon. Innumerable paintings depict people on rooftops looking eagerly at the dark clouds billowing out from over the horizon with flocks of herons flying in front. Of the many melodies of Indian music, *Raga Megha-Malhar* is the most popular because it brings to the mind distant echoes of the sound of thunder and the falling of raindrops. It brings the odour of the earth and of green vegetation to the nostrils; the cry of the peacock and the call of the koel to the ear. There is also the *Raga Desh* and *Hindole,* which invoke scenes of merry-making—of swings in mango groves and the singing and laughter of girls. Most Indian palaces had specially designed balconies from which noblemen could view the monsoon downpour. Here they sat listening to court musicians improvising their own versions of monsoon melodies, sipping wine and making love to the ladies of their harem. The most common theme in Indian songs is the longing of lovers for each other when the rains are in full swing. There is no joy greater than union during monsoon time; there is no sorrow deeper than separation during the season of the rains.

The Indian attitude towards clouds and rain remains fundamentally different from that of the Westerner. To the one, clouds are symbols of hope; to the other, of despair. The Indian scans the heavens and if nimbus clouds blot out the sun, his heart fills with joy. The Westerner looks up and if there is no silver lining edging the clouds, his depression deepens. The Indian talks of someone he respects and looks up to as a great shadow, like the one cast by the clouds when they cover the sun. The Westerner, on the other hand, looks on a shadow as something evil and refers to people of dubious character as shady types. For him, his beloved is like the sunshine and her smile a sunny smile. An Indian's notion of a beautiful woman is one whose hair is black as monsoon clouds and has eyes that flash like lightning. The Westerner escapes clouds and rain whenever he can to seek sunnier climes. An Indian, when the rains come, runs out into the street shouting with joy and lets himself be soaked to the skin.

THE MONSOON IN INDIAN LITERATURE

The monsoon has exercised the minds of Indian writers (as well as painters and musicians) over the centuries. Some of the best pieces of descriptive verse were composed by India's classical poets writing in Sanskrit. Amaru (date uncertain, but earlier than ninth century AD) describes the heat of the summer and the arrival of the monsoon (page 70, verse 68):

The summer sun, who robbed the pleasant nights,
And plundered all the water of the rivers,
And burned the earth, and scorched the forest-trees,
Is now in hiding; and the autumn clouds,
Spread thick across the sky to track him down.
Hunt for the criminal with lightning-flashes.

To be away from one's wife or sweetheart during the season
of rains can be a torture (page 76, verse 92):

At night the rain came, and the thunder deep
Rolled in the distance; and he could not sleep,
But tossed and turned, with long and frequent sighs,
And as he listened, tears came to his eyes;
And thinking of his young wife left alone,
He sobbed and wept aloud until the dawn.
And from that time on
The villagers made it a strict rule that no traveller
Should be allowed to take a room for the night in the village.[4]

Literary conceit and facetiousness have always been practiced
by Indian poets. Thus Sudraka (probably third–fourth century
AD) has a girl taunt a cloud (page 73, verse 81):

Thundercloud, I think you are wicked.
You know I'm going to meet my own lover,
And yet you first scare me with your thunder,
And now you're trying to caress me
With your rain-hands!

Bhartrihari[5] (AD 500 or a little earlier) went into erotic ecstasies
combining descriptions of the monsoon with dalliance (page 101,
verse 137):

Flashing streaks of lightning
Drifting fragrance of tropical pines,
Thunder sounding from gathering clouds,
Peacocks crying in amorous tones—

How will long-lashed maids pass
These emotion-laden days in their lovers' absence?

He writes of 'autumnal rains rousing men's lusts' (page 103, verse 140):

When clouds shade the sky
And plantain lilies mask the earth,
When winds bear lingering scents
Of fresh verbena and kadamba
And forest retreats rejoice
With the cries of peacock flocks;
Then ardent yearning overpowers
Loved and wretched men alike.

While the downpour lasts there is little that lovers can do besides stay in bed and make love (page 105, verse 142):

Heavy rains keep lovers
Trapped in their mansions;
In the shivering cold a lord
Is embraced by his long-eyed maid,
And winds bearing cool mists
Allay their fatigue after amorous play.
Even a dreary day is fair
For favoured men who nestle in love's arms.

Once the rains have set in good and proper, clouds, lightning and rain become a routine affair (page 79, verse 102):

Black clouds at midnight;
Deep thunder rolling.
The night has lost the moon:
A cow lowing for her lost calf.

Monsoon is not only trysting time for humans but also for animals and birds, above all India's national bird, the peacock.

Yogesvara (circa AD 800) describes the courtship dance in these beautiful lines (page 125, verse 216):

With tail-fans spread, and undulating wings
With whose vibrating pulse the air now sings,
Their voices lifted and their beaks stretched wide,
Treading the rhythmic dance from side to side,
Eyeing the raincloud's dark, majestic hue,
Richer in colour than their own throats' blue,
With necks upraised, to which their tails advance,
Now in the rains the screaming peacocks dance.

Subandhu[6] (late sixth century AD) in his *Vasavadatta* is exuberant in his welcome of the monsoon:

The rainy season had arrived. Rivers overflowed their banks. Peacocks danced at eventide. The rain quelled the expanse of dust as a great ascetic quells the tide of passion. The chataka birds were happy. Lightning shown like a bejewelled boat of love in the pleasure-pool of the sky; it was like a garland for the gate of the palace of paradise; like a lustrous girdle for some heavenly beauty; like a row of nailmarks left upon the cloud by its lover, the departing day.

The rain was like a chess player, while yellow and green frogs were like chessmen jumping in the enclosures of the irrigated fields. Hailstones flashed like pearls from the necklaces of heavenly birds. By and by, the rainy season yielded to autumn, the season of bright dawns; of parrots rummaging among rice-stalks; of fugitive clouds. In autumn the lakes echoed with the sound of herons. The frogs were silent and the snakes shrivelled up. At night the stars were unusually bright and the moon was like a pale beauty.

Poet Vidyapati[7] (1352–1448) of Mithila in the eastern state of Bihar used nature to highlight erotic scenes of love-making between Krishna and Radha. Of these many are set in the monsoon (page 57, verse 18):

How the rain falls
In deadly darkness!

O gentle girl, the rain
Pours on your path
And roaming spirits straddle the wet night.
She is afraid
Of loving for the first time.

O Madhava,
Cover her with sweetness.
How will she cross the fearful river
In her path?
Enraptured with love,
Beloved Radha is careless of the rest.
Knowing so much,
O shameless one,
How can you be cold towards her?
Whoever saw
Honey fly to the bee?

In another verse Vidyapati describes an empty house during the rainy season (page 100, verse 61):

Roaring the clouds break
And rain falls.
The earth becomes a sea
In a far land, my darling
Can think of nothing
But his latest love.
I do not think
That he will now return
The god of love rejects me.
A night of rain,
An empty house

And I a woman and alone
The streams grow to great rivers.
The fields lie deep in water.
Travellers cannot now reach home.
To all, the ways are barred.
May that god without a body

Strip me of my body too.
Says Vidyapati:
When he remembers, Krishna will return.

The prolonged monsoon can become tiresome for some people.
Vidyapati writes about their predicament (page 110, verse 7):

Clouds break.
Arrows of water fall
Like the last blows
That end the world.
The night is thick
With lamp-black for the eyes.
Who keeps so late a tryst?
The earth is a pool of mud
With dreaded snakes at large.
Darkness is everywhere,
Save where your feet
Flash with lightning.

But all said and done, the season of rains is one of exultation
(page 126, verse 87):

Clouds with lightning,
Lightning with the clouds
Whisper and roar.
Branches in blossom
Shower in joy
And peacocks loudly chant
For both of you.

Another body of literature where many references to monsoons
can be found are *Barahmasa* (twelve months) composed by
poets of northern India. We are not sure when the tradition
of composing *Barahmasa* came into vogue but by the sixteenth
century it had become well established and most poets tried their
hand at describing the changing panorama of nature through the

year. The Sikh's holy scripture, the Guru Granth Sahib, has two *Barahmasa* (Punjabi version of *Barahmasa*) of which the one composed by the founder of the faith, Guru Nanak[8] (1469–1539), *Raga Tukhari*[9] has some memorable depictions of the weather.

Since the monsoons in Punjab break sometimes after mid-July Nanak first describes the summer's heat in his verse on *Asadh* (June–July):

> *In Asadh the sun scorches*
> *Skies are hot*
> *The earth burns like an oven*
> *Waters give up their vapours*
> *It burns and scorches relentlessly*
> *Thus the landfalls not*
> *To fulfil its destiny*

> *The sun's chariot passes the mountain tops;*
> *Long shadows stretch across the land*
> *And the cicada calls from the glades.*
> *The beloved seeks the cool of the evening.*
> *If the comfort she seeks be in falsehood,*
> *There will be sorrow in store for her.*
> *If it be in truth,*
> *Hers will be a life of joy everlasting.*

Since monsoon is trysting time for lovers and thus engrossed they tend to forget their Maker, Nanak admonishes them in his verse of *Bhadon* (August–September):

> *In the month of Bhadon*
> *I lose myself in a maze of falsehood*
> *I waste my wanton youth*
> *River and land are one endless expanse of water*
> *For it is the monsoon the season of merry-making.*
> *It rains,*
> *The nights are dark,*
> *What comfort is it to the wife left alone?*
> *Frogs croak*

Peacocks scream
The papeeha calls 'peeoh, peeoh',
The fangs of serpents that crawl,
The stings of mosquitoes that fly are full of venom.
The seas have burst their bounds in the ecstasy of fulfillment.
Without the Lord I alone am bereft of joy
Whither shall I go?
Says Nanak, ask the guru the way
He knoweth the path which leads to the Lord.

The poetic tradition has continued to the present time. India's only Nobel Laureate in literature, Rabindranath Tagore (1861–1941), has two beautiful pieces in his most celebrated work, *Gitanjali*[10] (page 11, verse 18 and page 14, verse 23):

Clouds heap upon clouds and it darkens
Ah, love, why dost thou let me wait outside at the door all alone?
In the busy moments of the noontide work I am with the crowd,
But on this dark lonely day it is only for thee I hope
If thou showest me not thy face, if thou leavest me wholly
aside, I know not how I am to pass these long, rainy hours.
I keep gazing on the far-away gloom of the sky and my heart
wanders wailing with the restless wind.
Art thou abroad on this stormy night on the journey of love,
my friend? The sky groans like one in despair.
I have no sleep tonight.
Ever and again I open my door and look out on the
darkness, my friend!
I can see nothing before me,
I wonder where lies thy path!
By what dim shore of the ink-blackriver, by what far edge of
the frowning forest,
Through what mazy depth of gloom art thou treading the
course to come to me my friend?

These are but a few examples from Sanskrit and languages of northern India illustrating the impact the monsoons make on sensitive minds of poets and men of letters. Similar examples are available from all other languages and dialects spoken in the rest of the country.

THE MONSOON DESCRIBED BY
ENGLISH POETS AND NOVELISTS

Many foreign writers have given vivid descriptions of the monsoon. Of these there is a memorable one by L.H. Niblett in his *India in Fable, Verse and Story*,[11] published in 1938:

> The sky was grey and leaden: the Moon was dull and pale;
> Suspended high, the dust-clouds, in canopying veil,
> O'erlooked wide fields and hamlets of India's arid plains—
> Sun-baked and scorch'd and yellow—athirsting for the Rains.
> The atmosphere was stifling; the air was still as death,
> As the parched jheels emitted their foul and charnel breath.
> Stormclouded the horizon: a flash across the sky,
> A boom of far-off thunder, and a breeze like a distant sigh:
> 'Tis the dirge of a dying summer: the music of the gods;
> Dead leaves rise up and caper: the Melantolia nods:
> Tall trees to life awaken: the top-most branches sway
> And the long grass is waving along the zephyr way.
> A mantle of red shadow envelops all around—
> The trees, the grass, the hamlets, as the storm-clouds forward bound.
> Of a sudden, comes a whirlwind, dancing, spinning rapidly;
> Then gust on gust bursts quick, incessant, mad, rushing furiously.
> A crash—and the Monsoon's on us, in torrents everywhere,
> With the bellowing roar of thunder, and lightning, flare on flare.
> The tempest's now abated; a hush falls o'er the scene;
> Then myriad birds start chatt'ring and the grass again is green,
> The fields like vast, still mirrors, in sheets of water He,
> The frogs, in droning chorus, sing hoarse their lullaby,
> Each tank and pool is flooded, great rivers burst their banks,
> King Summer's reign is ended, the Monsoon sovereign ranks.

E.M. Forster, the celebrated author of *A Passage to India*, has an equally vivid portrayal of the rainy season in his *The Hill of Devi*.[12]

The first shower was smelly and undramatic. Now there is a new India—damp and grey, and but for the unusual animals I might think myself in England. The full monsoon broke violently and upon my undefended form. I was under a little shelter in the garden, sowing seeds in boxes with the assistance of two aged men and a little boy. I saw black clouds and felt some spots of rain. This went on for a quarter of an hour, so that I got accustomed to it, and then a wheel of water swept horizontally over the ground. The aged men clung to each other for support, I don't know what happened to the boy. I bowed this way and that as the torrent veered, wet, through of course, but anxious not to be blown away like the roof of palm leaves over our head. When the storm decreased or rather became perpendicular, I set out for the Palace, large boats of mud forming on either foot. A rescue expedition, consisting of an umbrella and a servant, set out to meet me, but the umbrella blew inside out and the servant fell down.

Since then there have been some more fine storms, with lightning very ornamental and close. The birds fly about with large pieces of paper in their mouths. They are late, like everyone else, in their preparations against the rough weather, and hope to make a nest straight off but the wind blows the paper round their heads like a shawl, and they grow alarmed and drop it. The temperature is now variable, becomes very hot between the storms, but on the whole things have improved. I feel much more alert and able to concentrate. The heat made me feel so stupid and sleepy, though I kept perfectly well.

It is strange that the monsoon did not exercise the minds of foreign writers as much as it did of the Indians. A large majority of them were birds of passage who did not stay long enough in the country to share the emotional response of the Indians. During British rule, in most government offices English officers with their families moved up to hill stations like Simla, Mussoorie, Darjeeling and Ooty from where they administered the country or went on holidays to Kashmir and so escaped the intense heat that enveloped the plains; consequently they were unable to sense the relief and the joy that came with the monsoon. In any event, they could not rid themselves of their inborn aversion to rain which spoiled their fun at home; for them monsoons were just a succession of rainy days.

THE MONSOON IN FOLK LITERATURE

A substantial portion of the folk literature of all of India's fourteen languages is devoted to the monsoons. What was observed in the changes of climate, formation of clouds, flora and fauna was put in doggerel or made into proverbs. And every village has its *sabjantawallah* (Mr Know-it-all) who could predict when the monsoon would break and how bountiful it would be.

PORTENTS

In every part of India peasants have their own way of predicting the monsoon. There is a general belief that the more intense the heat during April, May and June, the heavier will be the rains that follow. In northern India some varieties of thorny bushes like the karwand and heever break into tiny leaf a month before the rains break. The papeeha is loudest during the hot days and its cry is interpreted in Marathi as '*paos ala, paos ala*' meaning 'the rains are coming'. The peasants are also familiar with the monsoon bird (pied crested cuckoo, the *Clamator Jacobinus*), also known as megha papeeha—the song-bird of the clouds. Its natural habitat is in East Africa. Taking advantage of the monsoon winds, it flies across the Indian Ocean and the Arabian Sea to arrive on the western coast of India a day or so ahead of the rain-bearing clouds. It is rightly regarded as the monsoon herald. It flies at a more leisurely pace inland and is usually sighted in Delhi about fifteen days after the monsoon has broken over the Western Ghats.[13]

VILLAGE SOOTHSAYERS

Indians divide the few months of the summer monsoon into eight periods of thirteen to fourteen days each, depending on the signs of the zodiac known as *nakshatras*.

Of the twenty-seven nakshatras the fifteenth known as *svati* (late October) is considered the most auspicious. According to poets, the mythical bird Chatrik drinks only of the svati rain. And it is only the drops of the svati rain that turn to pearls when they fall into oysters. The svati falling on bamboo trees produces *vanslocham,* a precious medicament of Ayurveda, the indigenous Hindu system of medicine.

All Indian languages have innumerable proverbs stressing the importance of rains in their particular regions. For instance, the test of a good monsoon in Maharashtra is when the gunny sacks peasants drape over their heads and shoulders as they go out in the rain remain damp long enough to breed insects. For Punjab, comprehensive compilation has been made (thirteen). They are largely variations of the single theme 'if the rains are good, there will be no famine'. There are also proverbs about distribution of rains during the year:[14]

> Four months do not need even a rain of gold: (mid-November to mid-December), *chaitra* (mid-March to mid-April), *vaisakha* (mid-April to mid-May) and *jyestha* (mid-May to mid-June). Except for these four months, rain is desirable in all the other months of the year.

For some unknown reason people expect the monsoons to break over Bombay by the tenth of June. The onset of winter rain is calculated as following a hundred days after the end of the summer monsoon.

Despite the summer rains being the real monsoon, it is the short winter rains that the Punjabi farmer prizes more. 'Winter rain is gold, *hadha* (June–July) rains, silver, and *sawan-bhadon* (July–September), mere copper,' says a proverb. 'If there is a spell of rain in *margasirsa* (mid-November to mid-December) the wheat will have healthy colour'. There are parallel proverbs instructing farmers what to do during the winter monsoon months: 'If you do not plough your land in hadha you will be like a dry sawan and a child who learnt nothing at school.' 'If it rains on Diwali (the festival of lamps that falls early in November) the sluggard will be as well off as a conscientious tiller except that the tiller's crop will be more abundant.'

MONSOON PROVERBS IN HINDI

Most of these are ascribed to Ghagh (seventeenth century), a learned Brahmin poet–astrologer and his even more learned wife, Bhaddari, a low-caste girl he married because of her learning. Says Bhaddari:

> When clouds appear like partridge feathers and are spread across the sky, they will not go without shedding rain.

A similar proverb in Punjabi says exactly the opposite. Ghagh predicts:

> When lightning flashes in the northern sky and the wind blows from the east, bring oxen under shelter because it is sure to rain.
> When water in the pitcher does not cool, when sparrows bathe in dust and the ants take their eggs to a safer place, you can be sure of a heavy downpour.
> If the southern wind flows in the months of *magha* and *pausa* (i.e. January and February), the summer monsoon is bound to be good.
> Dark clouds in the sky may thunder without shedding a drop; where white clouds may be pregnant with rain.

However, some of their proverbs seemed to have been designed to keep hope alive. 'If the clouds appear on Friday and stay till Saturday,' Ghagh tells Bhaddari, 'be sure that it will rain.'

Ghagh–Bhaddari proverbs are on the lips of peasant folk in the Hindi-speaking belt stretching from Haryana and Rajasthan across

Uttar Pradesh, Madhya Pradesh to eastern boundaries of Bihar. Variations of the same proverbs exist in Bengal and Maharashtra.

NOTES

1. See, C. Carrington, *Rudyard Kipling, His Life and Work*, London, Macmillan, 1953, p.94.
2. See, *Rudyard Kipling's Verse 1885-1926*, London, Hodder and Stoughton, 1930, p.80.
3. See Aristophanes's *The Frogs* in the *Great Books of the Western World*, New York, Benton, 1952, p.566.
4. See, J. Brough, *Poems From the Sanskrit*, Harmondsworth, Penguin Books Ltd, 1968.
5. See, Bhartrihari: *Poems with the Transliterated Sanskrit Text of the. Satakatrayam*, trans. B.S. Miller, ed., William Theodore de Bary, New York and London, Columbia University Press, 1967.
6. See Subandhu's *Vasavaddatta in B.N. Pandey, ed., A Book of India—An Anthology of Prose and Poetry from the Indian Sub-Continent*, Delhi, Rupa, Vol. I, 1977, p.138.
7. See, W.G. Archer, *Love Songs of Vidyapati*, trans. D. Bhattacharya, London, Allen and Unwin, 1963.
8. For details see, Guru Nanak's *Raga Tukhari*, 1604, in Guru Arjun Dev, compiler, *Adi Granth*, SGPC, Amritsar, 1984, pp.1107–1110. Translated by Khushwant Singh in *A History of the Sikhs*, Princeton, Princeton University Press, Vol. I, 1963, pp. 351–57.
9. Khushwant Singh's translation of the *Baramah* is carried in full elsewhere in the book.
10. See, Rabindranath Tagore, *Gitanjali*, Delhi, Macmillan, 1980.
11. See L.H. Niblett's *India in Fable, Verse, and Story*, in B.N. Pandey ed., *A Book of India—An Anthology of Prose and Poetry from the Indian Sub-Continent*, Delhi, Rupa, Vol. I, 1977, p.138.
12. See E.M. Forster, *The Hill of Devi*, London, Edwin Arnold and Co., 1953, p.93.
13. For details see, S. Ali and S.D. Riply, *Handbook of the Birds of India and Pakistan*, Delhi, Oxford University Press, Vol. 3, 1984, pp. 194–200.
14. For details see, M.S. Randhawa ed., *Agricultural Proverbs of the Punjab, Chandigarh*. Directorate of Public Relations, 1962.

APRIL IN DELHI (FROM *NATURE WATCH*)

Delhi's short spring is over; summer is yet to come. Mornings and evenings are cool, the day at times unpleasantly warm. March flowers begin to wilt under the heat of the sun; summer blossoms are ready to take their place.

April inherits some of its unpredictability from the preceding month. All Fools Day is almost 12 hours long; to be precise, 12.26 hours. Baisakhi, thirteen days later, is 22 minutes longer. Both days can be equally unpredictable. I have known them to be as chilly as some in winter and I have known Baisakhi to be uncomfortably hot outdoors. I have also recorded Baisakhi celebrations at Majnoon da Tilla Gurdwara along the upper reaches of the Yamuna in north Delhi being washed out by unseasonal rain. The Bard was correct in comparing the vagaries of a new love affair with the eccentric weather of April:

Of how this spring of love resembleth
The uncertain glory of an April Day.

However, Delhi in April is indeed 'well-apparelled' and 'proud-pied'. Gardens continue to look like painters' easels. Flower shows in different parts of the city exhibit new strains of roses and bougainvillaeas.

One year, early in April, I happened to drive out of the city towards Jaipur. It was rugged country typical of the Aravalli range which extends across the Rajasthan desert and ends in the northern suburbs of Delhi; keekar (camel thorn), cactus,

226

wild thorny shrub (jujube) and other scrubby flora manage to survive in this waterless wasteland. However, flame trees lit up the countryside. And as I drove back in the evening the bitter-sweet perfume of keekar flowers wafted across the road. How well the poet Avimaraka caught the breath of a summer evening! How enchanting is the great variety of the world!

Gone is the heat of the day as the earth dresses for night;
The evening breeze of this strange world gently the body touches
Slowly she removes the sun from her forehead
Quietly puts around her neck a garland of stars
Scatters the brave throughout the sleeping city
And joins together the bodies of young lovers.
(Avimaraka, *Love's Enchanted World*, translated by J.L. Masson & D.D. Kosambi.)

I must have muddled my calendar of flowering trees in believing that the flame tree and the coral come into flower at the same time as the semul. They do not; the semul comes first. The coral and the flame blossom almost a month later. By Baisakhi (13 April) silk semuls have almost entirely shed their blossoms while the flame and the coral are in their best finery. By then bauhinia beans are ready for plucking. Trees that flower at the same time as flames and corals are jacarandas (their Indian name neelam—sapphire—is an apt description of their colouring), widely planted in New Delhi. You have to see them in a cluster to catch the lapis-la-zuli blue of their tiny bell-shaped flowers. There are a few in the roundabout facing Parliament House on Sansad Marg, avenues of them along the Safdarjung flyover, on Siri Fort Road and in new residential areas. They can be seen at their best between the first and third weeks of the month.

People often confuse the coral and the flame, since they are both the same colour. Coral's Latin name Erythrina means 'red', but there the resemblance ends. The flowers of the coral (Gul-e-Nastareen or Pangra in Hindi) stand erect; flame petals are curved like scimitars and resemble a parrot's beak. Their boles and leaves are also quite dissimilar. The coral tree can be seen in abundance in most of Delhi's parks. It has many uses, its wood being made into stakes to support betel (paan) and pepper vines. The flame is still largely wild. There are many flame trees on the Ridge and a whole forest of them beyond Surajkund. People don't care to grow this tree in their gardens because its glory lasts barely seven days; the rest of the year it is just a mass of leaves that make a clattering noise in the wind. In north India they sew flame leaves together to make donas (cups) and pattals (plates). A variety of astringent gum known as the Bengal Kino is extracted from its bark. For some reason the lac insect which breeds on flames is not cultivated on Delhi's trees. The tree, Butea frondosa, derives its Latin name from an eighteenth century botanist, the Karl of Bute. It has many Indian names; dhak, palas and tesoo. My friend the poet Jaseemuddin in Dhaka had many in his garden, so he named his house Palas Baari. It is said that the famous battle of Plassey (AD 1757) came to be so known because it took place in a jungle of flame (palas) trees.

One morning on the way to the Club I saw a whirl of kites dive-bombing an injured bat which had fallen on the road. It managed to elude them by dragging itself into a drain.

Since the poor bat could not fly, it would almost certainly be eaten up by dogs.

How had the bat come to grief? What makes bats choose certain trees in preference to others? In New Delhi their favourite perches are arjuna trees growing between Motilal Nehru Place and the roundabout where Janpath meets Maulana Azad Road. They can be seen and heard squabbling amongst themselves every morning. I used to see lots of them in my father's garden on Janpath. Their favourite trees were the fragrant maulsaris. When these were in fruit, bats were as thick as bees in a hive. There are other varieties of bats (or are they flying foxes?) which inhabit old monuments. They have many nests in the ancient seminary at Hauz Khas.

By more than trebling its population in the last forty years,

Delhi has lost a great deal of its bird life that I lived with in my school days. A weekend in Kurukshetra made me aware of nature's sights and sounds now rarely heard or seen in the Delhi of today. At the university guest house I was shaken out of my slumber by the trumpet call of a peafowl by my window: paon, paon, paon—very much like the way its name is pronounced in French. As I opened the window, it scuttled away. The eastern horizon had turned grey and it was drizzling. All at once a papeeha (hawk cuckoo) perched on a neighbouring tree, wound itself up and began to call 'brain-fever, brain-fever'. Besides peacocks and papeehas there were lapwings screaming as they flew about in the grey dawn, as also koels and drongos. No sooner had these birds fallen silent than the doves took over and the 'voice of the turtle' was heard over the campus. An hour later when the clouds lifted to reveal a deep blue sky, flocks of swallows chittered as they wheeled about in the high heavens.

Soon after Baisakhi, the first crop of mangoes grown around Delhi appear in the market. They are seldom very sweet or succulent. It takes the searing heat of summer to bring them to their full richness of taste and colour.

More trees are in the process of shedding old leaves and donning new ones, coming to flower and being deflowered (sic). What could have induced New Delhi's master-gardener, Lancaster, to import sausage trees (Kigelia pinata) from East Africa and plant them in Delhi? Sausage trees can be seen along Amrita Shergil Marg and many other avenues. It is a singularly ugly tree with scraggy red flowers which exude a malodorous oil and bear solid sausage fruit for which neither man nor bird nor beast have any use. Its flowers are said to open up at night and begin to close up by mid-morning. Apparently fruit-bats relish their taste. Some rural folk make a paste out of its fruit and use it against skin eruptions. How different is the siris! It is quick-growing but short-lived. It is leafless till spring. Then suddenly fresh, light green leaves appear, and soon its pale powder-puff flowers spread their fragrance far and wide.

The dual highway running from the airport to the city is divided by beds of bougainvillaeas and has siris growing on either side. There are two varieties of siris to be seen in Delhi: Albizia lebbek, the fragrant variety, and the much taller white Albizia procera (safed siris). The second variety has a pale, smooth bole with branches well above the ground. There are a few lining Man Singh road on either side of its intersection with Rajpath.

By the last week of April the days are distinctly warmer and the afternoon sun unbearable. It is time to put on air-coolers. As long as the air outside is dry, which it usually is through April, May and June, they effectively cool rooms blowing in dry air through wet khas screens. But beware! Damp air is the mother of body aches and pains and an invitation to mosquitoes and cockroaches. If you can afford it, use air-conditioners rather than coolers.

In the last days of the month the first gulmohar blooms begin to peep out of their green casings (my diary records some appearing as early as 15 April). The Gul ('gold') mohar derives its Latin name Ponciana regia from M. de Poinci, a governor of the French Antilles in the mid-seventeenth century. The tree is a native of Madagascar. It has become the great favourite amongst flowering trees because of its flamboyant display of fiery red and orange. Connaught Place has a cluster of these trees and they are now grown extensively in most new residential colonies.

Another flowering tree which resembles the gulmohar in colouring and is grown extensively in Delhi is the peacock tree, also known as the dwarf ponciana or Barbados pride. Why peacock? There is nothing of the peacock's blue about it. Its Latin name *Caesalpina pulcherrima* (most beautiful) is well-matched by its Indian ones, Krishna chura or Radha chura, the crest of Krishna or Radha.

Pink cassias, cherry-red and white are now in full bloom. So also are yellow elders and oleanders, both pink and white. At the same time neems shed their flowers like sawdust about their boles.

Semul pods burst and scatter their fluff which lies like snowflakes on the ground. The summer heat and damp rouse serpents from their hibernation. Delhi has all three species of the most venomous snakes; cobras, vipers and kraits. It also has others which are quite harmless to humans but prey on man's worst enemies—rats and mice. One warm afternoon I went to see Arpana Caur, a young painter working in the artists' colony at Garhi. The studios are built along the walls of this ancient robber fortress. In between is an open space, now lush with grass and cannas. As I entered I saw a gang of urchins hurling stones, brandishing sticks and yelling as they ran towards a snake basking on the lawn.

Before I could stop them they had beaten the poor reptile into a bloody mess. 'Saanp ka bachha (a baby snake),' they cried triumphantly. It was a small orange-coloured snake with diamond-shaped black spots—a full grown diadem (rajat). It was too late to tell the children that like many other snakes of Delhi it was not only harmless but also a well-meaning reptile.

WORSHIP OF THE GANGA

Of all the rivers of the world, none has received as much adoration as the Ganga. Though there is scant reference to it in the Vedas, it assumes a dominant position in the Puranas. She is the daughter of Himavat, the Himalayas, and Mena, the sister of Parvati, wife of Siva. Originally, the river was confined to the realms of paradise. When brought to earth to irrigate barren land, it came down in such a mighty torrent that it would have drowned everything but for Siva breaking its downfall on his head and allowing it to flow out into seven streams, *Sapta Sindhava*—the seven sacred rivers of India, the most sacred being the Ganga.

No one knows why or when Ganga's waters acquired powers of healing minds and bodies. But long before records started being kept, men who were disillusioned with life or were in search of eternal truths gave up other pursuits to retire into caves in valleys through which the Ganga ran to meditate in the silence of mountain fastnesses. At dawn, they stood in the icy-cold waters of the river to welcome the rising sun. At sunset, they floated leaf boats with flowers and oil lamps on its fast-moving streams.

Waters of the Ganga acquired the reputation of healing properties. They were undoubtedly the cleanest, clearest source of portable water near Delhi and Agra which were for centuries the seats of rulers of India. The fourteenth century ruler at Delhi, Mohammed bin Tughlaq, organized a regular supply of drinking water from Hardwar for inmates of his palace. The practice was followed from one dynasty to the next. The Mughal emperor Akbar drank only Ganga water and ordered it to be used in the royal kitchen. Though Muslims attached no religious significance to it, the Ganga found an important place in their thinking. Allama Iqbal, one of the founding fathers of Pakistan and the greatest Urdu poet of his times, had this to say:

Ai aab-e-rood-e-Ganga,
Voh din hai yaad tujh ko
Utra terey kinaarey
Jab kaarvaan hamaara?

(O, limpid waters of the Ganga,
remember you the day,
When our caravan stopped by your banks
And forever came to stay?)

For the Hindus, *Ganga jal* (Ganga water) has more spiritual than mundane significance. A newborn babe has a few drops put in its mouth. So has a dying person before he breathes his last. A dip in the river washes away all sins. Ashes of the dead are immersed in it.

The water of the Ganga is in great demand all over the country. As you go along the road to Hardwar, you pass long lines of *kanwarias* carrying pots containing Ganga jal slung on poles. At short distances, there are small platforms for them to rest their cargo, as the pots must never touch the ground. In Calcutta, there are *jal yatris,* water pilgrims. Soon after Shivratri, they can be seen taking water pots from the Tribeni in Howrah district, to the Tarakeshwar temple in Hooghly district, calling out *Baba Tarakeshwari serai nomo* (obeisance and service to Baba Tarakeshwari), or *Bholey Baba paar karega* (Lord Shiva will take you across) or simply, *Bom, bom bholey, Taraknath boley bom bom.*

The Ganga is sacred from its source, Gangotri, down the mountains past Rudraprayag, Devprayag, Badrinath and Rishikesh till it enters the plains at Hardwar. So far it is a fast-moving river, crystal clear and sparkling. After Hardwar, it slows down. By the time it reaches Allahabad for its *sangam* (confluence with the Yamuna), it becomes a sluggish stretch of water full of human garbage. It continues to gather debris as it goes past Benares and Patna to its junction with the mighty Brahmaputra to become the Hooghly and empty itself in the Bay of Bengal.

On its long journey from the Himalayas to the sea, many rivers join it while canals rob it of its waters. It is a strange phenomenon that though the water from the main stream is regarded sacred, the same water running in canals and taps is accorded no sanctity. Even in the places of pilgrimage, some small areas along the bank are more sacred than others. In Hardwar, Har-ki-paudi (Footsteps of the Lord), a 50-yard stretch on the right bank of the river, is about the most sacred place in India. Here, pilgrims throng in thousands from early hours of the dawn to late at night, to bathe, pray, make offerings and ask for favours. A never-to-be-forgotten sight is the *aarti*, worship with oil lamps, which takes places every evening at sunset.

Hardwar is a comfortable four-hour drive from Delhi. However, it is advisable to choose an appropriate time of the year for the visit. The best time is from January to April, preferably around Holi, when the countryside en route and the hills around Hardwar are ablaze with the flame of the forest and the coral. Choose a couple of days before the full moon and plan to spend at least one night in the town. It has plenty of hotels, small and big, *ashrams* and *dharamshalas*, lodges to suit your pocket. The menu everywhere is strictly vegetarian; there is also prohibition, but soda water is available and no one really bothers if you enjoy your drink in your room.

A short halt at a midway eatery, *Cheetal Grand*, outside village Khatauli, is a must. It is laid out in a spacious, well-kept garden. Large cages with roosters, ducks, geese, turkeys and guinea fowl call and cackle all day long. The service is fast, the food of gourmet quality. The owner, Urooj Nisar, does good business: he feeds upto 8,000 guests every day. It is a meeting place for people taking the ashes of their loved ones to immerse in the Ganga at Hardwar and those returning after having done so. It is also the favourite picnic spot for boys and girls from schools in Mussoorie, Dehra Dun, Hardwar and Ranipur.

Make sure you get to the *ghat* (embankment) well before sunset. Stroll along the banks of the river and you will meet many well-fed cows, ash-smeared sadhus smoking ganja and opium in their chillums. Every few yards, there will be a conclave of men and women—many more women than men—listening *topurvachans* being delivered to some holy personage. In Hardwar, holy men are nine to a dozen. So are *pandas* who can trace your lineage back to forefathers you have never heard of—for a fee. Also, men with receipt books asking for donations for *gaushalas* (cattle pens) and other worthy causes. Avoid them.

As the sun goes down over the range of hills in the west, a deep shade falls over Hardwar and the silvery moonlight takes over. It is time to find a vantage point from where you can see the aarti. There is a bridge along the right bank to an island facing Har-ki-paudi on which stands a clock tower. The bridge and the island give a splendid view of what is going on at Har-ki-paudi where the action takes place. Most pilgrims prefer to sit on the steps along Har-ki-paudi just above the stream because it is there that pandas take offerings from them. In return, they give them leaf boats full of flowers and lit oil lamps, and invoke the blessings of Mother Ganga—all for a fee.

Hardwar has hundreds of temples lining the bank, but not one of them of any architectural pretensions. Evening shadows envelop their ugliness and the skullduggery of pandas looting gullible pilgrims. Only the Ganga remains as pure as the snows which give it birth. Bathed in early moonlight, it assumes ethereal beauty. Suddenly, a cry goes up, *Bolo, bolo Ganga Mata Ki*, and thousands of voices yell in triumph, *Jai*— victory of the Mother Ganga. The aarti is about to begin. All the steps leading to and around Har-ki-paudi, the bridge and the clock-tower island, are crammed with pilgrims and sightseers.

Men start striking gongs with mallets: this is in honour of the lesser gods. Then, bells of temples start clanging. Men holding candelabras with dozens of oil lamps each, stand ankle-deep in the river and wave them over it. Conch shells are blown. Leaf boats with flowers and *diyas* bob up and down the fast-moving current and disappear from view. Above all this cacophony of light and the din of gongs and bells, rises the chant:

Om, Jai Gangey Mata
(Victory to Mother Ganga)

The spectacle lasts barely ten minutes. It transports you to another world. It will haunt you for the rest of your nights and days.

VILLAGE IN THE DESERT

It is safest to begin with the beginning.

Where I was born I have been told by people who were present at my birth. When I was born remains a matter of conjecture. I am told I was born in a tiny hamlet called Hadali, lost in the sand dunes of the Thar desert some thirty kilometres west of the river Jhelum and somewhat the same distance southward of the Khewra Salt Range. Hadali is now deep inside Pakistan. At the time I was born, my father, Sobha Singh, was away in Delhi with his father, Sujan Singh. When the news was sent to him, he did not bother to put it down in his diary. I was his second son. At that time records of births and deaths were not kept in our villages. Unlike Hindus who noted down the time of birth of their offspring so that their horoscopes could be cast, we Sikhs had no faith in astrology, and therefore attached no importance to the time and place of nativity. Several years later, when he had to fill a form for our admission to Modern School in Delhi, my father gave my elder brother's and my date of birth out of his imagination. Mine was put down as 2 February 1915. Years later, my grandmother told me that I was born in *Badroo*—some time in August. I decided to fix it in the middle of the month, to 15 August 1915 and made myself a Leo. Thirty-two years later in 1947, 15 August became the birthday of independent India.

Some time after I had been weaned, my father came to Hadali to take my mother and elder brother to Delhi, where he and his father had secured some building contracts. I was left with my grandmother. For the first few years of my life she was my sole companion and friend. Her name I later discovered was Lakshmi Bai. We called her Bhaabeejee. Like her, my mother also had a Hindu—Maharashtrian—name, Veeran Bai. The children knew her as Baybayjee.

I have hazy recollections of my childhood years in Hadali. The village consisted of about three hundred families, most of them Muslims of Baluch extraction. They were enormous men, mostly serving in the British Indian army, or having retired from it. A fair proportion of the Viceroy's bodyguard came from Hadali. Till recently, a marble plaque on a wall alongside the railway Station Master's office stated that Hadali had provided proportionately more soldiers from its population for World War I than any other village in India. There were about fifty Hindu and Sikh families engaged in trade, shopkeeping and moneylending. My ancestors —I can only trace them back to my great-grandfather, Inder Singh, and his father, Pyare Lal, who converted to Sikhism and became Sohel Singh—were tradesmen. They had camel caravans which took rock-salt from the Khewra mines, and dates, the only fruit of our desert homeland, to sell in Lahore and Amritsar. They brought back textiles, kerosene oil, tea, sugar, spices and other items to sell in neighbouring towns and villages. Later, my grandfather and father got into the construction business. They laid a part of the small-gauge railtrack and tunnels on the Kalka–Simla railway.

We were the most prosperous family of Hadali. We lived in a large brick-and-mud house with a spacious courtyard enclosing a buffalo shed and had a well of our own. The entrance was a massive wooden door which was rarely opened. It had a small aperture to let people in. A number of Hindus and Sikhs served us as clerks, and hired Muslim camel-drivers took our wares to the markets. Many Muslim families were our debtors.

Our family's prosperity was ascribed to a legend. It is said that one year, when it rained heavily on the Salt Range, flood waters swept down the rocky ridge, carrying with them a Muslim holy man named Shaida Peer, who had climbed on to the thatched roof of his hut. By the time he floated down to Hadali, he had nothing on him except his loin cloth. My grandfather, Sujan Singh, gave him clothes, made a hut for him near the Muslim graveyard and sent him food. Shaida Peer blessed him: 'I will give your two sons the keys of Delhi and Lahore. They will prosper.' And prosper they did—my father as a building contractor in Delhi; and his younger brother Ujjal Singh as one of pre-Partition Punjab's biggest landowners. He later became a member of the Legislative Assembly and, after Independence, finance minister of Punjab and still later its Governor. He ended his career as Governor of Tamil Nadu.

We Sikhs and Hindus of Hadali lived with the Muslims in an uneasy but peaceful relationship. Though we addressed their elders as uncles or aunts as they did ours, we rarely went to each other's homes except on marriages and deaths. We lived in slight awe of the Muslims because they were more numerous and much bigger built than us. Fortunately for us, they were split into different clans—Waddhals, Mastials, Awans, Janjuas, Noons and Tiwanas—and were often engaged in litigation over land, frequently murdering each other. We kept ourselves at a safe distance from them.

I recall passing their men striding down the village lanes. Most of them were over six feet tall and made as if of whipcord. They wore their well-oiled hair curling out behind their ears, stuck with small wooden or ivory combs. They normally twirled spindles with the fleece of sheep or camels to make yarn, or took their hooded falcons out for airing. Their women were also tall, slender and well proportioned. They could carry two pitchers full of water balanced on their heads, and one pitcher caught between the right arm and waist. Water splashed on their muslin shirts and ankle-length lungis, displaying the outlines of their taut, shapely, black-nippled breasts as well as their muscular, dimpled buttocks. They never looked up from the ground as they glided past, aware of men eating them up with their eyes. Though barely four years old, I became an inveterate voyeur.

Nothing very exciting happened in Hadali. Life had a soporific routine. My grandmother rose well before dawn to milk the buffaloes and put the milk in an earthen pot over smouldering embers of pats of buffalo dung. She went out into the open with neighbouring women to defecate. She pulled up a couple of buckets of water from the well and bathed herself under starlight as she mumbled the morning prayer, *Japji*. She spent the next half hour churning butter and butter-milk, reciting her prayers as she did so. Then she woke me up. I was allowed to defecate on the roof-top where the hot sun burnt up everything exposed to it. I washed myself. She combed my long hair and plaited it: being Sikhs we did not cut our hair. I got out my wooden *takhti* (slate) smeared over with yellow *gaachnee* (clay), my reed pen and earthen soot-inkpot. She got a bundle of stale chappatis left over from the previous evening's meal and wrapped them in her *dupatta*. We set out together for the Dharamsal-cum-school. Pi dogs awaited us at our threshold. We took turns tearing up pieces of chappati and throwing them to the dogs. We kept a few in reserve for our return journey.

The Dharamsal was a short distance from our home. I was handed over to Bhai Hari Singh who was both Granthi and teacher. I sat on the floor with other Hindu and Sikh boys and chanted multiplication tables in sing-song. My grandmother went to the large hall where three copies of the Granth Sahib were placed side by side on a low table. Beneath the table was an assortment of spectacles discarded by worshippers for the use of anyone they fitted. After chanting the tables, Bhai Hari Singh wrote the letters of the Gurmukhi alphabet on a board for us to copy. Though bent with age, he had a terrible temper. Any mistake he spotted on our wooden slates was rewarded with resounding kicks on our backsides. Mercifully, the lesson did not last more than an hour. My grandmother and I walked back, giving the village dogs all that remained of the chappatis. While she busied herself sweeping the floor, rolling up beds and cooking the midday meal, I went out to play hop-scotch or tip-cat *(gullee-dundaa)* with boys of my age.

What we did in the afternoons depended on the time of the year. Desert winters could be very cold and the days very short. There was more to do and less time to do it in. But the real winter lasted barely forty days. After a brief spring, the long summer was upon us. It became hotter day by day with temperatures rising to 125°F. We hardly ever had any rain. Our *tobas* (ponds) were filled with brackish rain-water coming down the Salt Range. Some of it percolated into the wells. Only a few of these wells, which were brick-and-cement lined, yielded potable water fit for human consumption. For some reason brackish wells were referred to by the male gender as *khaara khoo*; those which yielded sweet water were known by the diminutive, feminine gender as *mitthee khooee*. Most of us had pale yellow teeth with a brown line running horizontally across the upper set. This was ascribed to the impure water we drank. No matter what time of year it was, my grandmother spent her afternoons plying the charkha while mumbling Guru Arjun's *Sukhmani*—the Psalm of Peace. My memories of my grandmother are closely linked with the hum of the spinning wheel and the murmur of prayers.

The long summer months were an ordeal. The hot sands burnt the soles of one's feet. Going from one house to another we had to hug the walls to walk in their shadows, deftly avoiding blobs of shit left by children who too had found the shadows the coolest places in which to defecate. We spent most of the day indoors gossiping, or drowsily fanning away flies. It was only late in the afternoon that camels and buffaloes were taken to the tobas for watering. The buffaloes were happiest wallowing in the stagnant ponds. Boys used them as jumping boards. At sunset the cattle were driven back, the buffaloes milked and hearths lit. The entire village became fragrant with the aroma of burning camel-thorn and baking bread. Boys formed groups to go into the sand-dunes to defecate. While we were at it, dung beetles gathered our turds into little marble-sized balls and rolled them to their holes in the sand. We had a unique way of cleansing ourselves. We sat on our bottoms in a line. At a given signal we raised our legs and propelled ourselves towards the winning post with our hands. By the end of the race called *gheesee*, our bottoms were clean but full of sand. Later, in the night and during the early phases of the moon, we played *kotla chapakee*, our version of blind-man's buff. Full-moon nights on the sanddunes remain printed in my memory. We ran about chasing each other till summoned home for supper. The one threat that worked was that we might be kidnapped by dacoits. We were familiar with the names of notorious outlaws like Tora and Sultana who had spread terror in the countryside because of the number of murders and abductions they had committed.

Next to dacoits we most feared sand storms. We were used to living with dust-raising winds and spiralling dust-devils, but *haneyree* or *jhakkhar* were something else. They came with such blinding fury that there was little we could do besides crouching on the ground with our heads between our knees to prevent sand getting into our nostrils, eyes and ears. There were times when so much sand was blown that the rail track was submerged under it, and no trains ran till it was cleared. But it purged the air of flies and insects, and for the following day or two the air would be cleaner and cooler.

After the evening meal we went to our roof-tops to sleep. My grandmother, who had already said her evening prayer, Rehras, recited the last prayer of the day, *Kirtan Sohila*. She rubbed clotted cream on my back. If her gentle ministrations did not put me to sleep, she would tell me anecdotes from the lives of our Gurus. If I was still wide awake, she would point to the stars and reprimand me: 'Don't you see what time it is? Now *chup*—shut up.'

The nicest time in the summer was the early morning. A cool breeze blew over the desert, picking up the fragrances of roses and jasmine which grew in our courtyards. It was the time for half sleep and fantasizing. It was all too brief. The sun came up hot, bringing with it flies and the raucous caw-cawing of crows. The blissful half hour that Urdu poets refer to as the *baad-e-naseem*—zephyr of early dawn—came to an end all too suddenly.

Little happened in Hadali to relieve the tedium of our daily routine. There was a murder or two every other year. But since murders were confined to the Muslims, we never got overexcited about them. Once a year there were tent-pegging competitions on the open ground near the railway station. Competitors lined up on their horses and, at a given signal, galloped towards the stakes waving their spears and yelling '*Allah Beli Ho*'—Oh Allah is my best friend. After piercing the stakes they waved their spears triumphantly for all to see. They often raced passing railway trains and kept pace with them till their horses ran out of breath. I remember the first time a Sikh brought a bicycle to Hadali. He boasted that he would outrun any horse. Before a horseman could take up his challenge, we boys decided to take him on. Hadali had no metalled road and the cyclist was still wobbly on the wheels. He fared very poorly as his cycle got stuck in the sand. He became the laughing stock of the village and was thereafter mocked with the title 'Saikal Bahadur'—brave man of the bicycle.

I returned to Hadali three times after shifting to Delhi. The first time, to be initiated into reading the Granth Sahib. My elder brother, a cousin and I were made to read aloud the Japji in front of the congregation and asked to swear that we would read at least one hymn every day. None of us was able to keep our promise for very long. I went there next when practising law in Lahore. I drove to Hadali with a friend whose cousin was the manager of the salt mines. As we pulled up near the railway station tears welled up in my eyes. I resisted the urge to go down on my knees and kiss the earth. I walked up to the Dharamsal and to the house where I was born. A man who was Risaldar in the Viceroy's bodyguard recognized me and spread the news to the village. By the time I left, there was a crowd to see me off.

My last visit to Hadali was in the winter of 1987. The partition of India in 1947 had brought about a complete change in its population. Not a single Sikh or Hindu remained. Our homes were occupied by Muslim refugees from Haryana. Our family haveli was divided into three equal parts, each shared by Muslim refugees from Rohtak. A new generation of Hadalians who had never seen a Sikh were then in their forties. I was uncertain of the reception they would give me. My only contact with this generation was through meeting a few young soldiers taken captive in the Indo-Pakistan war of 1971 in the prisoner-of-war camp in Dhaka. I had sought them out and written to their parents that they were safe and in good health.

I drove from Lahore and reached Hadali early in the afternoon. Village elders awaited me on the roadside with garlands of silver and gold tassels with the words *Khoosh Amdeed*—welcome—inscribed on them in Urdu. I did not recognize any of the men whose hands I shook. I was escorted to the High School ground where a dais with the Pakistan flag fluttering over it had been put up. Over 2,000 Hadalians sat in rows on chairs and on the ground. Speeches in badly pronounced, florid Urdu were delivered acclaiming me as a son of Hadali. My heart was full of gratitude. I sensed that I would make an ass of myself. I did. I started off well. I spoke to them in the village dialect. I said that just as they looked forward to going on pilgrimage to Makka and Madina, coming back to Hadali at the time of the *Maghreb* (evening prayer) of my life was my *Haj* (big pilgrimage) and my *Umra* (small pilgrimage). And as the Prophet on his return to Makka as Victor had spent his first night wandering about the streets and praying beside the grave of his first wife, I would have liked nothing better than to be left alone to roam about the lanes of Hadali and rest my head on the threshold of the house in which I was born. Then I was overcome by emotion and broke down. They understood and forgave me. I was escorted to my former home with the entire village following me. Fireworks were let off; women standing on rooftops showered rose-petals on me. Who was the author of the perfidious lie that Muslims and Sikhs were sworn enemies? No animosity had soured relations between the Muslims, Hindus and Sikhs of Hadali. Muslims had left the Sikh–Hindu Dharamsal untouched because it had been a place of worship for their departed cousins.

The Rohtak families living in what was once our home had done up the haveli with coloured balloons and paper buntings. The elders of the village who once knew my father had a feast laid out in my honour. There was little that I saw of Hadali that I recognized. The sanddunes which had been the playgrounds of my childhood years were gone. A canal had greened the desert. The tobas had become swamps full of reeds. The marble plaque commemorating the services of the men who had fought in World War I had been removed. I left Hadali a little before sunset, aware that I would never return to it again.

Simba

I returned home to Delhi. Once again I was without a job and with very little money in my pocket or in my bank account. All I had on the credit side was a collection of short stories which brought me some good notices but no money, a short and, unsatisfactory *Short History of the Sikhs* which was condemned by orthodox Sikhs, and a novel which brought me money which I had spent. And the manuscript of a second novel which had yet to be accepted by a publisher.

Among those who greeted me at home was a one-month old Alsatian pup presented by a friend of my father's to my daughter, Mala. To start with, he resented me as an intruder in his tight little human family consisting of my wife and our two children. He slept in the same upstairs bedroom in my father's house and used the roof of the porch as his lavatory. Till then he had no name. I decided to name him Simba after the marmalade cat we had abandoned in Paris. As with most Alsatians, Simba was a one-person dog. He belonged to my daughter, my wife fed him, took him to the vet for his shots and for any ailment he had, but he adopted me as his master. He was as human a dog as I have ever known and shared our joys as he did our sorrows. By the time we moved into our own ground-floor apartment in Sujan Singh Park, he had got over his frisky puppiness and grown into a powerful full-sized German Shepherd. He still shared our bedroom, where he had his own cot. And for his sake more than ours we had an airconditioner put in the room. Often at night he would sniff into my ears and ask me to make room for him.

I did. He would heave himself on to the bed with a deep sigh of gratitude, and take over more than half of my bed for the rest of the night.

We would talk to him. If we pretended to cry, he would sniff soothingly in our ears and join us wailing: *booo, ooo ooo*. If he was naughty, we'd order him to the corner. He stayed there with his head down in penitence till we said, 'Okay, now you can come back.'

Simba developed a special relationship with Mala's ayah, the seventy-five-year-old Mayee. 'Vey Shambia,' she would greet him as she opened the door to let Simba out in the garden. She waited for him to do his business in the garden before going to the neighbouring gurdwara to say her prayers. He knew he was not allowed inside the gurdwara and sat outside guarding her slippers. Just as the morning prayer was about to end, he would take one of her slippers in his mouth, trot home and hide it under a bed. Mayee would follow him pleading, 'Vey Shambia! Where have you hidden my slipper?' He followed her from room to room wagging his tail till she found the missing slipper.

Simba was always impatient for his evening walk. He would put his head in my lap and look appealingly at me: 'Isn't it time?' his eyes asked. 'Not yet,' I would reply. Then he would bring his leash and put it at my feet. 'Now?' I would tell him not to be so impatient. Next he brought my walking stick and dropped it on the book I was reading. 'Surely now!' There was no escape. He whined and trembled with excitement as we left. As he jumped on to the rear seat of the car his whining became louder. He liked to put his head out of the window and bark challenges to every dog, cow or bull we passed on the road. He had to be let off at the entrance of the Lodhi gardens. He raced the car, stopping briefly to defecate, and resumed the race to the parking lot. At that time there used to be some hares in the park. He would sniff them out of the hedges and then go in hot pursuit, yelping as he tried to catch up with them. They were too fast and dodgy for him. But he became quite adept at hunting squirrels. He learnt that they ran to the nearest tree and went round its bole to evade pursuit. He would steal up to the tree and then go for them. In the open ground they had no escape. However much I reprimanded him and even beat him, he could not resist killing harmless squirrels.

On Saturday evenings he could sense from the picnic basket being packed that the next day would be devoted largely to him. Long before dawn he would start whimpering with excitement and wake everyone up. It was difficult to control him in the car. When we got to the open countryside near Suraj Kund, or Tilpat, we had to let him out to prevent him jumping out of the car. He would chase herds of cows and scatter them over the fields. Once he nearly got his face bashed in by the rear kick of a cow. And once he almost killed a goat.

Three to four hours in the open countryside chasing hares, deer or peafowl made him happily tired. It was a drowsy, sleepy Simba we brought back from our Sunday morning picnics. He was not so impatient now for his evening walk.

He was, again, restless for his after-dinner stroll round Khan Market, where we went to get paan. He would stop by the ice-cream man and plead with us to buy him one. He was passionately fond of ice-cream. He was also very possessive. Once somebody had two lovely pups for sale under a tree in the market. He resented our paying attention to them. Whenever we stopped by the tree he would savagely bite its bole. Everyone in and around Sujan Singh Park knew Simba. We came to be known by the children of the locality as Simba's parents.

Simba was also feared. Once when going out with my wife and daughter in the Lodhi gardens, a cyclist slapped my daughter on her back and sped on. My wife screamed, 'Simba get him!' Simba chased the man, knocked him off his bicycle and stood over him baring his fangs. The poor fellow folded the palms of his hands and pleaded forgiveness. Another time, as I was stepping out of my flat after dinner, I heard a girl shout for help. Two young lads were trying to molest her. I ran towards her with Simba following on my heels. The boys tried to run away. I ordered Simba to get them. He ran and brought one fellow down on the ground. He was a big fellow and much stronger than I. But with Simba at my side, I had no hesitation in slapping the man many times across his face and roundly abusing him, calling him a goonda and a budmaash. He asked to be forgiven and swore he would never make passes at women again.

We always took Simba with us to Mashobra or Kasauli. He was happiest in the mountains. I often put him on the leash to make him pull us up steep inclines. He liked Kasauli more than Shimla because of its herds of rhesus monkeys and langoors. He waged unceasing warfare against them, and against hill crows which flocked round when he was having his afternoon meal.

Most dogs have a sixth sense. Our Simba had seventh and eighth senses as well. I will mention only one episode to prove it. My wife and I had to go abroad for a couple of months. Our children were in boarding schools. We decided to give our servants leave and lock up our flat. Simba was to be housed with Prem Kirpal: the two were on very friendly terms, as Prem was always with us on our Sunday outings and a regular visitor to our home. He happily agreed to take Simba. Being a senior government official, he had a bungalow on Canning Lane with a large garden. Simba had been there many times and sensed that we meant to leave him there. He did not seem to mind very much.

My wife returned to Delhi a few days before me. She went to Canning Lane to fetch Simba. He greeted her joyfully but refused to get into her car. Prem was very pleased over his success in winning Simba's affections. My wife reluctantly gave in. 'If he is happy with you, he can stay here,' she said. Apparently they mentioned the date I was due to return, and Simba heard them. The evening before I returned to Delhi, Simba walked all the way from Canning Lane to Sujan Singh Park and scratched at the door with his paws to announce his arrival. He knew I was coming next morning. Prem was more dejected at Simba leaving him than he would have been had I stolen his mistress.

Simba aged gracefully. The hair about his mouth turned white. He developed cataracts in his eyes. Sometimes he got feverish: there were times when my wife spent whole nights with his head on her lap, stroking his head. He was then well over thirteen years old. When I got a three-month teaching assignment at Swarthmore College, we had to leave him in the care of his real mistress, my daughter Mala. She had to take him to the vet almost every day. He didn't get any better. His legs began to give in. She sent us a cable, 'Return immediately, Simba seriously ill.' The next day, we received another cable from Mala: 'Simba passed away peacefully.'

Apparently, the vet advised Mala that Simba was in pain, his legs were paralysed and he couldn't last much longer. With her permission he gave him a lethal dose of something which put him to sleep. If I had to talk of my close friendships, Simba would be amongst the top in my list. We never kept another dog. One can't replace friends.

KASAULI: MY MINI BAIKUNTH

I plan my summers to conform to nature's calendar. I stay in Delhi in July and August, go up to Kasauli in early September when the mountains are well-washed and green, and the hillsides flecked with wild flowers.

By the last week of August the monsoon is usually beating a retreat. So this year I left Delhi on 1 September, relying on the weather keeping its time-schedule, prepared to spend the month of September in my earthly paradise. It would not be as warm as Delhi and not too cold for comfort. Delhi was denuded of flowers, Kasauli's hills would still have its monsoon blossoms, chiefly the spectacular cactus, yucca gloriosa, with dozens of bell-shaped, ivory-pale white flowers suspended from one green stem and wild dahlias of various colours blazing away on the hill slopes.

But even before the Shatabdi Express had passed Sonepat (25 miles down the route), it began to rain and continued to pour all the way to Chandigarh. It seemed the rain had just been woken up after sleeping through June, July and most of August till alarm bells sounded, warning of a drought. Then it opened up its much delayed bags full of bountiful waters to make amends for its tardiness. The Sidhus, Poonam and Karanjit, were to drive us (my daughter, Mala, was with me) to Kasauli to spend the afternoon and evening with us. The downpour washed out their plans. Poonam had brought food and drink meant for four. My daughter and I ate it for four days.

We were not the only people to be fooled by the weather. There was heavy uphill traffic on the Chandigarh–Simla road, right into the heart of Kasauli. So instead of sitting out in the garden under the shade of the toon, and gazing into the blue heavens, I spent the first few days indoors by the fireside, wrapped up in a shawl, wishing I was back in Delhi.

It takes a day or two to get used to the solitude and all-pervading silence of the mountains. It takes an afternoon or two for the locals to know you are back so that they can drop in for some gup-shup. As for the total absence of the sounds of traffic and loudspeakers, I can only describe it as deafening except for the sound of the wind sloughing through the pine trees. Besides, the occasional plane going overhead, the siren from the Solan brewery and the peal of bells from Christ Church are all that I hear in the day. At this time of the year birds seldom sing. Their period of courtship is long over, the eggs have hatched and the parent birds are busy feeding their hungry chicks.

Being locked up indoors all day and all night can be boring beyond endurance. I want company, not necessarily human company because humans are demanding and talk too much. I found exactly what I was looking for—Billoo.

Two monsoons ago, when there was a short break in the downpour, I was sitting in my garden. I saw a tiny pup, black-and-white, fluffy and of no pedigree, stumbling along and shivering in the cold. I picked it up and cuddled it in my shawl. It looked up with its shiny black eyes to ask who I was. I rubbed its ears gently. It licked my hand to say thank you, made sweet moaning sounds, stopped shivering and fell asleep. There are few experiences more gratifying than to have a young thing fall asleep in one's arms.

Then its mother came along and I put it down on the ground. She scolded her pup for allowing strangers to take liberties with it and led it back home. I found out that the bitch belonged to the caretaker of the bungalow just below mine. It didn't take much for me to persuade them to give me the puppy as soon as it was weaned. The little one had been promised to my housekeeper, Prem Kumar. A month or so later, when it had been weaned, it was formally handed over. The puppy was a male; I named him Billoo. He spent an hour every evening in my lap nibbling at my cardigan buttons, pawing my hands and nipping my fingers with its pin-sharp teeth. I looked forward to its evening visits. He was a good listener and never talked back.

When I returned to Raj Villa the following summer, Billoo had grown to his full height. He did not recognize me. I had to bribe him with buttered toast and biscuits while having my afternoon tea. He had a nose for meat. Any evening he smelt chicken or mutton, he sat under the dining table waiting for his share.

Billoo was full of zest for life. Every evening his friends from the neighbouring bungalows assembled in my garden, waging mock battles. At times Billoo's mother also joined them. But Billoo proved to be a poor watchdog. When rhesus monkeys invaded my garden, he barked at them from a safe distance. When I egged him on, he made a brave show of attacking them but as soon as a big one turned to fight him, he ran back for protection. Now when monkeys come, he pretends not to see them. As for strangers, all he does is to bark to tell me: 'You have visitors.' As soon as they shake my hand, he wags his tail in welcome.

This time when I alighted from my car, Billoo was at the doorstep waiting for me. He licked my hands, jumped up on my legs and made me feel welcome. The third day, when Billoo was out for a morning stroll on the Upper Mall, he ran into a car. He howled in pain as he lay on the road. Prem's sister-in-law, Bhagwanti, and her son ran up to see what had happened. The car driver was good enough to take all of them to the vet. Mercifully, he had broken no bones.

He was brought home. He could not stand up and wailed in pain. It seemed as if the lights of Raj Villa had been switched off. For a day Billoo lay on the floor whining. The next day, he tried to drag himself down to the hill where his mother lived. He did not get far and howled for help. Bhagwanti took him in her arms and brought him back. His mother had heard him cry. She came trotting up to see him. Now she comes every morning and evening to be with her son. Billoo is on the mend. He is still unable to walk properly but manages to wobble up to my bedroom window and make his presence felt. It won't be long before he is able to join me for breakfast, tea and supper. The lights of Raj Villa have been switched on again.

My housekeeper in Kasauli kept two dogs to keep uninvited visitors and monkeys at bay, Neelo and Joojoo. Neither could claim any pedigree and both had been picked out of litters of bitches living in the vicinity. Both were ill-tempered but their barks were stronger than their bites. Their ill-temper was more in evidence when I happened to be in Kasauli.

As is common with most dogs, they sense who is the master of the house, and attach themselves to him rather than to those who feed them. No sooner had I arrived than the two would vie with each other to claim closeness to me. Neelo being the younger and the tougher of the two would sit by my chair and snarl at Joojoo if he came anywhere near me. But Joojoo found ways to get around his rival. Neelo did not like to go for a stroll in the evening and would wait for me at the gate. I did not like Joojoo coming with me because he was prone to pick up quarrels with any dog we met during our walks. While going through the small stretch of the bazaar, Joojoo would fight with half-a-dozen dogs belonging to shopkeepers. However, over the years, I got used to the temperaments of the two dogs and stopped fussing over them.

This went on for fourteen years. Both Neelo and Joojoo aged but not very gracefully. White hair sprouted round their mouths, they became slower in their movements. I noticed the signs of ageing in the two dogs but refused to admit to myself that I, too, had aged and was now reluctant to step out of the house. When I last came to Kasauli in June, Neeloo was missing. My servant told me that the dog catchers employed by the cantonment board had fed him poison because he wore no collar. Joojoo, who had spent his lifetime quarrelling with Neeloo, looked older than ever before. His skin sagged over his bones, his genitals hung like a dilapidated sack under his belly, his legs trembled as he walked and his eyes looked bleary and unseeing. He would join me at tea time to beg for a biscuit or two because he could not chew anything harder.

One morning he came and sat by my side while I was having my morning tea. When I got up, he stood up on his trembling legs and looked pleadingly at me. I spoke to him gently: 'Joojoo *tu buddha ho gaya. Joojoo main bhi buddha ho gayaa.*' (Joojoo, you have grown old, so have I.) He looked at me with uncomprehending eyes and slowly went away. An hour later one of the boys living in the house came and told me: 'Joojoo *mar gaya.*' (Joojoo is dead.) I saw him lying by the club house. The cantonment board took his body away in a cart. So ended our fifteen-year-long friendship.

My constant companions, ever since I have been coming to Kasauli, are a family of spiders. They live apart in three bathrooms. I have no phobia of spiders. So I never disturb them. But I am curious to know why they stay in dark, smelly bathrooms and what they live on. They do not spin webs to catch flies or other insects; in any case there aren't any to catch. They hardly ever move from their chosen spots on the wall; and when they do, they only scamper along to some place where they cannot be seen. However, one evening I spotted one along the seat of my WC. I didn't want to chance being bitten on my bum: some spiders are known to be venomous. I brushed it aside with a newspaper before I lowered my bare bottom on the seat.

My curiosity was aroused. Back in my study, I consulted my book on insects. Lo and behold, it said spiders are not insects at all but only insect-like. Insects have three parts—head, thorax and abdomen; spiders have only two—four pairs of legs and no antennae. 'Okay,' I said to them, 'you are no miserable insects, but belong to the species arachnida, but what on earth do you live on? Where and how do you breed? Do you have predators that live off you?' One day I hope to solve the mystery of the webless spider and the vagaries of the monsoon. I must also find out why Kasauli has no fireflies (jugnu) but lots of glow-worms.

After two days of absolute solitude with no one to talk to besides the caretaker's mongrel, I begin to miss human voices and welcomed a visitor or two. I had two in succession, neither of whom I had seen before. I was lucky both times. The first was Nagina Singh of the *Indian Express,* Chandigarh edition. A comely, elegantly dressed young lass with a diamond sparkling in her nose pin. And all of nineteen. A no-nonsense young lady who came armed with a photographer. It was a business-like interview about the changes I had seen in Kasauli over the eighty years I have been coming here. The interview over, she shut her notebook and departed. The other was Baljit Virk, a teacher at Pinegrove School not far from Kasauli. I expected a middle-aged, blue-stockinged, bespectacled person with a schoolmarmish manner. In walked a statuesque beauty wreathed in smiles. She was an ex-air hostess, tired of seeing the world and being a glorified waitress. She decided to stay grounded and teach English (she had an MA in literature) and sociology. She wanted me to see the manuscript of the second novel she had written. 'Just read a page or two and tell me if it is any good.' I kept the manuscript: 'I will read all of it. Give me a week and then collect it.' I did not want to miss the opportunity of another tête-á-tête with the air hostess turned pedagogue. I was surprised with the theme of her novel, *Jockstrapped.* It was based on a young dipsomaniac who drinks at all hours, gets into scraps, smashes cars, has affairs with women and does not have to work for a living. I could not understand why Baljit chose to write about a good-for-nothing, foul-mouthed character, when she herself is a strait-laced teetotaller of the type in whose mouth butter would not melt. I'll find out the truth on her next visit.

At tea time, a strapping sardar and his comely sardarni joined me. 'How did you come by a name like Likhari?' I asked him. 'One of my ancestors was a master calligrapher who wrote with his nail. So we came to be known by that name,' he replied. His wife said, 'He also has a beautiful handwriting. I preserve his letters.'

'They must be love letters,' I suggested. 'Yes,' she replied with a blush. 'From when he was courting me.'

I asked them another question that Ghalib might well have asked visitors calling on him. 'Are you drinking people?' Both nodded their heads indicating yes.

Among the visitors who descended on me in my hide-out in Kasauli was Rajni Walia who came all the way from Simla to spend a couple of hours with me. Rajni was colourful in every sense of the word. She was decked up like a filmstar ready to face the cameras: heavily made-up, a dupatta with the colours of the rainbow and a paisley-shaped bindi more colourful than any I had seen. She carried a handbag studded with stones and marbles of many hues.

'Where on earth did you get that?' I asked.

'Baghdad,' she replied. 'My dad was an adviser to the Iraqi government for some years, I spent quite some time with him and did a lot of shopping.'

'And what do you do?' I questioned her.

'I am the associate professor of English literature at the government college, Simla,' she replied.

'Why Simla? Why not Chandigarh or Delhi?'

'My husband is in the Himachal Pradesh forest services. Simla is his base.'

'Can you tell me the name of the tree under which we are sitting?' I asked her because I was still uncertain of its identity.

'Toon.'

'And that big one facing us?' I saw a lot of langurs on it eating its leaves.

She took one glance and replied, 'Himachalis call it Khirik. My husband will give you its Latin name. I have picked up information about trees because I often go out with him on tours into the hinterland.'

'Where else have you been?'

'Just about everywhere,' she replied and fished out a book from her handbag. 'I did this in Australia. It was written under the guidance of David Parker, professor of English at the Australian National University, Canberra.'

Rajni Walia has written the book *Women and Self: Fiction of Jean Rhys, Barbara Pym & Anita Brookner.* I had not read anything by these ladies; nor, I suspect, have many Indians. The one thing that they share (according to Rajni) is their disappointment in love and marriage: something most women in love, married or single, experience in their lives.

Rajni has an MA, an MPhil and a PhD from Punjab University, and is a first class first throughout. She is currently writing about contemporary Indo-American women's fiction. Appearances are deceptive. This lady, whom I took as a light-weight because of the care she had taken in decking up, is quite a scholar. Long after she left, the fragrance of the perfume she wore lingered in the pine-scented air of my little garden.

For reasons unknown to me, many of the younger generation look upon me as a man-eating ogre, a cannibal sardarji. They come to see me in droves but keep at a safe distance as they do when seeing a tiger in a zoo. It takes me quite a while to convince them that I will not bite them and am as harmless as a teddy bear. Then they relax and say what they want to in rapid machine gun fire speed till they have run out of breath. One such couple who paid me a visit in Kasauli will stay in my mind a long time.

I was sitting in the garden under the shade of the massive toon tree, reading the morning papers. I heard the sound of footsteps at some distance from me. I looked up. It was a couple, a strapping young sardar in his fifties and a buxom, cuddlesome lass in her thirties. 'Can we disturb you for a moment?' asked the man. 'Come,' I replied, 'I am only whiling away my time doing a crossword puzzle.' They approached me gingerly, took their seats and introduced themselves: 'I am Major Joginder Singh Aulakh, the security officer of Punjabi University, Patiala,' said he. 'And I am his wife, Ravinder Pal Kaur Bajwa,' she said. Then began a rapid fire of questions from him interspersed with him taking my snapshots with a camera. All I was able to gather in the interludes allowed to me was that the Major had fought in two wars against Pakistan and was proud of his record. He had also taken part in

Operation Bluestar under the command of Generals Sunderji and Brar, was witness to the destruction of the Akal Takht and had seen the bodies of Bhindranwale and General Shabeg Singh. He did not want to talk or even think about it. The episode had left deep scars on his psyche. He was an unhappy widower till he ran into Ravi Bajwa, equally unhappy because of her broken marriage and her two children in the custody of their father. They had a whirlwind romance: met one day, and got married the next, ignoring the twenty years' difference in their ages. They looked happy. I asked them to join me for a drink the next evening before they returned to Patiala.

They were much more relaxed the next day. Though the question-and-answer session was resumed, it was not as hectic as the day before. Ravi gave me a shawl to put over my knees and proceeded to scribble something on a greeting card her husband had given me. After they left, I read what she had written in Gurmukhi: a poem entitled 'China Dupatta' (white headcover). A rough translation would read as follows:

I am not a widow
Nor living in matrimonial bliss;
Nevertheless I drape myself in spotless white
White is a combination of many colours in display
White also combines other colours
As well as colours that lead one astray,
White is like milk
White the colour of purity
Bright as sunshine
And quiet as silence.
(Many things colourful white can hide)
I wear white because now I am a bride.

A welcome addition to Kasauli's landscape are refugees from Tibet. There are only about a dozen families who have opened up small kiosks made of gunny sacks, tarpaulin and wooden planks along the most frequented stretch of road extending from Jakki

Mull's building housing the main provision store, run by Guptaji, a tailor and photographer, to Kalyan Hotel with its statue of a black cocker spaniel and a liquor vend.

They sell woollen goods like sweaters, scarves and gloves. Tibetan refugees, wherever they are, manage to live amicably with the locals. They are courteous, ever-smiling and law-abiding. In the very short season extending from April till the end of October, they manage to sell enough to make both ends meet. Then they go down to the industrial township of Parvanoo for the winter. The cantonment executive board used to charge them Rs 10 per month per stall. The rental rates were raised to Rs 70 per month. They paid that as well as other taxes.

The board allowed vegetable and fruit sellers to set up stalls as well. The board has now served them notices to shut shop so that it can build permanent shops. There is nothing wrong with that provided those hapless victims of persecution are assured that they will get the first option to resume their trade where they were and the kiosks not auctioned to the highest bidders.

There is a lot of pressure from local shopkeepers who have a lot more money to take over the site. This would be unethical and unfair. The Tibetan refugees are our guests till as long as they can return to their homeland. And Kasauli will not be the same without their winsome smiles.

As often in the past, on most days that I was in Kasauli, it rained intermittently every day and night. But the morning I left, the sky was an azure blue and the hills looked rain-washed and bright green. I had to wear my sweater, dressing gown and a shawl against the cold. Half an hour down the hill, it became warm enough to shed the woollen garments.

An hour later we were caught in traffic jams at Parvanoo, Kalka and Pinjore. For many years I have been hearing of plans to build a bypass which would skirt around these growing towns but so far even blueprints have not been prepared. The chief ministers of the states concerned are taken up with more important matters like staying in power. By the time I got off at the Kalka railway station, I was sweating and trying to cool off under the hot breeze churned downwards by ceiling fans.

I had an uneasy feeling that I was being given a final farewell. In Kasauli, munshi Mohan Lal, our local millionaire who comes to me at least once every few weeks for my kadam bosi (feet kissing), came twice—the second time to invite me to a reception for his son-in-law who had been elevated to the rank of a brigadier in Lucknow.

At Kalka station there was quite a turn out of celebrities to shake hands with me: A.S. Deepak, Poonam (the editor of *Preet Lari)* and her husband, Gaur, and the pretty Nagina. Cold drinks were served all around.

I was escorted to my seat on the Shatabdi Express where Kaushik, conductor-cum-man of letters, took charge of me. They may have wanted to bid me a final farewell, but I had no intention of allowing them to do so. Come next spring, I will be back in the Shivaliks.

THE ROMANCE OF NEW DELHI

Once upon a time there was a boy who dreamed of great buildings. He made friends with a blind man whose ambition in life was to design a church. One evening the blind man told his young friend of his concept of the perfect cathedral. The boy got out his sketch-book and began to draw according to the specifications dictated by the blind man. The blind man's wife came in while this was going on. She put her finger to her forehead to indicate that her husband had a screw loose and should not be taken seriously. Then she went over to the boy. She was amazed to see the sketch of a magnificent cathedral.

We do not know who the blind man was, but the young boy who drew the picture of the cathedral from dictation rose to be the greatest architect of his time, Edwin Landseer Lutyens, the builder of New Delhi.

Lutyens was forty-two when he was called upon to design the city. His wife, Lady Emily, was the daughter of Lord Lytton. This aristocratic connection had in no small measure helped Lutyens in his professional career. It also helped him in securing the assignment of building New Delhi. But above all it was the man's innate genius and confidence that he was the master of his destiny that paved the way to success. On a casket that he had designed as an engagement present for his fiancée, he had inscribed his motto: 'As faith wills, fate fulfils.'

On 12 December 1911, King George and Queen Mary laid the foundation stones of the new capital on a hurriedly chosen site north of the old city of Shahjahanabad.

There was an outcry against the project. European business houses established in Calcutta were vociferous in their protests. Lord Curzon decried it as wasteful expenditure; so later did Mahatma Gandhi when he came to India. Age-old superstition about Delhi being 'the graveyard of dynasties' was revived. Didn't seven cities lie in ruins about Shahjahanabad? The Viceroy, Lord Hardinge, was strong enough to brush aside these objections. A committee under the chairmanship of Captain Swinton of the London County Council was appointed to examine the site and the Royal Institute of British Architects was asked to suggest names of architects: to design the city.

The Royal Institute recommended Edwin Lutyens. The government not only accepted the nomination but also Lutyens's own recommendation of a colleague—Herbert Baker, a man he had befriended in his student days and who had also designed buildings in South Africa.

In the summer of 1912 Lutyens arrived in India with the Swinton Committee. The committee was unanimous in condemning the site selected earlier and in recommending another south of Delhi with its centre on a low-lying rocky escarpment known as Raisina Hill. There was plenty of barren land available at low cost. There was also the ridge to give the main buildings necessary elevation and provide building material. Lord Hardinge agreed with the suggestion. One night under the cover of darkness, the two foundation stones so solemnly laid by Their Majesties amid the pomp and splendour of princely India were uprooted and conveyed by bullock cart ten miles south to be planted in the wilderness of cactus, acacia and camelthorn.

Lord Hardinge was strongly of the opinion that the chief buildings—the viceregal lodge, the secretariats and the Parliament—should be in the traditional Indian style. He was reinforced in his opinion by the King who had been deeply impressed by Mughal architecture. Both Lutyens and Baker were taken round to see India's famous buildings—the Buddhist stupas of Sarnath and Sanchi, the temples in South India, the Taj Mahal at Agra, the palaces of Bikaner and Mandu. Lutyens was fascinated by some of the buildings he saw but totally rejected Indian style. 'Personally I do not believe there is any real Indian architecture or any great tradition,' he wrote. 'These are just spurts by various mushroom dynasties.' His colleague agreed that despite its charm Indian architecture did not have 'the constructive and geometric qualities necessary to embody the idea of law and order which has been produced out of chaos by British administration'. However, in the rough sketches they made concessions to their patron's views by adapting some features of old Indian buildings, e.g., the sun-breaker *(chajja)*, the latticed window *(jali)*, the umbrella dome *(chattri)*. In Baker's words, the blueprints had 'the eternal beauty of classical architecture with appropriate features of Indian architecture grafted on it'. It was left to Lutyens to get the Viceroy and the King to agree. Lutyens was gifted with a honeyed tongue and had no difficulty in winning over Lady Hardinge to his point of view. The Vicereine persuaded the Viceroy who readily approved of the first sketches. Lutyens and Baker worked them out in greater detail on their voyage back to England. Lutyens presented them to the King at a dinner at Buckingham Palace and had no difficulty in getting royal approval.

Lutyens and Baker divided their work evenly. Lutyens took over the plan of the general outlay of the city with two big buildings, the viceregal palace and the war memorial arch. Baker designed the two secretariats and the Parliament. There were other public buildings and bungalows for officers, clerks' quarters etc., which were also equally shared. Assisting them was a string of talented juniors—Greaves, Shoosmith, Walter George and Medd. The execution of the plans was entrusted to the Public Works Department (PWD) then under Sir Hugh Keeling, the chief engineer. Keeling was also assisted by men who rose to become chief engineers—Sir Alexander Rouse and later Sir Teja Singh Malik[1] who became the first Indian incumbent of the post.

The going was not easy. Lord Hardinge's initial enthusiasm waned as Lutyens' estimates for the projected city mounted. Then

Hardinge soured of India altogether. Terrorists tried to murder him—and almost succeeded. He became peevish and began to find fault with everything, particularly the magnitude of Lutyens's plans. Lutyens hit back. 'The Viceroy thinks only of what the place will be like in three years' time—300 is what I think of.' Lutyens turned his courtly charm on the Vicereine. For some time Lady Hardinge became the chief patroness of the nebulous city. Once when she pulled up Lutyens for wilfully disobeying her instructions, he promised to make amends by washing her feet with his tears and drying them with his hair . . . 'It is true I have very little hair,' he added, 'but then you have such very little feet.' He was readily forgiven.

Lady Hardinge's patronage did not last long. Her son was wounded at Flanders. The over-anxious mother lost her health and died before her son succumbed to his injuries. Preoccupation with the war and the absence of viceregal enthusiasm put the plans for the building of New Delhi in cold storage. Only Lutyens and Baker continued to dream of the city they would raise on Raisina Hill. Herbert Baker records how one evening he and two of his friends stood on the ridge looking down 'the deserted cities of dreary and disconsolate tombs' and wondering how the new city would rise. The sky was overcast and it rained intermittently. Suddenly, the clouds lifted and the sun broke through. 'A brilliant rainbow formed a perfect arch on what was destined to be a great vista, where Lutyens's memorial arch now stands. We acclaimed it as a good omen.'

As soon as blueprints for New Delhi were ready, trouble began—and they came in the proverbial battalions. Lutyens, and Baker fell out. The main dispute was on the question of the level of the viceregal palace vis-a-vis the secretariats. Lutyens wanted the ruler of the country to be housed at a higher level than his civil servants. Baker wanted the acropolis—as the secretariats and the palace buildings had come to be known—to be on the same level to conform to the prevailing notions of democracy. Baker won, Lutyens next desired the road between the secretariats to be at a sharp gradient so that the viceregal palace was distinctly visible from a distance. Baker disagreed. And Baker won again. Lutyens became peevish and fought the 'battle of the gradient' to the bitter end. The two architects were not on speaking terms for many years.

The supply of raw material presented another problem. The architects had planned to quarry the ridge to make an amphitheatre and use the stone so dug up for other buildings. The quartzite on the ridge was found unsuitable; the plan to build open air amphitheatre was abandoned. It was decided to quarry Vindhyan stone used by the Mughals: white and buff stone from Dholpur; red from Bharatpur; marble from Makrana, Alwar, Jaisalmer, Baroda and Ajmer. To get Badarpur sand and rubble, a fifteen-mile light railway (Imperial Delhi Railway) with five miles of siding was made. Transportation costs upset all estimates. Lutyens's rough guess of ten million came closest to the mark. But even Lutyens did not expect that instead of four to five years, New Delhi would take almost sixteen to look like a city.

Lutyens's puckish sense of humour sustained his enthusiasm in those trying times. Once the Duke of Connaught asked him why he had hung bells from tops of columns, Lutyens replied, 'Did you never hear, Sir, of the Mogul superstition that the ringing of bells proclaimed the end of a dynasty? That is why my bells are made of stone.' Another time at a press conference a journalist asked him, 'What is the place of women in architecture?' Lutyens replied, 'As the wives of architects.'

Slowly a new city began to rise on the escarpment. By 1922 most of the stone had been delivered on the site. The stone yard at New Delhi was the biggest in the world; 3,500 stone masons worked in its sheds. Brick-kilns went up in the suburbs. The quantity of brick consumed was astronomical—700 million. Lutyens took interest in every detail. The most important was the planting of trees. W.R. Mustoe of the horticultural department established a nursery with 500 varieties of trees at Safdarjung. Most of them were indigenous; some imported from Australia or East Africa.

As soon as the roads had been marked, trees were planted. They began to rise with the public buildings and bungalows. Lutyens chose wood for viceregal furnishings and instructed cabinet makers. Likewise carpets, pictures and murals were made under his instructions. And all this was done with the cooperation of a succession of viceroys and civil servants.

The last day of the year 1929 was set as the target date for the completion of the three major buildings on the acropolis and the India Gate (bearing names of 13,516 of the 70,000 Indians killed in the great war). For many months, work went on round the clock.

The formal inauguration of New Delhi took place in January 1931. The kind of tragedy that had soured Hardinge against India was repeated. An attempt was made by terrorists to blow up the train in which Lord Irwin was coming to New Delhi. Fortunately, the Viceroy was unhurt and unshaken. He went through the inaugural ceremonies with British sangfroid. Lutyens records his entry into the viceregal palace: 'The ceremony proceeded. Then H.E. went up the stairway to the great portico, where I and others were presented to him. At a given signal the doors were opened (there was no key, as there was no lock). They went into the House, and for the first time in 17 years the house was closed on me.'

Lutyens was also present at the first official banquet given by the Viceroy. He believed this was to be his last visit to the place. He later confessed to a friend, 'I had not the nerve to say good-bye to Irwin. I just walked out, and I kissed the wall of the House.'

This was however not Lutyens's last visit. He was consulted many times for inscriptions that should go on some of the monuments. Could Lutyens suggest what should be inscribed on the Jaipur Column? asked Lord Irwin. This was too good an opportunity for Lutyens to miss. 'No dogs must be allowed on the ramp,' he wrote back. While the Viceroy was still digesting the quip, Lutyens forwarded a more serious suggestion:

Endow your thought with faith
Your deed with courage
Your life with sacrifice
So all men may know
The greatness of India.

Lord Irwin distilled from this the conciser version used:

In thought faith; in word wisdom
In deed courage; in life service
So may India be great.

The inscription on the thrones was suggested by the talented painter-wife of the engineer, Shoosmith. It was taken from *Proverbs:* 'Wisdom resteth in the heart of him that hath understanding.'

Lutyens's last visit to the city he had designed was in the autumn of October 1938. Lord Linlithgow invited him to repair the damage done by the wilful Lady Willingdon: she had the furniture and fittings of the palace changed to her favourite colour, mauve, and she had many of Mustoe's trees in the Mughal gardens uprooted and replaced by rows of cypress. Lutyens was very upset and did the best he could to restore the old design. But he could do nothing to the stadium built in Willingdon's regime. The stadium blocked Purana Qila from the view.

Much has been said and written on the architecture of New Delhi. Most of the criticism has been levelled against Baker's buildings. Lutyens's work has been universally acclaimed. And of Lutyens's buildings, the Rashtrapati Bhavan of today is a veritable masterpiece. Captain Swinton, who had first seen the barren escarpment and then the completed building exulted, 'There has now risen before us in all its majesty, the Viceroy's House—one looks, one accepts, one marvels.'

As one mounts up the central vista between the two secretariats the first thing that catches the visitor's eye are slabs of yellow sandstone fixed in alcoves bearing the names of the architects, engineers and builders of the acropolis. On the builders' tablet five names are listed in the following order: Sobha Singh,[2] Dharam Singh Sethi, Basakha Singh, Seth Haroon, Nawab Ali. Some of the other major buildings of New Delhi also have names of the men who conceived them and contracted to build them placed on tablets. There is, however, no record of the 30,000 workers who came from all parts of northern India to hew rock, mix mortar and carry brick and cement to its ultimate destination.

The largest group of unskilled workers came from Rajasthan. It was the Bagris as they were known who more than any others built New Delhi. They were paid at the rate of eight annas for the man and six for the woman per day. (Wheat sold at four rupees for a maund.) They lived in coolie camps where drinking water was supplied, latrines provided and medical attention given free of charge. Throughout the decade-and-a-half of building operations, there was never a labour strike. The other group of unskilled workers were the Bandhanis from the Punjab. They hauled loads too heavy for the frailer Rajasthani. There were also a variety of skilled craftsmen in marble and stone. The sangtarash (stonecutters) came from Agra, Mirzapur and Bharatpur and were largely descendants of people who had built the monuments for the Mughals. Slabs of stone, gravel and sand were transported by the Imperial Delhi Railway from Bada Badarpur near Tughlakabad right into what is today Vijay Chowk. Where the All India Radio (AIR) is today were a series of enormous corrugated iron sheds where electrically propelled saws cut stone into proper dimensions. For many years the citizens of New Delhi were awakened by the deafening roar of the *ara-masheen*. The artistic designs on stone were executed under the direction of a Scottish master mason, Cairns.

The fortunes of the families who took on the contracts for building would provide a writer rich material for a novel. With rare exceptions these pioneer builders were men of little or no education, no experience of building and of modest means. By the time New Delhi was half-built, they had taught themselves a brand of pidgin English, learnt the tricks of the building trade and due to the sudden boost in value of land become millionaires. One expression of this windfall were palatial mansions of stone and marble; another was indulgence towards their progeny. Many scions of these *nouveau riche* families remained as unlettered as their sires. But they were infinitely better dressed and owned the latest models of cars. And while their fathers sweated out their guts on Raisina Hill, they patronized the muses of song and dance in the red-light area of Chawri Bazar.

The first to arrive on the scene were the Sindhis, Rai Bahadur Fateh Chand of Sukkar built the Old Secretariat near Metcalfe House. He was not able to participate in the building of New Delhi, but another Sindhi, Khan Bahadur Seth Haroon, shared in the building of Rashtrapati Bhavan. A third Sindhi, Lachman Das, took a lion's share in the building of Parliament House. He became legendary for his honesty. He did not use cheap material, he was punctilious in the payment of his labour. He did not even cheat on income tax. It was the tax which finally broke him. Lachman Das retired to Hardwar where he died in the saffron robes of a sadhu.

The Punjabis wrested the initiative from the Sindhis. The first in the field was Narain Singh, a peasant from Sangrur (Jind). He was responsible for the arrangements for the Royal Durbar. Most of the roads and officers' bungalows were built by him. He also prepared the foundations of Rashtrapati Bhavan. He was made a Rai Bahadur. Of his many sons, the most successful is Ranjit Singh who not only multiplied the family fortunes by adding sugar to his building interests but also acquired real estate (including the Imperial Hotel) and became a member of Parliament. Dharam Singh Sethi, at one time a canal overseer and then a minor partner in the building firm of Ram Singh Kabuli and Co., rose to be one of the wealthiest builders of his time. He had virtual monopoly of the supply of stone and marble. Dharam Singh lived in a palatial house on Jantar Mantar Road which is now the office of the All India Congress Committee (AICC). He left most of his millions to the Guru Nanak Vidya

Bhandar Trust which to this day maintains innumerable schools and gurdwaras. Dharam Singh died of cancer in distant Vienna. Basakha Singh of village Mucchal (district Amritsar) also started as an overseer. He built the entire North Block of the secretariat and many officers' bungalows. Besides these men there were two Punjabi Muslims, Khan Bahadur Akbar Ali of Jhelum who built the National Archives, and Nawab Ali of Rohtak who had a big share in the laying out of the Mughal Gardens.

Without question the first place in the list of New Delhi's many building contractors belongs to Sujan Singh (of Sujan Singh Park) and his illustrious son, Sobha Singh (whose younger brother Ujjal Singh later became Governor of the Punjab and then Madras). The family was by comparison with other contractors rich and experienced. Besides owning land in Shahpur district, they had extensive camel transportation business in western Punjab. They had built some of Punjab's railways and laid most of the Kalka–Simla line. The family came to Delhi before the First World War. After a few insignificant ventures in cotton and textile they went in for building in a big way. The lion's share of the building of New Delhi was taken by Sobha Singh. Amongst the many buildings that are his handiwork are the South Block, the Court of Rashtrapati Bhavan, Vijay Chowk, India Gate, Baroda House, All India Radio, the National Museum and innumerable bungalows, chummeries and clerks' quarters. Sobha Singh shared with Lutyens and Baker a vision of the shape of things to come. When Raisina was a jungle of barren rock and kikar trees he bought large tracts of land at open auction. Some plots in what is now Karol Bagh were acquired at two annas a square yard. The highest he paid was two rupees per square yard for land in today's Connaught Circus. Like his other colleagues, Sobha Singh taught himself English, became president of the New Delhi Municipal Committee and member of the Council of States. He was later knighted by the British Government.

The building contractors of New Delhi were a close-knit fraternity. Despite the differences of religion, language and background there was much coming and going between them. Very seldom did they quarrel—profits made quarrels unnecessary. When they first came to Raisina they lived in a row of shacks along what is now Old Mill Road (it was Herbert Baker's modesty which saved it from being named Baker Street). *En bloc* they moved to more expansive houses on Jantar Mantar Road where they spent the next two decades. As the city grew, they dispersed to different parts of the town. And one after the other, they were gathered to their forefathers.

NOTES

1   Khushwant Singh's father-in-law.
2   Khushwant Singh's father.

ON HAPPINESS

I've lived a reasonably contented life. I've often thought about what it is that makes people happy—what one has to do in order to achieve happiness.

First and foremost is good health. If you do not enjoy good health, you can never be happy. Any ailment, however trivial, will deduct something from your happiness.

Second, a healthy bank balance. It need not run into crores, but it should be enough to provide for comforts, and there should be something to spare for recreation—eating out, going to the movies, travel and holidays in the hills or by the sea. Shortage of money can be demoralizing. Living on credit or borrowing is demeaning and lowers one in one's own eyes.

Third, your own home. Rented places can never give you the comfort or security of a home that is yours for keeps. If it has garden space, all the better. Plant your own trees and flowers, see them grow and blossom, and cultivate a sense of kinship with them.

Fourth, an understanding companion, be it your spouse or a friend. If you have too many misunderstandings it robs you of your peace of mind. It is better to be divorced than to be quarrelling all the time.

Fifth, stop envying those who have done better than you in life—risen higher, made more money, or earned more fame. Envy can be very corroding; avoid comparing yourself with others.

Sixth, do not allow people to descend on you for gup-shup.

By the time you get rid of them, you will feel exhausted and poisoned by their gossip-mongering.

Seventh, cultivate a hobby or two that will fulfil you—gardening, reading, writing, painting, playing or listening to music. Going to clubs or parties to get free drinks, or to meet celebrities, is a criminal waste of time. It's important to concentrate on something that keeps you occupied. I have family members and friends who spend their entire day caring for stray dogs, giving them food and medicines. There are others who run mobile clinics, treating sick people and animals free of charge.

Eighth, every morning and evening devote fifteen minutes to introspection. In the mornings ten minutes should be spent in keeping the mind absolutely still, and five minutes listing the things you have to do that day. In the evenings, five minutes should be set aside to keep the mind still and ten to go over the tasks you had intended to do.

Ninth, don't lose your temper. Try not to be short-tempered, or vengeful. Even when a friend has been rude, just move on. To carry on and live reasonably well you don't have to be rich or be socially up there—good health and some financial stability are important, but there has to be that focus.

ON GREAT TALKERS

Great talkers are drawn to me like iron filings to a magnet. I am a patient listener but after an exposure or two, I do my best to dislodge them without hurting their feelings; most crashing bores are also well-meaning, good people. The other day, having nothing better to do, I made a list of those who came into my life and what made them go on talking by the hour.

The first man, on the top of my list, was Danial Latin. A great gentleman and a great bore—that is how I thought of Danial. Good people tend to be somewhat tiresome and Danial was goodness personified. He never lied, or ever said a hurtful thing about anyone. We became friends in Lahore. He was the son of Sir Alma Latifi, ICS, one of a distinguished clan comprising the Tyabjis, Futtehallys and Salim Ali. He was a graduate from Oxford University and a barrister-at-law. Everyone expected him to start practice at the high court and end up as a judge. Instead, he joined the Communist Party of India and was in the bad books of the police and the Criminal Investigation Department.

One night he was caught pasting subversive posters on the city walls. He spent a while in jail. After his release he shifted to the party headquarters. He lived on daal and roti. He was always lean and fragile; he became leaner and frailer; his long nose appeared longer—he had a vulpine profile. I persuaded him to move in with me. I had reason to regret my offer of hospitality.

Every evening, as I sat down to enjoy my whisky, Danial, who was a teetotaller, would start an endless monologue on Marxism,

275

class struggle, imperialism, et al. It ruined the taste of my good Scotch. One day when my cook and I were away, my mother turned up unexpectedly. She took Danial to be my servant, reprimanded him for sitting on the sofa and ordered him to get her luggage from the tonga and bring it up. He did so without a word. When my mother discovered who he was, she was most embarrassed. He often teased her about it.

One point in favour of endless talkers is they do not interrupt their monologue by asking questions: the listener need not listen provided he or she keeps his or her eyes fixed on the monologist. Once some friends dropped in after dinner. Both of them were a little drunk. I introduced them to Danial and decided to take a stroll. When I returned Danial was propounding the theory of class struggle: both my friends were fast asleep.

It was in my flat that he met Sarah Itiyarah, a Syrian Christian teacher in Kinnaird College for Women and as ardent a communist as he. They fell in love and got married. Danial would often smile but rarely laugh. Sarah did neither. They were admirably suited to each other. The only thing they had in common was a passion for Marxism. They had no children.

Danial and Sarah did not live together very much. So when she died, he was not shattered. He was not designed for domesticity. So I was surprised when I heard a few years ago that he had married again—this time to a princess of royal blood, a descendant of the great Moguls.

After Partition, the Latifis moved to Delhi. My father gave them a flat in the block next to mine. Dodging Danial became a game of wits: another thing endless talkers share in common is that they disdain making appointments. Once I told him that I was pestered by uninvited visitors. He got me a spy glass to put in my door so that I could see the visitor and if I did not want to be seen I need not open the door. Danial was the first victim of his own gift.

Danial did not change except that he began to drink in modest quantities. The last time I ran into him was at a French Embassy reception. It was a buffet dinner and guests had to line up for their drinks and food. The French make their guests as uncomfortable as they can so that they do not overstay their welcome. No chairs or tables were provided so you had to keep standing while you ate and drank. I ran into Danial holding a plateful of food in one hand and a glass of red wine in the other. The crowd of guests jostled us for attention. I greeted Danial and remarked how nice it was to see him drinking wine. That was enough for him to launch on a long explanation of there being nothing in the Koran or the Hadith declaring alcohol to be haraam for a Muslim. We were interrupted many times but Danial kept going till it was time to depart.

Another great talker I got to know was General Nathu Singh. He was a tall strapping soldier, proud of his aristocratic Rajput lineage and his martial exploits. He used to often stay with my parents, and after they died, with my elder brother. When they were out, the old General would drop in on me (unannounced) and keep me in thrall like the ancient mariner with the wedding guest. I protested to my sister-in-law. 'We've inherited him from your parents, so you must be patient and polite with him,' she admonished me. But she also warned me of his arrival in Delhi, 'General Sahib will be staying with us all next week. Don't complain I didn't tell you well ahead of time.' I had to tell my servants to tell anyone who came that I was not at home. Now that General Nathu Singh is no longer with us, I feel ashamed of myself because despite him being long-winded, I liked him.

I could not say that for Ranbir Singh, once in our foreign service. After retiring he settled abroad with his foreign wife. But every winter he came to Delhi and made it a point to call on his old acquaintances (unannounced). I was not an old acquaintance but was acceptable to him as I was a Sikh. This was strange as Ranbir was a Christian descended from the branch of the Kapurthala family which had converted to Christianity. (Rajkumari Amrit Kaur was his aunt.) Ranbir was proud of his Sikh ancestry, notably Jassa Singh Ahluwalia, the founder of the house of Kapurthala. Winter after winter, he would regale me with exploits of the Ahluwalia Misl and the feats of valour his ancestor, Jassa Singh, had performed. He would flex his biceps to convince me that he had inherited his bulging muscles from his forefathers. Like others of his ilk, he never bothered to find out whether I was free to receive him. After having my morning schedule upset many times, I put my foot down and told my servant to tell him that he should ring up before coming. He was outraged. I heard him shout at my servant to tell his master that he would never see me again. Thank god!

It was different with Nazar Hayat Tiwana. He is the eldest son of Sir Khizr Hayat Tiwana, the chief minister of Punjab before its partition and one of the biggest landowners of his time. The Tiwanas' estate included Hadali, the village in which I was born. I had great respect and affection for them. Nazar fell out with his father, married a Hindu girl and migrated to the United States. He got a job as an assistant librarian at Chicago University. Every winter he came to India and Pakistan. Since his father was long dead, he revived his affection for his Tiwana ancestors. He had his father's biography written; he set up an organization to promote Indo-Pakistan amity. He was, and is, a very lovable character. Also, an endless talker. Once he got started you never knew when he would run out of breath. He sensed I had begun to avoid him. The last time he came to see me, he was his old self, going on and on till my head was dizzy with his words. He paused for a second or two before he delivered the punch line. 'You know what my wife says? She says I lose friends because I talk too much.' I did not contradict him.

One man who loves the sound of his own voice is Joginder Singh, the retired head of the CBI. One evening I was in Lodi Gardens sitting on a ledge below the Bara Gumbad mosque. It is my favourite spot to take a short rest between my perambulations because I tire easily. It has become my chosen resting place for two reasons: the dome of the Bara Gumbad is the most sensuously perfect of all domes I have ever seen; and from where I sit I can see people striding along the paved footpath without them noticing me. I can watch the trees, birds and clouds without being disturbed. However, one evening I saw a family of three break away from the stream of walkers and head across the lawn towards me. As they got closer, I recognized Joginder Singh with a lady he introduced as his wife and a young girl who was his daughter. Joginder had a Walkman dangling on his side. He took out the earplugs to talk to me.

'I am listening to my recorded speeches,' he told me.

'Listening to your own voice?' I remarked, dumfounded.

His wife, who heads the publication division, came to his rescue. 'Yes, they are full of wisdom. He reads lots of books, gets the best out of them and puts them in his speeches. You should listen to them sometime.'

I did not rise to the bait. My lady companion diverted the dialogue to another topic. 'Are you writing another book?' she asked him.

'Yes,' replied Joginder Singh in a triumphant voice. 'Bofors! You'll see, I will reveal everything about it.' Joginder Singh was evidently very pleased with himself.

On my way back home, I recalled another man who was in love with the sound of his own voice. This was the late A.S. Bokhari, who was a professor of English at Government College, Lahore. He was a great wit; his *Patras kay Mazaameen,* a collection of humorous articles, is still widely read and acclaimed in Urdu circles. He was also an excellent after-dinner speaker and was applauded wherever he spoke. He became the director general of All India Radio, then of Radio Pakistan before he joined the UN as the head of the department of mass communications.

Professor Bokhari died in New York. Though he had a family, he lived alone in a spacious apartment attended to by an elderly female housekeeper and cook. My friend, Shafqat Mahmood, a retired Pakistani diplomat, who also lived in New York and visited Bokhari regularly, was informed. He immediately went to Bokhari's apartment and as instructed by the late professor's family in Lahore proceeded to make an inventory of his belongings.

When he had finished with the main rooms, the housekeeper told him about the attic where she said the professor spent his evenings and did not allow even her to enter. Shafqat went into the attic. He was surprised with what he saw. There was a hi-fi system; the shelves were lined with tapes of the professor's speeches. He spent most of his evenings in the attic sipping his Scotch and listening to his own voice. It was a kind of vocal narcissism.

The champion of all talkers whom I had to suffer was my security guard, Sita Ram. He was a Jat from eastern UP and a follower of Chaudhary Mahinder Singh. Sita Ram was into religion and was prone to deliver long pravachans on spiritual matters. Though a Jat, his fellow policemen addressed him as Shastriji. Once travelling with me and a film crew to Jaipur, he talked all the way from Delhi to the Pink City. It did not do him much good. While others who joined the police force at the same time became head constables and SHOs, Sita Ram remained a constable.

While on the subject of great endless talkers, it occurs to me that I have never encountered a female of the species. Long-windedness, like the prostate gland, is a masculine phenomenon.

BILLO

My granddaughter Naina found a kitten lying on the road. It had been bitten and mauled by a dog and left for dead. It was in a state of shock. She brought it home and nursed it for several weeks cradling it in her arms like a new-born baby. Its face had been cut and one eye damaged seemingly beyond repair.

Slowly the kitten recovered. Its wound healed and its damaged eye recovered its golden sparkle. But it is scared to go out of the flat because of the dogs. Since my granddaughter has to be at the university for several hours of the day, it attached itself to her maid-servant, Kamla.

During the day, it remains close to Kamla and when my granddaughter comes back, it shuttles between the two, purring as it snuggles in their laps. When neither of her two foster mothers is at home, it sits in my ailing wife's lap and purrs louder to give her comfort. It refuses to respond to my overtures.

When I put it in my lap, it stops purring and is impatient to get away. It hurts my pride, because I am convinced all animals like me as much as I like them. I didn't know whether it is female or male—a *billee* or a *billa,* so I have named it 'Billo'. Cats do not respond to names; neither does Billo.

Billo has grown into a full-sized cat and spends most of its time in my apartment without coming too close to me except when I am having my meals. Then, it tries to grab whatever it can lay its paws or mouth on and runs away. It looks for tilings under sofas and chairs, examines all my bookshelves and artefacts and is particularly intrigued by the TV set.

Early one morning, when without switching on the lights I switched on the TV, I noticed a long tail dangling in front of the screen. It was Billo seated on the top surveying the room. As the sound came on, it went round the set looking for its source. Then it stared at the pictures and pawed the screen to make sure if the flattened images were of real people.

For many days the TV set became its favourite perch. Then one day as I was watching Discovery Channel, its hackles went up as a tiger appeared on the screen. The tiger roared and Billo fled for its life. Since then, it has not been near the TV set.

Not all people like cats. Some have even gone to the extent of wanting to pass laws to prevent them from wandering about. The classic example is of the state of Illinois considering a bill to ban their prowling about.

When it came for approval to Adelai Stevenson, Governor of the state, he wrote a dissenting note: 'I cannot agree that it should be the declared public policy of Illinois that a cat visiting a neighbour's yard or crossing the highway is a public nuisance. It is in the nature of cats to do a certain amount of unescorted roaming—to escort a cat on a leash is against the nature of the owners.

'Moreover, cats perform useful service, particularly in the rural areas. The problem of the cat versus the bird or the rat is as old as time. If we attempt to resolve it by legislation, who knows but what we may be called upon to take sides as well as on the age-old problems of dog versus cat, bird versus bird, or even bird versus worm. In my opinion, the state of Illinois and its local government bodies already have enough to do without trying to control feline delinquency.'

There must be something in my character which Billo does not like. Perhaps like Maneka Gandhi and a few others of her kind, Billo has come to the conclusion that I am not a nice man to know.

TRANSLATIONS

SHIKWA

Ever since *Shikwa* (The Complaint) was first recited by Iqbal in 1909 at Lahore, it had remained one of his most controversial and most quoted works—not because of its poetic qualities, which are undisputed, but because of its message. Its theme is the poet's complaint against Allah for having been unfair to the Muslim community; and while lauding the achievements of Muslim warriors and the civilizing role of Islam, Iqbal laments the decline of Muslim power and the taunts that infidels fling at them. *Shikwa* is regarded as the first manifesto of the two-nation theory, which was later elaborated and became the basis for the foundation of a separate state for Muslims, Pakistan, by Mohammad Ali Jinnah.

The excerpt below contains the first sixteen stanzas of *Shikwa* (the complete poem has thirty-one stanzas), translated by Khushwant Singh in 1980.

Why must I forever lose, forever forgo profit that is my due,
Sunk in the gloom of evenings past, no plans for the morrow pursue.
Why must I all attentive be to the nightingale's lament,
Friend, am I as dumb as a flower? Must I remain silent?
My theme makes me bold, makes my tongue more eloquent.
Dust be in my mouth, against Allah I make complaint.

We won renown for submitting to Your will—and it is so;
We speak out now, we are compelled to repeat our tale of woe.
We are like the silent lute whose chords are full of voice;

When grief wells up to our lips, we speak; we have no choice.
Lord God! We are Your faithful servants, for a while with us bear,
It is in our nature to always praise You, a small plaint also hear.

That Your Presence was primal from the beginning of time is true;
The rose also adorned the garden but of its fragrance no one knew.
Justice is all we ask for: You are perfect, You are benevolent.
If there were no breeze, how could the rose have spread its scent?
We Your people were dispersed, no solace could we find,
Or, would Your Beloved's[1] following have gone out of its mind?

Before our time, a strange sight was the world You had made:
Some worshipped stone idols, others bowed to trees and prayed.
Accustomed to believing what they saw, the people's vision wasn't
free,
How then could anyone believe in a God he couldn't see?
Do you know of anyone, Lord, who then took Your Name? I ask.
It was the muscle in the Muslim's arms that did Your task.

Here on this earth were settled the Seljuqs and the Turanians,
The Chinese lived in China, in Iran lived the Sassanians.
The Greeks flourished in their allotted regions,
In this very world lived the Jews and Christians.
But who did draw their swords in Your Name and fight?
When things had gone wrong, who put them right?

Of all the brave warriors, there were none but only we.
Who fought Your battles on land and often on the sea.
Our calls to prayer rang out from the churches of European lands
And floated across Africa's scorching desert sands.
We ruled the world, but regal glories our eyes disdained.
Under the shades of glittering sabres Your creed we proclaimed.

All we lived for was to battle; we bore the troubles that came,
And laid down our lives for the glory of Your Name.
We never used our strength to conquer or extend domain,
Would we have played with our lives for nothing but worldly gain?
If our people had run after earth's goods and gold,
Need they have smashed idols, and not idols sold?

Once in the fray, firm we stood our ground, never did we yield,
The most lion-hearted of our foes reeled back and fled the field.
Those who rose against You, against them we turned our ire,
What cared we for their sabres? We fought against cannon fire.
On every human heart the image of Your oneness we drew,
Beneath the dagger's point, we proclaimed Your message true.

You tell us who were they who pulled down the gates of Khyber?[2]
Who were they that reduced the city that was the pride of Caesar?
Fake gods that men had made, who did break and shatter?
Who routed infidel armies and destroyed them with bloody
slaughter?
Who put out and made cold the 'sacred' flame[3] in Iran?
Who retold the story of the one God, Yazdan?

Who were the people who asked only for You and no other?
And for You did fight battles and travails suffer?
Whose world-conquering swords spread the might over one and all?
Who stirred mankind with Allah-o-Akbar's clarion call?
Whose dread bent stone idols into fearful submission?
They fell on their faces confessing, 'God is One, the Only One!'

In the midst of raging battle if the time came to pray,
Hejazis turned to Mecca, kissed the earth and ceased from fray.
Sultan and slave in single file stood side by side,
Then no servant was nor master, nothing did them divide.
Between serf and lord, needy and rich, difference there was none.
When they appeared in Your court, they came as equals and one.

In this banquet hall of time and space, from dawn to dusk we
spent,
Filled with the wine of faith, like goblets round we went.
Over hills and plains we took Your message; this was our task.
Do you know of an occasion we failed You? is all we ask.
Over wastes and wildernesses of land and sea,
Into the Atlantic.Ocean[4] we galloped on our steed.

We blotted out the smear of falsehood from the pages of history,
We freed mankind from the chains of slavery.
The floors of Your Kaaba with our foreheads we swept.

The Koran You sent us we clasped to our breast.
Even so You accuse us of lack of faith on our part:
If we lacked faith, You did little to win our heart.

There are people of other faiths, some of them transgressors.
Some are humble; drunk with the spirit of arrogance are others.
Some are indolent, some ignorant, some endowed with brain,
Hundreds of others there are who even despair of Your Name.
Your blessings are showered on homes of unbelievers, strangers all.
Only on the poor Muslim, Your wrath like lightning falls.

In the temples of idolatry, the idols say, 'The Muslims are gone!'
They rejoice that the guardians of the Kaaba have withdrawn.
From the world's caravanserais singing camel-drivers have vanished;
The Koran tucked under their arms they have departed.
These infidels smirk and snigger at us, are You aware?
For the message of Your oneness, do You anymore care?

Our complaint is not that they are rich, that their coffers overflow;
They who have no manners and of polite speech nothing know.
What injustice! Here and now are houris and palaces to infidels
given;
While the poor Muslim is promised houris only after he goes to
heaven.
Neither favour nor kindness is shown towards us anymore;
Where is the affection You showed us in the days of yore?

NOTES

1. The Beloved refers to Prophet Mohammed.
2. Khyber was a stronghold of Jewish tribes near Medina and was captured by Hazrat Ali, the Prophet's cousin and son-in-law.
3. This refers to the sacred flame worshipped by the Zoroastrians of Persia.
4. *Behr-i-tulmat.* When Arab conquerors came to the westernmost shores of Africa which they considered the end of the earth, they are said to have exclaimed, 'Great God! Had there been land further we would have conquered it in Your name.'

Bara Mah

The practice of composing verses on the twelve months was once common amongst Indian poets. It gave them an opportunity to describe nature and human moods, and moralize at the same time. Several exist in the Punjabi language, of which Guru Nanak's is the most highly rated. It is believed to be amongst the last of the Guru's compositions.

CHET (MARCH–APRIL)
Chet basant bhala bhavar suhavde

It is the month of Chet
It is spring. All is seemly,
The beauteous bumble-bees
The woodlands in flower;[1]
But there is a sorrow in my soul
For away is the Lord my Master

If the husband comes not home, how can a wife
Find peace of mind?
Sorrows of separation waste away her body.

The koel calls in the mango grove,
Her notes are full of joy
But there is sorrow in my soul.

The bumble-bee hovers about the blossoming bough
(A messenger of life and hope)

But O Mother of mine, 'tis like death to me
For there is a sorrow in my soul.
How shall I banish sorrow and find blessed peace?
Sayeth Nanak: When the Lord her Master comes home to her
Then is spring seemly because she is fulfilled.

VAISAKH (April–May)
Vaisakh bhala sakhaves kare

Beauteous Vaisakh, when the bough adorns itself anew
The wife awaits the coming of her Lord
Her eyes fixed on the door.
'My love, who alone can help me cross
The turbulent waters of life,
Have compassion for me and come home,
Without thee I am as worthless as a shell.
Love, look thou upon me with favour
And let our eyes mingle
Then will I become priceless beyond compare.'

Nanak asks: 'Whither seekest thou the Lord?
Whom awaitest thou?
Thou hast not far to go, for the Lord
Is within thee, thou art His mansion.
If thy body and soul yearn for the Lord,
The Lord shall love thee
And Vaisakh will beautiful be.'

JETH (May–June)
Mah jeth bhala pritam kiu bisrai

Why forget the beloved Lord in the good month of Jeth?
The earth shimmers in the summer's heat
The wife makes obeisance and prays
Let me find favour in Thine eyes O Lord,
Thou art great and good
Truth manifest and unshakable,
Of attachments art Thou free.

And I, lowly, humble, helpless.
How shall I approach Thee?
How find the haven of peace?
In the month of Jeth, says Nanak,
She who knoweth the Lord
Becometh like the Lord.
She knoweth Him
By treading the path of virtue.

ASADH (JUNE–JULY)
Asadh bhala suraj gagan tapai

In Asadh the sun scorches.
Skies are hot
The earth burns like an oven
Waters give up their vapours.
It burns and scorches relentlessly
Thus the land fails not
To fulfil its destiny.

The sun's chariot passes the mountain tops;
Long shadows stretch across the land
And the cicada calls from the glades.
The beloved seeks the cool of the evening.
If the comfort she seeks be in falsehood,
There will be sorrow in store for her.
If it be in truth,
Hers will be a life of joy everlasting.

My life and its ending depend on the will of the Lord.
To Him says Nanak, I surrendered my soul.

SAVAN (JULY–AUGUST)
Savan saras mana ghan varsai rut ae

O my heart, rejoice! It's Savan
The season of nimbus clouds and rain,
My body and soul yearn for my Lord.

But my Lord is gone to foreign lands.
If He return not, I shall die pining for Him.

The lightning strikes terror in my heart.
I stand all alone in my courtyard,
In solitude and in sorrow.
O Mother of mine, I stand on the brink of death.
Without the Lord I have neither hunger nor sleep
I cannot suffer the clothes on my body.

Nanak says, she alone is the true wife
Who loses herself in the Lord.

BHADON (AUGUST–SEPTEMBER)
Bhadon bharam bhuli bhar joban pachtani

In the month of Bhadon
I lose myself in a maze of falsehood
I waste my wanton youth.
River and land are one endless expanse of water
For it is the monsoon, the season of merry-making.
It rains,
The nights are dark,
What comfort is it to the wife left alone?
Frogs croak
Peacocks scream
The papeeha² calls 'peeoh, peeoh'.
The fangs of serpents that crawl,
The stings of mosquitoes that fly
Are full of venom.
The seas have burst their bounds in the ecstasy
Of fulfilment.
Without the Lord I alone am bereft of joy,
Whither shall I go?

Says Nanak, ask the guru the way
He knoweth the path which leads to the Lord.

ASAN (September–October)
Asan au pira sadhan jhur mui

It's the month of Asan
O Master come to me
I waste and shall die.
If the Master wills,
I shall meet Him.
If He wills not,
In a deep well shall I be lost.

I strayed on to the paths of falsehood
And the Master forsook me.
Age hath greyed my locks
I have left many winters behind.
But the fires of hell still lie ahead.
Whither shall I turn?

The bough remaineth ever green
For the sap that moveth within day and night,
Night and day, reneweth life.
If the name of the Lord courseth in thy veins,
Life and hope will forever be green.
That which cooketh slowly cooketh best.

It is Asan, says *Nanak*,
It is trysting time, O Lord,
And we have waited long.

KATAK (October–November)
Katak kirat paiya jo prabh bhaia

In the month Katak
Will I get my due.
What pleases the Lord
Is all I merit.
The lamp of wisdom burneth steadily
If the oil that feeds it

Be reality.
If the oil that feeds the lamp
Be love,
The beloved will meet the Lord and be fulfilled.

Full of faults, she dies not
Nor gains release
It's death after virtuous life.
That doth the Lord please.

Those who are granted the worship of Thy name
Merge in Thee, for Thou art then
Their aim and end in life.

Nanak says: Lord, till Thou grant vision
And burst the bonds of superstition,
One watch of day will drag on like half a year.

MAGHAR (November–December)
Maghar mah bhata hari gun ank samave

The month of Maghar is bliss
For her who is lost in the Lord.
She singeth songs of joy and fulfilment.
Why not love the Lord who is eternal?

He who is eternal, wise, omniscient is also the master of destiny.
The world is agitated because it hath lost faith in Him.
She that hath knowledge and contemplates
Loses herself in Him.
She loveth the Lord, the Lord loveth her.

In song and dance and verse, let it be the name of Lord Rama
And sorrows will fly away.
Nanak says, only she is loved by her Lord
Who prayeth, not only with her lips
But worships Him with her soul.

POKH (December–January)
Pokh tukhar pade van trin raps sokhai

As in the month of Pokh
Winter's frost doth freeze
The sap in tree and bush, so does
The absence of the Lord
Kill the body and the mind.
O Lord, why earnest not Thou?

I praise through the guru's Word
Him that gives life to all the world,
His light shines in all life born
Of egg or womb or sweat or seed.
Merciful God and master! Thy vision grant
And grant me salvation.

Nanak says, only she mingles with Him
Who loves the Lord, the giver of life.

MAGH (January–February)
Magh punit bhai tirath antar ja nia

In the month of Magh
I made my ablution,
The Lord entered my being.
I made pilgrimage within myself and was purified.
I met Him.
He found me good
And let me lose myself in Him.

'Beloved! If Thou findest me fair
My pilgrimage is made,
My ablution done.
More than the sacred waters
Of Ganga, Yamuna and Triveni mingled at the
Sangam,
More than the seven seas.

All these and charity, alms-giving and prayer,
Are the knowledge of eternity that is the Lord.'

Nanak says, Magh is the essence of ambrosia
For him who hath worshipped the great giver of life.
Hath done more than bathe in the sixty and eight places of
pilgrimage.

PHALGUN (FEBRUARY–MARCH)
Phalgun man rahsi prem subha ea

In the month of Phalgun
She whose heart is full of love
Is ever in full bloom.
Day and night she is in spiritual exaltation
She is in bliss because she hath no love of self.

Only those that love Thee
Conquer love of self.
Be kind to me
And make my home Thy abode.
Many a lovely garment did I wear.
The Master willed not and
His palace doors were barred to me.
When He wanted me I went
With garlands and strings of jewels and raiments of finery.

O Nanak, a bride welcomed in the Master's mansion
Hath found her true Lord and Love.

NOTES

[1] In Chet the *Salvadora persica (pee loo)* is in blossom in the Punjab countryside.

[2] Common hawk-cuckoo *(Hierococcyx varius)* popularly known as the 'brain-fever' bird because of its call. To Indian ears, the same call sounds like *pee-kahan* (where is my husband?) or *papeeha*.

THE EXCHANGE OF LUNATICS

Translated from the Urdu by Saadat Hassan Manto

A couple of years or so after the partition of the subcontinent, the governments of Pakistan and India felt that just as they had exchanged their hardened criminals, they should exchange their lunatics. In other words, Muslims in the lunatic asylums of India should he sent across to Pakistan; and mad Hindus and Sikhs in Pakistani asylums be handed over to India.

Whether or not this was a sane decision, we will never know. But people in knowledgeable circles say that there were many conferences at the highest level between bureaucrats of the two countries before the final agreement was signed and a date fixed for the exchange.

The news of the impending exchange created a novel situation in the Lahore lunatic asylum. A Muslim patient who was a regular reader of the *Zamindar* was asked by a friend, 'Maulvi Sahib, what is this thing they call Pakistan?' After much thought he replied, 'It's a place in India where they manufacture razor blades.' A Sikh lunatic asked another, 'Sardarji, why are we being sent to India? We cannot speak their language.' The Sardarji smiled and replied, 'I know the lingo of the Hindustanis.' He illustrated his linguistic prowess by reciting a doggerel.

Hindustanis are full of shaitani
They strut about like bantam cocks.

One morning a mad Mussulman yelled the slogan 'Pakistan *Zindabad*' with such vigour that he slipped on the floor and knocked himself senseless.

Some inmates of the asylum were not really insane. They were murderers whose relatives had been able to have them certified and thus saved from the hangman's noose. These people had vague notions of why India had been divided and what was Pakistan. But even they knew very little of the complete truth. The papers were not very informative and the guards were so stupid that it was difficult to make any sense of what they said. All one could gather from their talk was that there was a man of the name of Mohammed Ali Jinnah who was also known as the *Qaid-i-Azam*. And that this Mohammed Ali Jinnah alias Qaid-i-Azam had made a separate country for the Mussulmans which he called Pakistan.

No one knew where this Pakistan was or how far it extended. This was the chief reason why inmates who were not totally insane were in a worse dilemma than those utterly mad: they did not know whether they were in India or Pakistan. If they were in India, where exactly was Pakistan? And if they were in Pakistan how was it that the very same place had till recently been known as India?

A poor Muslim inmate got so baffled with the talk about India and Pakistan, Pakistan and India, that he got madder than before. One day while he was sweeping the floor he was suddenly overcome by an insane impulse. He threw away his brush and clambered up a tree. And for two hours he orated from the branch of this tree on Indo-Pakistan problems. When the guards tried to get him down, he climbed up still higher. When they threatened him he replied, 'I do not wish to live either in India or Pakistan; I want to stay where I am, on top of this tree.'

After a while the fit of lunacy abated and the man was persuaded to come down. As soon as he was on the ground he began to embrace his Hindu and Sikh friends and shed bitter tears. He was overcome by the thought that they would leave him and go away to India.

Another Muslim inmate had a master of science degree in radio-engineering and considered himself a cut above the others. He used to spend his days strolling in a secluded corner of the garden. Suddenly a change came over him. He took off all his clothes and handed them over to the head constable. He resumed the peripatations without a stitch of clothing on his person.

And there was yet another lunatic, a fat Mussulman who had been a leader of the Muslim League in Chiniot. He was given to bathing fifteen to sixteen times during the day. He suddenly gave it up altogether.

The name of this fat Mussulman was Mohammed Ali. But one day he proclaimed from his cell that he was Mohammed Ali Jinnah. Not to be outdone, his cell-mate who was a Sikh proclaimed himself to be Master Tara Singh. The two began to abuse each other. They were declared 'dangerous' and put in separate cages.

There was a young Hindu lawyer from Lahore. He was said to have become unhinged when his lady-love jilted him. When he heard that Amritsar had gone to India, he was very depressed: his sweetheart lived in Amritsar. Although the girl had spurned his affection, he did not forget her even in his lunacy. He spent his time cursing all leaders, Hindu as well as Muslim, because they had split India into two, and made his beloved an Indian and him a Pakistani.

When the talk of exchanging lunatics was in the air, other inmates consoled the Hindu lawyer with the hope that he would soon be sent to India—the country where his sweetheart lived. But the lawyer refused to be reassured. He did not want to leave Lahore because he was convinced that he would not be able to set up legal practice in Amritsar.

There were a couple of Anglo-Indians in the European ward. They were very saddened to learn that the English had liberated India and returned home. They met secretly to deliberate on problems of their future status in the asylum: would the asylum continue to have a separate ward for Europeans? Would they be served breakfast as before? Would they be deprived of toast and be forced to eat chappaties?

Then there was a Sikh who had been in the asylum for fifteen years. And in the fifteen years he said little besides the following sentence: 'O, *pardi, good good di, anekas di, bedhyana di, moong di dal* of *di* lantern.'

The Sikh never slept either at night or in the day. The warders said that they had not known him to blink his eyes in fifteen years. He did not as much as lie down. Only on rare occasions he leant against the wall to rest. His legs were swollen down to the ankles.

Whenever there was talk of India and Pakistan, or the exchange of lunatics, this Sikh would become very attentive. If anyone invited him to express his views, he would answer with great solemnity, 'O *pardi, good good di, anekas di, bedhyana di, moong di dal* of *di* Pakistan government.'

Some time later he changed the end of his litany from 'of the Pakistan Government' to 'of the Toba Tek Singh government'.

He began to question his fellow-inmates whether the village of Toba Tek Singh was in India or Pakistan. No one knew the answer. Those who tried, got tied up in knots when explaining how Sialkot was at first in India and was now in Pakistan. How could one guarantee that a similar fate would not befall Lahore and from being Pakistani today it would not become Indian tomorrow? For that matter how could one be sure that the whole of India would not become a part of Pakistan? All said and done, who could put his hand on his heart and say with conviction that there was no danger of both India and Pakistan vanishing from the face of the globe one day!

The Sikh had lost most of his long hair. Since he seldom took a bath, the hair of the head had matted and joined with his beard. This gave the Sikh a very fierce look. But he was a harmless fellow. In the fifteen years he had been in the asylum, he had never been known to argue or quarrel with anyone. All that the older inmates knew about him was that he owned land in village Toba Tek Singh and was a prosperous farmer. When he lost his mind, his relatives had brought him to the asylum in iron fetters. Once in the month, some relatives came to Lahore to find out how he was faring. With the eruption of Indo-Pakistan troubles their visits had ceased.

The Sikh's name was Bishen Singh but everyone called him Toba Tek Singh. Bishen Singh had no concept of time—neither of days, nor weeks, nor of months. He had no idea how long he had been in the lunatic asylum. But when his relatives and friends came to see him, he knew that a month must have gone by. He would inform the head warder that 'Miss Interview' was due to visit him. He would wash himself with great care; he would soap his body and oil his long hair and beard before combing them. He would dress up before he went to meet his visitors. If they asked him any questions, he either remained silent or answered, '*O pardi, anekas di, bedhyana di, moong di dal* of *di* lantern.'

Bishen Singh had a daughter who had grown into a full-bosomed lass of fifteen. But he showed no recognition of his child. The girl wept bitterly whenever she met her father.

When talk of India and Pakistan came up, Bishen Singh began to question other lunatics about the location of Toba Tek Singh. No one could give him a satisfactory answer. His irritation mounted day by day. And now even 'Miss Interview' did not come to see him. There was a time when something had told him that his relatives were due. Now that inner voice had been silenced. And he was more anxious than ever to meet his relatives and find out whether Toba Tek Singh was in India or Pakistan. But no relatives came. Bishen Singh turned to other sources of information.

There was a lunatic in the asylum who believed he was God. Bishen Singh asked him whether Toba Tek Singh was in India or Pakistan. As was his wont 'God' adopted a grave mien and replied: 'We have not yet issued our orders on the subject.'

Bishen Singh got the same answer many times. He pleaded with 'God' to issue instructions so that the matter could be settled once and for all. His pleadings were in vain; 'God' had many pressing matters awaiting 'His' orders. Bishen Singh's patience ran out and one day he let 'God' have a bit of his mind 'O, pardi, good good di, anekas di, bedhyana di, moong di dal of Wahi-i-Guru Ji Ka Khalsa and Wahi-i-Guru di Fateh! Jo boley so nihal, Sat Sri Akal!'

This was meant to put 'God' in his place as God only of the Mussulmans. Surely if He had been God of the Sikhs, He would have heard the pleadings of a Sikh!

A few days before the day fixed for the exchange of lunatics, a Muslim from Toba Tek Singh came to visit Bishen Singh. This man had never been to the asylum before. When Bishen Singh saw him he turned away. The warders stopped him: 'He's come to see you; he's your friend, Fazal Din,' they said.

Bishen Singh gazed at Fazal Din and began to mumble. Fazal Din put his hand on Bishen Singh's shoulder. 'I have been intending to see you for the last many days but could never find the time. All your family have safely crossed over to India. I did the best I could for them. Your daughter, Roop Kaur . . .'

Fazal Din continued somewhat haltingly 'Yes . . . she too is well. She went along with the rest.'

Bishen Singh stood where he was without saying a word. Fazal Din started again. 'They asked me to keep in touch with you. I am told that you are to leave for India. Convey my salaams to brother Balbir Singh and to brother Wadhawa Singh . . . and also to sister Amrit Kaur . . . tell brother Balbir Singh that Fazal Din is well and happy. Both the grey buffaloes that they left behind have calved—one is a male, the other a female . . . the female died six days later. And if there is anything I can do for them, I am always willing. I have brought you a little sweet corn.'

Bishen Singh took the bag of sweet corn and handed it over to a warder. He asked Fazal Din, 'Where is Toba Tek Singh?'

Fazal Din looked somewhat puzzled and replied, 'Where could it be? It's in the same place where it always was.'

Bishen Singh asked again: 'In Pakistan or India?'

'No, not in India; it's in Pakistan,' replied Fazal Din. Bishen Singh turned away mumbling '*O pardi, good good di, anekas di, bedhyana di, moong di dal* of *di* Pakistan and Hindustan of *dur phittey moonh.*'

~

Arrangements for the exchange of lunatics were completed. Lists with names of lunatics of either side had been exchanged and information sent to the people concerned. The date was fixed.

It was a bitterly cold morning. Bus loads of Sikh and Hindu lunatics left the Lahore asylum under heavy police escort. At the border at Wagah, the superintendents of the two countries met and settled the details of the operation.

Getting lunatics out of the buses and handing over custody to officers of the other side proved to be a very difficult task. Some refused to come off the bus; those that came out were difficult to control: a few broke loose and had to be recaptured. Those that were naked had to be clothed. No sooner were the clothes put on them than they tore them off their bodies. Some came out with abuse, others began to sing at the top of their voices. Some squabbled; others cried or roared with laughter. They created such a racket that one could not hear a word. The female lunatics added to the noise. And all this in the bitterest of cold when people's teeth chattered like the scales of rattlesnakes.

Most of the lunatics resisted the exchange because they could not understand why they were being uprooted from one place and flung into another. Those of a gloomier disposition were yelling slogans 'Long Live Pakistan' or 'Death to Pakistan'. Some lost their tempers and were prevented from coming to blows in the very nick of time.

At last came the turn of Bishen Singh. The Indian officer began to enter his name in the register. Bishen Singh asked him, 'Where is Toba Tek Singh? In India or Pakistan?'

'In Pakistan.'

That was all that Bishen Singh wanted to know. He turned and ran back to Pakistan. Pakistani soldiers apprehended him and tried to push him back towards India. Bishen Singh refused to budge. 'Toba Tek Singh is on this side,' he cried, and began to yell at the top of his voice, 'O pardi, good good di, anekas di, bedhyana di, moong di of Toba Tek Singh and Pakistan.' They did their best to soothe him, to explain to him that Toba Tek Singh must have left for India; and that if any one of that name was found in Pakistan he would be dispatched to India at once. Bishen Singh refused to be persuaded. They tried to use force. Bishen Singh planted himself on the dividing line and dug his swollen feet into the ground with such firmness that no one could move him.

They let him be. He was soft in the head. There was no point using force; he would come round of his own—yes. They left him standing where he was and resumed the exchange of the other lunatics.

Shortly before sunrise, a weird cry rose from Bishen Singh's throat. The man who had spent all the nights and days of the last fifteen years standing on his feet, now sprawled on the ground face down. The barbed wire fence on one side marked the territory of India; another fence marked the territory of Pakistan. In the no-man's land between the two barbed wire fences lay the body of Bishen Singh of village Toba Tek Singh.

THE DEATH OF SHAIKH BURHANUDDIN

Translated from the Urdu by K.A. Abbas

My name is Shaikh Burhanuddin.

When violence and murder became the order of the day in Delhi and the blood of Muslims flowed in the streets, I cursed my fate for having a Sikh for a neighbour. Far from expecting him to come to my rescue in times of trouble, as a good neighbour should, I could not tell when he would thrust his kirpan into my belly. The truth is that till then I used to find the Sikhs somewhat laughable. But I also disliked them and was somewhat scared of them.

My hatred for the Sikhs began on the day when I first set my eyes on one. I could not have been more than six years old when I saw a Sikh sitting out in the sun combing his long hair. 'Look,' I yelled with revulsion, 'a woman with a long beard!' As I got older this dislike developed into hatred for the entire race.

It was a custom amongst old women of our household to heap all afflictions on our enemies. Thus for example if a child got pneumonia or broke its leg, they would say 'a long time ago a Sikh, (or an Englishman), got pneumonia'; or, 'a long time ago a Sikh, (or an Englishman), broke his leg'. When I was older I discovered that this referred to the year 1857 when the Sikh princes helped the feringhee (foreigner) to defeat the Hindus and Muslims in the War of Independence. I do not wish to propound a historical thesis but to explain the obsession, the suspicion and hatred which I bore towards the English and the Sikhs. I was more frightened of the English than of the Sikhs.

305

When I was ten years old, I happened to be travelling from Pelhi to Aligarh. I used to travel third class, or at the most in the intermediate class. That day I said to myself, 'Let me for once travel second class and see what it feels like.' I bought my ticket and I found an empty second class compartment. I jumped on the well-sprung seats; I went into the bathroom and leapt up to see my face in the mirror; I switched on all the fans. I played with the light switches. There were only a couple of minutes for the train to leave when four red-faced 'tommies' burst into the compartment, mouthing obscenities: everything was either 'bloody' or 'damn'. I had one look at them and my desire to travel second class vanished.

I picked up my suitcase and ran out. I only stopped for breath when I got into a third class compartment crammed with natives. But as luck would have it it was full of Sikhs—their beards hanging down to their navels and dressed in nothing more than their underpants. I could not escape from them; but I kept my distance.

Although I feared the white man more than the Sikhs, I felt that he was more civilized: he wore the same kind of clothes as I. I also wanted to be able to say 'damn', 'bloody fool'—the way he did. And like him I wanted to belong to the ruling class. The Englishman ate his food with forks and knives, I also wanted to learn to eat with forks and knives so that natives would look upon me as being as advanced and as civilized as the white man.

My Sikh-phobia was of a different kind. I had contempt for the Sikh. I was amazed at the stupidity of men who imitated women and grew their hair long. I must confess I did not like my hair cut too short; despite my father's instructions to the contrary, I did not allow the barber to clip off more than a little when I went to him on Fridays. I grew a mop of hair so that when I played hockey or football it would blow about in the breeze like those of English sportsmen. My father often asked me, 'Why do you let your hair grow like a woman's?' My father had primitive ideas and I took no notice of his views. If he had had his way he would have had all heads razored bald, and stuck artificial beards on people's chins. That reminds me that the second reason for hating the Sikhs was their beards which made them look like savages.

There are beards and beards. There was my father's beard, neatly trimmed in the French style; or my uncle's which went into a sharp point under his chin. But what could you do with a beard to which no scissor was ever applied and which was allowed to grow like a wild bush—fed with a compost of oil, curd and goodness knows what! And, after it had grown a few feet, combed like hair on a woman's head! My grandfather also had a very long beard which he combed . . . but then my grandfather was my grandfather and a Sikh is just a Sikh.

After I had passed my matriculation examination I was sent to the Muslim University at Aligarh. We boys who came from Delhi, or the United Provinces, looked down upon boys from the Punjab; they were crude rustics who did not know how to converse, how to behave at the table, or to deport themselves in polite company. All they could do was to drink large tumblers of buttermilk. Delicacies such as vermicelli with essence of *kewra* sprinkled on it, or the aroma of Lipton's tea was alien to them. Their language was unsophisticated in the extreme, whenever they spoke to each other it seemed as if they were quarrelling. It was full of '*ussi, tussi,* saadey, twhaadey'—Heaven forbid! I kept my distance from the Punjabis.

But the warden of our hostel (god forgive him), gave me a Punjabi as a room-mate. When I realized that there was no escape, I decided to make the best of a bad bargain and be civil to the chap. After a few days we became quite friendly. This man was called Ghulam Rasul and he was from Rawalpindi. He was full of amusing anecdotes and was a good companion.

You might well ask how Ghulam Rasul gate-crashed into a story about the Sikhs. The fact of the matter is that Ghulam Rasul's anecdotes were usually about the Sikhs. It is through these anecdotes that I got to know the racial characteristics, the habits and customs of this strange community. According to Ghulam Rasul the chief characteristics of the Sikhs were the following: All Sikhs were stupid and idiotic. At noon-time they lost their senses altogether. There were many instances to prove this. For example, one day at 12 noon, a Sikh was cycling along Hall Bazaar in Amritsar when a constable, also a Sikh, stopped him and demanded, 'Where is your light?' The cyclist replied nervously, 'Jemadar Sahib, I lit it when I left my home; it must have gone out just now.' The constable threatened to run him in. A passer-by, yet another Sikh with a long white beard, intervened: 'Brothers, there is no point in quarrelling over little things. If the light has gone out it can be lit again.'

Ghulam Rasul knew hundreds of anecdotes of this kind. When he told them in his Punjabi accent his audience was left helpless with laughter. One really enjoyed them best in Punjabi because the strange and incomprehensible behaviour of the uncouth Sikh was best described in his rustic lingo.

The Sikhs were not only stupid but incredibly filthy as well. Ghulam Rasul, who had known hundreds of them, told us how they never shaved their heads. And whereas we Muslims washed our hair thoroughly at least every Friday, the Sikhs who made a public exhibition of bathing in their underpamts, poured all kinds of filth like curd into their hair. I rub lime-juice and glycerine in my scalp. Although the glycerine is white and thick like curd, it is an altogether different thing—made by a well-known firm of perfumers of Europe. My glycerine came in a lovely bottle whereas the Sikhs' curd came from the shop of a dirty sweetmeat-seller.

I would not have concerned myself with the manner of living of these people except that they were so haughty and ill-bred as to consider themselves as good warriors as the Muslims. It is known over the world that one Muslim can get the better of ten Hindus or Sikhs. But these Sikhs would not accept the superiority of the Muslim and would strut about like bantam cocks, twirling their moustaches and stroking their beards. Ghulam Rasul used to say that one day we Muslims would teach the Sikhs a lesson that they would never forget.

Years went by.

I left college. I ceased to be a student and became a clerk; then a head clerk. I left Aligarh and came to live in New Delhi. I was allotted government quarters. I got married. I had children.

The quarters next to mine were occupied by a Sikh who had been displaced from Rawalpindi. Despite the passage of years, I remembered what Ghulam Rasul had told me. As Ghulam Rasul had prophesied, the Sikhs had been taught a bitter lesson in humility, at least in the district of Rawalpindi. The Muslims had virtually wiped them out. The Sikhs boasted that they were great heroes; they flaunted their long kirpans. But they could not withstand the brave Muslims. The Sikhs' beards were forcibly shaved. They were circumcized. They were converted to Islam. The Hindu press, as was its custom, vilified the Muslims. It reported that the Muslims had murdered Sikh women and children. This was wholly contrary to Islamic tradition. No Muslim warrior was ever known to raise his hand against a woman or a child. The pictures of the corpses of women and children published in Hindu newspapers were obviously faked. I wouldn't have put it beyond the Sikhs to murder their own women and children in order to vilify the Muslims.

The Muslims were also accused of abducting Hindu and Sikh women. The truth of the matter is that such was the impact of the heroism of Muslims on the minds of Hindu and Sikh girls that they fell in love with young Muslims and insisted on going with them. These noble-minded young men had no option but to give them shelter and thus bring them to the true path of Islam. The bubble of Sikh bravery was burst. It did not matter how their leaders threatened the Muslims with their kirpans, the sight of the Sikhs who had fled from Rawalpindi filled my heart with pride in the greatness of Islam.

The Sikh who was my neighbour was about sixty years old. His beard had gone completely grey. Although he had barely escaped from the jaws of death, he was always laughing, displaying his teeth in the most vulgar fashion. It was evident that he was quite stupid. In the beginning he tried to draw me into his net by professions of friendship. Whenever I passed him he insisted on talking to me. I do not remember what kind of Sikh festival it was, when he sent me some sweet butter. My wife promptly gave it away to the sweepers. I did my best to have as little to do with him as I could. I snubbed him whenever I could. I knew that if I spoke a few words to him, he would be hard to shake off. Civil talk would encourage him to become familiar. It was known to me that Sikhs drew their sustenance from foul language. Why should I soil my lips by associating with such people!

One Sunday I was telling my wife some anecdotes about the stupidity of the Sikhs. To prove my point, exactly at 12 o'clock, I sent my servant across to my Sikh neighbour to ask him the time. He sent back the reply, 'Two minutes after 12.' I remarked to my wife, 'You see, they are scared of even mentioning 12 o'clock!' We both had a hearty laugh. After this, many a time when I wanted to make an ass of my Sikh neighbour, I would ask him 'Well, Sardarji, has it struck twelve?' The shameless creature would grin, raring all his teeth and answer, 'Sir, for us it is always striking twelve.' He would roar with laughter as if it were a great joke.

I was concerned about the safety of my children. One could never trust a Sikh. And this man had fled from Rawalpindi. He was sure to have a grudge against Muslims and to be on the look-out for an opportunity to avenge himself. I had told my wife never to allow the children to go near the Sikh's quarters. But children are children. After a few days I saw my children playing with the Sikh's little girl, Mohini, and his other children. This child, who was barely ten years old, was really as beautiful as her name indicated; she was fair and beautifully formed. These wretches have beautiful women. I recall Ghulam Rasul telling me that if all the Sikh men were to leave their women behind and clear out of the Punjab, there would be no need for Muslims to go to paradise in search of houris.

The truth about the Sikhs was soon evident. After the thrashing in Rawalpindi, they fled like cowards to East Punjab. Here they found the Muslims weak and unprepared. So they began to kill them. Hundreds of thousands of Muslims were martyred; the blood of the faithful ran in streams. Thousands of women were stripped naked and made to parade through the streets. When Sikhs, fleeing from Western Punjab, came in large numbers to Delhi, it was evident that there would be trouble in the capital. I could not leave for Pakistan immediately. Consequently I sent away my wife and children by air, with my elder brother, and entrusted my own fate to god. I could not send much luggage by air. I booked an entire railway wagon to take my furniture and belongings. But on the day I was to load the wagon I got information that trains bound for Pakistan were being attacked by Sikh bands. Consequently my luggage stayed in my quarters in Delhi.

On the 15th of August, India celebrated its independence. What interest could I have in the independence of India! I spent the day lying in bed reading *Dawn* and the *Pakistan Times*. Both the papers had strong words to say about the manner in which India had gained its freedom and proved conclusively how the Hindus and the British had conspired to destroy the Muslims. It was only our leader, the great Mohammed Ali Jinnah, who was able to thwart their evil designs and win Pakistan for the Muslims. The English had knuckled under because of Hindu and Sikh pressure and handed over Amritsar to India. Amritsar, as the world knows is a purely Muslim city. Its famous Golden Mosque—or am I mixing it up with the Golden Temple!—yes of course, the Golden Mosque is in Delhi. And in Delhi besides the Golden Mosque there are the Jamma Masjid, the Red Fort, the mausolea of Nizamuddin and Emperor Humayun, the tomb and school of Safdar Jang—just about everything worthwhile bears imprints of Islamic rule. Even so this Delhi (which should really be called after its Muslim builder Shahjahan as Shahjahanabad) was to suffer the indignity of having the flag of Hindu imperialism unfurled on its ramparts.

My heart seemed rent asunder. I could have shed tears of blood. My cup of sorrow was full to the brim when I realized that Delhi, which was once the footstool of the Muslim Empire, the centre of Islamic culture and civilization, had been snatched out of our hands. Instead we were to have the desert wastes of Western Punjab, Sindh and Baluchistan inhabited by an uncouth and uncultured people. We were to go to a land where people do not know how to talk in civilized Urdu; where men wear baggy salwars like their womenfolk, where they eat thick bread four pounds in weight instead of the delicate wafers we eat at home!

I steeled myself. I would have to make this sacrifice for my great leader, Jinnah, and for my new country, Pakistan. Nevertheless the thought of having to leave Delhi was most depressing.

When I emerged from my room in the evening, my Sikh neighbour bared his fangs and asked, 'Brother, did you not go out to see the celebrations?' I felt like setting fire to his beard.

One morning the news spread of a general massacre in old Delhi. Muslim homes were burnt in Karol Bagh. Muslim shops in Chandni Chowk were looted. This then was a sample of Hindu rule! I said to myself, 'New Delhi is really an English city; Lord Mountbatten lives here as well as the commander-in-chief. At last in New Delhi no hand will be raised against Muslims.' With this self-assurance I started towards my office. I had to settle the business of my provident fund; I had delayed going to Pakistan in order to do so. I had only got as far as Gole Market when I ran into a Hindu colleague in the office.

He said, 'What on earth are you up to? Go back at once and do not come out of your house. The rioters are killing Muslims in Connaught Circus.' I hurried back home.

I had barely got to my quarters when I ran into my Sikh neighbour. He began to reassure me. 'Shaikhji, do not worry! As long as I am alive no one will raise a hand against you.' I said to myself: 'How much fraud is hidden behind this man's beard! He is obviously pleased that the Muslims are being massacred, but expresses sympathy to win my confidence; or is he trying to taunt me?' I was the only Muslim living in that block, perhaps I was the only one on that road.

I did not want these people's kindness or sympathy. I went inside my quarter and said to myself, 'If I have to die, I will kill at least ten or twenty men before they get me.' I went to my room where beneath my bed I kept my double-barrelled gun. I had also collected quite a hoard of cartridges.

I searched the house, but could not find the gun.

'What is huzoor looking for?' asked my faithful servant, Mohammed.

'What happened to my gun?'

He did not answer. But I could tell from the way he looked that he had either hidden it or stolen it.

'Why don't you answer?' I asked him angrily.

Then he came out with the truth. He had stolen my gun and given it to some of his friends who were collecting arms to defend the Muslims in Daryaganj.

'We have hundreds of guns, several machine guns, ten revolvers and a cannon. We will slaughter these infidels; we will roast them alive.'

'No doubt with my gun you will roast the infidels in Daryaganj, but who will defend me here? I am the only Mussulman amongst these savages. If I am murdered, who will answer for it?'

I persuaded him to steal his way to Daryaganj to bring back my gun and a couple of hundred cartridges. When he left I was convinced that I would never see him again.

I was all alone. On the mantlepiece was a family photograph. My wife and children stared silently at me. My eyes filled with tears at the thought that I would never see them again. I was comforted with the thought that they were safe in Pakistan. Why had I been tempted by my paltry provident fund and not gone with them? I heard the crowd yelling.

'Sat Sri Akal . . .'
'Har Har Mahadev.'

The yelling came closer and closer. They were rioters—the beares of my death warrant. I was like a wounded deer, running hither and thither with the hunters' hounds in full pursuit. There was no escape. The door was made of very thin wood and glass panes. The rioters would smash their way in.

'Sat Sri Akal . . .'
'Har Har Mahadev . . .'

They were coming closer and closer; death was coming closer and closer. Suddenly there was a knock at the door. My Sikh neighbour walked in—'Shaikhji, come into my quarters at once.' Without a second thought I ran into the Sikh's veranda and hid behind the columns. A shot hit the wall above my head. A truck drew up and about a dozen young men climbed down. Their leader had a list in his hand—'Quarter No. 8—Sheikh Burhanuddin.' He read my name and ordered his gang to go ahead. They invaded my quarter and under my very eyes proceeded to destroy my home. My furniture, boxes, pictures, books, druggets and carpets, even the dirty linen was carried into the truck. Robbers! Thugs! Cut-throats!

As for the Sikh, who had pretended to sympathize with me, he was no less a robber than they! He was pleading with the rioters: 'Gentlemen, stop! We have a prior claim over our neighbour's property. We must get our share of the loot.' He beckoned to his sons and daughters. All of them gathered to pick up whatever they could lay their hands on. One took my trousers; another a suitcase.

They even grabbed the family photograph. They took the loot to their quarters.

You bloody Sikh! If god grants me life I will settle my score with you. At this moment I cannot even protest. The rioters are armed and only a few yards away from me. If they get to know of my presence . . .

'Please come in.'

My eyes fell on the unsheathed kirpan in the hands of the Sikh. He was inviting me to come in. The bearded monster looked more frightful after he had soiled his hands with my property. There was the glittering blade of his kirpan inviting me to my doom. There was no time to argue. The only choice was between the guns of the rioters and the sabre of the Sikh. I decided, rather the kirpan of the old man than ten armed gangsters. I went into the room hesitantly, silently.

'Not here, come in further.' I went into the inner room like a goat following a butcher. The glint of the blade of the kirpan was almost blinding.

'Here you are, take your things,' said the Sikh.

He and his children put all the stuff they had pretended to loot, in front of me. His old woman said, 'Son, I am sorry we were not able to save more.'

I was dumbfounded.

The gangsters had dragged out my steel almirah and were trying to smash it open. 'It would be simpler if we could find the keys,' said someone.

'The keys can only be found in Pakistan. That cowardly son of a filthy Muslim has decamped,' replied another.

Little Mohini answered back: 'Shaikhji is not a coward. He has not run off to Pakistan.'

'Where is he blackening his face?'

'Why should he be blackening his face? He is in . . .'

Mohini realized her mistake and stopped in the middle of her sentence. Blood mounted in her father's face. He locked me in the inside room, gave his kirpan to his son and went out to face the mob.

I do not know what exactly took place outside. I heard the sound of blows; then Mohini crying; then the Sikh yelling full-blooded abuse in Punjabi. And then a shot and the Sikh's cry of pain 'Hai.'

I heard a truck engine starting up; and then there was a petrified silence.

When I was taken out of my prison my Sikh neighbour was lying on a charpoy. Beside him lay a torn and blood-stained shirt. His new shirt also was oozing with blood. His son had gone to telephone for the doctor.

'Sardarji, what have you done?' I do not know how these words came out of my lips. The world of hate in which I had lived all these years, lay in ruins about me.

'Sardarji, why did you do this?' I asked him again.

'Son, I had a debt to pay.'

'What kind of a debt?'

'In Rawalpindi there was a Muslim like you who sacrificed his life to save mine and the honour of my family.'

'What was his name, Sardarji?'

'Ghulam Rasul.'

Fate had played a cruel trick on me. The clock on the wall started to strike . . . one . . . two . . . three . . . four . . . five . . . The Sikh turned towards the clock and smiled. He reminded me of my grandfather with his twelve-inch beard. How closely the two resembled each other!

. . . six . . . seven . . . eight . . . nine . . . we counted in silence.

He smiled again. His white beard and long white hair were like a halo, effulgent with a divine light . . . 10 . . . 11 . . . 12 . . . The clock stopped striking.

I could almost hear him say: 'For us Sikhs, it is always 12 o'clock!'

But the bearded lips, still smiling, were silent. And I knew he was already in some distant world, where the striking of clocks counted for nothing, where violence and mockery were powerless to hurt him.

FICTION

A Bride for the Sahib

'What can I do for you, gentlemen?'

Mr Sen asked the question without looking up. He pushed the cleaner through the stem of his pipe and twirled it around. As he blew through it, his eyes fell on the rose and marigold garlands in the hands of his callers. So they knew that he had been married that morning! He had tried to keep it as quiet as possible. But as he had learned so often before, it was impossible to keep anything a secret for too long in his nosey native land.

He screwed on the bowl to the stem and blew through the pipe again. Through his lowered eyes, he saw his visitors shuffling their feet and nudging each other. He unwrapped his plastic tobacco pouch and began filling his pipe. After an uneasy minute of subdued whispers, one of the men cleared his throat.

'Well, Mr Bannerjee, what is your problem?' asked Mr Sen in a flat monotone.

'Saar,' began the superintendent of the clerical staff, 'Whee came to wheesh your good shelph long liphe and happinesh.' He beckoned to the chaprasis: 'Garland the Sahib.'

The chaprasis stepped in front with the garlands held aloft. The Sahib stopped them with a wave of his pipe. *'Mez par'*—on the table, he commanded in his gentle but firm voice. The chaprasis' hands came down slowly; their fawning smiles changed to stupid grins. They put the garlands on the table and stepped behind the semi-circle of clerks.

'If that is all,' said Mr Sen standing up, 'we can get back to our work. I thank you, gentlemen, for your good wishes.' He bowed slightly to indicate that they should leave. 'Bannerjee, will you look in later to discuss the redistribution of work while I am away?'

'Shuttenly, Saar.'

The men joined the palms of their hands, murmured their 'namastes' and filed out.

Sen joined his hands across his waistcoat and watched the smoke from his pipe rise in a lazy spiral towards the ceiling. A new chapter in his life had begun. That's how Hindus described marriage—the third of the four stages of life according to the Vedas. It was alarming, he reflected, how his thought processes slipped into cliches and how Hinduism extended its tentacles in practically every sphere of life. His father had not been a particularly orthodox Hindu and had sent him to an Anglo-Indian school where the boys had changed his name from Santosh to Sunny. Thereafter he had gone to Balliol. He had entered the administrative service before the independent Indian government with its new-fangled nationalist ideas had made Hindi and a vernacular language compulsory. His inability to speak an Indian language hadn't proved a handicap. As a matter of fact, it impressed most Indians. Although his accent and mannerisms made him somewhat of an outsider, it was more than compensated for by the fact that it also put him outside the vicious circle of envy and back-biting in which all the others indulged. They sought his company because he was an un-Indian Indian, because he was a brown British gentleman, because he was what the English contemptuously described as a wog—a Westernized oriental gentleman.

Sen's main contact with his country was his mother. Like an orthodox Hindu widow she shaved her head, only wore a plain white sari and went about in bare feet. He was her only child so they both did the best they could for each other. She ran his home. He occasionally ate rice, curried fish and the sticky over-sweetened confections she made on special occasions. Other times she had the bearer cook him the lamb chops and the shepherd pies he liked better. She had converted one of the rooms into a temple where she burnt incense and tinkled bells to a diminutive image of the black-faced, red-tongued goddess, Kali. But she never insisted on his joining her in worship. Although he detested Indian movies, he made it a point to take her to one every month. She, at her end, did not object to his taking his evening Scotch and soda or smoking in her presence. She never questioned him about his movements. They got on extremely well till she started talking about his getting married. At first he had laughed it off. She became insistent and started to nag him. She wanted to see him properly settled. She wanted to fondle a grandson just once before she died, she said with tears in her eyes. At last he gave in. He did not have strong views on marriage or on whom he would marry. Since he had come back to settle in India, he could not do worse than marry one of his countrywomen. 'All right, Ma, you find me a wife. I'll marry anyone you want me to marry,' he said one day.

His mother did not bring up the subject again for many days. She wrote to her brother living at Dehra Dun, in the Himalayan foothills, to come down to Delhi. The two drafted an advertisement for the matrimonial columns and asked for insertions in two successive Sunday editions of the *Hindustan Times*. It read: 'Wanted a fair, good-looking virgin of a high class respectable family for an Oxford-educated Bengali youth of 25, drawing over Rs 1,000 p.m. in first class gazetted government service. Applicant should be conversant with H.H. affairs. C and D no bar. Correspond with horoscope. P.O. Box No. 4200.'

The first insertion brought over fifty letters from parents who enclosed not only the horoscopes of their daughters but their photographs as well to prove that they were fair and therefore good-looking. A fortnight later the applications were sorted out and Sunny's mother and uncle triumphantly laid out nearly a hundred photographs on the large dining table. Their virginity and capacity to deal with household affairs had, of necessity, to be taken on trust. But despite the professed indifference to

C and D, the applicants selected for consideration were of the same caste as the Sens and those whose fathers had made offers of substantial dowries. Now it was for Sunny to choose.

This was the first time that Sunny had heard of the matrimonial advertisement. He was very angry and acutely embarrassed as some anxious parents had travelled up all the way from Calcutta, bribed the clerks concerned at the newspaper office and called on him at the office. He told his mother firmly that if it did not stop, he would call off the whole thing. But as he had given his word, he would accept anyone chosen for him. His mother and uncle quickly settled the matter by selecting a girl whose father promised the largest dowry and gave a substantial portion of it as earnest money at the betrothal ceremony. The parties took the horoscopes of the affianced couple to a pandit who consulted the stars and, having had his palm crossed with silver, pronounced the pair ideally suited to each other and the dates that suited the parties to be most auspicious. That was as much as Sunny Sen could take. He told them quite bluntly that he would be married at the Registry or not at all. His mother' and uncle sensed his mounting irritation and gave in. The bride's parents made a nominal protest: the cost of a wedding on the traditional pattern, which included feasting the bridegroom's party and relations, giving presents and paying the priests, could run into thousands of rupees. The registrars fee was only five rupees. That was how Srijut Santosh Sen came to marry Kumari Kalyani, the eldest of Srijut Profulla and Srimati Protima Das's five daughters. Mr Das was, like his son-in-law, a first class gazetted government servant.

The honeymoon also created difficulties. His mother blushed as if he had said something improper. The Das's were outraged at the suggestion that their daughter should go away for a fortnight unaccompanied by a younger sister. But they resigned their daughter to her fate. Her husband had been brought up as a Sahib and she must follow his ways.

Sen's thoughts were interrupted by his colleague Santa Singh bursting into the room. The Sikh was like the rest of his race, loud and aggressive: 'Brother, you think you can run away without giving us a party?' he yelled as he came in. 'We insist on having a feast to welcome our sister-in-law.'

Sen stood up quickly and put his hand across the table to keep the Sikh at arm's length. Santa Singh ignored the preferred hand, came round the table and enveloped his friend in his arms. He planted his wet and hirsute kisses on the Sahib's cheeks. 'Congratulations, brother, when are we to meet our sister-in-law?'

'Soon, very soon,' replied Sen, extricating himself from the Sikh's embrace and wiping his cheeks. And before the words were out of his mouth, he knew he had blundered: 'As soon as we get back from our honeymoon.'

'Honeymoon!' exclaimed Santa Singh with a leer; he took Sen's hands in his and squeezed them amorously. 'I hope you've had yourself massaged with chameleon oil; puts more punch into things. You should also add crushed almonds in your milk. Above all, don't overdo it. Not more than . . . There was no stopping the Sikh from giving unsolicited advice on how to approach an inexperienced virgin and the proper use of aphrodisiacs. Sen kept smiling politely without making comment. When he had had enough, he interrupted the Sikh's soliloquy by extending his hand. 'It was very kind of you to have dropped in. We will call on you and Mrs Singh as soon as we are back in Delhi.'

Santa Singh took Sen's hand without any enthusiasm. 'Goodbye. Have a nice time,' he blurted and went out. Sen sat down with a sigh of relief. He knew he had not been rude. He had behaved with absolute rectitude—exactly like an English gentleman.

A minute later the chaprasi raised the thick curtains to let in Mr Swami, the director of the department. Sen again extended his hand across the table to keep the visitor at arm's length; the native's desire to make physical contact galled him. 'Good morning, sir.'

The director touched Sen's hand with his without answering the greeting. His mouth was full of betel saliva. He raised his face to hold it from dribbling out and bawled out to the chaprasi: 'Hey, spittoon *lao.*'

The chaprasi ran in with the vessel which Sen had ordered to be removed from his room and held it under the director's chin. Mr Swami spat out the bloody phlegm in the spittoon. Sen opened his table drawer and pretended he was looking for his match box. The director sat down and lit his beedi. 'Eh, you Sen, you are a dark harse. By god, a pitch black harse, if I may say so.' Mr Swami fancied his knowledge of English idiom. 'So quietly you go and get yourself hitched. My steno says "Sir, we should celebrate holiday to celebrate Sahib's marriage!" I say, "What marriage, man?" "Sir, Mr Sen got married this morning." "By god," I said, "I must get the truth, the whole truth and nothing but the truth right from the harse's mouth—the dark harse's mouth."' The director stretched his hand across the table. 'Clever guy you, eh?' he said with a smirk. Sen touched his boss's hand with the top of his fingers, 'Thank you, sir.'

'What for thank you? And you come to the office on the day you get married. Heavens won't fall if you stay away a few days. I as your boss order you to go back home to your wife. I will put in a demi-official memo. What do you say?'

The director was pleased with himself and extended his hand. Sen acknowledged his boss's wit by taking his hand. 'Thank you, sir. I think I will go home.'

'My god, you are a Sahib! I hope your wife is not a Memsahib. That would be too much of a joke.'

The director left but his betel-stained smirk lingered on like the smile of the Cheshire cat and his last remark began to go round and round in Sen's head with an insistent rhythmic beat. 'I hope your wife isn't a Memsahib, not a Memsahib, not a Memsahib. I hope your wife is not a Memsahib.'

Would his wife be a Memsahib, he mused as he drove back home for lunch. It was not very likely. She claimed to be an MA in English literature. But he had met so many of his countrymen with long strings of firsts who could barely speak the English language correctly. To start with, there was the director himself with his 'okey dokes' and 'by gums' who, like other South Indians, pronounced eight as 'yate', and egg as 'yagg', and who always stumbled on words begining with an 'M'. He smiled to himself as he recalled the director instructing his private secretary to get Mr M.M. Amir, member of Parliament, on the phone. 'I want Yum Yum Yumeer, Yumpee.' The Bengalis had their own execrable accent; they added an airy 'h' whenever they could after a 'b' or a 'w' or an 's'. A 'virgin' sounded like some exotic tropical plant, the 'vharjeen', 'will' as 'wheel', and 'simple' as 'shimple'.

~

There was much crying at the farewell and the bride continued to sniffle for a long time afterwards in the car. She had drawn her sari over her forehead down to her eyes and covered the rest of her face with a silk handkerchief into which she blew her nose. When Sen lit his pipe, she firmly clamped the handkerchief on her nostrils. 'Does the smoke bother you?' was the first sentence he spoke to his wife. She replied by a vigorous shake of the head.

They stopped at a mango orchard by the roadside to have lunch. His mother I had made two separate packets with their names in Bengali pinned on them. The one marked 'Sunny' had roasted chicken and cheese sandwiches. The other contained boiled rice and pickles in a small brass cup with curried lentils. His wife poured the lentils on the rice and began to eat with her fingers.

They ate without speaking to each other. Within a few minutes they had an audience of anxious passers-by and children from a neighbouring village. Some sat on their haunches; others just stood gaping at the couple or commenting on their being newly married. Sen knew how to deal with the rustic. 'Are you people hungry?' he asked sarcastically.

The men turned away sheepishly; but the urchins did not budge. 'Bugger off, you dirty bastards,' roared Sen, raising his hand as if to strike. The children ran away to a safe distance and began to yell back at Sen, mimicking his English. 'Buggeroff, Buggeroff,' they cried. '*Arey* he is a Sahib, a big Sahib.'

Sen ignored them and spoke politely to his wife. 'Pardon the language,' he said with a smile. 'Would you like to sample one of my sandwiches? I don't know whether you eat meat; take the lettuce and cheese; it is fresh cheddar.'

Mrs Sen took the sandwich with her curry-stained fingers. She tore a strip off the toast as if it were a chapatti, scooped up a mixture of rice, curry and cheddar and put it in her mouth. She took one bite and stopped munching. Through her thick glasses she stared at her husband as if he had given her poison. She turned pale and, being unable to control herself any further, spat out the food in her mouth. She turned her face the other way and brought up the rice and curry.

'I am dreadfully sorry,' stammered Sen. 'The cheddar upset you. I should have known.'

Mrs Sen wiped her mouth with the end of her sari and asked for water. She rinsed her mouth and splashed it on her face. The lunch was ruined. 'We better be on our way,' said Sen, standing up. 'That is if you feel better.'

She tied up her brass cup in a duster and followed him to the car. They were on the road again. She fished out a silver box from her handbag and took out a couple of betel leaves. She smeared one with lime and catechu paste, put in cardamom and sliced betel nuts, rolled it up and held it out for her husband.

'I'm afraid I don't touch the stuff,' he said apologetically. 'I'll stick to my pipe if you don't mind.' Mrs Sen did not mind. She slipped the leaf in her own mouth and began to chew contentedly.

They got to the rest-house in good time, The rest-house bearer took in the luggage and spread the bedding rolls. He asked Mrs Sen what they would like for dinner. She referred him to her husband. 'Just anything for me,' he replied, 'omelette or anything. Ask the Memsahib what she would like for herself. I will take a short walk before dinner.'

'Don't go too far, Sahib,' continued the bearer. 'This is wild country. There is a footpath down to the river which the Sahibs who come to fish take. It is quite safe.'

Sen went into the bedroom to ask his wife if she would like to come out for a walk. She was unpacking her things. He changed his mind. 'I'll go for a short stroll towards the river. Get the bearer to put out the Scotch and soda in the veranda; there's a bottle in my suitcase. We'll have a drink before dinner.'

His wife nodded her head.

The well-beaten fisherman's footpath snaked its way through dense foliage of *sal* and flame of the forest, ending abruptly on the pebbly bank of the river. The Ganges was a magnificent sight; a broad and swift-moving current of clear, icy-blue water sparkling in the bright sun. It must have been from places like where he stood, he thought, that the sages of olden times had pronounced the Ganges the holiest of all the rivers in the world. He felt a sense of kinship with his Aryan ancestors, who worshipped the beautiful in nature, sang hymns to the rising sun, rised goblets of fermented soma juice to the full moon and who ate beef and were lusty with full-bosomed and large-hipped women. Much water had flowed down the Ganges since then and Hinduism was now like the river itself at its lower reaches—as at Calcutta where he was born. At Calcutta it was a sluggish expanse of slime and sludge, carrying the excrement of millions of pilgrims who polluted it at Hardwar, Benaras, Allahabad, Patna and other 'holy' cities on its banks, and who fouled its water by strewing charred corpses for the fish and the turtles to eat. It had become the Hinduism of the cow-protectors, prohibitionists—and chewers of betel leaves. That must be it he thought cheerfully. His was the pristine Hinduism of the stream that sparkled before him; that of the majority, of the river after it had been sullied by centuries of narrow prejudices. He walked over the pebbled bank, took up a palmful of the icy-cold water and splashed it on his face.

The shadows of the jungle lengthened across the stream and the cicadas began to call. Sen turned back and quickly retraced his steps to the bungalow. The sun was setting. It was time for a sundowner.

Tumblers and soda were laid out on the table in the veranda. The bearer heard his footsteps and came with a bunch of keys in his open hand. 'I did not like to open the Sahib's trunk,' he explained. 'Please take out the whisky.'

'Why didn't you ask the Memsahib to take it out?'

The bearer looked down at his feet. 'She said she could not touch a bottle of alcohol. She gave me the keys but I don't like to meddle with the Sahib's luggage. If things are misplaced . . .'

That's all right. Open my suitcase. The bottles of whisky and brandy are right on the top. And serve the dinner as soon as the Memsahib is ready.'

It was no point asking his wife to sit with him. He poured himself a large Scotch and lit his pipe. Once more his thoughts turned to the strange course his life had taken. If he had married one of the English girls he had met in his university days how different things would have been. They would have kissed a hundred times between the wedding and the wedding night; they would have walked hand-in-hand through the forest and made love beside the river; they would have lain in each other's arms and sipped their Scotch. They would have nibbled at knick-knacks in between bouts of love; and they would have made love till the early hours of the morning. The whisky warmed his blood and quickened his imagination. He was back in England. The gathering gloom and the dark, tropical forest, accentuated the feeling of loneliness. He felt an utter stranger in his own country. He did not hear the bearer announcing that dinner had been served. Now his wife came out and asked in the quaint Bengali accent, 'Do you want to shit outshide?'

'What?' he asked gruffly, waking up from his reverie.

'Do you want to shit inshide or outshide? The deener ees on the table.'

'Oh I'll be right in. You go ahead. I'll join you in a second.' Good lord! What would his English friends have said if she had invited them in this manner! The invitation to defecate was Mrs Sen's first communication with her husband.

A strong sweet smell of coconut oil and roses assailed Sen's nostrils as he entered the dining room. His wife had washed and oiled her hair; it hung in loose snaky coils below her waist. The parting was daubed with bright vermilion powder to indicate her status as a married woman. He had no doubt that she had smeared her body with the attar of roses as her mother had probably instructed. She sat patiently at the table; being a Hindu woman, she could not very well start eating before her husband.

'Sorry to keep you waiting. You should have started. Your dinner must be cold.'

She simply wagged her head.

They began to eat: he, his omelette and buttered slice of bread with fork and knife; she, her rice and lentil curry mashed in between her fingers and the palm of her right hand. Sen cleared his throat many times to start a conversation. But each time the vacant and bewildered look behind the thick lenses of his wife's glasses made him feel that words would fail to convey their meaning. If his friends knew they would certainly have a big laugh. 'Oh Sunny Sen! How could he start talking to his wife? He hadn't been properly introduced. Don't you know he is an Englishman?'

The dinner was eaten in silence. Kalyani Sen emitted a soft belch and took out her betel-leaf case. She rolled a leaf, paused for a split-second and put it in her mouth. Sunny had promised himself the luxury of expensive Havana cigars over his honeymoon. He took one out of its phallic metal case, punctured its bottom with a gold clipper and lit it. The aromatic smoke soon filled the dining room. This time his wife did not draw the fold of her sari across her face; she simply clasped her hands in front of her mouth and discreetly blocked her nostrils with the back of her hands.

They sat in silence facing each other across the table; she chewing her leaf—almost like a cow chewing the cud, thought Sen. He, lost in the smoke of his long Cuban cigar. It was oppressive—and the barrier between them, impassable. Sen glanced at his watch and stood up. 'News,' he exclaimed loudly. 'Mustn't miss the news.' He went into the bedroom to fetch his transistor radio set.

Two beds had been laid side by side with no space between them; the pillows almost hugged each other. The sheets had been sprinkled with the earthy perfume of khas fibre and looked as if they also awaited the consummation of the marriage performed earlier in the day. How, thought Sen, could she think of this sort of thing when they hadn't even been introduced! No, hell, barely a civil word had passed between them? He quickly took out his radio set and hurried back to the dining room.

He tuned in to Delhi. While he listened to the news, the bearer cleared the table and left salaaming, 'Good night, sir.' Mrs Sen got up, collected her betel-leaf case and disappeared into the bedroom.

The fifteen minutes of news was followed by a commentary on sports, Sen had never bothered to listen to it. He was glad he did because the commentary was followed by the announcement of a change in the programme. A concert of vocal Hindustani music by Ustad Badey Ghulam Ali Khan had been put off to relay a performance by the Czech Philharmonic Orchestra from New Delhi. Ghulam Ali Khan was the biggest name in Indian music and even the Anglicized natives had to pretend that they admired the cacophony of gargling sounds he produced from the pit of his stomach. Members of the diplomatic corps were known to sit through four hours of the maestro's performance lest they offend their Indian hosts or be found less cultured than staffs of rival embassies. The Czech Philharmonic had come to

India for the first time and the wogs who ran Delhi's European Music Society had got away with it. Pity, thought Sen, he wasn't in town; he could have invited the right people for dinner (tails, of course!) followed by the concert. How would his wife have fitted into a party of this sort?

The sound of applause came over the air, followed by an announcement that the opening piece was a selection from Smetana's *The Bartered Bride*. Sen was transported back to the glorious evenings at Covent Garden and the Festival Hall. Smetana was followed by Bartok. The only thing that broke the enchantment was the applause between the movements. How could one expect the poor, benighted natives to know that the end of a movement was not the end of the symphony!

There was an interval of ten minutes. The last piece was Sen's favourite—Dvorak's Symphony No. 5 in E minor. He poured himself a liqueur brandy (VSOP), drew a chair and stretched his legs on it. He had never heard Dvorak as well performed even in Europe. A Cuban cigar, an excellent Cognac and the world's greatest music, what more could one ask for! He gently decapitated the cigar of its ashy head, lay back in the armchair and closed his eyes in complete rapture. By the final movement he was fast asleep with the cigar slowly burning itself out between his lips.

Neither the applause, at the end of the concert, nor the silence and the cackling of the radio woke Sen from his slumber. When the cigar got too hot, he opened his mouth and let it drop on his lap. It slowly burnt through his shirt and trouser then singed the hair on his under-belly. He woke with a start and threw the butt on the ground.

Although the cigar had only burnt a tiny hole near a fly button, the room was full of the smell of burning cloth. That was a narrow escape, thought Sen. He switched off the transistor and glanced at his watch. It was well after midnight. He blew out the oil lamp and went to the bedroom.

An oil lamp still burned on the table. His wife had fallen asleep—obviously after having waited for him. She had not changed nor taken off her jewellery. She had put mascara in her eyes. Her tears had washed some of it on to her cheeks and the pillow had a smudge of soot.

Sen changed into his pajamas and slipped into his bed. He stared at his wife's gently heaving bosom and her open mouth. How could he? In any case, he didn't have the slightest desire. He turned the knob on the lamp. The yellow flame turned to a blue fluting on the edge of the wick, spluttered twice, then gave up the struggle and plunged the room into a black solitude.

The bearer came in with the tea-tray and woke him up. 'Sahib, it is after nine. Memsahib has been up, for the last four or five hours. She has had her bath, said her prayer and has been waiting for you to get up to have her chota hazri.'

Sen rubbed his eyes. The sun was streaming through the veranda into the room. His wife had made a Swiss roll of her bedding and put it away on the top of her steel trunk. 'I'll have my tea in the veranda,' he replied, getting up. He went to the bathroom, splashed cold water on his face and went out.

'Sorry to keep you waiting, I seem to do it all the time. You should really never wait for me.' He stretched himself and yawned. 'I am always . . . what on earth.'

His wife had got up and, while his face was still lifted towards the ceiling, bent down to touch his feet. He was her husband, lord and master. He looked down in alarm. She looked up; tears streamed down both her cheeks. 'I am unworthy,' she said half-questioning and half-stating her fears. And before he could reply, she drew the flap of her sari across her eyes and fled inside.

'What the hell is all this?' muttered Sen and collapsed into an armchair. He knew precisely what she meant. He sat a long while scratching his head with his eyes fixed in a hypnotic stare on the sunlit lawn. He had no desire to go in and make up to his wife.

The bearer came, looked accusingly at the untouched tray of tea and announced that breakfast was on the table. Sen got up reluctantly. She would obviously not have anything to eat unless he cajoled her. And he was damned if he was going to do it. Again he was wrong. She was at the table. He avoided looking at her. 'Tea?' he questioned and filled her cup and then his own. Once again they ate their different foods in their different ways without saying a word to each other. And as soon as the meal was over, she went to her betel leaves and he to his pipe. She retired to her bedroom. He took his transistor and returned to the veranda to listen in to the morning news.

The arrival of the postman at noon put the idea in his head. It was only a copy of the office memorandum sanctioning him leave for a fortnight. He walked in waving the yellow envelope bearing the legend—'On India Government Service Only.'

'I am afraid we have to return at once. It's an urgent letter from the minister. He has to answer some questions in Parliament dealing with our department. I'll get the bearer to help you pack while I give the car a check up. Bearer, bearer,' he yelled as he walked out.

Half an hour later they were on the road to Delhi; a little before sunset, Sen drove into his portico. The son and mother embraced each other and only broke apart when the bride knelt down to touch her mother-in-law's feet. 'God bless you, my child,' said the older woman, touching the girl on the shoulder, 'but what . . .'

Her son pulled out the yellow envelope from his pocket and waved it triumphantly. 'An urgent summons from the minister. These chaps don't respect anyone's private life. I simply had to come.'

'Of course,' replied his mother, wiping off a tear. She turned to her daughter-in-law. 'Your parents will be delighted to know you are back. Why don't you ring them up?' A few minutes later Mrs Sen's parents drove up in a taxi. There were more tears at the re-union, more explanations about the letter from the minister. There was also relief. Now that the bride had spent a night with her husband and consummated the marriage, she could return to her parental home for a few days.

Sen spent the next morning going round the local bookshops and coffee houses. The weekend followed. On Sunday morning, when his mother was at prayer, he rang up the director at his home to explain his return and ask for permission to resume work. 'My mother has been keeping indifferent health and I did not want to leave her alone for too long.' He knew this line of approach would win both sympathy and approval. The director expressed concern and spoke warmly of a Hindu son's sacred duty towards his widowed mother. 'And we must celebrate your wedding and meet your wife . . . as soon as your mother is better.'

'Yes, sir. As soon as she is up to the mark, we will invite you over.'

The mother being 'a bit under the weather' and 'not quite up to the mark' became Sen's explanation for cancelling his leave and not having a party. It even silenced Santa Singh who had planned a lot of ribaldry at Sen's expense.

Days went by—and then weeks. Kalyani came over with her mother a couple of times to fetch her things. She came when her husband was in the office and only met her mother-in-law. It was conveyed to Sunny Sen that, under the circumstances, it was for the husband to go and fetch his wife from her home. Sen put off doing so for some time—and then had to go away on a tour of inspection to southern India. It was a fortnight after his return that his parents-in-law learnt that he was back in town. The relations between the two families became very strained. Nothing was said directly but talk about the Sen's being dowry-seekers and Sen's mother being a difficult woman started going round. Then Sunny got a letter from his father-in-law. It was polite but distinctly cold. From the contents it was obvious that it had been drafted and written on the advice of a lawyer with a carbon copy made for use if necessary. It referred to the advertisement in the matrimonial columns and the negotiations preceding the marriage, the money given on betrothal and in the dowry, the wedding and its consummation in the forest rest-house on the Ganges. Sen was asked to state his intentions.

For the first time, Sen realized how serious the situation had become. He turned to his mother. A new bond was forged between the mother and son. 'It is a matter of great shame,' she said firmly. 'We must not let this business go too far. You must fetch her. I will go away to my brother at Dehra Dun for a few days.'

'No, Ma, I will not have anyone making insinuations against you,' he replied, and pleaded, 'in any case you must not leave me.'

'No one has made any insinuations and I am not leaving you. This will always be my home; where else can I live except with my own flesh and blood. But you must get your wife. Let her take over the running of the house and become its mistress as is her right. Then I will come back and live without worrying my head with servants and cooking and shopping.'

Sen flopped back in his chair like one exhausted. His mother came over behind him and took his head between her hands, 'Don't let it worry you too much. I will write to my brother to come over to fetch me. He will go to your father-in-law's and bring over your wife. Before we leave, I will show her everything, give her the keys and tell the servants to take orders from her. When you come back from the office you will find everything running smoothly.' She kissed her son's half. 'And do be nice to her, she is only a child. You know how much I am looking forward to having a grandson to fondle in my lap!'

Sen found the whole thing very distasteful. He felt angry with himself for allowing things to come to such a pass. And he felt angrier with his wife for humiliating his mother and driving her out of her home. He would have nothing to do with her unless she accepted his mother. He instructed his cook-bearer about the arrangements of the bedrooms. If the new mistress asked any questions, he was to say that those were his master's orders.

On Monday morning, when the bearer brought him his morning tea, he told him not to expect him for lunch and to tell his wife not to wait for him for dinner as he might be working late in the office. He had breakfast with his mother and uncle.

He promised to write to his mother every day to tell her how things were going. 'You must try and understand her point of view,' admonished his mother. 'She has been brought up in a different world. But love and patience conquer all.'

Sen was the last to leave his office. He drove straight to the Gymkhana Club. For an hour he sat by the bathing pool, drinking ice-cold lager and watching the bathers. There were European women from the diplomatic corps with their children; there were pretty Punjabi girls in their pony tails and bikinis; there were swarthy young college students showing off their Tarzan-like torsos as they leapt from the diving board. This surely was where he belonged—where the east and the west met in a sort of minestrone soup of human limbs of many pigments, black, brown, pink and white. Why couldn't he have married one of these girls, taught her proper English instead of the Americanized chi-chi which they thought was smart talk.

The bathers went home. Sen got up with a sigh and went to the bar. He was greeted by several old friends. 'Hi, Sunny, you old bastard. What's this one hears about you?'

Sunny smiled. 'I don't have to proclaim everything I do from the housetops, do I?'

'Like hell you do. You stand drinks all round or we'll debag you and throw you out in front of all the women.' Three of them advanced towards him.

'Lay off, chaps. Bearer, give these B.F.s what they want. What's the poison?'

They sat on the high stools and downed their drinks with 'Cheers', 'here's mud in your eye' and 'bottoms up'.

'Where is your wife?' asked one. 'Don't tell me you are going to keep her in the seclusion of the purdah like a native!'

'No ruddy fears,' answered Sen. 'She's gone to her mother's. Would you chaps like another?'

One round followed another till it was time for the bar to close. One of the men invited him home for dinner. Sen accepted without a murmur.

It was almost one a.m. when Sen drove back into his house. He was well fortified with Scotch to gloss over any awkwardness. He switched on the light in the hall and saw trunks piled up against the wall. His wife had obviously come back. There was no light in her bedroom. She must have gone to sleep many hours earlier. He switched off the hall light, tiptoed to his bedroom, switched on the table-lamp, went back and bolted the door from the inside. A few minutes later, he was fast asleep.

The bearer's persistent knocking woke him up. His head rocked as he got up to unfasten the bolt. What would the bearer think of the Sahib bolting his door against his wife? He couldn't care less. The throbbing in his head demanded all his attention.

'Shall I take tea for the Memsahib?' he asked.

'She does not have bed-tea,' replied Sen. 'Isn't she up yet?'

'I don't know Sahib; she had also bolted her door from the inside.'

Sen felt uneasy. He swallowed a couple of aspirins and gulped down a cup of strong tea. He lay back on his pillow to let the aspirins take effect. His imagination began to run away with him. She couldn't. No, of course not! Must have waited for him till midnight, was scared of being alone and must have bolted the doors and was sleeping late. But he had been nasty to her and she might be oversensitive. He decided to rid himself of the thought. He got up and knocked at the door. There was no response. He went to the bathroom and then tried her door again There was no sound from the inside. He went to the window and pressed it with both his hands. The two sides flew apart and crashed against the wall. Even that noise did not waken her. He peered in and caught the gleam of her glasses on her nose.

With a loud cry Sen ran back into the house and called for the bearer. The master and servant put their shoulders to the door and battered against it. The bolt gave way and they burst into the room. The woman on the bed didn't stir. A white fluid trickled from her gaping mouth to the pillow. Her eyes stared fixedly through the thick glasses. Sen put his hand on her forehead. It was the first time he had touched his wife. And she was dead.

On the table beside her bed was an empty tumbler and two envelopes. One bore her mother's name in Bengali; the other was for him. A haunted smile came on his lips as he read the English address.

'To,

Mr S. Sen, Esq.'

THE PORTRAIT OF A LADY

My grandmother, like everybody's grandmother, was an old woman. She had been old and wrinkled for the twenty years that I had known her. People said that she had once been young and pretty and had even had a husband, but that was hard to believe. My grandfather's portrait hung above the mantelpiece in the drawing-room. He wore a big turban and loose-fitting clothes. His long white beard covered the best part of his chest and he looked at least a hundred years old. He did not look the sort of person who would have a wife or children. He looked as if he could only have lots and lots of grandchildren. As for my grandmother being young and pretty, the thought was almost revolting. She often told us of the games she used to play as a child. That seemed quite absurd and undignified on her part and we treated it like the fables of the Prophets she used to tell us.

She had always been short and fat and slightly bent. Her face was a criss-cross of wrinkles running from everywhere to everywhere. No, we were certain she had always been as we had known her. Old, so terribly old that she could not have grown older, and had stayed at the same age for twenty years. She could never have been pretty; but she was always beautiful. She hobbled about the house in spotless white with one hand resting on her waist to balance her stoop and the other telling the beads of her rosary. Her silver locks were scattered untidily over her pale, puckered face, and her lips constantly moved in inaudible prayer. Yes, she was beautiful. She was like the winter landscape in the mountains, an expanse of pure white serenity breathing peace and contentment.

My grandmother and I were good friends. My parents left me with her when they went to live in the city and we were constantly together. She used to wake me up in the morning and get me ready for school. She said her morning prayer in a monotonous sing-song while she bathed and dressed me in the hope that I would listen and get to know it by heart. I listened because I loved her voice but never bothered to learn it. Then she would fetch my wooden slate which she had already washed and plastered with yellow chalk, a tiny earthen inkpot and a reed pen, tie them all in a bundle and hand it to me. After a breakfast of a thick, stale chapatti with a little butter and sugar spread on it, we went to school. She carried several stale chapatties with her for the village dogs.

My grandmother always went to school with me because the school was attached to the temple. The priest taught us the alphabet and the morning prayer. While the children sat in rows on either side of the veranda singing the alphabet or the prayer in a chorus, my grandmother sat inside reading the scriptures. When we had both finished, we would walk back together. This time the village dogs would meet us at the temple door. They followed us to our home growling and fighting each other for the chapatties we threw to them.

When my parents were comfortably settled in the city, they sent for us. That was a turning-point in our friendship. Although we shared the same room, my grandmother no longer came to school with me. I used to go to an English school in a motor bus. There were no dogs in the streets and she took to feeding sparrows in the courtyard of our city house.

As the years rolled by we saw less of each other. For some time she continued to wake me up and get me ready for school. When I came back she would ask me what the teacher had taught me. I would tell her English words and little things of Western science and learning, the law of gravity, Archimedes' principle, the world being round, etc. This made her unhappy. She could not help me with my lessons. She did not believe in the things they taught at the English school and was distressed that there was no teaching about god and the scriptures. One day I announced that we were being given music lessons. She was very disturbed. To her music had lewd associations. It was the monopoly of harlots and beggar—and not meant for gentle folk. She rarely talked to me after that. When I went up to university, I was given a room of my own. The common link of friendship was snapped. My grandmother accepted her seclusion with resignation. She rarely left her spinning wheel to talk to anyone. From sunrise to sunset she sat by her wheel spinning and reciting prayers. Only in the afternoon she relaxed for a while to feed the sparrows. While she sat in the veranda breaking the bread into little bits, hundreds of little birds collected round her creating a veritable bedlam of chirrupings. Some came and perched on her legs, others on her shoulders. Some even sat on her head. She smiled but never shooed them away. It used to be the happiest half-hour of the day for her.

When I decided to go abroad for further studies, I was sure my grandmother would be upset. I would be away for five years, and at her age one could never tell. But my grandmother could. She was not even sentimental. She came to leave me at the railway station but did not talk or show any emotion. Her lips moved in prayer, her mind was lost in prayer. Her fingers were busy telling the beads of her rosary. Silently she kissed my forehead, and when I left I cherished the moist imprint as perhaps the last sign of physical contact between us.

But that was not so. After five years I came back home and was met by her at the station. She did not look a day older. She still had no time for words, and while she clasped me in her arms I could hear her reciting her prayer. Even on the first day of my arrival, her happiest moments were with her sparrows whom she fed longer and with frivolous rebukes.

In the evening a change came over her. She did not pray. She collected the women of the neighbourhood, got an old drum and started to sing. For several hours she thumped the sagging skins of the dilapidated drum and sang of the home-coming of warriors. We had to persuade her to stop to avoid overstraining. That was the first time since I had known her that she did not pray.

The next morning she was taken ill. It was a mild fever and the doctor told us that it would go. But my grandmother thought differently. She told us that her end was near. She said that, since only a few hours before the close of the last chapter of her life she had omitted to pray, she was not going to waste any more time talking to us.

We protested. But she ignored our protests. She lay peacefully in bed praying and telling her beads. Even before we could suspect, her lips stopped moving and the rosary fell from her lifeless fingers. A peaceful pallor spread on her face and we knew that she was dead.

We lifted her off the bed and, as is customary, laid her on the ground and covered her with a red shroud. After a few hours of mourning we left her alone to make arrangements for her funeral.

In the evening we went to her room with a crude stretcher to take her to be cremated. The sun was setting and had lit her room and veranda with a blaze of golden light. We stopped half-way in the courtyard. All over the veranda and in her room right up to where she lay dead and stiff wrapped in the red shroud, thousands of sparrows sat scattered on the floor. There was no chirping. We felt sorry for the birds and my mother fetched some bread for them. She broke it into little crumbs, the way my grandmother used to, and threw it to them. The sparrows took no notice of the bread. When we carried my grandmother's corpse off, they flew away quietly. Next morning the sweeper swept the bread crumbs into the dust bin.

POSTHUMOUS

I am in bed with fever. It is not serious. In fact, it is not serious at all, as I have been left alone to look after myself. I wonder what would happen if the temperature suddenly shot up. Perhaps I would die. That would be really hard on my friends. I have so many and am so popular. I wonder what the papers would have to say about it. They couldn't just ignore me. Perhaps the *Tribune* would mention it on its front page with a small photograph. The headline would read 'Sardar Khushwant Singh Dead'—and then in somewhat smaller print:

We regret to announce the sudden death of Sardar Khushwant Singh at 6 p.m. last evening. He leaves behind a young widow, two infant children and a large number of friends and admirers to mourn his loss. It will be recalled that the Sardar came to settle in Lahore some five years ago from his home town, Delhi. Within these years he rose to a position of eminence in the Bar and in politics. His loss will be mourned generally throughout the Province.

Amongst those who called at the late Sardar's residence were the P.A. to the Prime Minister, the P.A. to the chief justice, several ministers and judges of the high court.

In a statement to the press, the Hon'ble Chief Justice said: 'I feel that the Punjab is poorer by the passing away of this man. The cruel hand of death has cut short the promise of a brilliant career.'

At the bottom of the page would be an announcement:

The funeral will take place at 10 a.m. today.

I feel very sorry for myself and for all my friends. With difficulty I check the tears which want to express sorrow at my own death. But I also feel elated and want people to mourn me. So I decide to die—just for the fun of it as it were. In the evening, giving enough time for the press to hear of my death, I give up the ghost. Having emerged from my corpse, I come down and sit on the cool marble steps at the entrance to wallow in posthumous glory.

In the morning I get the paper before my wife. There is no chance of a squabble over the newspaper as I am downstairs already, and in any case my wife is busy pottering around my corpse. The *Tribune* lets me down. At the bottom of page three, column one I find myself inserted in little brackets of obituary notices of retired civil servants—and that is all. I feel annoyed. It must be that blighter Shafi, special representative. He never liked me. But I couldn't imagine he would be so mean as to deny me a little importance when I was dead. However, he couldn't keep the wave of sorrow which would run over the Province from trickling into his paper. My friends would see to that.

Near the high court the paper is delivered fairly early. In the house of my lawyer friend Qadir it is deposited well before dawn. It isn't that the Qadirs are early risers. As a matter of fact, hardly anyone stirs in the house before 9 a.m. But Qadir is a great one for principles and he insists that the paper must be available early in the morning even if it is not looked at.

As usual, the Qadirs were in bed at 9 a.m. He had worked very late at night. She believed in sleep anyhow. The paper was brought in on a tray along with a tumbler of hot water with a dash of lime juice. Qadir sipped the hot water between intervals of cigarette smoking. He had to do this to make his bowels work. He only glanced at the headlines in bed. The real reading was done when the cigarette and lime had had their effect. The knowledge of how fate had treated me had to await the lavatory.

In due course Qadir ambled into the bathroom with the paper in one hand and a cigarette perched on his lower lip. Comfortably seated, he began to scan it thoroughly and his eye fell on news of lesser import. When he got to page three, column one he stopped smoking for a moment, a very brief moment. Should he get up and shout to his wife? No, he decided, that would be an unnecessary demonstration. Qadir was a rationalist. He had become more of one since he married a woman who was a bundle of emotions and explosions. The poor fellow was dead and nothing could be done about it. He knew that his wife would burst out crying when he told her. That was all the more reason that he should be matter-of-fact about it—just as if he was going to tell her of a case he had lost.

Qadir knew his wife well. He told her with an air of casualness, and she burst out crying. Her ten-year-old daughter came running into the room. She eyed her mother for a little while and then joined her in the wailing. Qadir decided to be severe.

'What are you making all this noise for?' he said sternly. 'Do you think it will bring him back to life?'

His wife knew that it was no use arguing with him. He always won the arguments.

'I think we should go to their house at once. His wife must be feeling wretched,' she said.

Qadir shrugged his shoulders.

'I am afraid I can't manage it. Much as I would like to condole with his wife—or rather widow—my duty to my clients comes first. I have to be at the tribunal in half an hour.'

Qadir was at the tribunal all day and his family stopped at home.

Not far from the city's big park lives another friend, Khosla. He and his family, consisting of a wife, three sons and a daughter, reside in this upper-class residential area. He is a judge and very high up in the bureaucracy.

Khosla is an early riser. He has to rise early because that is the only time he has to himself. During the day he has to work in the courts. In the evenings he plays tennis—and then he has to spend some time with the children and fussing with his wife. He has a large number of visitors, as he is very popular and enjoys popularity. But Khosla is ambitious. As a lad he had fancied himself as a clever boy. In his early youth his hair had begun to fall off and had uncovered a large bald forehead. Khosla had looked upon it as nature's confirmation of his opinion about himself. Perhaps he was a genius. The more he gazed upon his large head in the mirror, the more he became convinced that fate had marked for him an extraordinary career. So he worked harder. He won scholarships and rounded off his academic career by topping the list in the Civil Service examination. He had justified the confidence he had in himself by winning laurels in the stiffest competitive examination in the country. For some years he lived the life of a contented bureaucrat. In fact, he assured himself that he was what people called 'a success in life'.

After some years this contentment had vanished. Every time he brushed the little tuft at the back of his head and ran his hands across his vast forehead he became conscious of unrealized expectations. There were hundreds of senior civil servants like him. All were considered successes in life. The Civil Service was obviously not enough. He would work, he would write—he knew he could write. There it was written in the size of his head. So Khosla took to writing. In order to write well he took to reading. He amassed a large library and regularly spent some hours in it before going to work.

This morning Khosla happened to be in a mood to write. He made himself a cup of tea and settled in a comfortable armchair by the electric radiator. He stuck the pencil in his mouth and meditated. He couldn't think of what to write. He decided to write his diary. He had spent the previous day listening to an important case. It was likely to go on for some days. The courtroom had been packed and everyone had been looking at him—that seemed a good enough subject. So he started to write.

Khosla was disturbed by the knock of the bearer bringing in the paper. He opened the news-sheet to read the truths of mundane existence.

Khosla was more interested in social affairs, births, marriages and deaths, than events of national or international import. He turned to page three, column one. His eye caught the announcement and he straightened up.

He just tapped his notebook with his pencil, and after a wake-up cough informed his wife of the news. She just yawned and opened her large dreamy eyes wide.

'I suppose you will close the high court today?' she said.

'I am afraid the high court doesn't close at just any excuse. I'll have to go. If I have any time I'll drop in on the way—or we can call on Sunday.'

The Khoslas did not come. Nor did many others for whose sorrow at my demise I had already felt sorrowful.

At 10 o' clock a little crowd had collected in front of the open space beneath my flat. It consisted mainly of people I did not expect to see. There were some lawyers in their court dress, and a number of sightseers who wanted to find out what was happening. Two friends of mine also turned up, but they stood apart from the crowd. One was a tall, slim man who looked like an artist. With one hand he kept his cigarette in place, the other he constantly employed in pushing his long hair off his forehead. He was a writer. He did not believe in attending funerals. But one had to hang around for a little while as a sort of social obligation. It was distasteful to him. There was something infectious about a corpse—so he smoked incessantly and made a cigarette smoke-screen between himself and the rest of the world.

The other friend was a communist, a short, slight man with wavy hair and a hawkish expression. His frame and expression belied the volcano which they camouflaged. His approach to everything was coldly Marxist and sentiment found no place in it. Deaths were unimportant events. It was the cause that mattered. He consulted the writer in a polite whisper.

'How far are you going?'

'I plan dropping off at the coffee house,' answered the other. 'Are you going the whole way?'

'No ruddy fear,' said the communist emphatically. 'Actually I had to be at a meeting at ten, and I was planning to be free of this by 9.30—but you know our people haven't the foggiest idea about time. I'll get along to the Party office now and then meet you at the coffee house at 11.30. Incidentally if you get the opportunity, just ask the hearse-driver if he is a member of the Tongawalla Union. Cheers.'

A little later a hearse, drawn by a bony brown horse arrived and pulled up in front of my doorstep. The horse and his master were completely oblivious of the solemnity of the occasion. The driver sat placidly chewing his betel nut and eyeing the assembly. He was wondering whether this was the type likely to produce a tip. The beast straightaway started to piddle and the crowd scattered to avoid the spray which rebounded off the brick floor.

The crowd did not have to wait very long. My corpse was brought down all tied up in white linen and placed inside the hearse. A few flowers were ceremoniously placed on me. The procession was ready to start.

Before we moved another friend turned up on his bicycle. He was somewhat dark and flabby. He carried several books on the carrier and had the appearance of a scholarly serious-minded professor. As soon as he saw the loaded hearse, he dismounted. He had great respect for the dead and was particular to express it. He put his bicycle in the hall, chained it, and joined the crowd. When my wife came down to bid her last farewell he was visibly moved. From his pocket he produced a little book and thoughtfully turned over its pages. Then he slipped through the people towards my wife. With tears in his eyes he handed the book to her.

'I've brought you a copy of the Gita. It will give you great comfort.'

Overcome with emotion, he hurriedly slipped back to wipe the tears which had crept into his eyes.

'This,' he said to himself with a sigh, 'is the end of human existence. This is the truth.'

He was fond of thinking in platitudes—but to him all platitudes were profound and had the freshness and vigour of original thought.

'Like bubbles,' he said to himself, 'human life is as momentary as a bubble.'

But one didn't just die and disappear. Matter could not immaterialize—it could only change its form. The Gita put it so beautifully, 'Like a man casts off old garments to put on new ones . . . so does the soul, etc., etc.'

The professor was lost in contemplation. He wondered what new garments his dead friend had donned.

His thoughts were disturbed by a movement between his legs. A little pup came round the professor's legs licking his trousers and looking up at him. The professor was a kind man. He involuntarily bent down and patted the little dog, allowing him to lick his hands.

The professor's mind wandered—he felt uneasy. He looked at the corpse and then at the fluffy little dog at his feet, who after all was part of god's creation.

'Like a man casts off old garments to put on new ones . . . so does the soul . . .'

No, no, he said to himself. He shouldn't allow such uncharitable thoughts to cross his mind. But he couldn't check his mind. It wasn't impossible. The Gita said so, too. And he bent down again and patted the pup with more tenderness and fellow feeling.

The procession was on the move. I was in front, uncomfortably laid within the glass hearse, with half a dozen people walking behind. It went down towards the river.

By the time it had passed the main street, I found myself in solitude. Some of the lawyers had left at the high court. My author friend had branched off to the coffee house, still smoking. At the local college, the professor gave me a last longing, lingering look and sped up the slope to his classroom. The remaining six or seven disappeared into the district courts.

I began to feel a little small. Lesser men than myself had had larger crowds. Even a dead pauper carried on a municipal wheelbarrow got two sweepers to cart him off. I had only one human being, the driver, and even he seemed to be oblivious of the enormity of the soul whose decayed mansion he was transporting on its last voyage. As for the horse, he was positively rude.

The route to the cremation ground is marked with an infinite variety of offensive smells. The climax is reached when one has to branch off the main road towards the crematorium along a narrow path which runs beside the city's one and only sewer. It is a stream of dull, black fluid with bubbles bursting on its surface all the time.

Fortunately for me, I was given some time to ruminate over my miscalculated posthumous importance. The driver pulled up under a large peepul tree near where the road turns off to the cremation ground. Under this peepul tree is a tonga stand and a water trough for horses to drink out of. The horse made for the water and the driver clambered off his perch to ask the tonga-drivers for a light for his cigarette.

The tonga-drivers gathered round the hearse and peered in from all sides.

'Must be someone rich,' said one. 'But there is no one with him,' queried another. 'I suppose this is another English custom—no one to go to funerals.'

By now I was thoroughly fed up. There were three ways open to me. One was to take the route to the cremation ground and, like the others that went there, give myself up to scorching flames, perhaps to be born again into a better world, but probably to be extinguished into nothingness. There was another road which forked off to the right towards the city. There lived harlots and other people of ill-repute. They drank and gambled and fornicated. Theirs was a world of sensation and they crammed their lives with all the varieties which the senses were capable of registering. The third one was to take the way back. It was difficult to make up one's mind. In situations like these the toss of a coin frequently helps. So I decided to toss the coin; heads and I hazard the world beyond; tails and I go to join the throng of sensation seekers in the city; if it is neither heads nor tails and the coin stands on its edge, I retrace my steps to a humdrum existence bereft of the spirit of adventure and denuded of the lust for living.

THE MULBERRY TREE

Vijay Lall was an early riser. He awoke to the harsh cawing of the first crows, and when he drew the curtains of his study window, he could see nothing except street lights glimmering in the distance. During the last few mornings of the waning moon, the apartment blocks around the square patch of lawn in his colony were bathed in soft moonlight. Then they made a pleasant sight. But at all other times they looked squat, staid and lifeless, like middle-aged women who had let themselves go. For some years now, the hour or two before sunrise was the only time he could gaze out of his window without being mildly irritated by what he saw.

Facing his window was a large mulberry tree, which had been planted at the time the apartment blocks were built and was over fifty years old, perhaps exactly as old as he. Vijay had developed a special relationship with this tree. Most of the winter it was without any leaves and its dry branches stuck out like the quills of a giant porcupine. During these months only the crows and sparrows visited it. Their cawing and twittering were his dawn chorus. Sometime in mid-February, usually the eighteenth, he noticed tiny green specks sprout from the seemingly dead brown branches. In recent years he had been watching out for this event and noted it down carefully in his diary. A week after they first became visible, the green specks turned into green leaves. And as spring turned to summer, the tree was covered with so thick a foliage that he could not see the branches. It became host to a variety of birds. Even before the eastern horizon turned grey

352

and the call for the Fajr prayer floated in from the tall minaret of the mosque across the road, a family of spotted owlets set up a racket—chitter-chitter-chatter-chatter—and roused the crows and sparrows roosting there for the night. Then came the green barbets. They wound themselves up with a low kook-kook-kook before exploding into an incessant katrook-katrook. Most afternoons koels, as shy as barbets, hid behind the foliage and called intermittently till the sun went down and the call for the Maghrib prayer rose from the mosque. As it got dark, the spotted owlets set up their racket again, which was a signal that it was time for his sundowner.

The mulberry came into its full glory at the time of the water festival, Holi, in March. Its invisible flowers turned into light green caterpillar-like fruit full of sweet juice. Humans vied with parakeets to be the first to get them. Street urchins threw sticks and stones to knock them down. Within a week the tree was denuded of all its fruit and then all it had to offer man, bird and beast was its cool shade. Stray dogs were chased away by the people living in the block closest to the tree, who tried to grab space under it for their cars against the scorching sun. Since Vijay was an early riser and worked at home, he did not have much problem getting the shadiest spot directly under a huge branch for his twenty-year-old car, a beige-coloured, temperamental Fiat called Annie. Although his car was regularly messed up by bird droppings, it remained cool through the day. It was during the long summer months that Vijay strengthened his personal relationship with the mulberry tree. He greeted it with a 'Hi' when he went to take Annie out for a drive and a 'Cheerio' when he parked her there for the night.

The mulberry tree was a constant in Vijay's life. He awoke to the bird-babble rising from its branches and had his first drink every evening at the hour when the owlets announced sunset. He brought out his woollens when its branches became bare, and began using his air-conditioner when they were heavy with foliage. It was a comfortable, sedate routine.

Then one day the tree almost killed Vijay, and his life was thrown out of gear.

~

It was the month of June; temperatures had soared into the forties. One way of remaining cool was to stay in an air-conditioned room. Another, and a healthier way, was to spend an hour or two in a swimming pool which cooled one off for the evening. Though Vijay felt lethargic after his siesta, he forced himself out of his apartment one particularly hot afternoon and walked to his car under the mulberry tree. It was oppressive and still. Not a breath of air; not a leaf stirred. The sky was a bleached grey. It looked ominously like a lull before a storm. He saw a wall of muddy brown advancing from the west, with kites wheeling above it. At this time of the year, dust storms were common; they blew in and out with blind fury, uprooting trees and telegraph poles and spreading layers of dust everywhere. Vijay thought it wise to get away as fast as he could. He had barely reversed ten yards when a dust-laden gale swept across the colony at devilish speed. He heard a loud crack, like that of thunder following lightning, and the enormous branch under which his car had been parked came crashing down on the tarmac. The earth trembled beneath him.

Vijay switched off the engine and sat still in the car for several minutes. The two chowkidars of the colony ran up to check if he was all right. He waved them away without rolling down his window, and just to prove that he was not rattled, turned Annie around and drove out. His hands were shaking. It was best to be somewhere else for a while.

The storm had blown away as fast as it came. Branches of trees littered the roads. An auto-rickshaw had turned turtle on Mathura Road and a small crowd had gathered around it. Vijay slowed down, wanting to know if the driver had survived, then changed his mind. By the time he got to the club pool, a cool, clean breeze was blowing. For an hour he had the pool all to himself. When other members and their children started streaming in, he came out of the water and stretched himself out on a poolside chair. He covered his face with his bath towel and went over the scene of destruction caused by the storm.

He had had the narrowest of escapes. Instead of being comfortably stretched out on a deck chair, he could have been in the morgue of some hospital with a smashed skull, and every bone in his body broken. What was even more unsettling was the manner in which he had escaped certain death: he did not remember a single day when his old Fiat had warmed up and started in less than half a minute at the very least, but today it had started instantly. A few seconds later and both he and Annie would have been crushed. Was it god's will that he should live a little longer?

Vijay was not sure about god, nor about providence. He had never given these things much thought. Now he did. Half-forgotten stories of providential escape from certain death came to his mind. Some instances that he remembered reading about were extremely bizarre. One was of a plane flying from Dublin to London's Heathrow Airport. It caught fire as it was approaching London. The pilot decided to make an emergency landing on an airstrip near a suburb called Mill Hill. As it descended, the plane hit the chimney of a house and broke into two. All the passengers and crew were killed, except a stewardess who was sitting at the tail end of the plane. She was thrown out of the burning aircraft and into the swimming pool in the garden of the house. Not a bone broken, not a scratch on her body. Why was she singled out for survival, and by whom?

Some years later there was the case of a man standing on the crowded platform of a London Underground station. He fell on the tracks as the train was coming out of the tunnel. The train came to an abrupt halt just as its wheels touched the man's body. The authorities decided to reward the train driver for his vigilance, but he was an honest man and refused to accept the reward. He had not stopped the train, he said; someone in the train must have pulled the emergency cord, though he couldn't imagine why, since no one in the enclosed compartments could have seen what lay ahead on the tracks. Enquiries were made, but no passenger claimed to have pulled the emergency cord. Whose was the unseen hand that had brought the train to a sudden halt in the nick of time? Why had the man's life been spared? Was it to allow him time to finish some task left unfinished? Or was it to compensate him for some good deed he had done?

But the most mind-boggling was a case in Vijay's own country. A man was travelling in a crowded bus along a narrow mountain road. He took a window seat in the last row. Since it was autumn and the weather had turned chilly, he wrapped himself in his shawl and soon fell asleep. He awoke a few hours later when he felt something slimy around one of his ankles. It was a small snake which had found the man's leg a warm place to hibernate for the winter. The man screamed. The bus came to a screeching halt. The driver, conductor and passengers rushed to the back of the bus but shrank back at the sight of the snake curled around the man's ankle. No one had any idea what to do about it. The driver ran out of patience and suggested that the man slowly step out of the bus and sit on the parapet of the road with his leg exposed to the sun. It would induce the snake to leave him and find another dark, warm place and he could then get on the bus following them. The man did as he was told. The bus moved on. The snake behaved as had been predicted: it uncurled itself and slithered down the hillside. The man got on the following bus. A mile or so ahead they noticed the parapet of the road knocked down. The bus ahead of them was lying upside-down in the khud at the bottom of the hill. There were no survivors. The only one to escape was the man who had got off the bus because of the snake curled around his ankle.

Vijay went over and over these incidents. He felt disoriented. He left the club as the evening came on. When he reached his colony, he parked his car just inside the gate and walked up to examine the damage the mulberry tree had suffered. The branch which had been wrenched out had left a nasty gash exposing a hollow trunk. The fallen branch had been hacked into pieces to be used as firewood and its leaves stripped off to feed goats. Lots of twigs were littered about the tarmac. No one had dared to park their cars under the tree. Though not superstitious, Vijay also avoided leaving his car near it. He found another place, close to his window. This time the old mulberry tree had failed to demolish him or his car, but he had an uneasy feeling that it had turned malevolent towards him. As he entered his dark apartment and fumbled for the light switch, the strange thought came to him that the tree was in the last leg of its life and had meant to take him with it.

By the next morning everyone in the blocks of flats around the square was talking of Vijay's miraculous escape from what must certainly have been the end of his life. They were used to seeing Annie occupy pride of place under the mulberry tree; they now saw her parked alongside his apartment, without a dent or even a scratch on her body. His neighbours came to congratulate him and get details of the story. With every narration he made it sound more and more dramatic. 'It was the will of the Ooperawala,' some of his neighbours said, pointing heavenwards. 'Inscrutable are His ways. If the good lord is your protector, no one can touch a hair on your head.' A silver-haired great grandmother, whom Vijay knew to be close to a hundred years old, added, 'No one can go before his time; no one can live a second beyond the span allotted to him.' Most were agreed that Vijay must have done some good karma in his previous life and had been rewarded for it. God is your protector, they said. God is good and merciful. A faint smile came over Vijay's face at this, as he recalled the lines of a popular film song:

Ooperwala—very good very good
Nicheywala—very bad very bad . . .

It was an absurd song. But what he felt was no less absurd: till this morning he would have described himself as an agnostic; now, though not quite a believer, he felt like god's chosen one.

The morning papers had pictures of the havoc caused by the dust storm on their front pages. A huge neem tree had been uprooted in Chanakyapuri. It lay diagonally across the road and there was a Maruti under it, reduced to a crumpled sheet of metal. Fortunately, there had been no one in the car. A peepal stretched across another road in the Delhi University campus with three mangled cars under it. Four men and two women had been seriously injured and taken to hospital. A small child in one of the cars had escaped unscathed. The storm had taken a toll of five lives: two labourers sleeping under a tree, two cyclists hit by a hoarding which had collapsed on them, and an elderly lady who ran to save her pet Pekinese from a falling eucalyptus only to be crushed under it. Their deaths made news, but among his friends Vijay's narrow escape was the bigger news. They came morning and evening, all with stories of their own: of people who did not get to the airport on time and missed their flights that went down; trains that people had missed that went off the tracks.

The more Vijay heard these tales, the more he was convinced that he was someone special, above the common run of humanity. This added to his state of disorientation, because for as long as he could remember nothing very special had happened to him.

From the block of flats in which Vijay lived, his story spread to the neighbouring Khan Market. The shops were agog with talk of his incredible luck.

Vijay was known to most of the shopkeepers as he was seen in the market almost every evening, peering into shop windows, flipping through magazines displayed on the footpath, going into one bookshop after another and browsing around the shelves but rarely buying any books—they had become too expensive, and, in any case, as a freelance newspaper columnist he got more books to review than he could read. In the two antique shops, he examined figurines of Hindu gods and goddesses, garnet necklaces and brass artefacts, asked their price but never bought anything. In the music shops he hung about listening to tapes being played at the request of buyers. At the greengrocer's he gaped awestruck at monstrous Korean apples, small-sized honey-sweet Japanese watermelons, avocado pears from Bangalore, fresh broccoli, baby corn, asparagus and artichokes. Their buyers were largely European and American diplomats and journalists who in Vijay's opinion drew unacceptably large salaries and spoiled the market rates.

Vijay did not like the shop-owners of Khan Market. They were single-minded in their pursuit of money: everything here was more expensive than in any other market in the city. There were other reasons why Vijay had no time for them. Most shop-owners were Punjabi refugees from Pakistan—in one of his columns he had described them as semi-literate parvenus who had converted their hatred for Pakistan to prejudice against all Muslims. They supported one or the other of the Hindu fundamentalist parties. Between them they had built a small temple behind the main market which represented their religious beliefs. Ostensibly it was a Krishna temple, Shri Gopal Mandir, named after the deity, and life-size statues of Krishna and his consort, Radha, were put up on the altar. But the temple also accommodated several other deities favoured by the shopkeepers who were masters at hedging their bets. So there was the monkey-god, Hanuman, on one side of the entrance gate and Goddess Durga, astride a lion, on the other. Inside, the left wall had the Sai Baba of Shirdi, with stubble on his chin, one leg over the other and peering into space, and next to him the Sai Baba of Puttaparti with his halo of fuzzy hair and a pudgy hand raised in blessing. There was also a black granite Shivalinga, and in the cubicle next to it, idols of Shiva's consort Parvati and his elephant-headed son, Ganesha. 'To every Hindu his or her own god or goddess' was the market motto. The only one on whom all were agreed as the supreme divinity was Lakshmi, the Goddess of Wealth.

Vijay did not need the blessings of the many deities housed in the temple, just as he had no need for much of what was sold in Khan Market. The only things he bought were a packet of cigarettes and a couple of paans. He put one paan in his mouth, kept another in his pocket to chew after dinner, lit a cigarette and launched upon his hour-long wanderings through the market. When anyone asked him why he made the rounds of Khan Market every evening, he answered, 'To see the raunaq. I like watching the happy crowds.' And he would quote the Urdu poet Zauq: 'I pass through the bazaar (of the world) / There is nothing I want to buy.'

There were others who, like Vijay, came to Khan Market every evening for the raunaq of multicoloured lights, fancy cars and trendy people going from shop to shop. Vijay recognized many of the regulars and even exchanged smiles with a few, but rarely spoke to them. There was a woman, in particular, who attracted Vijay's attention and curiosity. She was not a regular but came to the market two or three times a week, not to see the raunaq but to do her shopping. She came in a chauffeur-driven car which was parked at the end of the market, facing the temple. She emerged from the car, always carrying a plastic handbag, crossed the road and went past the temple to another market which had a liquor store. She returned shortly afterwards to dump the bag full of liquor bottles in her car. Then she took out another bag, this time of black canvas, and strolled along the shops at a leisurely pace, stopping at every bookshop window. The only shop she entered was The Book Shop, which was classier than the others and played soft Western classical music at all hours of the day. It warmed Vijay towards the woman, since this was his favourite bookshop too, though he only ever bought his weekly magazines from it. He never entered the shop while the woman was inside. He loitered near the entrance till she emerged, usually half an hour later, and tailed her as she proceeded round the market to the greengrocer's and the butcher's.

When she returned to her car, she handed over the shopping bag to her driver, leaned against the bonnet and lit a cigarette. She surveyed the scene around her as she smoked, unbothered by the looks some of the people coming from the temple gave her. When she had finished her cigarette, she stamped the stub under her sandals—the same bright red pair each time, Vijay had noticed—and ordered the driver: 'Chalo'. Two doors slammed shut and the Honda City eased out of the parking lot and sped away.

Vijay could not make out why this woman attracted his attention more than other visitors to Khan Market. It was true that he was immediately drawn towards Indian women who smoked and drank: to him, they were liberated women, possibly amenable to entering into frankly sexual relationships, no strings attached. Yet there were several other women he met at parties who also smoked and drank nonchalantly but left no impression on him. What was it about this woman? She had cropped black hair, thicker than any he had seen on another head, and while it was true that he liked short hair on women, that could not be the only reason for the attraction. As for looks, though she had a pleasant face, shapely breasts and an impressive posterior that protruded invitingly, a good number of women who came to the market were better looking.

Why did he follow her around, then? And why was it that he looked forward to seeing her but did not want to get any closer to her and strike up a conversation? It was as if he was afraid of ruining something. His infatuation was a mystery to him. So was she. He tried to guess facts about her life. She usually wore a salwar-kameez, but no bindi on her forehead nor sindhoor in the parting of her hair. At first he thought she might be Muslim or Christian, till he noticed she had a mangalsutra around her neck. Evidently she was Hindu and married. He could not make out where in India she came from: she could be Punjabi, Rajasthani, from UP or Maharashtra. He gave her names: Usha, Aarti, Menaka. Some evenings, having his drinks, he thought of her and felt warm and mellow. But it never occurred to him to do anything more than follow her around quietly.

A few evenings after the branch of the mulberry tree tried but failed to kill him, things changed.

Vijay saw the woman in the market a little earlier than her usual time. He followed her, as usual, a few steps behind. She went inside The Book Shop. And without thinking about it, he walked into the shop after her. He pretended to browse, picking out a book, reading the blurb, putting it back and pulling out another, as he kept inching closer to her. He heard her ask the proprietress, 'I'm looking for a suitable birthday gift for a boy of fifteen.'

'We have quite a selection for his age group,' replied the young proprietress. The proprietress was a tall and attractive young girl who wore a diamond nose pin. She reminded Vijay of another girl he had known in his youth whom he had wanted vaguely to spend the rest of his life with, but the romance had fizzled out at the prospect of marriage.

'What are his interests?' she asked the woman. 'Stamps, photography, wildlife, shikar, computers?'

'I'm not sure. He reads a bit of everything. Perhaps good fiction . . . about wildlife?'

'What about Joy Adamson's *Born Free*, about her pet lioness Elsa?'

'I think he read that a couple of years back.'

Vijay heard himself say, 'Why not Kipling's *Jungle Book*? It has all kinds of animals: Sher Khan, the tiger, Baloo, the bear. And there is Mowgli, the wolf-boy.'

The woman turned towards him, 'You must be kidding! That is kid's stuff. He read it when he learned to read English.' To soften the snub she beamed a smile at him.

Vijay persisted. 'What about Jim Corbett's books on his encounters with man-eating tigers and leopards?'

'He has read all of Corbett's books,' replied the woman, cutting him short.

Vijay did not give up. He was feeling a little reckless. 'I bet he hasn't read Gerald Durrell's *My Family and Other Animals*.'

The girl from the shop lent her support. 'It has long been one of our best-sellers, ma'am. I'm sure the young man will enjoy it as well.'

So it was Durrell's book that won the evening. Both the women thanked Vijay for suggesting it. He felt strangely elated. The woman paid for the book and as she was leaving, turned to Vijay and said, 'Thanks for everything. Goodnight.'

'My pleasure,' he beamed like a schoolboy.

On his second drink later that evening, Vijay found himself thinking of the woman and felt restless. The mellow, quiet feeling of the past had vanished. Had it been a mistake to talk to her? He knew that he could not follow her around silently as he used to. He had crossed an invisible line and now he must get to know her better. He decided that he would do so. He was aware that she must be at least twenty, perhaps twenty-five years younger than him, and he could be snubbed badly, but life was too short not to take chances. The thought of taking chances excited him.

Vijay ran into her again three days later. He was not sure if she recognized him. He took the liberty of greeting her and asked, 'So, how did you like Durrell?'

She gave him a broad smile and replied, 'Hi there! Enjoyed it hugely—both of us. Thanks for suggesting it.'

'You live around here?' he asked. 'I see you almost every other evening.'

'Not far. I like to do my shopping here. I can get everything I want, and it is so cheerful. And you?'

'I live in the block of flats across the road. A poky little flat crammed with books. I have no other hobbies. I'm a boring man. I'll be honoured if you'll drop by some evening for a cup of chai or whatever.'

'Thanks, but not today,' she replied brusquely. 'I may take you up on your invitation some other time. Nice meeting you.' She extended her hand to bid him farewell. It was the first time he touched her. He liked the feel of her soft, warm hand. He wanted to hold it for longer but she did not encourage him. Pulling her hand out of his discreetly, she said, 'See you. I must get things before the shops close.' And she disappeared in the crowd of shoppers.

Another surprise awaited Vijay in his pursuit of his newfound passion. One afternoon he was loitering in the Masjid Nursery looking at plants for sale. There were three such nurseries close to his apartment. Although he bought nothing as he had not enough space in his flat for plants, he liked looking at them, finding out their names and prices. Masjid Nursery, so named because it was next to a mosque, had the largest display of flowers and cacti. While he was going around the nursery, he spotted the woman come to the mosque. She came on foot, there was no sign of her car. She took her sandals off at the entrance and went in. Vijay had assumed that she was Hindu; what was she doing in a mosque? Perhaps he was wrong. But then, Muslim women did not come to pray in mosques. Perhaps her son was at the madrasa reading the Quran and she had come to pick him up. Vijay hung around in the nursery for over half an hour. He heard the call for the Maghrib prayer. Men trooped in, taking their shoes inside with them, and fifteen minutes later, streamed out. It began to turn dark. Vijay could not hold his curiosity much longer. He went up to the entrance of the mosque. Only the lady's bright red sandals lay close to the threshold. He peered in. There was a lone man sitting close to the pulpit, reciting from the Quran. To his right was another small door. Possibly she had entered from the main door and left by the side door, forgetting about her sandals. Vijay paused for a few moments, then picked up the sandals and brought them home.

It was a curious, inexplicable sense of triumph—like a scientist making a breakthrough in his research for the lodestone by which base metal could be turned into gold. He now had an excuse to invite her to his flat and get to know her name, to find out who she was and what she did. He put the sandals in a gap in one of his book shelves, next to the leather-bound volumes of *Inferno*, *Don Quixote* and *Rubaiyat* that were his prized possessions. Strange things were happening to Vijay Lall.

The next three evenings he went to the market and spent longer than usual going around the shops. The raunaq of Khan Market was no longer enough. He waited, but there was no sign of her. He bought two packets of cigarettes and a couple of paans. He wandered agitatedly for some time. He returned home defeated.

He was luckier on the fourth day. Returning from The Book Shop with copies of *Outlook* and *India Today*, he saw her coming towards him with a bag full of groceries. She was barefoot. Vijay stopped right in front of her and greeted her.

'Good evening.'

'Hi there,' she replied with a distant smile.

'What's happened to your red sandals?' he asked.

She looked down at her bare feet, as if noticing them for the first time, and replied, 'I have lost them. How did you know they were red?'

'I am a very observant man. You must not walk barefoot on these dirty roads and pavements. You might step on a sharp pebble or piece of glass. Surely you must have other footwear at home?'

'Nope. Maybe I should buy a new pair.'

'You can save your money. I have your sandals in my flat.'

She looked him full in the face, visibly alarmed. 'In your flat? Where did you find them? And how did you know they were mine?'

'I am observant and I am also a good spy,' he replied. 'I happened to be in the Masjid Nursery when I saw you take off your sandals and go into the mosque. You probably went out by the side door forgetting about them. I picked them up and took them home. I've taken good care of them. Don't you want them back?'

'Of course I do,' she replied. Her brow gathered in a frown. 'I'll send my driver to pick them up when I'm done with my shopping. Where do you live?'

'No,' he said firmly. 'I will return your sandals only to you and no one else. I've told you, I live just across the road. Besides, you might forget to send the driver. I can tell that you are very absent-minded.'

He half expected to be told to buzz off. But she seemed to like what she heard and smiled. 'That I am. A little off my rocker, as they say. Eccentric and moody.'

'Sounds charming. So, do I have the pleasure of your company?'

She laughed and nodded her head. He accompanied her to her car. She asked her driver to turn around and take her and the sahib to the block of flats across the road. They had no conversation in the car as Vijay kept instructing the driver where to turn to park the car. 'Wait for a few minutes,' she told the driver as they stepped out. Vijay opened the door of his flat and ushered her in.

She looked around the room. 'Books, books, books. You could not have read them all.'

'No, it will take more than a lifetime to read all of them. I just like surrounding myself with books. Do be seated,' he said, pointing to the sofa. 'I'll get your sandals.'

She sat down. She looked sheepishly at her dirty feet resting on the expensive Bukhara carpet. 'I'm afraid I'll dirty your kaaleen,' she said.

'Don't you worry about that, it has suffered much worse,' he assured her. 'Stay right where you are, I'll be back in a minute.'

Vijay came back not with her shoes but a basin of water and a towel thrown over his shoulder.

'What's this for?' she asked nervously.

'You'll find out,' he replied. 'See what a mess your feet are—black with gravel and dust. Put them in the basin, I'll clean them.'

A look of alarm returned to her face, but she submitted tamely and put her feet in the basin. The water was warm. He pulled a moorha and sat in front of her. 'Relax,' he said gently. She leaned back, rested her head on the blue sofa and shut her eyes. He soaped her feet and sponged them. He took his own time doing this. Then moving the basin out of his way, he put her feet on his knees by turns and rubbed them with a towel. 'Lovely arches,' he said, kneading her feet with his thumbs. 'You may open your eyes. See how clean and soft they look.'

She opened her eyes. She saw the basin full of muddy black water and her feet looking fresh and clean. The thin gold chain around her right ankle was gleaming after the wash. So was the silver ring she wore on one of her toes. 'You seem to be a nice gentleman. But why are you doing all this for me?' she asked. 'I don't even know your name.'

'All in good time,' he replied with a grin. He picked up the basin of dirty water and soapsuds and took it to his bathroom, poured down its contents in the loo and pulled the flush. He washed his hands and came back with the red sandals. Once again he sat on the moorha facing her and slipped the sandals on her feet. 'Don't go about leaving them at the doorsteps of mosques again. They may never come back. Even I might not return them the next time, since they've brought me good luck.'

'What do you mean? What luck have they brought you?'

'Made you visit my poky den. I hope not for the first time, or the last.'

She blushed and brushed the hair off her forehead. 'I don't even know your name,' she said, looking straight at him.

'Vijay. And yours?'

'Karuna.'

'Karuna, meaning compassion. A lovely name. But Karuna what?'

'Karuna, that's all,' she said curtly.

'I only asked because I am curious. You have a Hindu name, so what were you doing in a mosque?'

'Nosey, aren't we? Anyway, if it is so important for you to know, I went because I had never seen the inside of a mosque.' She rose abruptly. 'I must go home now. Thanks for everything. I still don't know why you took all the trouble, though.' He walked her to the door. He hoped to linger there a while, to hold her back, but she was in no mood to oblige. 'Bye,' she said without turning back as she hurried away. He heard her car start up and go out of his block of apartments.

An odd character, this Karuna woman! mused Vijay. She was obviously somewhat soft in the head. Or why would a woman who went about in a chauffeur-driven car not buy herself a new pair of sandals and go about barefoot instead? She probably had a well-to-do husband and children. How was it that none of them bothered to notice her waywardness?

More difficult to explain was his sudden desire to get to know her. She was clearly unpredictable—warm and approachable one moment, brusque and distant the next. He would normally not have any patience with such people—he never did, and years of living alone had made him even less tolerant. But despite her erratic behaviour his infatuation with Karuna kept getting stronger. He was not entirely sure of what he wanted: Was he content to just have her around him to talk to and touch furtively once in a while? Or did he want her in his bed for wild sex, the kind he had not experienced in years? All that he was certain of was that the days when he did not see her were unreal and incomplete. Now he found himself thinking: The episode of the lost-and-found sandals must have conveyed my feelings for her. Will she respond?

He went to Khan Market every evening. He pottered around in The Book Shop, looking disinterestedly at new books. He peered inside other bookstores, the grocer's and the butcher's. She was nowhere. Then one evening, for no reason, he went to the Krishna temple at the rear of the market. It was time for the sandhya prayer. The scent of agar incense floated out of the temple and through the clanging of bells he could hear worshippers sing

Jai Jagdish Hare! He had never been inside a temple before, or any place of worship for that matter, but something compelled him to enter the courtyard and take a closer look at what was going on. One side of the courtyard was lined with the shoes and chappals of worshippers. A caretaker sat on a stool keeping watch over them. In the second row was a pair of red sandals that Vijay recognized so well. He stayed in the courtyard till the prayer was over and worshippers started streaming out with prasad in their palms. As she stepped out of the crowd, he accosted her.

'What are you doing here?' he asked. 'One evening at a mosque, another evening at a temple.'

'Hi there!' she responded. 'And what are you doing loitering outside?'

'I spotted the red sandals but could not steal them. That man with the stick had his hawk eyes on them. So I thought I might wait for their owner and invite her for a cup of tea or coffee.'

'You may not,' she replied matter-of-factly. 'I have another date.' She took a quick glance at her wristwatch. 'Omigod! I'm half an hour late!' She slipped on her sandals and ran across the road to her car.

A month after his miraculous escape from death, Vijay heard of another miracle but did not witness it, though it happened no further from his little flat than Khan Market's Shri Gopal Mandir. One evening when he went there, hoping to run into the elusive Karuna, he saw a long queue, starting at the temple and snaking around the entire market. Everyone in the queue was carrying a tin can, a tumbler, a lota or a thermos flask. He did not like this disruption of the market routine; besides, all these people would make it more difficult for him to spot the object of his affection. He broke through the queue to get to The Book Shop. It was closed for some reason. Disappointed, he walked over to another bookstore, owned by an earthy, robust man who sported a thick, curled moustache, like those worn by men in advertisements for aphrodisiacs. Vijay had named him Hakim Tara Chand. The bookstore owner greeted him affably and as usual asked, 'Some coffee-shoffee, chai-vai?' Vijay waved a 'No thanks' with his hand and asked, 'What is going on here? Who are all those people outside?'

'Andh vishvas, sir,' Hakim Tara Chand said, shaking his head but wearing an indulgent smile. 'Apparently the gods are accepting milk from worshippers. Those people are waiting to make their offerings to the idols.'

'What? Stone and metal idols drinking milk?' Already disappointed at not having found Karuna in the market, Vijay sounded more irritated than incredulous.

Hakim Tara Chand was taken aback by Vijay's tone and was apologetic. 'As I said, sir—blind faith. I know you don't believe in these things, nor do I . . . but why deny people the right to believe in whatever they want to believe? My wife went to the temple with a jug of milk this morning and poured it on Ganeshji's idol. The milk disappeared. Where, why, only Bhagwan knows.'

'Good business for milkmen,' sneered Vijay. 'Who started all this?'

'I don't know. But a Hindi paper says that Shreeswamy claims he invoked Ganeshji to accept offerings of milk.'

'Shreeswamy! That crook who has a dozen criminal cases pending against him and has been jailed a few times?'

Hakim Tara Chand put his hands together and replied, 'Forgive me, but I won't say anything against a man who is worshipped by so many—presidents, prime ministers, multimillionaires, film stars. Every other leader of ours goes to him for advice. So I think, there must be something to him . . . Not that I believe in these things.'

'He's said to provide call girls to Arab sheikhs.'

'Tauba! Maybe the papers say so. I have no knowledge.'

Vijay sensed Hakim Tara Chand was not keen to talk on the subject, so he moved on: 'Achha ji, I'll see you soon.' He decided to go back home, but then he thought there might be some chance of finding Karuna at the temple. She seemed to have an unusual interest in places of worship. He didn't think she herself would offer milk as the others did, but she might want to witness the spectacle. So he went along the queue around the corner facing the temple. From the way they were dressed, the people in the queue seemed middle class and educated. Marching up and down, swaying his baton, was a senior police officer in uniform, perhaps a superintendent. There was a large red tilak on his forehead, indicating that he had already made his offering. He had four of his constables with him, walking briskly along the queue and asking people not to be impatient. 'You will get your turn,' the officer assured the eager worshippers. 'Be patient, the miracle will go on for some days.' Vijay thought of asking him how he knew, but he did not want to get into an argument with a policeman.

Pye dogs along the queue were licking up the milk that spilled out of the containers. A boy of seven or eight years was warding off a puppy jumping on his leg, wagging his tail furiously and yapping for a few drops. The boy tried to kick the puppy away and spilt some of his milk as he did so. The grateful puppy lapped it up, now wagging his tail in gratitude.

'You can't offer this milk to Shri Ganesh. It has been polluted by a dog,' growled a man standing behind the boy. 'Go and get another jug from the milkman.' The boy burst into tears, poured the rest of the milk on the ground and gave the puppy a vicious kick before going off to look for fresh milk.

Briefly distracted by the commotion, Vijay walked on towards Shri Gopal Mandir. Three constables barred the way to the road that separated the market from the temple. When those who had made their offerings came out, the policemen stopped all traffic to allow a dozen or so people from the queue to cross the road and enter the temple. Vijay came to the end of the queue. Standing right in front, awaiting her turn to cross the road, was Karuna. She had a large steel tumbler in her hand.

'I had a feeling I would find you here,' he said happily, resisting a strong impulse to reach out and hold her hand.

'Hi there!' she said, genuinely surprised, then looked away. The policemen who had blocked vehicular traffic on the road urged the queue to move on: 'Chalo, chalo, chalo.' About twenty worshippers, Karuna among them, sped across the road to the temple.

Vijay's spirits plummeted as abruptly as they had risen. She hadn't even bothered to wave goodbye, or ask him to wait while she made her offering and returned. Or even suggest that he come with her—it was not the kind of thing he would normally do, but he would have gone if she had asked. He waited for close to an hour to catch her as she came out. Worshippers in the queue kept moving in batches of ten or twenty into the temple and came out with their faces beaming. There was no sign of the one Vijay was looking for. It reminded him of her disappearance in the mosque. She had found another side door.

It was already past his drink hour, a ritual he was very particular about. But today he did not go back home. He looked for her car. The police had ordered all cars to be parked on the road to make room for the crowd of worshippers. The queue seemed unending, as more people kept coming to join it. Vijay walked distractedly through the crowds.

He did not find Karuna's car, so he hung about a paanwala's kiosk, unable to decide what he should do next. His mood had soured. He felt like picking a fight. The paanwala was waxing eloquent about the miracle of the gods to a group of young men in saffron kurtas who were waiting their turn to be served.

'Lalaji, your gods are moody,' Vijay said to the paanwala, 'I have a stone Ganpati outside my flat. I put a cupful of milk to his tusk and his trunk but he did not drink a drop.'

'You have to have faith for miracles to happen,' said one of the young men. 'Faith can move mountains. Lord Krishna held up a hill on his little finger to save his village from a cloudburst. Hanuman uprooted a mountain to get the Sanjeevini herb. So what is unusual about the gods showing their pleasure by accepting offerings of milk from people of all castes, from the highest to the lowest—even mlechhas? It is indeed a chamatkar.' He looked pleased with his oration.

'This is what makes India great,' added another man. Then he quoted the Urdu poet Iqbal's lines: 'Greek, Egyptian and Roman rulers have all been wiped off the face of the earth; there must be some reason that India still shines in all its pristine glory.'

Vijay felt his temper rise. 'Greece, Egypt and Rome continue to flourish as they ever did in the past; only India remains buried under the debris of ignorance and superstition. Stone and metal imbibing milk is the latest example of our continuing backwardness. This trickery is the best our gods can do!' he proclaimed in a loud voice.

'Stop this bakwas!' barked the young man with the caste mark on his forehead. 'If you want to buk-buk, do it elsewhere, not so close to our temple. Are you a Mussalman?'

Soon the argument had become a shouting match. Vijay yelled, 'You are a bunch of chootiyas, you make India a laughing stock of the world!'

The young man grabbed Vijay by his shirt collar and shouted, 'Saale, you dare call us chootiyas! I'll split your arse right here!'

The paanwala jumped down from his seat and separated the two. 'Babuji, don't create a hangama in front of my shop,' he pleaded with Vijay. 'Please go home. Here, take your packet of cigarettes. It is a gift from me. May god be kind to you and teach you to overcome your anger.'

Vijay felt humiliated. The boys were almost half his age. He had made an ass of himself by losing his temper.

Vijay had many pet hates, with religious superstition, astrology, horoscopy, numerology and other such methods of forecasting the future topping the list. But mostly he lived peacefully enough with the fools of his world. Even donkeys, he believed, had a right to have their opinions and bray about them. So he was surprised by his outburst at the paanwala's, especially since it had degenerated into physical violence, which he abhorred. He could not understand what had come over him.

He also wondered at Karuna. It seemed strange to him that an otherwise educated, Westernized woman who smoked and drank openly and was seemingly free of religious bias would go about pouring milk over marble and bronze statues, expecting them to drink it up. Perhaps she was doing it for a lark. There was a news item in the papers about two girls who had offered whiskey to Ganpati. There was an uproar and the girls had to beg forgiveness. It was the kind of thing Karuna would do.

After the episode of Ganpati drinking milk and the altercation at the paanwala's, Vijay stayed away from Khan Market for a few days. When he went back, he resolved to walk around the market without stopping outside or entering any shop. He wanted to avoid every place where he might lose his temper with the devout and end up embarrassing himself. He even found a different paanwala for his cigarettes and paan.

On the fourth evening after he ended his short exile, as he was walking past the less-frequented part of Khan Market occupied by a bank which closed its doors to customers, Vijay heard somebody call out, 'Jai ho!' He turned around and saw a bearded man with long shoulder-length hair carrying a brass plate with flowers, kumkum powder and a tiny silver oil lamp.

'Something for Shani devta,' the man demanded, thrusting the plate forward. Vijay realized it was Saturday and the exalted beggar was asking for alms to appease Saturn. There were many others of his ilk around railway stations and bus stands and at road crossings, making money from the gullible. Vijay was not one of the gullible. But what the man said next before Vijay could brush him aside made him pause.

'You have someone on your mind, a young lady may be. So what is the problem? She is not responding, hain? I will give you something to win her affections. Close your fist.'

Almost despite himself Vijay clenched his fist and extended his arm.

'Now open your hand,' the man said. Vijay did so. There was a big black ring in the middle of his palm. 'See: it is rahu, the evil planet. I can abolish him. Give me a little dakshina, say ten rupees, and I will give you foolproof advice on how to gain your heart's desire.' After a short pause during which the fellow transfixed Vijay with his kohl-lined sparkling eyes, he continued, 'Janaab, I know you do not belive in jyotish or palm-reading. But I can read your face like an open book. Why not try out my predictions and formula for gaining what your heart seeks? Ten rupees won't make you poor nor me rich.'

Without pondering over the matter Vijay took out a ten-rupee note and put it in the man's brass tray.

'Let's sit down somewhere where we are not disturbed by people,' suggested the Shani-man. The only secluded place they could find was a narrow passage between the public lavatory and the market boundary wall. It was malodorous but unfrequented. The man put his tray on the wall, the ten-rupee note in his pocket and asked Vijay to hold out his right hand.

Everyone enjoys being the object of attention. So did Vijay, even when the bearded Shani-man's gentle prodding and squeezing of his palm, as he examined every line, thumb and finger, assumed erotic overtones.

'There are two marriages in your life,' pronounced the sage.

'I had better get started soon. I haven't a wife yet and I'm not young anymore,' Vijay said.

'A man is never too old for marriage and sex,' the sage assured Vijay, then continued, 'I see a large home, double-storeyed and with many motorcars.'

'That's nice to know. I live in a one-room flat and ride a motorcycle,' Vijay lied.

Undeterred, the man went on. 'There is money, lots of money, name and fame.'

Vijay snubbed him again: 'I could do with both. My bank balance is very low and my name is not known beyond my block of flats and this little market.'

'There is also phoren travel soon,' the man went on.

'When? Both the American Embassy and the British High Commission turned down my visa applications. Forget about name, fame, money and foreign travel. Can you tell me anything about my present problem?'

'Date and place of birth,' demanded the soothsayer as he pulled a pencil and small notebook out of his pocket. Vijay told him. He drew several lines, parallel and horizontal. He counted on his fingers and inserted figures in the squares and triangles he had made. Then he shut his eyes and pronounced, 'Her name begins with K.'

Vijay was taken aback. 'How did you know?'

'It's all written in your stars. She pretends indifference but she loves you. I will now give you a magic formula to make her hungry for you and you hungry for her.' The man paused and looked meaningfully at Vijay.

'I already am hungry for her,' Vijay said impatiently.

'But you must be hungrier, then she too will pant for you without shame. I can guarantee it. For that I charge fifty rupees. If my formula fails, I'll give your money back with fifty from my own pocket. I'll give you my card, with my name and address. If the formula fails, you send me the card by post and I'll come and return the money.' He fished out a grimy visiting card. It had the letter Om on top with a figure of Ganpati beneath and then his name: Natha Singh, World-famous Master of Science of Jyotish, Astrologer, Numerologist, Specialist in Love Potions.

Now that he had let himself in for the hocus-pocus, Vijay said to himself: What the hell, let's go the whole hog. The fellow got the girl's initial right. He may just get her to take more interest in me.

'Okay, here's another fifty rupees, and if it does not work I'll get the police after you. Okay?'

'Okay, janaab, okay. Hundred times okay. My formula is foolproof.' He lowered his voice to a whisper, 'All you have to do, janaab, is pluck two hairs from your jhaant and two from her jhaant, mix them up, swallow one pair yourself and give her the other pair to drink up with a cup of tea. Both of you will be on fire. Guaranteed.'

Vijay was speechless. He looked at the Shani-man disbelievingly.

'You doubt my formula?' the man challenged him. He patted his crotch and declared, 'Don't underestimate the power of the jhaant. It is the strongest aphrodisiac known to man.'

Blood rushed to Vijay's head but he kept his cool. He did not want to create another scene. 'What kind of love formula is this?' he snapped. 'If I could get close enough to pluck her pubic hair, I need no help from you. How do I get her to bare her privates before me, anyway?'

'You can do that if you try,' said the Shani-man as he picked up his brass plate and walked away.

Vijay realized it had cost him sixty rupees to learn that he was as big a chootiya as all those people offering milk to the idol of Ganpati. He weaved his way through the closely parked cars to make his way home and walked straight into Hakim Tara Chand.

'You should be careful of charlatans like that man, Lall Sahib,' he said with a chuckle. 'He is not really a sadhu, just a thug who exploits people's weaknesses.'

He had obviously seen Vijay talking to the Shani-man and handing him money. Vijay's ears went red. He felt as if he had exposed himself in public. His humiliation was complete.

Vijay pondered over the events of the past few days and felt very depressed. He described his mood in his diary: 'Pissed off with the world' and then added, 'Pissed off with myself.' Khan Market had lost its raunaq; he avoided going there for another few days. But the itch to have it out with Karuna got the better of him. Did she know what she was doing to him?

After a week, one Saturday evening, he was back in the market hoping to run into her. He went around her usual haunts, the bookstores, the grocer's and the butcher's. She was not there. Ultimately he went to The Book Shop to get his magazines and ask the proprietress if Karuna had been around. He broached the subject very casually. 'That lady who bought Durrell from you, has she been around lately?'

'You mean Karuna Chaudhury? Yes, she came in one evening to settle her account. She said her husband had been transferred to some other city—she did not say where.'

Vijay was lost for words. He took his magazines and slowly walked back to his apartment. He sensed he might never see her again. And the name Chaudhury yielded no clue. Chaudhurys could be found across the country, from Punjab to Assam, down to the Southern states, and they could be Hindus, Muslims, Sikhs, even Christians. The search would be as futile as that of Majnu sifting the sands of the desert to find his Laila. And that was what he felt like—a lovesick Majnu. Which made him an old fool: he was fifty-four. He tried to console himself—that it was an infatuation that would fade away in time. There would be other women. Or there would not.

It was still too early for his sundowner. Nevertheless, he poured himself a stiff one and switched on his TV to divert his mind to things other than a woman who had slipped out of his hands; a woman he should have left well alone. He pressed the buttons of the remote control and tried one channel after another. Nothing held his attention for more than a few seconds. Suddenly the lights went out and the entire complex of apartments was plunged in gloom. The sun had set but through the twilight he could see the outlines of the mulberry tree, already beginning to lose much of its foliage. The sudden darkness prompted a pair of spotted owlets perched on its branches to break into their pointless racket, chitter-chitter-chatter-chatter.

Most residents of the apartment complex slept late the next morning. It was a Sunday. There were only two old ladies out in the lawn when Vijay returned from his walk in Lodhi Gardens. They saw him drive in and park Annie in her old spot under the mulberry tree.

TRAIN TO PAKISTAN

First published in 1956, and now regarded as a classic of modern Indian fiction, *Train to Pakistan* is set in the summer of 1947 in a Punjab village, Mano Majra, where Sikhs and Muslims have always lived peaceably together. Then one day a train comes over the bridge, full of dead bodies, and Mano Majra too is engulfed in the violence and bloodshed of the Partition. The extract below reflects the novel's moving portrayal of the human dimensions of this momentous historical event.

The peasants thought about their problem. They could not refuse shelter to refugees: hospitality was not a pastime but a sacred duty when those who sought it were homeless. Could they ask their Muslims to go? Quite emphatically not. Loyalty to a fellow-villager was above all other considerations. Despite the words they had used, no one had the nerve to suggest throwing them out, even in a purely Sikh gathering. The mood of the assembly changed from anger to bewilderment.

After some time the lambardar spoke.

'All Muslims of the neighbouring villages have been evacuated and taken to the refugee camp near Chundunnager. Some have already gone away to Pakistan. Others have been sent to the bigger camp at Jullundur.'

'Yes,' added another. 'Kapoora and Gujjoo Matta were evacuated last week. Mano Majra is the only place left where there are Muslims. What I would like to know is how these people asked their fellow-villagers to leave. We could never say anything like that to our tenants, any more than we could tell our sons to get

379

out of our homes. Is there anyone here who could say to the Muslims, "Brothers, you should go away from Mano Majra"?'

Before anyone could answer another villager came in and stood on the threshold. Every one turned round to see, but they could not recognize him in the dim lamplight.

'Who is it?' asked the lambardar, shading his eyes from the lamp. 'Come in.'

Imam Baksh came in. Two others followed him. They also were Muslims.

'Salaam, Chacha Imam Baksh. Salaam Khair Dina. Salaam, salaam.'

'*Sat Sri Akal*, lambardara. *Sat Sri Akal*,' answered the Muslims

People made room for them and waited for Imam Baksh to begin.

Imam Baksh combed his beard with his fingers.

'Well, brothers, what is your decision about us?' he asked quietly.

There was an awkward silence. Everyone looked at the lambardar.

'Why ask us?' answered the lambardar. 'This is your village as much as ours.'

'You have heard what is being said! All the neighbouring villages have been evacuated. Only we are left. If you want us to go too, we will go.'

Meet Singh began to sniff. He felt it was not for him to speak. He had said his bit. Besides, he was only a priest who lived on what the villagers gave him. One of the younger men spoke.

'It is like this, Uncle Imam Baksh. As long as we are here nobody will dare to touch you. We die first and then you can look after yourselves.'

'Yes,' added another warmly, 'we first, then you. If anyone raises his eyebrows at you we will rape his mother.'

'Mother, sister and daughter,' added the others.

Imam Baksh wiped a tear from his eyes and blew his nose in the hem of his shirt.

'What have we to do with Pakistan? We were born here. So were our ancestors. We have lived amongst you as brothers,' Imam Baksh broke down. Meet Singh clasped him in his arms and began to sob. Several of the people started crying quietly and blowing their noses.

The lambardar spoke: 'Yes, you are our brothers. As far as we are concerned, you and your children and your grandchildren can live here as long as you like. If anyone speaks rudely to you, your wives or your children, it will be us first and our wives and children before a single hair of your heads is touched. But Chacha, we are so few and the strangers coming from Pakistan are coming in thousands. Who will be responsible for what they do?'

'Yes,' agreed the other, 'as far as we are concerned you are all right, but what about these refugees?'

'I have heard that some villages were surrounded by mobs many thousands strong, all armed with guns and spears. There was no question of resistance.'

'We are not afraid of mobs,' replied another quickly. 'Let them come! We will give them such a beating they will not dare to look at Mano Majra again.'

Nobody took any notice of the challenge; the boast sounded too hollow to be taken seriously. Imam Baksh blew his nose again. 'What do you advise us to do then, brothers?' he asked, choking with emotion.

'Uncle,' said the lambardar in a heavy voice, 'it is very hard for me to say, but seeing the sort of times we live in, I would advise you to go to the refugee camp while this trouble is on. You lock your houses with your belongings. We will look after your cattle till you come back.'

The lambardar's advice created a tense stillness. Villagers held their breath for fear of being heard. The lambardar himself felt that he ought to say something quickly to dispel the effect of his words.

'Until yesterday,' he began again loudly, 'in case of trouble we could have helped you to cross the river by the ford. Now it has been raining for two days; the river has risen. The only crossings are by trains and road bridges—you know what is happening there! It is for your own safety that I advise you to take shelter in the camp for a few days, and then you can come back. As far as we are concerned,' he repeated warmly, 'if you decide to stay on, you are most welcome to do so. We will defend you with our lives.'

No one had any doubts about the import of the lambardar's words. They sat with their heads bowed till Imam Baksh stood up.

'All right,' he said solemnly, 'if we have to go, we'd better pack up our bedding and belongings. It will take us more than one night to clear out of homes it has taken our fathers and grandfathers hundreds of years to make.'

The lambardar felt a strong sense of guilt and was overcome with emotion. He got up and embraced Imam Baksh and started to cry loudly. Sikh and Muslim villagers fell into each other's arms and wept like children. Imam Baksh gently got out of the lambardar's embrace. 'There is no need to cry,' he said between sobs. 'This is the way of the world—'

Not forever does the bulbul sing
In balmy shades of bowers,
Not forever lasts the spring
Nor ever blossom flowers.
Not forever reigneth joy,
Sets the sun on days of bliss,
Friendships not forever last,
They know not life, who know not this.

'They know not life, who know not this,' repeated many others with sighs. 'Yes, Uncle Imam Baksh. This is life.'

Imam Baksh and his companions left the meeting in tears.

Before going round to other Muslim homes, Imam Baksh went

to his own hut attached to the mosque. Nooran was already in bed. An oil lamp burned in a niche in the wall.

'Nooro, Nooro,' he shouted, shaking her by the shoulder. 'Get up, Nooro.'

The girl opened her eyes. 'What is the matter?'

'Get up and pack. We have to go away tomorrow morning,' he announced dramatically.

'Go away? Where?'

'I don't know . . . Pakistan!'

The girl sat up with a jerk. 'I will not go to Pakistan,' she said defiantly.

Imam Baksh pretended he had not heard. 'Put all the clothes in the trunks and the cooking utensils in a gunny bag. Also take something for the buffalo. We will have to take her too.'

'I will not go to Pakistan,' the girl repeated, fiercely.

'You may not want to go, but they will throw you out. All Muslims are leaving for the camp tomorrow.'

'Who will throw us out? This is our village. Are the police and the government dead?'

'Don't be silly, girl. Do as you are told. Hundreds of thousands of people are going to Pakistan and as many coming out. Those who stay behind are killed. Hurry up and pack. I have to go and tell the others that they must get ready.'

Imam Baksh left the girl sitting up in bed. Nooran rubbed her face with her hands and stared at the wall. She did not know what to do. She could spend the night out and come back when all the others had gone. But she could not do it alone; and it was raining. Her only chance was Jugga. Malli had been released, maybe Jugga had also come home. She knew that was not true, but the hope persisted and it gave her something to do.

Nooran went out in the rain. She passed many people in the lanes, going about with gunny bags covering their heads and shoulders. The whole village was awake. In most houses she could see the dim flickers of oil lamps. Some were packing; others were helping them to pack. Most just talked with their friends. The

women sat on the floors hugging each other and crying. It was
as if in every home there had been a death.

Nooran shook the door of Jugga's house. The chain on the
other side rattled but there was no response. In the grey light
she noticed the door was bolted from the outside. She undid the
iron ring and went in. Jugga's mother was out, probably visiting
some Muslim friends. There was no light at all. Nooran sat down
on a charpoy. She did not want to face Jugga's mother alone
nor did she want to go back home. She hoped something would
happen—something which would make Jugga walk in. She sat
and waited and hoped.

For an hour Nooran watched the grey shadows of clouds
chasing each other. It drizzled and poured and poured and
drizzled alternately. She heard the sound of footsteps cautiously
picking their way through the muddy lane. They stopped outside
the door. Someone shook the door.

'Who is it?' asked an old woman's voice.

Nooran lost her nerve; she did not move.

'Who is it?' demanded the voice angrily. 'Why don't you
speak?'

Nooran stood up and mumbled indistinctly, 'Beybey.'

The old woman stepped in and quickly shut the door behind
her.

'Jugga! Jugga, is it you?' she whispered. 'Have they let you
off?'

'No, Beybey, it is I—Nooran. Chacha Imam Baksh's daughter,'
answered the girl timidly.

'Nooro? What brings you here at this hour?' the old woman
asked angrily.

'Has Jugga come back?'

'What have you to do with Jugga?' his mother snapped. 'You
have sent him to jail. You have made him a budmash. Does
your father know you go about to strangers' houses at midnight
like a tart?'

Nooran began to cry. 'We are going away tomorrow.' That did not soften the old woman's heart.

'What relation are you to us that you want to come to see us? You can go where you like.'

Nooran played her last card. 'I cannot leave. Jugga has promised to marry me.'

'Get out, you bitch!' the old woman hissed, 'You, a Muslim weaver's daughter, marry a Sikh peasant! Get out, or I will go and tell your father and the whole village. Go to Pakistan! Leave my Jugga alone.'

Nooran felt heavy and lifeless. 'All right, Beybey, I will go. Don't be angry with me. When Jugga comes back just tell him I came to say "*Sat Sri Akal*." The girl went down on her knees, clasped the old woman's legs and began to sob. 'Beybey, I am going away and will never come back again. Don't be harsh to me just when I am leaving.'

Jugga's mother stood stiff, without a trace of emotion on her face. Inside her, she felt a little weak and soft. 'I will tell Jugga.'

Nooran stopped crying. Her sobs came at long intervals. She still held on to Jugga's mother. Her head sank lower and lower till it touched the old woman's feet.

'Beybey.'

'What have you to say now?' She had a premonition of what was coming.

'Beybey.'

'Beybey! Beybey! Why don't you say something?' asked the woman, pushing Nooran away. 'What is it?'

The girl swallowed the spittle in her mouth.

'Beybey, I have Jugga's child inside me. If I go to Pakistan they will kill it when they know it has a Sikh father.'

The old woman let Nooran's head drop back on her feet. Nooran clutched them hard and began to cry again

'How long have you had it?'

'I have just found out. It is the second month.'

Jugga's mother helped Nooran up and the two sat down on the charpoy. Nooran stopped sobbing.

'I cannot keep you here,' said the old woman at last. 'I have enough trouble with the police already. When all this is over and Jugga comes back, he will go and get you from wherever you are. Does your father know?'

'No! If he finds out he will marry me off to someone or murder me.' She started crying again.

'Oh, stop this whining,' commanded the old woman sternly. 'Why didn't you think of it when you were at the mischief? I have already told you Jugga will get you as soon as he is out.'

Nooran stifled her sobs.

'Beybey, don't let him be too long.'

'He will hurry for his own sake. If he does not get you he will have to buy a wife and there is not a pice or trinket left with us. He will get you if he wants a wife. Have no fear.'

A vague hope filled Nooran's being. She felt as if she belonged to the house and the house to her; the charpoy she sat on, the buffalo, Jugga's mother, all were hers. She could come back even if Jugga failed to turn up. She could tell them she was married. The thought of her father came like a dark cloud over her lunar hopes. She would slip away without telling him. The moon shone again.

'Beybey, if I get the chance I will come to say *Sat Sri Akal* in the morning. *Sat Sri Akal.* I must go and pack.' Nooran hugged the old woman passionately. '*Sat Sri Akal*,' she said a little breathlessly again and went out.

Jugga's mother sat on her charpoy staring into the dark for several hours.

Not many people slept in Mano Majra that night. They went from house to house—talking, crying, swearing love and friendship, assuring each other that this would soon be over. Life, they said, would be as it always had been.

Imam Baksh came back from his round of Muslim homes before Nooran had returned. Nothing had been packed. He was too depressed to be angry with her. It was as hard on the young as the old. She must have gone to see some of her friends. He started pottering around looking for gunny bags, tin cannisters and trunks. A few minutes later Nooran came in.

'Have you seen all your girl friends? Let us get this done before we sleep,' said Imam Baksh.

'You go to bed. I will put the things in. There is not much to do—and you must be tired,' she answered.

'Yes, I am a little tired,' he said sitting down on his charpoy. 'You pack the clothes now. We can put in the cooking utensils in the morning after you have cooked something for the journey.' Imam Baksh stretched himself on the bed and fell asleep.

There was not much for Nooran to do. A Punjabi peasant's baggage consists of little besides a change of clothes, a quilt and a pillow, a couple of pitchers, cooking utensils, and perhaps a brass plate and a copper tumbler or two. All that can be put on the only piece of furniture they possess—a charpoy. Nooran put her own and her father's clothes in a battered grey steel trunk which had been with them ever since she could remember. She lit a fire in the hearth to bake a few chapatties for the next day. Within half an hour she had done the cooking. She rinsed the utensils and put them in a gunny bag. Flour, salt and the spices that remained went in biscuit and cigarette tins, which in their turn went inside an empty kerosene oil can with a wood top. The packing was over. All that remained was to roll her quilt round the pillow, put the odds and ends on the charpoy and the charpoy on the buffalo. She could carry the piece of broken mirror in her hand.

It rained intermittently all night. Early in the morning it became a regular downpour. Villagers who had stayed up most of the night fell asleep in the monotonous patter of rain and the opiate of the fresh morning breeze.

The tooting of motor horns and the high note of truck engines in low gear ploughing their way through the slush and mud woke the entire village. The convoy went around Mano Majra looking for a lane wide enough to let their trucks in. In front was a jeep fitted with a loudspeaker. There were two officers in it—a Sikh (the one who had come after the ghost train) and a Muslim. Behind the jeep were a dozen trucks. One of the trucks was full of Pathan soldiers and another one full of Sikhs. They were all armed with sten-guns.

The convoy came to a halt outside the village. Only the jeep could make its way through. It drove up to the centre and stopped beside the platform under the peepul tree. The two officers stepped out. The Sikh asked one of the villagers to fetch the lambardar. The Muslim was joined by the Pathan soldiers. He sent them out in batches of three to knock at every door and ask the Muslims to come out. For a few minutes Mano Majra echoed to cries of 'All Muslims going to Pakistan come out at once. Come! All Muslims. Out at once.'

Slowly the Muslims began to come out of their homes, driving their cattle and their bullock carts loaded with charpoys, rolls of bedding, tin trunks, kerosene oil tins, earthen pitchers and brass utensils. The rest of Mano Majra came out to see them off.

The two officers and the lambardar were the last to come out of the village. The jeep followed them. They were talking and gesticulating animatedly. Most of the talking was between the Muslim officer and the lambardar.

'I have no arrangement to take all this luggage with bullock carts, beds, pots and pans. This convoy is not going to Pakistan by road. We are taking them to the Chundunnager refugee camp and from there by train to Lahore. They can only take their clothes, bedding, cash and jewellery. Tell them to leave everything else here. You can look after it.'

The news that the Mano Majra Muslims were going to Pakistan came as a surprise. The lambardar had believed they would only go to the refugee camp for a few days and then return.

'No, Sahib, we cannot say anything,' replied the lambardar. 'If it was for a day or two we could look after their belongings. As you are going to Pakistan, it may be many months before they return. Property is a bad thing: it poisons people's minds. No, we will not touch anything. We will only look after their houses.'

The Muslim officer was irritated. 'I have no time to argue. You see yourself that all I have is a dozen trucks. I cannot put buffaloes and bullock carts in them.'

'No, Sahib,' retorted the lambardar stubbornly. 'You can say what you like and you can be angry with us, but we will not touch our brothers' properties. You want us to become enemies?'

'Wah, wah, lambardar Sahib,' answered the Muslim laughing loudly. 'Shabash! Yesterday you wanted to kill them, today you call them brothers. You may change your mind again tomorrow.'

'Do not taunt us like this, Captain Sahib. We are brothers and will always remain brothers.'

'All right, all right, lambardara. You are brothers,' the officer said. 'I grant you that, but I still cannot take all this stuff. You consult the Sardar Officer and your fellow-villagers about it. I will deal with the Muslims.'

The Muslim officer got on the jeep and addressed the crowd. He chose his words carefully.

'We have a dozen trucks and all you people who are going to Pakistan must get on them in ten minutes. We have other villages to evacuate later on. The only luggage you can take with you is what you can carry—nothing more. You can leave your cattle, bullock carts, charpoys, pitchers, and so on with your friends in the village. If we get a chance, we will bring these things out for you later. I give you ten minutes to settle your affairs. Then the convoy will move.'

The Muslims left their bullock carts and thronged round the jeep, protesting and talking loudly. The Muslim officer who had stepped off the jeep went back to the microphone.

'Silence! I warn you, the convoy will move in ten minutes— whether you are on it or not will be no concern of mine.'

Sikh peasants who had stood apart heard the order and went to the Sikh officer for advice. The officer took no notice of them; he continued staring contemptuously over the upturned collar of his raincoat at the men, cattle, carts and trucks steaming in the slush and rain.

'Why, Sardar Sahib,' asked Meet Singh nervously, 'is not the lambardar right? One should not touch another's property. There is always danger of misunderstanding.'

The officer looked Meet Singh up and down.

'You are quite right, Bhaiji, there is some danger of being misunderstood. One should never touch another's property; one should never look at another's woman. One should just let others take one's goods and sleep with one's sisters. The only way people like you will understand anything is by being sent over to Pakistan: have your sisters and mothers raped in front of you, have your clothes taken off, and be sent back with a kick and spit on your behinds.'

The officer's speech was a slap in the face to all the peasants. But someone sniggered. Everyone turned around to look. It was Malli with his five companions. With them were a few young refugees who were staying at the Sikh temple. None of them belonged to Mano Majra.

'Sir, the people of this village are famous for their charity,' said Malli smiling. 'They cannot look after themselves, how can they look after other people? But do not bother, Sardar Sahib, we will take care of Muslim property. You can tell the other officer to leave it with us. It will be quite safe if you can detail some of your soldiers to prevent looting by these people.'

There was complete confusion. People ran hither and thither shouting at the tops of their voices. Despite the Muslim officer's tone of finality, villagers clamoured around him protesting and full of suggestions. He came up to his Sikh colleague surrounded by his bewildered co-religionists.

'Can you make arrangements for taking over what is left behind?'

Before the Sikh could answer, a babel of protests burst from all sides. The Sikh remained tight-lipped and aloof.

The Muslim officer turned around sharply. 'Shut up!' he yelled.

The murmuring died down. He spoke again, punctuating each word with a stab of his forefinger.

'I give you five minutes to get into the trucks with just as much luggage as you can carry in your hands. Those who are not in will be left behind. And this is the last time I will say it.'

'It is all settled,' said the Sikh officer, speaking softly in Punjabi. 'I have arranged that these people from the next village will look after the cattle, carts and houses till it is over. I will have a list made and sent over to you.'

His colleague did not reply. He had a sardonic smile on his face. Mano Majra Sikhs and Muslims looked on helplessly.

There was no time to make arrangements. There was no time even to say good-bye. Truck engines were started. Pathan soldiers rounded up the Muslims, drove them back to the carts for a brief minute or two, and then on to the trucks. In the confusion of rain, mud and soldiers herding the peasants about with the muzzles of their sten-guns sticking in their backs, the villagers saw little of each other. All they could do was to shout their last farewells from the trucks. The Muslim officer drove his jeep round the convoy to see that all was in order and then came to say goodbye to his Sikh colleague. The two shook hands mechanically, without a smile or a trace of emotion. The jeep took its place in front of the line of trucks. The microphone blared forth once more to announce that they were ready to move. The officer shouted 'Pakistan!' His soldiers answered in a chorus 'Forever!' The convoy slushed its way towards Chundunnagar. The Sikhs watched them till they were out of sight. They wiped the tears off their faces and turned back to their homes with heavy hearts.

~

Mano Majra's cup of sorrow was not yet full. The Sikh officer summoned the lambardar. All the villagers came with him—no one wanted to be left alone. Sikh soldiers threw a cordon round them. The officer told the villagers that he had decided to appoint Malli custodian of the evacuated Muslims' property. Anyone interfering with him or his men would be shot.

Malli's gang and the refugees then unyoked the bullocks, looted the carts, and drove the cows and buffaloes away.

All that morning, people sat in their homes and stared despondently through their open doors. They saw Malli's men and the refugees ransack Muslim houses. They saw Sikh soldiers come and go as if on their beats. They heard the piteous lowing of cattle as they were beaten and dragged along. They heard the loud cackle of hens and roosters silenced by the slash of the knife. But they did nothing but sit and sigh.

A shepherd boy, who had been out gathering mushrooms, came back with the news that the river had risen. No one took any notice of him. They only wished that it would rise more and drown the whole of Mano Majra along with them, their women, children and cattle—provided it also drowned Malli, his gang, the refugees, and the soldiers.

While the men sighed and groaned, the rain fell in a steady downpour and the Sutlej continued to rise. It spread on either side of the central piers which normally contained the winter channel, and joined the pools round the other piers into one broad stream. It stretched right across the bridge, licking the dam which separated it from the fields of Mano Majra. It ran over the many little islands in the river-bed till only the tops of the bushes that grew on them could be seen. Colonies of cormorants and terns which were used to roosting there flew over to the banks and then to the bridge—over which no trains had run for two days.

In the afternoon, another villager went around to the houses shouting 'Oi Banta Singh, the river is rising! Oi Daleep Singha, the river has risen! Oi listen, it is already up to the dam!' The people just looked up with their melancholy eyes signifying, 'We have heard that before.'

Then another man came with the same message, 'The river has risen.' Then another, and another, till everyone was saying, 'Do you know, the river has risen!'

At last the lambardar went out to see for himself. Yes, the river had risen. Two days of rain could not have caused it; it must have poured in the mountains after the melting of the snows. Sluice gates of canals had probably been closed to prevent the flood from bursting their banks; so there was no outlet except the river. The friendly sluggish stream of grey had become a menacing and tumultuous spread of muddy brown. The piers of the bridge were all that remained, solid and contemptuously defiant of the river. Their pointed edges clove through the sheet of water and let it vent its impotent rage in a swirl of eddies and whirlpools. Rain beat upon the surface, pockmarking it all over. The Sutlej was a terrifying sight.

By evening, Mano Majra had forgotten about its Muslims and Malli's misdeeds. The river had become the main topic of conversation. Once more women stood on the rooftops looking to the west. Men started going in turns to the embankment to report on the situation.

Before sunset the lambardar went up again to see the river. It had risen more since his visit in the afternoon. Some of the clusters of pampas which had been above the water level were now partly submerged. Their stalks had gone limp and their sodden snow-white plumes floated on the water. He had never known the Sutlej to rise so high in so short a time. Mano Majra was still a long way off and the mud dam looked solid and safe. Nevertheless he arranged for watch to be kept all through the night. Four parties of three men each were to take turns and be on the embankment from sunset to sunrise and report every hour. The rest were to stay in their houses.

The lambardar's decision was a quilt under which the village slept snug and safe. The lambardar himself had little sleep. Soon after midnight the three men on watch came back talking loudly in a high state of excitement. They could not tell in the grey muffled moonlight whether the river had risen more, but they had heard human voices calling for help. The cries came from over the water. They might have been from the other side or from the river itself. The lambardar went out with them. He took his chromium-plated flashlight.

The four men stood on the embankment and surveyed the Sutlej, which looked like a sheet of black. The white beam of the lambardar's torch scanned the surface of the river. They could see nothing but the swirling water. They held their breath and listened, but they could hear nothing except the noise of the rain falling on the water. Each time the lambardar asked if they were sure that what they had heard were human voices and not jackals, they felt more and more uncertain and had to ask each other: 'It was clear, wasn't it, Karnaila?'

'Oh yes. It was clear enough. "*Hai, hai*"—like someone in pain.'

The four men sat under a tree, huddled around a hurricane lamp. The gunny sacks they used as raincoats were soaking wet; so were all their clothes. An hour later there was a break in the clouds. The rain slowed down to a drizzle and then stopped. The moon broke through the clouds just above the western horizon. Its reflection on the river made a broad path of shimmering tinfoil running from the opposite bank to the men under the tree. On this shining patch of moonlight even little ripples of water could be seen distinctly.

A black oval object hit the bridge pier and was swept by the stream towards the Mano Majra embankment. It looked like a big drum with sticks on its sides. It moved forward, backward and sideways until the current caught it again and brought it into the silvery path not far from where the men were sitting. It was a dead cow with its belly bloated like a massive barrel and its legs stiffly stretched upward. Then followed some blocks of thatch straw and bundles of clothing.

'It looks as if some village had been swept away by the flood,' said the lambardar.

'Quiet! Listen!' said one of the villagers in a whisper. The faint sound of a moan was wafted across the waters.

'Did you hear?'

'Quiet!'

They held their breath and listened.

No, it could not have been human. There was a rumbling sound. They listened again. Of course, it was a rumble; it was a tram. Its puffing became clearer and clearer. Then they saw the outlines of the engine and the train itself. It had no lights. There was not even a headlight on the engine. Sparks flew out of the engine funnel like fireworks. As the train came over the bridge, cormorants flew silently down the river and terns flew up with shrill cries. The train came to a halt at Mano Majra station. It was from Pakistan.

'There are no lights on the train.'

'The engine did not whistle.'

'It is like a ghost.'

'In the name of the Lord do not talk like this,' said the lambardar. 'It may be a goods train. It must have been the siren you heard. These new American engines wail like someone being murdered.'

'No, lambardar, we heard the sound more than an hour ago; and again the same one before the train came on,' replied one of the villagers.

'You cannot hear it any more. The train is not making any noise now.'

From across the railway line, where some days earlier over a thousand dead bodies had been burned, a jackal sent up a long plaintive howl. A pack joined him. The men shuddered.

'Must have been the jackals. They sound like women crying when somebody dies,' said the lambardar.

'No, no,' protested the other. 'No, it was a human voice as clear as you are talking to me now.'

They sat and listened and watched strange indistinguishable forms floating on the floodwaters. The moon went down. After a brief period of darkness the eastern horizon turned grey. Long lines of bats flew across noiselessly. Crows began to caw in their sleep. The shrill cry of a koel came bursting through a clump of trees and all the world was awake.

The clouds had rolled away to the north. Slowly the sun came up and flooded the rain-soaked plain with a dazzling orange brilliance; everything glistened in the sunlight. The river had risen further. Its turbid water carried carts with the bloated carcases of bulls still yoked to them. Horses rolled from side to side as if they were scratching their backs. There were also men and women with their clothes clinging to their bodies; little children sleeping on their bellies with their arms clutching the water and their tiny buttocks dipping in and out. The sky was soon full of kites and vultures. They flew down and landed on the floating carcases. They pecked till the corpses themselves rolled over and shooed them off with hands which rose stiffly into the air and splashed back into the water.

'Some villages must have been flooded at night,' said the lambardar gravely.

'Who yokes bulls to carts at night?' asked one of his companions.

'Yes, that is true. Why should the bullocks be yoked?'

More human forms could be seen coming through the arches of the bridge. They rebounded off the piers, paused, pirouetted at the whirlpools, and then came bouncing down the river. The men moved up towards the bridge to see some corpses which had drifted near the bank.

They stood and stared.

'Lambardar, they were not drowned. They were murdered.'

An old peasant with a grey beard lay flat on the water. His arms were stretched out as if he had been crucified. His mouth was wide open and showed his toothless gums, his eyes were covered with film, his hair floated about his head like a halo. He had a deep wound on his neck which slanted down from the side to the chest. A child's head butted into the old man's armpit. There was a hole in its back. There were many others coming down the river like logs hewn on the mountains and cast into streams to be carried down to the plains. A few passed through the middle of the arches and sped onward faster. Others bumped into the piers and turned over to show their wounds till the current turned them over again. Some were without limbs, some had their bellies torn open, many women's breasts were slashed. They floated down the sunlit river, bobbing up and down. Overhead hung the kites and vultures.

The lambardar and the villagers drew the ends of their turbans across their faces. 'The Guru have mercy on us,' someone whispered. 'There has been a massacre somewhere. We must inform the police.'

'Police?' a small man said bitterly. 'What will they do? Write a First Information Report?'

Sick and with heavy hearts, the party turned back to Mano Majra. They did not know what to say to people when they got back. The river had risen further? Some villages had been flooded? There had been a massacre somewhere upstream? There were hundreds of corpses floating on the Sutlej? Or, just keep quiet?

When they came back to the village nobody was about to hear what they had to say. They were all on the rooftops looking at the station. After two days a train had drawn up at Mano Majra in the daytime. Since the engine faced eastward, it must have come from Pakistan. This time too the place was full of soldiers and policemen and the station had been cordoned off. The news of the corpses on the river was shouted from the housetops. People told each other about the mutilation of women and children. Nobody wanted to know who the dead people were, nor wanted to go to the river to find out. There was a new interest at the station, with promise of worse horrors than the last one.

There was no doubt in anyone's mind what the train contained. They were sure that the soldiers would come for oil and wood. They had no more oil to spare and the wood they had left was too damp to burn. But the soldiers did not come. Instead, a bulldozer arrived from somewhere. It began dragging its lower jaw into the ground just outside the station on the Mano Majra side. It went along, eating up the earth, chewing it, casting it aside. It did this for several hours, until there was a rectangular trench almost fifty yards long with mounds of earth on either side. Then it paused for a break. The soldiers and policemen who had been idly watching the bulldozer at work were called to order and marched back to the platform. They came back in twos carrying canvas stretchers. They tipped the stretchers into the pit and went back to the train for more. This went on all day till sunset. Then the bulldozer woke up again. It opened its jaws and ate up the earth it had thrown out before and vomitted it into the trench till it was level with the ground. The place looked like the scar of a healed-up wound. Two soldiers were left to guard the grave from the depredations of jackals and badgers.

I Shall Not Hear The Nightingale

I Shall Not Hear the Nightingale is set in Amritsar in 1942–43. The central theme of this richly-textured novel, contained in the extract below, is the agonizing conflict between personal loyalties and the calls of conscience and duty. It is also a remarkably perceptive study of the behaviour of human beings under stress.

The main characters in the novel, most of whom are Sikh, are:

Buta Singh	Senior Magistrate
Sabhrai	Buta Singh's wife
Sher Singh	Buta Singh's son, a student leader involved in anti-British activities
Champak	Sher Singh's wife
Beena	Buta Singh's daughter
Jhimma Singh	Village headman and police informer
John Taylor	British ICS officer, Deputy Commissioner of the district
Dyer	Sher Singh's Alsatian dog

Jhimma Singh was one of many brothers. Being the eldest, he inherited the official function of headman of the village from his father. Thereafter he acquired possession of most of his father's property. He loved his brothers and arranged marriages and employment for them as farm labourers in newly-colonized lands a few hundred miles away to the north-west. Malicious tongues spread poison and turned the brothers against him. They took him to court to get possession of their share of the land. But providence, assisted by clever lawyers, triumphed over their evil designs. Then tried violence. That too went against them. They were imprisoned on charges of attempted murder and Jhimma Singh was given a revolver to defend himself. He gained the confidence of the local police officials by his hospitality; they let him look after the affairs of the village and Jhimma Singh became virtually its ruler. Anyone who has had to live the hard way, literally fighting for survival at every step, doesn't set much store by values like truth, honesty, loyalty or patriotism. Neither did Jhimma Singh. Each little success meant more envy and more danger from the envious. He had to seek the help of the police to protect him. In turn they expected him to keep an eye on miscreants. He became a paid informer.

It wasn't very surprising that for a week no one should have bothered about his disappearance. He was known to go away to the city for two or three days without telling his wives. As in the past, they assumed he had been called away on urgent business. After a week they became anxious and started going round to other homes asking the women to find out from their menfolk if they had seen Jhimma Singh. When no one came forth with any news of him for another week, the anxiety changed to alarm and a report was lodged at the police station by one of the tenants at the urging of Jhimma Singh's first wife. It mentioned the enmity of his brothers and their previous attempts to murder him. Once again the brothers were arrested, interrogated and beaten up. Nothing came of it. No corpse, no case. They were set at liberty. The police commissioner was notified that the most trusted informer in the district had disappeared—probably murdered by one of his many relations and no trace could be found of either the victim or the murderer. The commissioner sent the file to the deputy commissioner to have the case closed as 'untraced'. He was a little surprised to find that instead of the usual words 'Seen. File', with the illegible initials, there was an order asking him to come over to discuss the case. What followed startled the police commissioner.

The deputy commissioner handed the police commissioner a warrant to search the house of Sardar Buta Singh, the seniormost Indian magistrate of the district. He gave him another one, to arrest Sher Singh. Taylor refused to disclose his source of information. All he said was: 'Be gentle to the old man. I suggest you send him over to see me and then search the house. You may find something. In any case, take his son to the police station and give him the works. Get some of your tough Anglo-Indian sergeants to handle him. It will not be hard to make him talk.'

~

Buta Singh had firmly decided to speak to his son after the headman had left. That evening Sher Singh came home early but straight away retired to bed complaining of a severe headache. Next morning, he did not turn up for breakfast and Buta Singh went to see him in his room. The boy looked pale and jaundiced and would not speak at all. A doctor was sent for but he could not diagnose anything. Nevertheless it was plain to anyone that he was very sick; one could scarcely bring up a delicate subject with him in that state of health. After many days in bed, his health improved and he started moving about the house. He still wore a sallow, furtive look and avoided meeting people. Buta Singh waited patiently. At last came the first of the month. The father came to the conclusion that matters had been allowed to drift for too long and the time had come to settle the business once and for all. He would talk to his son after the morning ceremony.

Autumn had set in and there was a nip in the morning air. Inside the gurdwara it was cozy because of the thick carpet and the incense. Sher Singh, Champak and Shunno were inside. Mundoo, as usual, was lording it over the children and the dog outside. Buta Singh uncovered the Holy Book to start reading. He saw the figure of a policeman through the chick. He kept his temper under control and proceeded to look for the appropriate passage. He pressed his forehead reverently to the Book and looked up once more. There was yet another policeman outside talking excitedly to Mundoo. He took off his shoes and came into the gurdwara. This was too much for Buta Singh. He hollered angrily at the top of his voice: 'What is your business?' The constable saluted and said: 'Huzoor, the police commissioner is waiting for you outside in his car. The deputy commissioner has sent him to fetch you. It is most urgent. I crave forgiveness for disturbing you in the gurdwara; I was ordered to do so.'

The reference to the police commissioner and Mr Taylor changed Buta Singh's tone. He did not proceed with the reading. He left at once and asked Champak to carry on. Shunno followed her master; she wasn't going to be left out of things.

'You do the reading instead of your father,' said Champak with a smile.

Sher Singh did not smile back. 'I can't. I am not feeling too well.'

'What is the matter?' asked Champak.

'I don't know. I don't feel well.'

Champak put her hand on his forehead. 'You have no fever but you have cold-sweat. I'll get Mundoo to make your bed. You come and lie down. Mundoo, Oi Mundoo,' she cried. 'The policemen seemed to have frightened away the servants.'

She went out and shouted for the boy again. Mundoo came wailing. 'A policeman beat me. They have come inside the house. When I asked them what they were doing, one fellow slapped me.'

Sher Singh went deathly pale. Had they found out? Had one of the boys told on him? His wife looked at him for some explanation. 'I will see what is happening,' he said weakly. 'You go to your room.'

There were policemen all over the place: in the courtyard and the sitting-room; in the garden and at the gate. Sher Singh came out in the veranda followed by Dyer. Two white sergeants were sitting in the armchairs with their legs on the table, smoking. A head constable stood by them with handcuffs dangling from his belt. A policewoman in a khaki sari was leaning on a Black Maria in the porch. 'You want to see my father?' asked Sher Singh timidly.

'You Buta Singh's son?' asked one of them knocking the ash off his cigarette.

'Yes . . . sir,'

'Head constable, search this fellow. And send someone inside to search his woman.'

The two resumed their smoking. The policewoman went inside. The head constable took Sher Singh by the hand. Sher Singh felt he ought to protest. He mustered up all the courage he had and spoke: 'What is this about? How dare you put your hands on me! What authority . . .'

One of the sergeants got up slowly from his chair and came up to him. 'You want to know what authority we have to search you?'

'Yes,' answered Sher Singh through the spittle that clogged his throat.

'Man, this bugger wants to know why we want to search him,' said the sergeant turning to his companion. 'We better tell him.'

Without warning the sergeant struck his knee sharply into Sher Singh's privates. As he doubled over with pain, the sergeant hit him on the face with the back of his hand. Sher Singh's turban came off and fell on the ground; his long hair scattered about his face and shoulders.

'Cheeky nigger. That'll teach . . .'

The sergeant could not complete the sentence. Dyer leapt at him with savage fury and knocked him down. He tore the collar off the white man's coat and went for his throat. The constable lashed out with his iron handcuffs; the other sergeant laid about with his swagger stick and kicked the dog with his hobnailed boots. Policemen came running with their iron-shod bamboo-poles to beat him. At last the Alsatian gave up. Blood flowed from his face and back, the bone of one of his legs had been fractured.

'I'll shoot the bloody pariah,' raged the sergeant getting up and drawing his pistol. His coat was torn, his face scratched and bitten.

The other sergeant put his hand on the pistol. 'No, mun. Old Deecee will kick up a hell of a row if you shoot the bloody cur. You know how mad these f. . . . Englishmen are about dogs!'

The sergeant put back his pistol in the holster and wiped the blood off his face: 'Suppose I'll have to have anti-rabies shots. A Sikh's dog is bound to be mad.'

It look two constables with their long bamboo-poles to keep the battered Alsatian at bay.

Sher Singh slumped on the floor of the veranda with his arms covering his face and began to cry. He hated himself for crying but he could not stop. The two people he feared and loathed most, Anglo-Indians and Muslim policemen from northern Punjab, had insulted and beaten him in his own home and all he could do was to cry like a child. Even his dog had shown more fight.

'Take this bloody patriot to the station and put some red hot chillies up his arse,' ordered the sergeant to the head constable. 'If he has any illusions of being a magistrate's son, knock them out of him.'

The head constable put the handcuffs on Sher Singh's hands and said gently: 'Come along, Sardar Sahib.' Sher Singh rolled up his hair into a chignon and picked up his turban. His eyes were inflamed with hate and humiliation. When he tried to stand there was a stab of pain in his testicles. He held them with his manacled hands and slumped down again. The head constable took the turban from him and put his arm round his waist and helped him up on to his feet. He whispered in his ears: 'Be a man. Don't degrade yourself before these white bastards.' Sher Singh limped into the van.

The search lasted an hour. They ransacked every room in the house. A man was sent down the well. They found nothing—not even the rifle for which Taylor had made out a licence in Sher Singh's name. The illicit arms remained unnoticed in the pit in the centre of the empty garage.

The policewoman came out to report that she had searched Champak and her belongings but had recovered nothing. The sergeants rode off on their motor-cycles. The two policemen who had been keeping the Alsatian at a safe distance took their seats in the van. Sher Singh heard the defiant barking and snapping of the dog following the Black Maria till it gathered speed on its way to the police station.

~

The police commissioner dropped Buta Singh at Taylor's house. There were no other magistrates present nor were there any chairs laid out for them. Taylor's bearer came out and held open the wire-gauze door. 'The Sahib is at chota hazri and wants you to join him.'

Buta Singh had been inside Taylor's drawing room but no farther. Mrs Taylor came in to greet him. 'Come in, Sardar Sahib, and join us for breakfast.' She led him to the dining-room.

'Very kind of you, madam. I had my tea before coming,' answered Buta Singh lying. 'Very kind of you. Good morning, sir.'

'Good morning, Buta Singh,' answered Taylor putting down the morning paper. 'Come and join us. You have met my wife before, haven't you? Joyce, you know Mr Buta Singh.'

'Of course! One more cup of tea won't do you any harm.'

'No harm,' sniggered Buta Singh. 'No harm. Thank you. Very kind of you, madam.' Buta Singh sat down and allowed himself to be talked into having eggs and bacon, toast and marmalade, and three cups of tea. He could now bring up Taylor's breakfast menu casually with his colleagues and his family. It would be fun talking about bacon in front of the Muslim magistrates. Had Taylor some special favour to ask for this reception? Probably to pursue the subject of getting information from Sher Singh.

When breakfast was over, Taylor conducted Buta Singh to his study. He didn't light a cigarette to time the interview but took out his pipe and tin of tobacco.

'Sahib seems to have something special on his mind this morning. What service can I render?'

Taylor lit his pipe. 'I wanted to have a general talk with you about things; one seldom gets the time to do that. I also have to ask you about a particular subject which we will come to later on. I hope you don't mind my being personal. How long . . .'

'Nothing personal, sir,' interrupted Buta Singh. 'I have no secrets to keep from you. Ask me anything you like.'

'I was going to ask how long had your family been connected with the British government?'

'Sir,' warmed Buta Singh. 'Sir, we can almost go back to the days of Sikh rule. On the annexation of the Punjab and the disbanding of the Sikh forces my great-grandfather, who was a subedar and had fought against the British in the Anglo-Sikh wars, joined the British army. He served under John Lawrence. He also fought under Nicholson in the Mutiny of 1857 and was awarded a medal for the capture of Delhi; we still have it in the family. My grandfather was also in the British army. He rose from the ranks and retired as a Jemadar. In those days to be a Jemadar was a big thing for an Indian. My father did not join the army, but he recruited many soldiers in the 1914–18 war and our family was given lands in the Canal Colonies. I have kept up the tradition of loyalty to the British Crown and will do so till the day I die.' He became breathless with the excitement he had generated in himself. It did not seem to affect Taylor who coolly lit his pipe once more.

'What about your son?'

'What about my son? He may hobnob with the nationalists but he will have to be loyal to the British as long as Buta Singh lives,' he replied, smacking his chest. 'Otherwise I will disown him. After I am dead, he can do what he likes.'

Taylor still seemed unimpressed. 'I appreciate your sentiments of loyalty, Buta Singh, but I do not agree with you about the future of India; and I am British. I feel we should pull out of this country as soon after the war as we can and let you Indians manage your own affairs. I, for one, have no intention of continuing in the Indian Civil Service a day after the cease-fire. In fact I am not on the side of Mr Churchill but on that of Mr Gandhi and Mr Nehru—except, and this is important, I do think the war has to be won first. Otherwise the Nazis and the Fascists will put the clock back for you and for us. I may be wrong, but that is my belief.'

Englishmen like Taylor confused Buta Singh. It wasn't entirely his fault. He had only known Englishmen who believed in the British Empire as they did in the Church of England; who stood to attention even if a bar of their national anthem came over the air while somebody was fiddling with the knob of a radio set; who believed that 'natives' were only of two kinds—the Gunga Dins, whom they loved like their pet dogs because of their dogged devotion to the Sahibs, and the Bolshies, whom they hated.

'Mr Taylor, you may be right. I am an old man and I cannot change. I am for the British Raj. If it goes, there will be chaos in this country as there was chaos before the British came.' Buta Singh felt mean. There were limits beyond which flattery should not go; his frequently did. Only if the Englishman accepted it, he would feel better.

'What does your son have to say on the subject?'

That gave Buta Singh the opportunity to redeem himself.

'Of course he disagrees with me and is more of your point of view. He is young and you know what youth is!'

'Yes,' answered Taylor absent-mindedly. 'But what do you do when there is a conflict of loyalties? What would you do if you discovered that he had been mixed up not only with the Nationalists but also with terrorists?'

Insinuations about duplicity made Buta Singh angry. 'I would disown him. I would throw him out of the house,' he replied emphatically.

'You are a harsh judge, Buta Singh. Children are meant to be understood, not thrown out when there is a difference of opinion.'

'We teach our children to respect and obey their parents,' said Buta Singh. 'I am sure European parents do the same, sir.'

'It may be a hard thing to say, but, despite the close living in joint families and the formal respect paid to the elders, there is less contact, understanding, or friendship between parents and their children in India than in Europe.'

Buta Singh didn't understand the trend of the conversation. Taylor seemed to be beating about the bush. Then out of the blue he came out with a wholly irrelevant question. 'Did you know Jhimma Singh, headman?'

'Jhimma Singh? No, who is he?'

'I hope he is; he certainly was. A big, burly, black chap. Apparently he knew your son and was on visiting terms with him.'

'Oh yes, sir, I know,' answered Buta Singh. 'I think he came to my house some time ago when I was at prayer in the gurdwara. I remember him. I didn't know his name was Jhimma Singh. What about him, sir?'

Taylor went through the process of emptying, refilling, and relighting his pipe. Sometimes these tactics worked.

'What about Jhimma Singh, sir?'

'I have reason to believe that the day he came to your house was the last day he was seen alive. Further, I have reason to believe that your son, Sher Singh, was perhaps the last man to see him alive.'

Buta Singh's face fell, 'What is this you say, Sahib?'

'Jhimma Singh was a headman and a police informer. He had been informing me about your son's activities with a group of boys who practiced rifle shooting near his village. You recall I gave you a licence for one! I hoped that it would bring the whole business out in the open and you would have put a stop to it. Well, it didn't work out that way. These lads then tried to blow up a bridge on the canal. Jhimma Singh told me about that too. The only one of the gang he knew was your son. Then suddenly he disappeared. I am pretty certain he has been murdered. I may, of course, be wrong.'

Buta Singh sank back in his chair and covered his face with his hands. Large tears rolled down his cheeks and disappeared in his beard. 'My nose has been cut. I can no longer show my face to the world,' he sobbed.

Taylor took the Sikh magistrate's hairy hand in his own. 'Buta Singh, this is extremely unpleasant for me but I have to do my duty. Let me tell you all. Your house is being searched in your absence now. I have also ordered Sher Singh to be taken into custody. We have nothing to go on except what Jhimma Singh has told me and that, you as a magistrate know, is not enough. If Sher Singh had anything to do with the headman's disappearance it is for him to tell. It is on him we have to rely for information about his accomplices as well. If he gives it, I may consider granting him a King's pardon. Of course, if he had nothing to do with the affair, or refuses to talk, the case will not be reopened.'

'How shall I face the world?' moaned Buta Singh and again covered his face with his hands. Taylor got up and asked the bearer to get a cold drink. Mrs Taylor came in carrying a tray with three glasses of orange juice. She put it on the table and sat down on a chair beside the magistrate. She put her hand gently on his knee. 'Mister Buta Singh, pull yourself together and have a drink. I was told the Sikhs were brave people! This is not being very brave, is it?'

Buta Singh blew his nose and wiped his tears with his handkerchief. Mrs Taylor held the glass of orange juice for him 'Come along, drink it. And don't fret. What's happened has happened.'

The magistrate's hand shook as he gulped down his glass of orange juice. He brought up a deep sigh. 'How can I thank . . . .' He broke down again and started to sob in his handkerchief. The Taylors sat quietly and let him cry his heart out. Then Taylor spoke in a firm voice: 'Buta Singh, I have given you fifteen days' leave. Your house will continue to be guarded as before. If you want to be spared the embarrassment of visitors you can tell the policeman to keep them out. You can see your son as often as you want to. You can give him whatever advice you deem fit; it is for you to decide. I repeat, if he is willing to give us the names of his accomplices, he will be made a Crown witness and be granted the King's pardon. If not, he must face the consequences of his act.'

In the Himalayas it is not the advent but the end of the monsoon which is spectacular. There are not months of intense heat which turn the plainsman's longing for rain into a prayer for deliverance from a hot purgatory. People of the hills look upon the monsoon as they do on other seasons. One brings snow, one the blossoms, one the fruit; also one brings the rain. For another, in the mountains the monsoon is heavier and for days the hills and valleys are blotted out by sheets of rain. It is misty, damp and cold, and people pray for the sunshine. Their prayers are answered some time in September or October. The monsoon is given a grand farewell with fireworks. Thunder explodes like firecrackers and lightning illumines the landscape as if flares were being dropped from the heavens. The sky is no longer a mass of shapeless grey; it is an expanse of aquamarine full of bulbous white clouds which change their shapes and colours as they tumble away. The mists lift as if waved away by a magic wand. Unfolding rain-washed scenery of snow-capped mountains on one side and an infinity of brown plains intersecting a thousand golden streams on the other. The air is cleaner. It has the crispy cold of the regions of perpetual snows; it also has the insinuating warmth of the regions of perpetual sunshine.

Some days of autumn have more of 'God's in His Heaven' than others. This was one of them. When they came out into the garden, the sun had just come up over the hills and touched the snow range across the valley with a glow of pink. The forests of deodar stood on the mountainside patiently waiting for a long day of mellow sunshine. There wasn't a cloud in the deep blue sky: only lammergeyers drifting lazily with the noiseless ease and grace of gliders. It was too good to be true; and like all times that are too good to be true, there was mixed with the sense of elation, an apprehension that it would not last long, and perhaps, not end as well as it had begun.

They had their breakfast in the garden where the dew lay like whitewash on the lawn. The borders were thick with chrysanthemums, sunflowers and hollyhocks. After breakfast they went for a stroll on the Mall. The crowds had considerably thinned as most of the government offices had shifted back to the plains and some of the larger stores had closed down for the month. They walked up and down the road a couple of times and then went into Davicos for coffee. After the coffee, Madan took the girls with him to watch the finals of a football tournament played on the race-course in the valley at Annandale. Sabhrai went down to the temple in the lower bazar to spend the rest of the day.

When Sabhrai returned home late in the afternoon, the servant handed her a telegram; it had been delivered some hours earlier. She tore it open and looked at the hieroglyphics. 'What does it say?' she asked anxiously.

'I can't read English,' replied the boy, a little surprised that she should ask him.

'Go and ask somebody to read it and come back quickly.'

The boy went to the neighbours' homes and came back half-an-hour later to say that the masters were out and none of the servants could read. Sabhrai took the telegram from him. She paced up and down the veranda; she walked up to the gate and came back; she went down the road a little distance, came back home, and paced up and down the veranda again. She looked at the telegram over and over again. The only letters she could piece together were those that spelled her husband's name; the rest made no sense to her. At long last Madan and the girls came home. Sabhrai met them at the gate with the telegram. Madan read it out aloud first in English and then translated it for her in Punjabi. She was right, it was from her husband.

'Return immediately. Buta Singh.'

~

Sabhrai's sixth sense told her nothing about the drama that had taken place. She realized that nothing could be wrong with her husband because he had sent the telegram. Whatever had happened had happened to her son. If he were sick or had met with an accident, his wife was there to look after him. Why should Buta Singh send for her in this manner unless Sher Singh was dying or was already dead? The more she thought of it, the more certain she became that the telegram had something to do with her son; and that he was either in mortal danger or had succumbed to it. She sat up in her bed and prayed all through the night. Next day on her way down to the plains and again all night in the train, her thoughts and prayers were for her Shera.

It was still dark when she woke up Beena and asked her to wash, change and roll up the beddings. She asked her to come and sit beside her. 'Pray for your brother,' she said to indicate that she had an inkling of what had happened. They sat cross-legged on the berth wrapped in their shawls and recited the morning prayer. The black nothingness outside the window pane became a dimly-lit landscape beyond continuous waves of telegraph wires which rose and fell from pole to pole. The sun came up over the flat land and lit up the yellow squares of mustard, the solid greens of sugarcane and blocks of mud villages. They came to the suburbs of the city. Mud huts gave way to brick buildings, and open fields to evil-smelling ditches where men sat on their haunches, shamelessly baring their bottoms and relieving themselves.

The train drew in on a noisy crowded platform full of coolies in red uniforms. Sabhrai and Beena looked for a familiar face, but could not recognize anyone. The orderly came from the servants' compartment and took charge of the luggage. They were counting their pieces when an Englishwoman approached them. She touched Beena on the arm and asked, 'Are you Sardar Buta Singh's daughter?'

'Yes.'

'I am Mrs Taylor. Good morning. And this I presume is your mother. *Sat Sri Akal*, Sardarni Sahiba. We have met before.'

Sabhrat joined her hands and answered the Englishwoman's greeting. It took the mother and daughter some time to realize that the deputy commissioner's wife had come to receive them. Sabhrai lost her composure and whispered agitatedly into her daughter's ear. Joyce Taylor saw the consternation on their faces. 'Don't be alarmed Sardarni Sahiba, all is well,' she said putting her hand on Sabhrai's shoulder. 'Your husband and son are in the best of health; you will see them soon. I had nothing to do this morning so I thought I'd come along to fetch you and spare you a long tonga ride.'

Beena translated this to her mother and they smiled gratefully at Mrs Taylor. Things must have changed for an English deputy comissioner's wife to take the trouble to receive the family of an Indian subordinate. They were too bewildered to think that there might be other reasons. Beena gave the coolies more than twice their due to prevent them nagging and making a scene in front of the Englishwoman.

There was nothing at home to indicate a crisis. There were two policemen on duty, instead of one. They came to attention and saluted as the car went in. Nobody came out to receive them while they were unloading their luggage. That didn't surprise them. Buta Singh was likely to be at the Courts; Sher Singh would be

out somewhere and Champak in her room. But where was Dyer?
He was always the first to greet members of the family returning
home and had to be restrained from putting his paws on their
shoulders and licking their faces. As soon as Mrs Taylor had said
goodbye and left, Beena shouted for the dog. He came round the
house, hopping on three legs; the fourth was in plaster. There
was a gash on his nose on which flies were clustered. He whined
as he came to his mistress and let out a long piteous howl. 'Hai,
Dyer, what's happened to you? Who's hurt my little son?' Sabhrai
fanned the flies off with her headpiece and put her arms round
the dog. 'Didn't Sher take you to the doctor?'

Champak came out of the wire-gauze door. Her hair was
scattered untidily on her face. Her eyes were red and swollen.
She wore a plain white cotton sari without any make-up or
jewellery—like a widow in mourning. Sabhrai's heart sank. Was
her son dead? Hadn't the Englishwoman said he was in good
health!

'What has . . .?'

Champak clasped her mother-in-law round the waist and
burst out crying. Sabhrai, who had never particularly cared for
Champak, stroked her head. 'The True, the True, the Great
Guru,' she chanted.

Beena could not stand it any more. 'What has happened? Why
don't you tell?' she shrieked.

Buta Singh came out in the veranda. He, too, was shabbily
dressed in a white shirt and pajamas. His beard had not been
pressed and he wore no turban. 'What is all this crying for?' he
asked at the top of his voice. 'You behave as if he were dead.
Perhaps that might have been better.'

'The True, the True. The Great Guru. What words are these?
Where is my son, my moon, my little ruby. Where is he?' Tears
streamed down Sabhrai's face. 'Why don't you tell me?'

Even her tears did not appease Buta Singh's temper. 'My nose
has been cut; I can no longer show my face to anyone.'

'What has he done? Why don't you tell me where he is.'

'He's in jail. Where else can he be?'

'The Great Guru. The Great Guru. Who has been born to put my child in jail! What did he do?'

'Murder, what else! I can no longer show my face to anyone. All my life's work has been thrown into a well.'

'The True, the True, the Great Guru.'

They went into the sitting-room. After a few minutes, Sabhrai regained her composure and asked her husband to explain what had happened. Buta Singh did so in a bitter voice, mincing no words. He ended on a note of self-pity. 'All my years of loyal service thrown into the well . . . Just when I am due to retire and expect to be rewarded, my son cuts my nose. I wouldn't be surprised if the little land we have in reward for services, were confiscated and I were given no pension. I do not understand this complete lack of regard for one's parents. And Champak must have known about his goings-on with these bad characters. I wouldn't be surprised if that rascal Madan were one of them. To whom can I show my face now?'

Champak began to sob once more. Sabhrai spoke sharply: 'You are only concerned with yourself. Don't you want to save your child's life?'

The snub had a salutary effect on Buta Singh's temper. He relapsed into a sullen silence.

'What are we to do?' asked Beena at last.

'I don't know. I've gone mad,' replied her father.

'We shall have a non-stop reading of the Granth for two days and nights. The Guru will be our guide,' said Sabhrai quietly.

'Yes, yes,' commented Beena impatiently, 'we will do that, but we must do something about getting Sherji out of jail. Have you been to see him?' she asked her father.

'No, I don't want to see him.'

Champak's sobs became louder. Sabhrai put her arms round her. Buta Singh felt guilty. 'If the deputy commissioner had not been so kind to me, the police would have beaten him straight.

Even now, he has promised that if Sher tells them all about the crime, he will grant him the King's pardon.'

'Will he have to give the names of his accomplices?' asked Sabhrai.

'The police already know about them; they know everything. These other chaps were probably the ones to implicate Sher. It is only by the deputy commissioner's kindness that Sher can avail himself of the King's pardon. The others would give anything to have the offer made to them.'

'Will he have to become an informer?' asked Beena.

Buta Singh got angry again. 'These are stupid words. I am telling you that the police don't need an informer; they know everything. They are only willing to give Sher an excuse to save his life because the deputy commissioner is keen to help him.'

'Why haven't you told Sher of this offer?' asked Sabhrai. Buta Singh felt cornered. 'I've been out of my senses. If it hadn't been for the Taylors, I don't know what would have happened to me! What more can a man do than offer your son's life back to you?'

'You must see Sherji,' said Beena, 'and tell him about Mr Taylor's offer.'

'We will first do the non-stop reading of the Granth,' said Sabhrai firmly. 'The Guru will guide us. We will do what He commands.'

~

Being the only son, Sher Singh had been pampered in his childhood and allowed to have his own way in his adolescence. Despite this, the two things he hankered after were affection and esteem. The one he sought through popularity amongst friends; the other through leadership. The applause that came from his family and his colleagues was offset by his early marriage. Champak, despite her expressions of admiration, gave him an uneasy feeling of being a failure. To impress her became an obsession. The form it took was to hold out visions of a successful political career by which he would take her to dizzy heights of eminence along with him. The more his physical inadequacy gnawed his insides, the more daring he became in his political acitivity. From fiery speeches, he went on to uniforms and discipline; from those to belief in force: the worship of tough men and love for symbols of strength, like swords crossed over a shield. These, with the possession of guns, pistols, cartridges, and the handsomely masculine Alsatian as a companion, completed his partial padding. Living with these symbols of strength and among people who vaguely expected him to succeed, Sher Singh came to believe in his own future and his power. He did not realize that strength was not a natural development of his own personality but nutured behind the protection provided by his father's position as a senior magistrate and a respected citizen. He was like a hot-house plant blossoming in a greenhouse. The abuse, beating, and arrest were like putting that plant out in a violent hailstorm. His bluster and self-confidence withered in the icy cold atmosphere of the police station.

Sher Singh had never been beaten before in his life. Being kicked in the groin and hit in the face had been a shattering experience. He touched the depths of humiliation and anger. He had always feared and hated Anglo-Indians. They did the Englishman's dirty work, spoke his language in their own ugly Hobson-Jobson, full of vulgar abuse, but had none of his cricketing spirit. They were the Hydes of the English Dr Jekyll. He had also envied and hated Punjabi Mussulmans. They were physically stronger and more virile than his type of Sikh. And on that fatal morning an Anglo-Indian sergeant had hit him in the face with the back of his hand and a Mussulman constable had told him to face his ordeal like a man. He had wept from fear; he had wept in anger; he had wept in hate. At the end of two days of weeping, his system was drained of anger and hate; only fear remained: the fear of another thrashing and the greater one of death by hanging.

After a few days, life in the police station became such a routine that it seemed to Sher Singh as if he had been there all his life. Every hour a brass gong was struck, it told the time and regulated the life of the station. At the stroke of six, the reveille was sounded and everyone had to get up. There was much sucking of keekar twigs, spitting and gargling around the taps where policemen and prisoners took turns to bathe. An hour later they were given highly brewed tea and stale bread. Thereafter the courtyard rang with exercise and drill orders. Anglo-Indian sergeants drove in on their noisy motor-cycles and took charge. Policemen went out in batches for traffic duty or investigation or to make arrests. Black Marias were brought in; prisoners were handcuffed, fettered and taken to the law courts. They were brought back in the evening, locked up and fed. Anglo-Indians drove out more noisily than when they came. After the evening roll-call, there was another call of the bugle and the lights were switched off everywhere except in the reporting room. Then it was silent except for an occasional shriek or cry for mercy from the cells behind the courtyard where prisoners were interrogated. Through all this the brass gong marked the hours.

What Sher Singh dreaded most was a visit from his father. He had ruined the latter's career and he would now have no chance of getting an extension of service or a title in the next Honours list. The government might even deprive him of his pension. Buta Singh was sure to denounce him and refuse to let him come back home—if ever he got away alive. Without Buta Singh there was no chance of reconciliation with the rest of the family. Sabhrai was the type of Indian woman who believed that her husband was a god and would do little more than plead for her son after the initial outburst was over. Champak would probably be sent away to her parents and not be heard of till he came out of jail—if that ever happened. It was an amazing thought that he had hardly missed her. His sister, Beena, did not really matter. The only one he really missed was his dog. Dyer's defence of his master had made a deep impression on his mind. He had often visualized his picture in uniform on large posters with his handsome Alsatian beside him. Now he visualized the same picture of himself as a sad disillusioned man with a distant philosophic look, loved by no one except his dog, who fixed his doting eyes on his master. He wished they would let Dyer share his cell.

Then there was the interrogation. Sher Singh knew his turn would come soon. The sergeant who had hit him said so every morning when he went round the cells. 'Well, Sardar, how are your plans for turning the British out of the country getting on? We must discuss them soon; perhaps I can help you, hmm?'

How much did the police know?

Sher Singh tried to work that out hour after hour, day after day. It was obvious that he was the only one of the group they had arrested so far. Madan who had got him in this mess, was back in Simla having a good time; the others were scattered in different places. Could one of them have been a spy? No, because then his arrest would have followed immediately after the murder. Unless one of the gang had also been arrested and had talked, the police could not possibly know anything about it.

How much should he tell to get away without a beating?

~

One afternoon a constable came to the cell, put two cane chairs against the wall, and said casually: 'The Sahibs want to talk to you.' The 'Sahibs' came slapping their putteed legs with their swagger sticks. They were the same two who had arrested him. Sher Singh got up from his chair—more out of fear than out of politeness. He did not greet them because he knew the greeting would not be answered. The sergeants sat down. One of them pulled Sher Singh's chair nearer him with his toes and put his feet on it. Sher Singh's only option was to squat on the floor or to keep standing. He kept standing. He was conscious of his arms hanging at his sides as if he were at attention.

'Well, Sardar, are you still plotting to get the British out?' He turned to his companion. 'Great leader this chap, mun. You wouldn't know looking at him, would you?'

The other nodded his head slowly, scrutinizing Sher Singh from head to foot. 'One never knows with these niggers.'

'One doesn't, does one!'

'Not unless one sticks a greased pole up their bums.'

They had their eyes fixed on him; they scratched their chins as if contemplating the course of violence. Sher Singh could do nothing except look down at his hands or at their feet.

'Is this chap also involved in the killing of that fat Sikh lambardar?'

'No, mun! He's after bigger game. He wants to shoot the Guv or the Viceroy. Don't you? Speak, you big leader of the revolution! Don't you?'

Sher Singh felt the blood drain out of his system. Were they going to beat him? Why didn't they ask him a specific question and give him a chance to answer?

'Oi,' shouted one of them to the constable outside, 'ask the sub-inspector to *juldi karo*. We can't waste the whole afternoon with this fellow.'

The constable ran across the courtyard. The sub-inspector came with a sheaf of yellow files tucked under his arm. They got into a huddle. Sher Singh watched them carefully as they whispered into each other's ear. The older of the two sergeants pushed aside the file with disdain: 'Wot you wasting your time for on this chap if the other fellows have already given us all the names?'

'I don't know, Sahib,' answered the sub-inspector feigning surprise. 'Mr Taylor, deputy commissioner, say he Sardar Buta Singh son, give him chance to be informer and save his life.'

'So that's it! You hear, mister? The Deecee wants to give you a chance to save your bloody neck from hanging because of your old *bap*. We have all the information we want from your pals. It's a water-tight case. You confirm what they have said and we might consider granting you pardon. Otherwise you hang with the rest of the buggers.'

Sher Singh found his voice with great difficulty: 'What did they say?'

'The bugger wants to know what the others have said? Clever fellow isn't he? Don't try tricks with us, old chap. We've known too many like you.'

The Indian sub-inspector was more polite, obviously wanting to curry favour with Buta Singh. 'Sardar Sahib,' he said in Punjabi, 'as the Sahibs have told you, we have all the information we need from your associates. This is a very serious case, you can be sentenced to death for conspiracy to wage war against the King Emperor. Mr Taylor wants to reward the loyal services of your respected father and has ordered us to give you the chance to be a Crown witness. If your statement confirms what the other conspirators have said and is truthful about the crimes you have committed, the government may decide to grant you pardon. Do you understand?'

'Yes.'

Three pairs of eyes were fixed on him.

'Could I consult a lawyer?'

'Rape your sister,' exploded one of the sergeants. 'We want to give you a chance to save your neck and you want to bring lawyers here! Give him the rod properly greased.'

The Indian sub-inspector again took charge of the situation with a mixture of servility and firmness. 'Sardar Sher Singh, you have not appreciated our point. We know everything already and really have no need of your statement. It is only for your own good. If Taylor Sahib insists on sparing your life because of Sardar Buta Singh, we can make you talk; you know that, don't you?'

Sher Singh made no answer to the threat.

Three pairs of eyes continued to transfix him. He did not know what to say. But he knew that if they used any violence he would tell all he knew without considering the rights or wrongs of making the confession. He made one last attempt to postpone the decision. 'Could I at least see my father?'

'Now he wants to see his bap. What's wrong with this fellow?'

'Perhaps he will want to see his ma too,' added the other.

'You don't believe what we say?' asked the Indian sub-inspector angrily. 'It is because your father has been rubbing his nose at Mr Taylor's threshold every day that you are being given this opportunity!'

'It is very kind of you but I would like to speak to my father before making any statement.' For the first time Sher Singh spoke firmly, and that because an Indian subordinate had dared to talk disparagingly of his father.

The three officers went back into a huddle and then rose up together. The one with his feet on the chair kicked it towards Sher Singh. 'Okay. You see your bloody bap. We'll talk to you later.'

'And if you want our advice on how to kick the British out of India, don't hesitate to ask.'

They roared with laughter and left.

~

The non-stop reading of the Granth did not bring any peace in Buta Singh's home. What was worse, the Guru did not indicate the line of action as Sabhrai had promised. And soon after the cermonial reading was over, Buta Singh resumed his sulking and self-pity. He refused to see Sher Singh in the lock-up, and would not let anyone else see him. He began to insinuate that Champak must have known of her husband's activities and had done nothing to stop him. When Champak's parents heard of it, they came over and took her back home. At last Sabhrai's patience came to an end. One morning she boldly announced her intention to see her son. Buta Singh was adamant. The crisis was averted by the arrival of the officer in charge of the police station. He told them that Sher Singh had expressed the desire to see his father before making a statement and that Mr Taylor had specially requested Buta Singh to comply with his son's wishes.

Buta Singh refused to comply. He thought that, in the circumstances, the refusal to obey Taylor would more than ever prove his loyalty to the government and disapproval of his disloyal son. The responsibility fell automatically on Sabhrai. She accepted it readily, not because she had any advice to give her son on the statement he was to make, but because her heart ached to see her son and to clasp him to her bosom. She asked her husband to tell her what she was to say to Sher Singh about the confession.

Buta Singh explained the legal situation to her again. She asked: 'If the police already know the names of his associates why do they want them all over again from Sher?' He explained, as he said, for the twentieth time, because they wanted to give him a chance to get away. Why, she went on, were they so keen on letting him get away? For the hundredth time, answered her husband, because Mr Taylor was so kind and friendly to a family which had a long record of loyalty. Why, persisted Sabhrai, if the police really knew the names of Sher's associates hadn't they arrested any of them? Oh really, Buta Singh couldn't be bothered to go over things again and again. Sabhrai had developed a stubborn indifference to rudeness and irritation and asked her husband point blank: 'What will happen if he refuses to make a confession?'

'What will happen? As far as I am concerned, my service, pension and the land granted by the government all go. But that is a small matter; in addition, the boy will be hanged.'

Sabhrai shut her eyes: 'The True, the True. The Great Guru, the Great Guru.'

She turned to her daughter: 'Have you any advice for your brother?'

'I only want him back,' she replied full of emotion. 'I don't care what he says or does, but he must come home now.'

Buta Singh felt that he should not let the matter be postponed indefinitely. 'Will you go tomorrow morning? I have to tell the sub-inspector.'

'What is the hurry. We have waited so many days. We should think about it a little more,' answered Sabhrai.

Buta Singh launched into another tirade. When he finished telling her how little she appreciated the gravity of the situation, how stubborn and stupid she had become of late, Sabhrai got up. 'I will talk to the inspector myself,' she said.

The sub-inspector stood up and saluted Sabhrai.

'Have you come from the police station where my son is kept?'

'Yes, Mataji, your son is in our care.'

'Tell your senior officer I will come to the police station four days from now. I will come, not my husband. I would also like to bring my son's dog with me. He has missed his master very much.'

'Very good, Mataji. I will tell the inspector Sahib. Is there anything you want to send to your son or any message you want me to give him?'

Sabhrai thought for a while. 'If you wait for a moment, I will give you something for him.' She went into the house and came back with a small prayer book wrapped in velvet. 'Give this to my little ruby and tell him to say his prayers regularly. Tell him that the Guru is with him in body and in spirit. *Sat Sri Akal.*'

The sub-inspector was a Muslim. Nevertheless he put the Sikh prayer book reverently to his forehead and then kissed it. 'Mataji, I will give it to him myself. Allah will protect your son from harm.' For the next three days Sabhrai shut herself away from the world. Her sanctuary was not the gurdwara but her own bedroom. She sat in her armchair with her legs tucked beneath her and murmured her prayers. Her only companion was Dyer. She had never taken much notice of the dog but since her son's arrest she had tried to give him the affection Sher Singh had given. Dyer sat in front of his mistress with his chin stretched on the floor and his eyes dolefully fixed on her. After each prayer she would speak to him: 'Dyer, son, will you come with me to see Sher?' Dyer would prick up his ears at his master's name and cock his head inquiringly from side to side. 'Nobody takes you out for walks these days?' Like all dogs. Dyer knew the word 'walk'. He would get up with a whine and come to his mistress wagging his big tail. 'That's all right, son. Mama will take you out when you are well. And when my moon comes home, we will all go for walks together, won't we?' And Dyer would again be full of questions cocking his head from left to right, right to left. Sometimes he would get too excited, put his paws in his mistress' lap, and lick her face. She would push him away gently, for this she did not like. She would wipe her face with her headpiece, wash her hands in the bathroom, and start praying again. An hour later the whole thing would be repeated: 'Dyer, son, will you come with me to see my Shera?'

The evening before the interview, she had her dinner with her husband and daughter and told them she was going to spend the night at the temple in the city. They did not ask her any questions. She wrapped herself in her Kashmiri shawl, for it had become bitterly cold, and went away on a tonga.

When Sabhrai took off her slippers outside the main gate, the man in charge of shoes was already packing up. 'Brother, keep my shoes for the night; I will take them in the morning.' He gave her a ticket, put out his hurricane lantern, and locked the shoe-shed.

Not many people stay in the temple after the evening service is over. Visitors from other towns retire to the quarters provided for them: beggars are driven away by armed guards who patrol the sacred premises. Only those stricken with sorrow spend the midnight hours in different corners crying and praying for peace. These no one disturbs.

Sabhrai washed her hands and feet in the cistern at the entrance and went down the marble stairs gripping the silver railing on the side. The waters of the sacred pool and the milk-white of the marble walls glistened in the moonlight. The gilded dome of the shrine had a ghostly pallor. Sabhrai bowed towards the shrine, walked along the side-walk and up the narrow passage, which ran level with the water, to the central place of worship. The room was dimly-lit by a blue electric bulb; the diamonds and rubies in the ceiling twinkled like stars on a dark night. In the centre of the floor the sacred Granth lay wrapped on a low cot. In the corners of the room were huddled figures of men and women, some asleep, some in prayer. Sabhrai made her obeisance and went out. She found a spot from where she could see the dome of the temple and the reflection of the moon and the stars in the dark waters of the sacred pool. She sat down on the hard and cold marble floor. An icy wind blew over the water, through the trellised fence, into her bones. But it was absolutely still and peaceful. The city was asleep; only the gentle clop clop of ripples on marble and the boom of the tower clock striking the hours disturbed the heavy silence.

Sabhrai did not know what prayer one recited during the night; so she went through all she knew by heart. When she had finished, the clock struck two. But the tumult in her mind was not stilled. They were going to hang her son if he did not mention the names of the other conspirators. Hang her little Shera whom she had borne and fed by her own breasts. She began to sob. She stifled her sobs and tried to meditate. How could she meditate with Shera crying for help: 'Mother, they will hang me and I am only twenty-one . . .'

Tears coursed down her cheeks, hot and unceasing. She wiped them with the hem of her shirt and blew her nose. She felt her son's presence between her arms, and more tears flooded down. Why did she feel alone in this awful predicament? Her husband had no doubts; he wanted Shera to confess. So, obviously, did her daughter and daughter-in-law. Shera mattered as much to them as he did to her. Did they really believe that the police knew everything or were they doping their consciences with the thought? And what did Shera himself want to do? Surely it was really for him to decide rather than for her! And if she were the only one with doubts, couldn't she be mistaken?

So the tumult continued and the tears continued to course down her cheeks. Her grey head was full of dew and her limbs stiff with cold and damp. Why did the Guru not guide her in her hour of need? Had she lost faith? She recalled the time when she had come to this very temple to take part in the cleaning of the sacred pool. The water had been pumped out and the enormous carp that ate out of people's hands had been put away in another tank. Millions of Sikhs had volunteered to carry on their heads the slime which had accumulated for over a hundred years. People said that the hawk of the last Guru would come to see the cleaning. Non-believers had laughed their vulgar laughter, shrugged their shoulders, and said: 'What can you do to people like that?' But the hawk had come. With her own eyes she had seen it swoop down from the heavens, scattering the thousands of pigeons that nested in the temple precincts. It had perched on the pinnacle of the golden dome, preened its lustrous white plumage, and looked down on the throng waist-deep in slime and mire. The people had wept and prayed. Over and over again men had hurled the Guru's challenging cry: 'Ye who seek salvation, shout'; and the crowd had roared back: 'God is Truth'.

People with faith had seen; those without faith neither saw nor believed that others had seen. Sabhrai also recalled the terrible days when the Sikhs wanted to take over their shrines from the clutches of corrupt priests and the police had decided to help the priests against the people. They had killed and tortured passive resisters. But for each one who was killed, beaten or imprisoned, another fifty had come. Word had gone round that whenever a band of passive resisters prayed with faith, the Guru himself would appear in their midst and all the lathi blows the police showered on them would fall on him and not on them. That was exactly how it had happened. Frail men and women, who had not known the lash of a harsh tongue, had volunteered and taken merciless beatings without wincing. The police had tired and the priests had panicked. The faith of the Sikhs had triumphed. Was her faith shaking? She tried to dismiss all other thoughts and bring the picture of the last warrior Guru to her mind. He came as he was in the colour print on her mantelpiece: a handsome bearded cavalier in a turban, riding his roan stallion across a stream. On his right hand was perched his white falcon with its wings outspread. There was a man. He had lost all his four sons and refused to give in to injustice. She was to lose only one. How had the Guru faced the loss of his children? She began to recite his stirring lines:

> Eternal God, who are shield
> The dagger, knife, the sword we wield
> To us protector there is given
> The timeless, deathless Lord of Heaven . . . .

It went on in short staccato lines infusing warm blood into her chilled veins and making her forehead hot with anger. She was a Sikh; so was her son. Why did she ever have any doubts?

By the time the prayer ended, the grey light of dawn had dimmed the lesser stars—only the morning star shone a pure, silvery white. At last there was peace in her soul. She got up and went to the women's enclosure to bathe. The water was bitterly cold and she shuddered as she went down the steps. She bobbed up and down naming members of her family with each dip with five extra ones for her Shera. She had brought no towel and dried herself in the breeze. She got back into her clothes, wrapped the warm shawl about her shoulders, and went to the inner shrine where the morning prayer was about to begin.

The priest unwrapped the Granth and read the passage for the day.

> Lord, thou art my refuge
> I have found Thee and doubts are dispelled.
> I spoke not, but Ye knew my sorrow
> And made me to meditate on Thy holy name.
> Now I have no sorrow; I am at one with Thee
> You took me by arm
> And led me out of Maya's winding maze
> You set me free of the trap of attachment.
> Spake, the Guru: Thy fetters are fallen
> Thou who wert estranged
> Are united to Thy Lord.

Sabhrai made her obeisance to the Granth and went out. At the entrance to the temple she scraped a palmful of dust that had come off the feet of pilgrims and tied it up in a knot in her headpiece. She took her slippers from the shoe-stand and went home. The silence at the breakfast table was broken by the sound of a car drawing up in the porch. Mundoo came in to say that the deputy commissioner had sent his car to take Sabhrai to the police station. Buta Singh was very moved: 'What fine people these Taylors are! They have taken the trouble to find out and sent their car. Almost as if Sher were their own son.'

'The Guru will reward them for their kindness,' said Sabhrai. 'Those who are with you in your sorrow are your real friends. God bless them.'

The entire household, including the servants and orderlies, came to see Sabhrai off on her mission. Dyer, who had missed a car ride ever since the jeep had been taken away, cocked his unbelieving ears when his mistress asked him to come along. He gave a bark of joy and hopped onto the seat beside her. They drove off to the police station.

The deputy commissioner's car with its Union Jack and chauffeur in police uniform was well known to the staff of the police station. The sentries saluted as it went through the gates and the Anglo-Indian sergeants sprang to attention. Taylor's personal bodyguard stepped out of the front seat and opened the door. Dyer hopped out, followed by Sardarni Buta Singh.

The sergeants recognized the dog. They also realized that the native woman was Buta Singh's wife. The chauffeur enlightened them. They slunk away to the reporting room and let the Indian staff take over. The Muslim sub-inspector conducted Sabhrai to her son's cell.

Dyer was the first to greet his young master. He rushed at him, barking deliriously. He went round in circles, whining, pawing and licking, and would not let Sabhrai get near her son. Sher Singh patted the dog on the head and pushed him aside gently. Mother and son clasped each other in a tight embrace.

Sher Singh's pent up emotions burst their bounds and he began to cry loudly in his mother's arms. Sabhrai hid his unmanly tears by holding him to her bosom. She kissed his forehead again and again. They rocked in close embrace with the dog leaping about the cell, yapping and barking joyously.

'Could you leave us alone, sub-inspector Sahib?' asked Sabhrai addressing the officer.

'Certainly, Mataji,' he replied, drying his eyes. 'Stay here as long as you like. Can I bring you some tea or something to eat?'

'No, son, just leave me here for a few minutes. I won't be long.'

The sub-inspector went out and ordered the inquisitive group of constables back to their barracks.

Mother and son sat down on the charpoy. Dyer put his head in his master's lap.

'How pale you are! Do they give you enough to eat?'

'They give me all I want; I don't feel hungry. I could not even eat the food you sent me.'

'I did not send you anything.'

'Oh? The deputy commissioner's orderly brought it every day. I thought it was from home; it was Indian.'

'God bless him and his wife. Son, your father would not let me send you anything.'

'Is he very angry with me?'

'He had to be angry. You have poured water over all his ambitions.'

'What does he want me to do? The police tell me he wants me to make a statement naming the boys who were with me.'

'Yes. He thinks that is the only thing that will save you.'

'Have you all thought the matter over?'

'We have talked of nothing else. Everyone says that if the police already know about the others, there is no harm in making a statement. And Taylor Sahib is showing you a special favour in letting you be the only one to get away.'

After a long pause Sher Singh asked: 'Has Champak said anything?'

'What can she say except to want you back! Her eyes are inflamed with too much weeping. She would accept any course which would bring you back home as soon as possible. What is your own opinion?'

'. . . I . . .' said Sher Singh hesitantly, 'I have no opinion. I will do exactly what you people tell me to do. If it is true they know all about the affair, there seems no point in hiding anything any more.'

Sabhrai shut her eyes and rocked to and fro. After a while she asked, 'Son! Have they been beating you?'

Sher Singh looked down at his feet. The memory of the first thrashing came back to him. 'No, but they beat everyone who comes here. I can hear their cries at night.'

Sabhrai shut her eyes again and chanted as she rocked: The Great Guru! The True . . . Are you afraid?'

'Who is not afraid of a beating? Only those who get it know. It is easy to be brave at the expense of other people.' He stroked Dyer's head and tickled him between his front legs. 'Then are you all agreed that I should make a statement? What do you advise me?'

'I am an illiterate native woman. What advice can I give in these matters, son? I only ask the Guru to guide you. What He says is my advice.'

Sher Singh gave her time to tell him what the Guru had to say on the subject. Sabhrai simply closed her eyes and resumed rocking herself and chanting, 'The True, the True, the Great Guru.' Tears began running down her cheeks. Sher Singh put his hand on her knees: 'Mother, what do you want me to do?'

She dried her tears and blew her nose. 'Son, I spent last night at the Golden Temple asking the Guru for guidance, I do not know whether I got it right. In any case His orders were for me; not for you.'

'What did He say, Mother? Why don't you tell me?'

'He said that my son had done wrong. But if he named the people who were with him he would be doing a greater wrong. He was no longer to be regarded as a Sikh and I was not to see his face again.'

She undid the knot in her headpiece in which she had tied the dust collected at the temple and pasted it on her son's forehead with her palm. 'May the Guru be with you in body and in spirit.'

Delhi

In Khushwant Singh's vast, erotic, irreverent *magnum opus* on the city of Delhi, the principal narrator of the saga, which extends over 600 years, is a bawdy, ageing reprobate who loves Delhi as much he does the hijda whore Bhagmati—half man, half woman, with the sexual inventiveness and energy of both the sexes.

Travelling through time, space and history to discover his beloved city, the narrator meets a multitude of characters—in this extract, set in the eleventh century, the Kayastha scribe Musaddi Lal, the Sufi saint Hazrat Nizamuddin and the formidable Emperor Balban.

Today is the 15th of June. Delhi had its first pre-monsoon shower. It has cleansed the atmosphere of the dust that has been hanging in the air for the past three days. A fresh breeze drives snow-white clouds across the blue sky. The earth is fragrant. The air smells of more rain. How can anyone stay indoors on a day like this?

The choice is between Mehrauli and Okhla. Mehrauli has the Qutab Minar with its gardens, monuments and acres of mango orchards. Okhla has no monuments but it has lots of water. The Jamuna has a weir from which a canal branches off. At monsoon time the river is an awesome sight. She is then Triyama, the sister of the ruler of Hades. Delhiwallahs who have a death-wish come to Okhla during the monsoons to hurl themselves into the Jamuna's muddy arms. Those who have a zest for living come with baskets full of sucking mangoes. They suck them and see how far into the river they can throw their stones. Whether it is Mehrauli or Okhla you have to have a *mashooka* to share the experience: a mashooka in whose ears you can whisper, 'I want to take you in the rain till your bottom is full of mud and mine full of the monsoon.'

I hear a tonga pull up outside. I hear argument between the tongawalla and the passenger. The tongawalla shouts, 'There is more money in buggery than in plying a tonga.' The passenger replies in a louder voice, '*Abeyja!* Who would want to bugger you! Nobody will spit on your dirty arse.'

Who could it be except Bhagmati!

Before she can ring the bell I open the door. She comes in swaying her hips and abusing the tongawalla, 'Sala, *bahinchod!* I give the sister-fucker one rupee from Lal Kuan to this place and he wants to bugger me for more. There is no justice in the world.' She turns on me. 'Is this a day to sit indoors like a woman in a burqa? I thought you'd like to take me out in your motor car to eat some fresh air and mangoes.'

I am waiting for an excuse to get out. There is no one I'd like to be with more than Bhagmati. But not with her dressed in that red and blue sari and her head looking like a nest of butterflies. I've bought her a pair of stretch-pants and an open-collared shirt which she keeps in my apartment. 'I'll change into my vilayati clothes,' she says as she strides on into my bedroom.

She washes off the powder, rouge and lipstick. She plucks out the butterfly-clips from her hair, combs out the waves and ties it up in a bun at the back of her head. Now it is a different Bhagmati: a sprightly little gamine in a canvas kepi, half-sleeved sports shirt and bum-tight stretch-pants. Very chic! No one can tell whether she is a hijda or a boy who looks like a girl.

We start with an argument. Bhagmati says, 'It's a day for Okhla. When it rains the entire world goes to suck mangoes by the weir.'

'Not Okhla,' I reply. 'I don't like crowds: least of all Punjabis. There will be a crowd there screaming, shouting, eating, making litter everywhere.'

'If you are ashamed of being seen with me, I'll stay in the motor car,' retorts Bhagmati. It's true. But I am not going to spoil her day. 'I swear by the Guru that is not true! Okhla has too many people, too many monkeys, too many snakes. Once I killed five snuggling behind the water-gauge. Five! One after the other.'

Snakes settle the argument in favour of Mehrauli.

The road to Mehrauli has an endless procession of cycles, tongas, scooters, cars and people on foot. Everyone is shouting ho, ho or singing film songs.

A two-wheeled open cart jammed with women in veils and children comes tearing through the crowd and passes us. The driver puts the handle of his whip on the spokes of the wheel to make them rattle. He yells to everyone to get out of his way. He almost knocks down a Sikh with his wife and four children piled on one bicycle. The Sikh is very shaken. He lets out the foulest abuse he can for a family of Mussalmans. 'Progeny of pigs! You want to kill us?' Out of the huddle of burqas rises a six-year-old David. He loosens his red jock strap, sticks out his pelvis and flourishes his tiny circumcized penis. He hurls back abuse like pellets from a sling. '*Abey Sikhrey! Harami* (bastard), you want to sit on my Qutab Minar?'

Daood *Mian's* Qutub is a mighty two-a-half inches long. The other Qutub only 283 feet!

Bhagmati breaks into a helpless giggle. 'What a lovely little penis he has! So much nicer than the tapering things of the Hindus. Is your fellow circumcized?'

'You should know.'

'They all look the same when they are up. Next time I will look when it is asleep.'

We get to the Qutub. The car park is full of cars, the gardens are full of people. While we are trying to make up our minds where to go there is a heavy shower and everyone scurries for shelter. 'Not there,' I say and drive on. We go past the ruins of Metcalfe's mansion, Jamali-Kamali's mosque and enter Mehrauli town. I pull up in the car park alongside Auliya Masjid. The shower turns into a downpour. The Shamsi Talab becomes a part of the cascade pouring into it. We sit in the car playing with each other. Bhagmati slithers down the seat and parts my legs. I am nervous. Any moment someone may peep in the window and want to know what she is up to. 'Not here,' I tell her, pushing away her head. 'We'll try Jahaz Mahal.'

I take the car a few feet further up the road and park it alongside Jahaz Mahal. We make a dash for the building. There is a crowd of rustics—obviously caught by the rain on their way home. They make way for us. I take Bhagmati down the stairs to the floor which is almost level with the water of the pool. Not a soul. I take Bhagmati in my arms and crush her till she can't breathe. 'You want to break my bones? You want to murder me?' she protests. 'If you die here you would go straight to paradise. The waters of the Shamsi Talab have been blessed by many saints.'

'Acchaji, now you want to finish me! I'll go and tell them I was murdered by my lover. Allah will forgive my sins. In my next birth I will be born as Indira Gandhi and become a famous daughter of India.'

We resume our flirting. But when you have only one ear, one eye and half-a-mind to spare for sex and have to keep the other ear, eye and half-of-the-mind to confront anyone who suddenly bursts upon you, it is not much fun. Twice we try to have a quickie but both times we are interrupted by voices coming down the steps. In that light no one can tell whether Bhagmati is a boy or a girl—or both. Indians are very understanding about boys amusing each other. Only when it comes to straightforward fucking do they get censorious. We pretend we are deeply interested in archaeology, history, architecture. I light matches, examine the tiles and try to decipher inscriptions on stones.

The downpour continues. Not a break anywhere in the leaden sky. We continue strolling in the cellars examining dark corners by matchlight. I find a stone lying on the ground with some writing on it. I pick it up and bring it to the light. It has a swastika on top, two lotus flowers on either side with 'Allah' inscribed on it in Arabic. Beneath it is the legend in Persian:

Musaddi Lal Kayasth, son of Chagan Lal Kayasth, disciple and slave of Peer Hazrat Khwaja Nizamuddin, Beloved of God by whose blessing he received the gift of a son, Kamal Kayasth. In the reign of Sultan Ghiasuddin Balban, King of Kings, Shah-in-Shah of Hindustan.

I Musaddi Lal, son of Lala Chagan Lal, Hindu Kayastha of Mehrauli in the city of Delhi, having lost the light in one eye due to the formation of a pearl and fearing the same fate befalling the other, herewith record some events of my days upon this earth. May Ishwar who is also Allah, and Rama who is also Rahim, bear witness that what I have written is true, that nothing has been concealed or omitted.

I was born in 633 Hijri corresponding to the year 1265 of the Christian calendar. It was the beginning of the reign of Sultan Ghiasuddin Balban. My ancestors had been scribes in the service of the rulers of Delhi. They had served Raja Anangpal, the Tomara Rajput, who built Lal Kot and planted the sacred iron pillar of Vishnu Bhagwan in the middle of the city. They had also served Raja Prithvi Raj Chauhan who renamed the city Qila Rai Pithoras. When Mohammed Ghori defeated and slew Raja Prithvi Raj and became ruler of Delhi my ancestors acquired knowledge of Turki, Arabic and Persian and continued in the service of the new ruler. My great-grandfather served under Sultan Qutubuddin Aibak and with his own eyes saw the destruction of Hindu and Jain temples, the building of the Jamia Masjid later called Quwwat-ul-Islam on their ruins and the beginnings of the tower of victory, the Qutab Minar. My grandfather served under Qutubuddin's son-in-law and successor Sultan Altamash. Like a common labourer he dug the earth for the Shamsi Talab at the site where the Sultan had seen footprints of the Holy Prophet's horse, Buraq, and carried stones on his head to build the mausoleum of the Saint Qutubuddin Bakhtiyar Kaki. He saw the Qutub Minar completed in AD 1220.

It was my grandfather who built the stone house along the Shamsi Talab where I was born and spent most of my life. He also served under Sultan Altamash's daughter Razia Sultana who ruled over Hindustan for three-and-a-half years. My father, Lala Chagan Lal, was a clerk in the Kotwali (police station) of Mehrauli under the mighty Sultan Ghiasuddin Balban and served him for fifteen of the twenty years of his reign which lasted from AD 1265 to AD 1287. (My father died in the year AD 1280.)

Like my Kayastha forefathers, I was trained to be a scribe. A pandit taught me Sanskrit and Hindi. Through my father's influence I was admitted to a madrasa to learn Arabic, Turki and Persian. At first I was treated roughly by the Turkish boys and sons of Hindu converts to Islam. But when I learnt to speak Turki and dress like a Turk, they stopped bullying me. To save me being harassed, the Maulvi Sahib gave me a Muslim name, Abdul. The boys called me Abdullah.

I was the only child of my parents. I had been betrothed to a girl, one of a family of seven who lived in Mathura. We were married when I was nine and my wife, Ram Dulari, only seven. Four years later, when I was old enough to cohabit, my parents sent the barber who had arranged my marriage to fetch my wife from Mathura. For reasons I will explain later, her parents refused to comply with our wishes. Then tragedy struck our home. My father died and a few days later my mother joined him. At thirteen I was left alone in the world.

The Kotwal Sahib was very kind to me. When he came to offer his condolence, he also offered my father's post to me.

It was at that time my Muslim friends suggested that if I accepted conversion to Islam my prospects would be brighter; I could even aspire to become Kotwal of Mehrauli. And I would have no trouble in finding a wife from amongst the new converts. If I was lucky I might even get a widow or a divorcee of pure Turkish, Persian or Afghan stock. 'If you are Muslim,' said one fellow who was full of witticisms, 'you can have any woman you like. If you are up to it, you can have four at a time.'

A Turk for toughness, for hands that never tire;
An Indian for her rounded bosom bursting with milk;
A Persian for her tight crotch and her coquetry;
An Uzbeg to thrash as a lesson for the three.

There was something, I do not know what, which held me back from being converted to Islam. I suspected that the reason why my wife's parents had refused to send her to me was the rumour that my parents had adopted the ways of the Mussalmans. If I became a Muslim, they would say, 'Didn't we tell you? How could we give our daughter to an unclean *maleecha?*'

On the last day of the obsequial ceremony for my mother, my wife's uncle came from Mathura to condole with me. His real object was to find out what I was like and whether I observed Hindu customs. With his own eyes he saw that I had my head shaved, wore the sacred thread and fed Brahmins. I asked the barber to speak to him about sending my wife to me. The uncle did not say anything and returned to Mathura.

After waiting for some days I approached the Kotwal Sahib. At that time people felt that fate had dealt harshly with me and were inclined to be sympathetic. The Kotwal Sahib made me write out a complaint against my wife's parents for interfering with my conjugal rights. He forwarded it to the Kotwal of Mathura with a recommendation for immediate execution. If the family raised any objection, they were to be arrested and sent to Mehrauli.

A week later my wife escorted by her younger sister and uncle arrived at my doorstep. After a few days her uncle and sister returned to Mathura.

Ram Dulari behaved in a manner becoming a Hindu wife. She touched my feet every morning and wore vermilion powder in the parting of her hair. But she cried all the time and if I as much as put my arm on her shoulder to comfort her she shrank away from me. One night when I went to her bed she started to scream. Our neighbour woke up and shouted across the roof to ask if all was well. I felt very foolish.

Even after one month I did not know what she looked like because she kept her face veiled with the end of her dupatta. It was only from her neck and hands that I made out that she was fair. I also noticed that her bosom was full and her buttocks nicely rounded.

It took me several weeks to realize that my wife did not intend to cohabit with me. She cooked her food on a separate hearth and ate out of utensils she had brought with her. For her I was an unclean, Muslim maleecha. I tried to take her by force. I beat her. It was no use. I asked her whether she would like to return to her parents. She said that she would only go if I threw her out or when she was taken away on her bier. What was I to do? Could I go to the Kotwal Sahib and ask him to order my wife to spread her legs for me! Gradually, I reconciled myself to my fate. We slept under the same roof but never on the same charpoy.

One morning I took Ram Dulari to see the Qutub Minar. We climbed up to the first storey and I pointed out the mausoleum of the Saint Qutubuddin Bakhtiyar Kaki, the Auliya Masjid alongside the Shamsi Talab, our own little home on the other side. And right below us the tomb of Sultan Altamash. I showed her the slab on which a Hindu stonemason had inscribed *Sri Visvakarme Prasade Rachita* and stuck it into this Muslim tower of victory. We came down and I took her towards the Quwwat-ul-Islam mosque. I explained to her how the Turks had demolished twenty-seven Hindu and Jain temples and buried the idols of Vishnu and Lakshmi beneath the entrance gate so that Muslims going in to pray could trample on them. She refused to enter the mosque. As we were retracing our steps, she noticed that the figures of Hindu gods and goddesses on the pillars of what had once been a Hindu temple had been mutilated: noses sliced off, arms broken, breasts chopped off. She put her head against a pillar and began to cry. A small crowd collected. I pretended she was not feeling well and pushed her along. If it hadn't been for the fact that I was dressed like a Mussalman and my wife wore a burqa (all Hindu women of rank wore burqas) it could have been very awkward. When we got home I reprimanded her very severely.

The Hindus hatred of the Mussalmans did not make sense to me. The Muslims had conquered Hindustan. Why hadn't our gods saved us from them? There was that Sultan Mahmud of Ghazni who had invaded Hindustan seventeen times—not once or twice but seventeen times. He had destroyed the temple of Chakraswamy at Thanesar and nothing happened to him. Then Somnath. They said that even the sea prostrated itself twice every twenty-four hours to touch the feet of Somnath. But even the sea did not rise to save Somnathji from Mahmud. They said that Mahmud used to chop off the fingers of the Hindu rajas he defeated in battle; his treasury was full of Hindu fingers. He styled himself as Yaminuddaulah—the right hand of god and Zili-e-Illahi—the Shadow of God on earth.

The Muslims had become masters of Hindustan. They were quite willing to let us Hindus live our lives as we wanted to, provided we recognized them as our rulers. But the Hindus were full of foolish pride. 'This is our country!' they said. 'We will drive out these cow-killers and destroyers of our temples.' They were especially contemptuous towards Hindus who had embraced Islam and treated them worse than untouchables.

The Hindus lived on the stale diet of past glory. At every gathering they talked of the great days of the Tomaras and the Chauhans.

'*Arrey bhai!* Who can deny our ancients were great!' I told my Hindu friends a hundred times. 'But let us think of today. We cannot fight the Mussalmans; they are too big, too strong and too warlike for us. Let us be sensible and learn to live in peace with them.' But reason never entered the skull of the Hindu. Everyone in the world knows that if you put the four Vedas on one side of the scale and commonsense on the other, commonsense will be heavier. But not so with the Hindus. They would look contemptuously at me and call me a pimp of the Mussalmans. Their great hero was Prithivi Raj Chauhan who had defeated Ghori once at Tarain in AD 1191. But the very next year, on the same battlefield, he had been defeated and slain by the same Ghori. They had an answer to that too. 'Prithvi Raj's only mistake was to spare the life of the maleecha when he had first defeated him,' they would reply. Nobody really knows the truth about this Prithvi Raj. A poet fellow named Chand Bardai had made a big song-and-dance about him. This great hero Prithvi Raj married lots of women and even abducted the daughter of a neighbouring raja. But you could not say a word against him to the Hindus. Next to Sri Ramchandraji, it was Samrat Prithvi Raj Chauhan who they worshipped.

I realized that I belonged neither to the Hindus nor to the Mussalmans. How could I explain to my wife that while the Brahmins lived on offerings made to their gods, the Rajputs and the Jats had their lands, Aheers and the Gujars their cattle, the Banias their shops, all that the poor Kayasthas had were their brains and their reed pens! And the only people who could pay for their brains and their pens were the rulers who were Muslims!

I was disowned by the Hindus and shunned by my own wife. I was exploited by the Muslims who disdained my company. Indeed I was like a hijda who was neither one thing nor another but could be misused by everyone.

Then I heard of Nizamuddin. 'Go to the dervish of Ghiaspur on the bank of the river Jamuna and all your troubles will be over,' people said. They called him auliya (prophet) and also Khwaja Sahib. But there were many learned Mussalmans who called him an imposter who would soon meet the fate he deserved. As becomes a good Kayastha I did not express any opinion and waited to see which way the wind was blowing.

In due course this Nizamuddin was summoned by the Sultan to answer charges of heresy levelled against him. On the day of the trial I took leave from my job and went to the palace.

The very name of Ghiasuddin Balban made people urinate with fear. He had a terrible temper and was known to execute anyone who as much as raised his eyes to look at him. He kept two huge Negroes beside him to hack off the heads of people he sentenced to death.

What a sight it was! The great Sultan on his couch flanked by his Abyssinian bodyguards; black djinns with drawn swords! Hundreds of bearded Turkish generals! On one side of the throne-couch stood five ulema dressed in fine silks. Facing them on the other side was a young man not much older than I. He wore a long shirt of coarse black wool and had a green scarf tied round his head. With him were three of his followers dressed as poorly as he. This was Nizamuddin, the Sufi dervish of Ghiaspur.

The Sultan first addressed Nizamuddin. 'Dervish, the ulema have complained that you make no distinction between Mussalmans and infidels; that you pose as an intermediary between god and man; that you use words which obliterate the difference between man and his Maker; that your followers indulge in music and dancing in the precincts of the mosque and thus contravene the holy law of the *shariat*. What do you have to say in your defence?'

Nizamuddin smiled and replied: 'O mighty Sultan, it is true that I do not make any distinction between Mussalmans and Hindus as I consider both to be the children of god. The ulema exhort Your Majesty in the name of the Holy Messenger (upon Whom be peace) to destroy temples and slay infidels to gain merit in the eyes of Allah. I interpret the sacred law differently. I believe that the best way to serve god is through love of his creatures. As for the charge of posing as an intermediary between man and his Maker, I plead guilty. God's Messenger (on Whom be peace) said: "Whoever dies without an Imam dies the death of a pagan." We Sufis follow this precept and believe that he who has no Shaikh is without religion. The ulema know not that god often manifests himself in His creatures. They also do not know that Allah cannot be understood through knowledge of books or through logic. His Messenger (peace upon Him) when asked whether even he did not know god replied, "No, not even I. God is an experience."'

The Sultan nodded towards the ulema. Their leader went down on his knees and kissed the ground in front of the throne. *'Jahan Panah* (Refuge of the World),' he addressed the Sultan, 'you who are the wisest and the most just of all monarchs do not need such insects as we are to expound the holy law. Your Majesty must know that this man, Nizamuddin, talks of love only to throw dust in the eyes of innocent people.' He unwrapped a copy of the Quran, touched it to his forehead and read out a passage. The crowd broke into a chorus of applause *'Wah! Wah! Subhan Allah!'* Few of them understood Arabic. Even fewer understood what the words meant when translated into Turki.

The Sultan turned to the dervish and asked him about his claiming unity with god. Nizamuddin replied in very poetic language, 'O Sultan! And O you ulema learned of the law! And all of you people assembled here! Do you know what it is to love and be loved? Perhaps all you have known and enjoyed is the love of women. We Sufis love god and noone else. When we are possessed by the divine spirit we utter words which to the common man may sound like the assumption of godhood. But these should not be taken seriously. You may have heard of the story of the dove that would not submit to her mate. In his passion the male bird said, "If you do not give in to me, I shall turn the throne of Solomon upside down." The breeze carried his words to Solomon. He summoned the dove and asked it to explain itself. The dove replied, "O Prophet of Allah! The words of lovers should not be bandied about." The answer pleased Solomon. We hope our answer will please the Sultan Balban.'

A murmur of Wah! Wah! went round.

The Sultan asked the ulema for authority on the subject of music. The ulema opened another book (they had brought many bundles of books with them). Their leader again read of something in Arabic and then translated it into Turki. He looked back at the crowd and a section applauded Wah! Wah!

The Sultan again turned to Nizamuddin. The dervish had not brought any books. From memory he quoted a tradition of the

Prophet about music and dancing. 'When Allah's grace enters one's person it manifests itself by making that person sing and dance with joy. If this be a manifestation of being possessed by Allah, I say Amen.'

The Sultan pondered over the matter for a while. He brushed his beard and examined the hair that came off in his hand. The silence was terrible. At last he cleared his throat and spoke in a clear, loud voice, 'We dismiss the ulema's charges against Nizamuddin, dervish of Ghiaspur.'

The crowd broke into loud applause praising the Sultan's sense of justice. Many rushed to the dervish and kissed the hem of his coarse, woollen shirt.

The next morning I asked the Kotwal Sahib about Nizamuddin. 'He's gone up there,' he replied pointing up to the sky. 'He has shown many infidels the true path. Go to him any Thursday or on the eve of the new moon and you'll see what miracles he can perform!'

The following Thursday I hired an ekka to go to Ghiaspur which was more than a kos from Mehrauli. When I got to the hospice and asked an attendant whether I could see the man who was at the palace some days earlier, he replied, 'Khwaja Sahib is meditating in his cell. He only recives visitors in the evening. You can go and eat the langar (free kitchen).

I went to the langar. It was crowded with Muslims and Hindus, rich and poor, clamouring for a leaf-cup of lentils and a morsel of coarse bread. I had to fight my way through the crowd to grab a chappati. I came out and sat in the courtyard where a party of qawwals were singing in Hindi. I was told that the song had been written and composed by one Abdul Hassan, who was very close to the holy man.

Late in the afternoon word went round that the dervish had emerged from his cell. People buzzed round him like bees round a crystal of sugar. I pushed my way through the throng and when I got to him I kissed the hem of his shirt. Suddenly tears came gushing into my eyes. The dervish put his hand on my head. I felt a tingling sensation run down my spine and the fragrance of musk enveloping my frame. He tilted my tear-stained face upwards and said, 'Just as Allah has let my tunic drink your tears, so may he make your sorrows mine!' As he spoke those words I felt as light as a piece of thistledown floating in the air.

'Abdullah, my son,' he continued, 'you live near the mausoleum of Hazrat Qutubuddin Bakhtiyar Kaki. Go there every morning and recite the ninety-nine names of Allah. Your wishes will be granted. Come whenever your heart is heavy. The doors of our hut of poverty are never bolted against anyone.'

It was on my way back to Mehrauli that I asked myself, 'How does he know that I live near the mausoleum of Bakhtiyar Kaki? How does he know that my Muslim friends call me Abdullah? And if somebody has told him who I am and where I live, is it that he does not know that I am a Hindu and may not know the ninety-nine names of Allah?'

I could not contain myself. Since there was no one else I could unburden myself to I told my wife all that had passed. For the first time since we had been married, Ram Dulari showed some interest in me. When I ran out of words she asked very timidly, 'Why don't you take me along one day?' In my enthusiasm I took her hand. It went limp in my grasp.

On the first day of the new month of the Muslim lunar calendar I took Ram Dulari to Ghiaspur. Our ekka was one in a long line on the dusty road. We passed bullock carts loaded with women and children, the men striding along barefoot with their shoes hung on their staves.

There was an immense crowd. A whole bazaar of bangle-sellers, sweet-meat vendors, cloth-dealers and medicine-sellers had gone up. I feared Ram Dulari would not get a chance to have darshan of the holy man. I did not take her to the langar as she would not touch anything cooked by Muslims. We wandered round the stalls, watched jugglers and acrobats, dancing bears and monkeys. We sat down under a tree. I began to despair. In an hour the sun would set and the ekka-driver would insist that we return to

Mehrauli before it became dark. I was lost in my thoughts when a dervish came to me and said: 'Abdul! Isn't your name Abdul or Abdullah? The Khwaja Sahib has been enquiring after you.' He led us through a door at the back of the mosque into a courtyard where the holy man was receiving visitors. The dervish forced his way through the crowd with us following close on his heels.

I kissed the hem of the holy man's shirt. Ram Dulari prostrated herself on the ground before him. Khwaja Sahib stretched his hand and blessed her. 'Child, Allah will fulfil your heart's desire. If He wills your womb will bear fruit. Go in peace.' That was all. The crowd pushed us away.

Her womb bear fruit? This man of god who was said to read people's minds like a book had not read Ram Dulari's. From the way she turned away her face I could tell she was embarrassed. On the way back to Mehrauli she avoided touching me. We got off opposite the Auliya Masjid. We walked home as if we had nothing to do with each other. I in front looking at the shuttered doors of shops as if I had never seen them before; she behind me enveloped in her burqa.

As soon as we stepped into our courtyard she lit the hearth to warm up food she had cooked in the morning. I lit an oil lamp in the niche and wrote down the events of the day. She gave me my meal and went back to the kitchen to eat hers. After I had finished I gave her my empty brass plate and went to the bazaar to get a paan-leaf.

By the time I came back Ram Dulari had rinsed the utensils and was lying on her charpoy with her face towards the wall. I blew out the oil-lamp and stretched myself on my charpoy. I could not sleep. I kept thinking about the holy man's promise that we would have children. How could Ram Dulari have them unless I gave them to her? I wondered if she was thinking the same thing. After an hour of turning from side to side I called softly to her, 'Ram Dulari!'

'*Hun!*'

'Are you asleep?'

'No.'

The gong of the kotwali struck the hour of midnight. Once again I asked Ram Dulari if she was asleep; she said 'No'.

Something said she might not be averse to my touching her. I got up and went over to her charpoy. 'Can I lie with you?' I asked, 'I feel cold.' She made room for me and replied, 'If you wish.'

I lay beside her. The passion that I had stored up over the months welled in my body. Just as a torrent carries away everything that comes in its way my lust swept aside my fears. I fell on her like a hungry lion. I tore away her sari and tried to enter her. She spread out her thighs to receive me. But no sooner did I reach between them than my seed was spent. I felt ashamed of myself.

Ram Dulari got up to clean herself. She poured water from the pitcher into her brass lota. She put aside her sari and began to splash water between her thighs. Under the light of the stars I saw her pale body, the outlines of her rounded breasts and her broad hips. She dried herself with the same sari and wrapped it around her body. She hesitated, not sure which charpoy to go to. I stretched out my hand to her. She took it and let me pull her beside me. My passion was roused again. She let me remove her damp sari and warm her naked flesh in my embrace. This time I was able to hold myself longer. And she more eager to receive me. A cry of pain escaped her lips. I knew that I had at long last made Ram Dulari mine.

I re-lit the oil-lamp and helped her wash the stains of blood on the bedsheet. By the time we had finished our bodies were again hungry for each other. So passed the whole night.

I was woken by the sun on my face and flies buzzing in my ears.

Ram Dulari had bathed and cooked the morning meal. She was wearing the red sari she had worn when she had come to Mehrauli as a bride. She did not cover her face against me and blushed as she saw me get up from her bed. She ran indoors. I followed her and bolted the door from the inside.

Thereafter I could not have enough of Ram Dulari. I could not take my eyes off her. Every movement she made fired me with desire to take her. Every moment I was away from her was a torment and I hurried back home to be in her embrace. And she became coquetish, *'Ajee,* I am not a whore you can have anytime you like—not unless you pay me for it.' I bought her a nose-pin with a red ruby; I bought her glass bangles of all the colours I could find in the bazaar. For some months our world was narrowed to a small charpoy on which we sported night and day.

Ram Dulari and I became members of a community which worshipped both in Hindu temples and in Sufi hospices. We celebrated Hindu festivals as well as the Muslim. At Dassehra we went to see Ram Lila, on Diwali we lit oil-lamps on the parapet of our house, at Holi we squirted coloured water on our Hindu friends. On Id we exchanged gifts with Muslims we knew; on the death anniversaries of Muslim saints we went to the mausoleum of Qutubuddin Bakhtiyar Kaki. And at least once a month we went to Ghiaspur and watched the sky at dusk to see if the new moon had risen.

Ram Dulari continued to dress as other Hindu women did. She wore crimson in the parting of her hair, a red dot on her forehead, and a mangalsutra (a necklace of black and gold beads). I continued to dress like a Turk with a skull cap and turban. Like the Turks I sported a neatly trimmed beard and moustache. And I spoke the way they did. If they said, *'As Salaam-Valai-kum'* (peace be with you) I replied, *'valai-kum-As-Salaam'* (and with you too be peace). If they asked me how I was, I replied *'Al-hamdu-illah'* (well, by the grace of god). But if they asked me 'Abdullah when will you become a true Muslim?' I would reply, 'Soon, if that be the will of god—Inshallah.' If anyone asked me whether we were Hindus or Mussalmans, we would reply we were both. Nizamuddin was our umbrella against the burning sun of Muslim bigotry and the downpour of Hindu contempt.

So passed the days, weeks and months. By the end of the year Ram Dulari was pregnant and had to go to her parents in Mathura for her confinement. When news of the birth of a son was brought to me I sent plates full of sweets to the Kotwal Sahib and to all our Muslim and Hindu friends. After a few weeks I went to Mathura to bring back my wife and son. Ram Dulari's sisters made a lot of fuss over me. They teased me, 'Are you going to have the boy circumcized? Are you going to name him Mohammed or Ali or something like that?' I let them say what they liked. I had great fun with them.

I did not have my son circumcized. I had his head shaved and got a Brahmin to recite mantras. I chose the name Kamal for him—it could be either Hindu or Muslim. In Hindi it meant the lotus flower. In Arabic, pronounced with a longer accent on the second 'a', it meant excellence. We took the child to Jogmaya temple and had the priest daub sandalpaste on his forehead. Then we took him to Ghiaspur and had the Khwaja Sahib bless him. I recorded my gratitude to my *peer* by having his name inscribed on stone as my benefactor and embedding the stone in the outer wall of our home.

Lodhi Gardens (from *The Sunset Club*)

My story begins on the afternoon of Monday, the 26th of January 2009, the 59th anniversary of the founding of the independent Indian Republic. Although India gained independence from the British on the 15th of August 1947, its leaders wisely decided that mid-August was too hot and humid for outdoor celebrations and late January was a better time of the year to do so. So they picked the 26th of January, the day they gave the country its new Constitution. They declared it a national holiday and named it Republic Day—Ganatantra Divas.

By the end of January, winter loosens its grip; by sunrise, foggy dawns turn into sunny mornings; the time for flowers and the calling of barbets is round the corner.

Republic Day is the biggest event in India's calendar. It is the only one celebrated throughout the country by all of India's communities—Hindus, Muslims, Christians, Buddhists, Sikhs, Jains and Parsis. In every state capital they have flag hoistings, and parades of troops, police and schoolchildren.

However, there is nothing to match the grand spectacle in the capital city, with its display of India's military might and cultural diversity. Tanks, armoured cars, rocket launchers roll by; cannons boom; massed squads of soldiers, sailors, airmen march past, dipping their swords in salute; cavalrymen mounted on camels and horses are followed by floats of different states highlighting their achievements, with folk dancers dancing round them. People start assembling from the early hours of dawn, to line up along both sides of Rajpath. This broad avenue runs from Rashtrapati Bhavan—the President's Palace—atop Raisina Hill, down the slope between the two huge Secretariat buildings, North and South Blocks, to the massive War Memorial Arch known as India Gate, which bears the names of Indian soldiers who fell in the First World War, the Third Afghan War in 1919, and the 1971 confrontation with neighbouring Pakistan. In the centre of India Gate burns a celestial flame all day and night, in honour of men who laid down their lives for their Motherland.

You may well ask why India, which prides itself as the land of Gandhi, the apostle of peace and non-violence, celebrates the national day with such a display of lethal arms and fighting prowess. The truth is, we Indians are full of contradictions: we preach peace to the world and prepare for war. We preach purity of mind, chastity and the virtues of celibacy; we are also obsessed with sex. That makes us interesting. However, we do make up for the vulgar display of arms by having a Beating Retreat ceremony on Vijay Chowk (Victory Square) facing the Secretariat buildings. Here massed bands of the army, navy and air force bear no arms but trumpets, flutes, clarinets, drums and bagpipes, and march up and down the Square. The function ends with bells ringing out Gandhi's favourite hymn, 'Abide with Me'. A day later, on the 30th of January, the day we murdered Gandhi, our leaders assemble at Rajghat where we cremated him, and strew flowers on a slab of black marble where we reduced him to ashes. That's the kind of people we are. And that is why we are interesting.

Let me get back to my story. Around noon, the parade on Rajpath is over and crowds begin to disperse. Some go to the nearby Purana Qila, the Old Fort, to picnic on the lawns and doze in the sun. There are other ancient monuments which provide similar space and quiet. The most popular of them is Lodhi Gardens. It is within easy walking distance from Rajpath, and has a vast variety of trees, birds and medieval monuments. It is perhaps the most scenic historic park in India. At one time it was a scatter of tombs and mosques in a village called Khairpur.

In the 1930s the villagers were moved out and the monuments taken under government protection.

Then the Vicereine, Lady Willingdon, who was somewhat batty and wanted her name to go down in posterity, had the scattered monuments enclosed within walls and an entrance gate erected on the north side, bearing the inscription 'Lady Willingdon Park'. She also had a cinder track laid out for the Sahibs and their Mems to ride on. All that is history. No one now calls it Lady Willingdon Park, the cinder track has become a cobbled stone footpath, and the park is known as Lodhi Gardens because most of its monuments were built during the rule of the Lodhi dynasty. Today it has three more entrances. A second one is also in the north, with a small car park. People have to walk across an old stone bridge called *aathpula* (eight-spanned), over a moat which once guarded the walled enclosure of the tomb of Sikandar Lodhi, built in 1518, through an avenue of maulsari trees to the centre of the park. There is another entrance on the eastern side, along the India International Centre, and one more in the south, close to a palm-lined avenue leading to the oldest tomb in the complex, that of Muhammad Shah Sayyid, built in 1450.

For good reason, the most popular place in the park is the extensive lawn on the southern side of what must have been the main mosque, the Jami Masjid, built in 1494. The reason for its popularity is its dome, which is an exact replica of a young woman's bosom including the areola and the nipple. Most mosques and mausolea have domes but they have metal spires put on top of them which rob them of their feminine charm. Not the Bara Gumbad, the Big Dome. You can gape at it for hours on end and marvel at its likeness to a virgin's breast. You will notice that men sprawled on the lawns have their face towards it; their womenfolk sit facing the other way. It also has a bench facing it. Regular visitors to the park call it Boorha Binch, old men's bench, because for years, three old men have been sitting on it after they have hobbled round the park. While they talk, their gaze is fixed on Bara Gumbad. English-speaking Indians call them the 'Sunset Club' because the three men who occupy the bench are seen on it every day at sunset. All three are in their late eighties, the sunset years of their lives.

Let me introduce you to the members of the Sunset Club. First Pandit Preetam Sharma, because he is the eldest of the three. He is a Punjabi Brahmin, an Oxford graduate who served as cultural counsellor in London and Paris and rose to the highest position in the ministry of education before he retired. He is well preserved, bald in front but with white locks flowing down his skull and curling up around his shoulders. They give him a scholarly look. He is in good health but needs glasses to read, hearing aids to hear and dentures to eat. He believes in Ayurveda and homeopathy. Although there were a succession of women, foreign and Indian, in his life, he narrowly escaped marrying one. He lives with his spinster sister, Sunita, who is almost twenty years younger than him and works with an NGO. They live in a ground-floor flat close to Khan Market. It has two bedrooms and two bathrooms, a large drawing–dining room, a study and two verandas.

One wall of the drawing room has a bookshelf packed with books which he has not read, nor intends to read. They create the impression that he is a man of learning. Other walls have paintings he made after he retired from service. No one except he understands what they are about but they do create the impression that he is a man of culture. He writes long poems in blank verse. He has them printed in Khan Market and gives copies freely to his visitors. Having risen to the top in the ministry of education, he is chairman of many cultural and social organizations and school boards. He makes a very good chairman as he makes profound statements like 'Culture knows no frontiers; all religions teach truth and love', etc., etc. He has no enemies. All the men and women who know him love him. For company he has had a succession of Apsos named Dabboo One, Two and Three. He has a car and a chauffeur provided by a school whose chairman he is. It takes him, his servant Pavan and Dabboo Three to the northern entrance of Lodhi Gardens. He does a round of the park followed by Pavan and the dog before he takes his seat on the Boorha Binch. His servant and dog sit behind him on the lawn.

Second is Nawab Barkatullah Baig Dehlavi. He is a Sunni Mussalman whose Pathan ancestors settled in Delhi before the British took over the country. They combined soldiering with the practice of Yunani (Greek) medicine. They were granted land close to what is today Nizamuddin. Barkatullah's father set up a chain of Yunani *dawakhanas* (pharmacies) in the old city but preferred living in his large house in Nizamuddin. It is a spacious mansion named Baig Manzil. It has many rooms, verandas, a large garden in front and staff quarters at the back. Baig does not believe in amassing books; he finished with them after school and college. He has a few *diwans* of Urdu poets and an impressive collection of artefacts from Mughal times which are on display in his sitting room. He is a powerfully built six-footer with grey-white hair, a handlebar moustache and a short clipped beard.

Like all good Muslims from well-to-do families, Baig went to Aligarh Muslim University before he took over his father's business and, on his demise, his mansion. He is married to his cousin Sakina. They have a brood of children. But for occasional visits to Chawri Bazaar, the courtesans' street, and bedding his wife's maidservants in his younger days, he has been a faithful husband. After the partition of the country in 1947, he stayed on in India, joined the Congress Party and is a supporter of the Nehru–Gandhi dynasty. For over forty years he has been a regular stroller in Lodhi Gardens. The chauffeur of his Mercedes-Benz drops him at the southern entrance of the park. He does his rounds of the monuments followed by a servant pushing a wheelchair, before he takes his seat on the bench facing Bara Gumbad. Even in his eighties, Baig is in good shape: no glasses, no hearing aids, no false teeth, though he is occasionally short of breath.

Third is Sardar Boota Singh. He is a stocky Sikh with a paunch. The unshorn hair on his head is snow-white. Instead of tying a six-yard-long turban he has taken to wearing a cotton or woollen cap. He dyes his beard and looks younger than his eighty-six years. He suffers from many ailments: chronic constipation, incipient diabetes, fluctuating blood pressure, enlarged prostate and periodic bouts of gout. He has been wearing glasses since his schooldays, half a denture as all his lower teeth are gone, and for some years, hearing aids as well. He professes to be an agnostic sybarite, but every morning when he gets up around 4 a.m. he prays for his health and repeats *Aum Arogyam* many times, followed by the Gayatri Mantra and a Sikh hymn designed to keep sorrows at a distance:

> *May ill-winds not touch me, the Lord is my Protector.*
> *Around me Rama has drawn a wall to protect me;*
> *No harm will come to me, brother.*
> *The True Guru, who put the Universe together*
> *Gave me Rama's name as panacea against all ills;*
> *Meditate on Him and Him alone.*
> *He saves those who deserve saving; He removes all doubts*
> *Says Nanak, the Lord is merciful. He is my helper.*

He explains the contradictions in his agnosticism and hedonism by saying: 'Who knows! They say prayers can work miracles. No harm in trying them out.'

Prayers seldom help him, so he supplements them with a variety of pills from dawn to after dinner.

Boota had his higher education in England and served with Indian missions in London and Paris before he returned to Delhi and took to writing for newspapers. He lives in a flat close to Sharma's. The walls of his sitting room are lined with books: works of fiction, anthologies of poetry, biographies and books banned as pornographic. His favourites are books of quotations and anthologies of poetry, both Urdu and English. He has memorized quite a few and comes out with them at every opportunity. People think he is a man of learning but he knows he is a bit of a fraud.

Boota is a widower with two children. His son has migrated

to Canada. His daughter, who is widowed, lives close by with her daughter. Though he lives alone, he is never lonely; he has a constant stream of ladies visiting him in the evening when he opens his bar. He is a great talker and a windbag. He makes up salacious stories of his conquests, which keep his audience spellbound. He uses bad language as if it was his birthright. When he is tired of company, he simply says, 'Now bugger off.' If he disapproves of a person, he calls him '*phuddoo*', which is Punjabi for fucker. And every other person including himself is a '*chootia*'—cunt-born. Every evening he drives down to the India International Centre. He spends an hour there sipping coffee, then enters Lodhi Gardens through its eastern entrance past the Kos Minar. He too takes a couple of rounds of the park before he joins the other two on the bench facing Bara Gumbad.

How the three men got to form the Sunset Club is a long story. Sharma and Boota knew each other since their days in Lahore; by coincidence, both happened to be posted in London and then Paris at the same time. Back in Delhi both met in Lodhi Gardens every evening. Sharma was interested in meeting important people, Boota in trees and birds. Baig did not know either of them. For years he passed them as he did others. After some time they began to raise their hands in recognition. And still later, when they found themselves sitting on the same bench, introductions were made. They became friends and the Sunset Club came into being.

On the afternoon of the 26th of January 2009, Lodhi Gardens is more crowded than on other days. On its many lawns men and women lie sprawled on the grass. Around each group is a debris of paper plates and cups, with stray dogs wagging their tails, begging for leftovers.

One after another the three members of the Sunset Club arrive and take their seats on the Boorha Binch. Each one in turn puts out both hands with palms open as if pushing something—an all-India gesture asking if all is hunky-dory. After they have greeted each other with *aji aao* (come, come), *sab theek thaak* (is all okay?), Sharma replies: *'Bhagwan ki daya hai*—God is merciful.' Baig says: *'Alhamdulillah*—Allah be praised.' Boota says: *'Chalta hai*—life goes on.' Baig opens the dialogue: *'Ganatantra Divas mubarak ho*—congratulations for Republic Day.' Sharma returns the greetings in the same words: *'Aap ko bhi mubarak ho.'* Boota strikes a sour note: 'What is there to be congratulated about? We have made a bloody mess of our country. Murders, massacres, rapes, corruption, robberies like nothing we have ever seen before. Shame on us.'

Baig changes the subject. 'Did you watch the parade on TV? I never miss it.'

'Nor do I,' says Sharma. 'Grand display. Makes you feel proud of being Indian.'

'It is the same thing year after year, crores of rupees down the Yamuna,' snarls Boota.

'It is not the same year after year,' protests Baig. 'This is the first time our Prime Minister was unable to attend as he was in hospital after heart surgery. It is the first time we have had the President of Kazakhstan as our honoured guest.'

'Did you notice how bored he looked?' asks Boota. 'Most of the time he had his eyes shut as if falling off to sleep.'

'Arrey bhai,' protests Baig, 'he did not have his eyes shut. He is Mongoloid; they have narrow eyes like the Chinese.'

'Boota, does it never occur to you that this is one event in the year that everyone across the country watches every year? It generates a feeling of oneness in people of diverse religions, languages and races,' says Sharma raising his voice.

'Okay, okay bhai, you win. Two against one. Happy Ganatantra Divas to both of you,' responds Boota in a voice loaded with sarcasm.

'So what's new?' asks Baig.

'What's new is that last night I had a wet dream. You are a *hakeem*. I wanted to ask you if it is okay for a man of my age to have wet dreams.'

Before Baig can reply Sharma breaks in: 'That's because you

have dirty thoughts. What you can't do, you imagine you are doing. I bet you can't even get an erection any more. Anyhow, who was it who wet your pajamas?'

'I won't tell you. You know her very well. And I sought Hakeem Sahib's opinion, not yours,' Boota snaps back.

Baig ponders over the matter before he replies, 'You must be constipated. Constipation often induces night discharge of semen.'

Boota is taken aback. 'I've always had problems with my stomach. I have been taking laxatives since I left college.'

'You have a problem of gas in the stomach?' asks Baig.

'Yes, lots. I can't do anything about it.'

Boota tells Baig only half the truth. The truth is that Boota does not want to do anything about it because he enjoys farting. His wife's death relieved him from the bondage of good manners. When alone, he lets himself go—bhoom, phatas, phuss. And he revels in inhaling the stink he produces. 'My stomach is full of gas till the evening. When I take Scotch it seems to subside,' he adds.

'I don't like telling you this, but you could not have been a great performer. People who have gas problems don't make great lovers. They rarely succeed in bringing a woman to her climax. Am I right?'

Boota winces. He recalls that in his earlier years in college in England, he often came in his trousers while kissing girls passionately. Even later it was only when he was a little drunk that he lasted fifteen to twenty minutes, and once in a while brought a woman to a climax.

'Talk about something else,' says Sharma. 'Don't always have sex on your mind. It's bad for your health, particularly when you are old and can't do anything.'

'Okay bhai, we will postpone it till tomorrow evening. Let's talk about god and life hereafter of which we know nothing,' replies Boota.

By that time the sun has gone down behind Bara Gumbad. It has begun to turn chilly. Lights on footpaths have been switched on, Bara Gumbad lit up. Baig's servant puts a shawl on his master's lap. 'Sahib, it is getting cold. We better go home,' he says in a tone of authority. 'See, most people have already left.'

All three get up. Sharma says, 'Cheerio,' Boota says, 'Sleep well,' Baig says, '*Allah Hafiz*—God protect you.' They go back the way they came.

Sharma gets back to his ground-floor apartment followed by Dabboo Three and his servant. Dabboo Three announces their return with a couple of barks, Sharma's sister Sunita lets them in with her usual words of welcome: 'You are back.' Sharma makes no response. He puts his walking stick in its usual corner and sits down in his padded armchair. There is a roaring log fire in the grate—he likes to keep warm. His servant takes off his shoes and slips his woollen bedroom slippers on to his feet.

'Who-who was there?' asks Sunita.

Sharma's temper rises. 'How many times have I told you not to say who-who? One who is enough.'

Sunita protests, 'I did not go to Balliol. I was in Hindu College. Who-who for *kaun-kaun*. What is so wrong with it?'

'It is not English and when speaking English, use English; when speaking Hindi, speak Hindi. Don't make a *khichdi* of both.'

'*Achha bhai*, who was there?'

'Boota and Baig.'

'What did you talk about?'

'This and that.'

Sunita senses he is not in a mood to talk to her. 'I hope that Boota does not barge in. He is always one for a free drink. He also uses dirty language. His servant says he doesn't bathe for two-two, three-three days. He must smell.'

'Again two-two, three-three days! You will never learn.'

Sunita decides to end the debate. 'You take it from me, this is the kind of English we Indians will speak—Hinglish.'

Pavan pours out whisky, soda and two cubes of ice in a tumbler and places it on the side table beside his master's chair. A bowl of peanuts is already there. Sunita turns her back and joins the servants, their wives and children to watch a serial on Zee TV.

Sharma takes a couple of sips of whisky–soda, stretches his legs and shuts his eyes. He goes over Baig's analysis of Boota's wet dream. He has never suffered from constipation. As a matter of fact, he often boasted to Boota how his stomach worked like clockwork: two motions every morning, one before and another after breakfast. Every time, he announced it to everyone around in French, using two words he had picked up in his six years spent in Paris: *deuxieme fois*—second time. And yet, his first intimate contact with a female was little short of a disaster. It was monsoon time. He was later than usual working in his office to dispose of some urgent files to be sent to his minister. By the time he finished, it was dark. As he was leaving the Secretariat building he saw one of his lady deputy secretaries in the crowd, waiting for the rain to stop. He had often exchanged flirtatious dialogue with her.

'Lakshmi, can I give you a lift? It's drizzling,' he asked. She beamed a smile and replied, 'Please. I don't want to get drenched.' A chaprasi opened his umbrella and escorted the two to Sharma's office car. Sharma was tired. He sat with his legs stretched and his right arm resting on the back of the seat above Lakshmi's head. By accident his arm fell on her shoulder. She turned her face to him and kissed him on his lips. He was taken aback but responded passionately. They kept their lips glued together for a long time. He got a hard erection. He could not hold back and slipped his hand up to the middle of her thighs. 'Not today,' she whispered, 'I am not well. I have my periods.' He did not know anything about periods and thought she was making excuses. He pushed his hand further, found a padded obstruction, oozing blood. 'I told you so, darling. Be patient. You can have as much of it as you like after we are married.'

That is as close as Sharma ever got to having sex. Later in the evening he went to consult Boota on the subject. 'I thought she was making excuses to keep me off till I marry her. But she was really wounded and bleeding.' The only comment Boota made on his friend's misadventure was, 'Phuddoo! Chootia! How old are you?'

Sharma feels drowsy, his head droops on his chest. Sunita notices it and asks, 'Will you eat here or at the table?'

'Here.'

His servant brings a bowl of boiled rice, dal, a couple of karelas, and puts the food beside the bowl of peanuts. Sharma does not relish the food his sister gives him but has stopped complaining, because she then reminds him of the adage he often uses—'simple living, high thinking'. So she gives him a tasteless but belly-filling *bhojan*. Sharma gulps down the whisky, gobbles up the food, goes to the bathroom to rinse his mouth, urinates and goes to bed. His evenings have become deadly boring.

Boota returns home to a brightly lit fire, his single malt whisky, soda and bucket of ice cubes on a tray. He pours himself a double Patiala in a crystal cut-glass tumbler he uses only for himself, adds ice and soda. He munches some wasabi peas and cashewnuts, then fills his mouth with whisky and rolls it round with his tongue before letting it trickle down his throat. He wants to see if he can feel it go down to his intestines. When his stomach is clean, he can; when it is not, he cannot. He switches on the TV for a few minutes, watches cheetahs chasing deer, and some Australian wrestling with crocodiles and pythons, then switches it off, shuts his eyes and lets his mind drift back to his affairs with women in his younger days. He was never a great performer but the variety he performed with is impressive: whites, browns, blacks, Canadians, Americans, Germans, French, and of course Indians from all communities and parts of the country: Christians, Jews, Hindus, Muslims, Sikhs. Only a few encounters have stayed in his mind, others have faded from his memory.

One, particularly, keeps repeating itself. He was staying with friends in England. They had a young, attractive, English governess for their daughter. It was Christmas time. His hosts and their daughter had gone calling on friends. He was lying on a sofa when the governess brought him a glass of sherry. They exchanged 'Merry Christmas' greetings with light kisses on each other's cheeks. That was the prelude. The hosts returned with a couple of their friends for the Christmas feast—roast turkey, French wine, pudding loaded with rum, followed by cognac and Drambuie. Everyone was a little tipsy by the end of the evening. He bade them goodnight and returned to his bedroom on the top floor, which was next to that of the governess. Some minutes later he heard her footsteps going into her bedroom. Sleep would not come to him. He tiptoed to her bedroom. She made room for him as if expecting him. He laid himself on her and glued his lips to hers. She opened her thighs to let him in. He entered her. They lay in silence for what seemed like divine eternity. At long last he came with violent jerks and pumped half a gallon of his semen into her without bothering about the consequences. Mercifully there were none. He concluded that those who found English women cold had never sampled one. They continued to meet in different places and made love every time.

Boota's wife had kept an excellent table. She consulted a lot of cookery books: French, Italian, Chinese and Indian. She spent a good half-hour instructing the cook how to go about preparing various recipes. He turned out to be a master craftsman in the art of cooking. She had gone eight years ago but the cook was still with him and gave him a gourmet dinner every evening. Boota relishes good food, a glass of French wine, followed by a digestive Underberg. He swallows a dozen pills prescribed for his age for various ailments. Then he switches off for the night. He sleeps fitfully as he has to get up two or three times to empty his bladder. Nevertheless, he is up by 4 a.m. to start the day's work.

By the time Baig's Mercedes-Benz gets to Nizamuddin, street lights have been switched on. Hazrat Nizamuddin's shrine, which allows worshippers of all communities, has in its complex tombs of the poets Amir Khusrau and Mirza Ghalib, as well as bazaars all around, which attract large crowds. Baig's car leaves the main

Delhi–Agra road to enter the elite residential area, Nizamuddin West. The headlights of his car catch the two marble slabs on either side of the gates. One in English reads 'Baig Manzil', the other in Arabic '*Hada bin Fazl-e-Rabbee*—this by the Grace of God'. On top of the house is a circular marble slab with the numerals 786 in Arabic. God has certainly been good to the Baig family. The double-storeyed mansion is brightly lit. People refer to it as Baig's *daulat khana*—abode of wealth; he calls it *ghareeb khana*—house of poverty.

Begum Sakina awaits him in the veranda. He is helped to his armchair in the sitting room. A coal fire is glowing, his armchair has a small pillow to cushion his large frame, a *moorha* (cane stool) in front to rest his feet, a bottle of Black Label Scotch, a tumbler, ice bucket and a plate of shaami kababs on the side table. Sakina Begum sees him settle down comfortably, orders two of her maids to press his legs and retires to the neighbouring room from where she can see him as well as the *saas–bahu* TV serials to which she is addicted. She does not approve of his drinking as the Koran forbids consumption of alcohol to Muslims. But she refrains from reminding her husband about it.

Baig pours himself a generous peg; his servant adds soda and two cubes of ice. He takes a big swig of the whisky–soda, bits of shaami kabab, and stretches his legs out on the moorha. The maids sit on their haunches on either side of the moorha and begin to press his legs. That's all they do during the day for the Begum Sahiba and have become expert masseuses. First his feet. They press the insteps with their thumbs; then by turn every toe with their thumbs and index fingers. Then his legs with their palms. And back to his feet. They do not stop till told to do so. Baig is transported to another world. What more would he get in paradise than good Scotch and houris pressing his limbs: Paradise is a man-made fantasy; this is for real. He recalls Mirza Ghalib's lines: 'We know the truth about Paradise: it is a good idea to beguile the mind.' However, he knows that these pleasures will also not last very long as old age robs life of the fun of living.

Ghalib was a man after Baig's own heart: hard drinker, lover of women, only prayed on Fridays, never fasted during Ramadan. And yet, not only Muslims but all Urdu-knowing people of the world swear by his name as one of the greatest poets of all time. Baig recalls one of his favourite Ghalib couplets:

Where are the frivolities of yesteryear?
Where has your youth fled?

Where indeed had his youth fled? He recalled the early days of his married life. He was eighteen, Sakina sixteen. They had played together as children, teased each other in their early teens. He had noticed her bosom take shape and her buttocks get rounder. They had got down to real business on the first night they were left alone. She had called him Barkoo Bhaiyya and he had called her Sakki. Overnight, he became Janoo—sweetheart—and she became Begum.

What a volcano of passion she had in her little frame! They were at it every time they were on their own—at times, six times in one day. She found him too heavy and suggested she come on top. He found that even pleasanter and lay on his back with his massive circumcised penis up like the Qutub Minar. She mounted him, directed his erect member inside her till it disappeared between her thighs. She did most of the work, kissing his eyes, his lips, heaving up and down. It was her groaning with ecstasy that brought him to a climax. What bliss it was! As expected, she was pregnant by the second month. She had morning sickness and went back to her parents for a week's break.

That was too long for Baig. Sex had become compulsive. So he took her maids to bed in turn: one when she brought his early morning cup of tea, the other when she brought him the glass of hot milk he took before retiring for the night. The girls took it as a part of their duty. He didn't have any qualms of conscience. He repeated the exercise whenever his wife was far gone in her pregnancy and went to her parents for the delivery.

Occasionally he visited courtesans in Chawri Bazaar to watch their *mujra* and dance. The evening ended with his having sex with one of them. He tipped them handsomely. Sakina had a woman's sixth sense about her husband's infidelities but never questioned him. As long as he did not bring in a second wife, it was okay by her. That was the way of nawabs, rajas and rich businessmen. He was both a nawab and a man of substance.

Baig's reverie is disturbed by his wife's gentle query, 'Khana?'

'*Haan*,' he mumbles in reply.

Whisky, soda and tumbler are removed along with the side table. A larger table is brought with a couple of plates on it. Sakina Begum joins him.

'What was the *gup-shup* about this evening?' she asks.

'Not for your ears, Begum. That Sardar uses language not proper in polite society. Most of it is about his exploits with women.'

'*Chheeh! Chheeh!* Why do you talk to him?'

'He can be quite entertaining. Knows a lot of Urdu poetry.'

Dinner is laid on the table by a relay of servants: mutton biryani flavoured with saffron, three kinds of mutton and chicken curries, baghaara baigan (aubergines cooked in Hyderabadi style), chapattis and naans. Every night it is a royal feast. Sakina piles biryani on his plate till he says '*bas*—enough'. Mutton curry? Chicken curry? She heaps his plate till he raises his hand to say no more. Sakina spreads a napkin on his lap and hands him his plate. He waits for her to fill her plate and sit down. 'Bismillah,' he intones. They eat with their fingers: spoons and forks rob food of its taste.

Every evening large quantities of food are removed from the table. It is never wasted because the entire staff of six servants and their families are fed. So are beggars from Nizamuddin who cluster round the entrance gate. For dessert there is phirni covered with silver *varq* in an earthen cup, kulfi, ice cream and a variety of fruits of the season. Both take phirni—this time scooped up with spoons. The fruit goes untouched.

A servant brings a jug of warm water, soap, towels and a basin. They wash their hands, rinse their mouths and spit the contents into the basin. Baig lets out a loud *dakar* (belch) to express thanks for the delicious meal. The servants remove the table and put back the side table with a box of Romeo y Julieta cigars, clipper and lighter on it. Baig clips the end of his cigar and lights it. Sakina disapproves of smoking as much as of drinking, and quietly retires to another room.

It takes nearly half an hour for Baig to finish his Havana cigar, each costing around five hundred rupees. It is worth every paisa as it gives him time to digest his dinner. He tosses the butt into the grate of dying embers and growls '*chalo*—let's go'. Two servants help him go to the bathroom to brush his teeth, urinate, change into his night kurta–pajama and get on his bed. He takes two pinches of digestive *chooran* made of pomegranate seeds. He switches on his table lamp, reads a few couplets of Ghalib which he knows by heart. By then he is heavy with sleep. He switches off the table lamp, lays his head down on his pillow and begins to snore. That is one reason Sakina has given up sharing his bedroom. She sleeps in the next room where her husband's snoring does not disturb her, yet assures her all is well with the world.

The outside lights are kept lit throughout the night. The chowkidar keeps strolling between the entrance and exit gates, thumping his lathi on the tarmac surface, *thak-thak*, shouting periodically *Khabardar raho*—remain alert!

For old people, mornings are an ordeal. No matter what age-related ailments they suffer from, it is usually in the mornings from sunrise to noon that they succumb to them. More old people die during these hours than at others. This is a blessing in disguise as in tropical climates relatives dispose of their dead before sunset. And many deaths are related to bowel movements because they weigh heavily on their minds. Some have to strain at their stools, which takes a toll on their hearts. Others have breathing problems and are short of breath; their exertions on the commode also strain the heart till it gives way.

Though Sharma never had problems with his bowels he had an enlarged prostate which blocked his urine. Medical examination showed early stages of cancer. He was operated on in good time. He got rid of the cancer but it made his bladder uncontrollable. He has to get up twice or thrice at night to empty it in the pisspot that is kept under his bed.

Boota Singh is bowel-obsessed. He takes laxatives, enemas, glycerine suppositories up his rectum. For the last few years he has been taking three heaped teaspoonfuls of Isabgol in a glass of warm milk every morning. Sometimes he has a good clearance. But more often nothing works.

Baig, though he eats richer food, takes little exercise, and is overweight, has no complaint about his bowels.

Sharma gets up after daylight, stretches out his arms and loudly intones *Hari Om Tat Sat* a few times, coming down to just *Hari Om, Hari Om*. He goes to the bathroom to urinate and rinse his mouth. Then he downs a tumbler of warm water and a mug of tea. He goes on to recite the Gayatri Mantra at the top of his voice:

Almighty God: Creator of the Earth and the firmament
Blessed be Thy Name
And blessed be the Sun that gives us light and life
May thou endow me with similar qualities
May such thoughts enlighten my mind.

He waits for a few minutes till pressure builds up in his bowels. Thereafter he has his bath and gets into fresh clothes. He has a good breakfast of cereal, a couple of fried eggs, and is ready to face the day. He does not believe in subscribing to newspapers as he can read them all in the library of the India International Centre. Soon after his sister leaves for her office, his driver takes him to the Centre. He spends his mornings there, has a bite in the coffee lounge and returns home for a long siesta.

For Boota mornings are, as he says, a pain in the arse. He is up before 4 a.m. He swallows a couple of pills with a tumbler of orange juice. He sits down on a well-cushioned armchair. He says he does not believe in prayer but he prays for his bowels to move smoothly: 'Aum Arogyam.' He repeats the mantra many times. He keeps looking at the three table clocks in his bedroom and his pocket watch lying on the table. He looks through the window to see if dawn has come. From 5.30 a.m. newspapers start arriving. He subscribes to six. In the *Hindustan Times* and the *Times of India* he only reads the headlines and turns the pages of their supplements to see the tits and bums of Bollywood starlets. His morning preoccupation is solving crossword puzzles. With breakfast of a tumbler of warm milk with Isabgol he takes eight more pills prescribed for his fluctuating blood pressure, enlarged prostate, wind in the stomach and other age-related ailments. If his fake prayers and the pills do what they are meant to and he succeeds in filling the toilet bowl with his shit, he hears koels calling from the mango groves. If not, it is the kaw-kaw of crows all day long.

Baig's household are early risers. As the call for the Fajr prayer, *Allah-o-Akbar*, wafts across from the mosque in Nizamuddin, Begum Sakina and all the servants turn towards Makka, raise their hands to their ears and offer namaaz. Nawab Sahib's day begins much later. He announces it by stretching his arms wide with a loud cry, 'Ya Allah.' It is a signal for the household to get down to their daily chores. He goes to the bathroom to urinate and rinse his mouth. As he sits in his armchair by the fireplace, Sakina joins him with the greeting, '*Salaam Alaikum*. Did you sleep well?' He replies: '*Valaikum Salaam*. Allah be praised, I slept soundly.' A servant greets his master likewise, brings a silver tray with two Spode china cups on saucers, with silver spoons, a bowl of sugar cubes and a silver teapot covered by a tea cosy to keep it hot. Sakina pours tea, milk and sugar in the two cups, and hands one to her husband. She takes her seat with cup in hand. 'What is the programme for the day?' she asks.

'The same,' he replies. 'Some business, meeting people, eating the air in Lodhi Gardens and back home. Comes the morning, comes the evening and the day is done. This is the way in which our lives end.'

The tea tray is removed. Another servant brings an ornate silver hookah with an earthenware bowl full of live embers and fragrant tobacco. Baig takes a few pulls and utters a loud 'ah' at the end of each puff. A few puffs of his hookah is all he needs to activate his bowels. He doesn't care a fig about what goes on in the world. He gets one English paper, the *Hindustan Times*, for no better reason than that his father used to get it. He scans the headlines and the obituary columns and puts it aside. He used to subscribe to the Urdu journal, *Qaumi Awaaz*. Since it closed down, he gets *Roznama Rashtriya Sahara*, *Hindustan Express* and *Sahafat*. Also several magazines—*Nai Duniya*, *Sahara Times* and *Pakeeza Aanchal*. He never reads any of them; Begum Sakina goes over every one of them before she passes them on to her servants, all of whom can read Urdu. Baig gets his news second-hand from his wife, with suitable comments: *Besharam!* (shameless), *Goonda kahin ka!* (no-good thug), *Naalaik* (stupid) or just *Thoo!* Her *wah-wah*s are reserved for tennis star Sania Mirza and Muslims in India's Cricket Eleven.

Members of the Sunset Club do not normally meet on the evening of Beating Retreat. All three watch the spectacle on their TV sets. This year it was cancelled as a mark of respect for ex-President Venkataraman who had died two days earlier—all public ceremonies were cancelled for eleven days and flags flown at half-mast.

Indians have enormous respect for the dead. If the head clerk of an office dies, the entire office staff takes the day off. They have different ways of expressing their grief. Some take their families to the cinema, others take them to the zoo or for picnics to the Qutub Minar or to Okhla, where there is a barrage from where the Yamuna canal takes off. The next day they have a meeting. The boss makes a short speech, extolling the qualities of head and heart of their departed colleague. They stand in silence for a minute with their heads lowered. Then they go back to their desks and shuffle files, drink relays of tea or coffee. And gossip.

That afternoon there were lots of picnickers in Lodhi Gardens. As they took their seats, Baig remarked, 'There is a lot of raunaq in the garden today.'

'Has to be,' says Boota, 'Venkataraman died the day before yesterday. So there have to be *shok sabhas*—condolence meetings. This is as nice a place as any to hold one. Let's forget Venkataraman. What do you make of the Chandra Mohan–Anuradha affair in Chandigarh? The papers are full of it.'

Sharma is the first to answer: 'Shameful! A Brahmin girl from a respectable family marrying a married fellow with two children. And a Bishnoi at that. The founder of the sect, Guru Jambeshwar, was a noble soul, a visionary, a century ahead of his time, the first environmentalist. Don't kill trees, don't kill animals, don't hurt people, don't tell lies—that's what he preached. He even sanctioned selecting handsome, healthy males to service married women whose husbands could not impregnate them. That's the reason why the Bishnois are a handsome people. And see what happened to them. At one time the British intended to declare them a criminal tribe. They have a very high rate of murders and violent crimes. And we had this fellow's father Bhajan Lal who was once chief minister of Haryana. Overnight he changed sides and bribed MLAs to join him. Now his son has gone one better than his father—he deserts his family to have illicit relations with an upper-caste woman.'

Baig speaks next. 'Sharmaji, there is nothing Bishnoi or Brahmin about it. Love crosses all barriers of race, religion, caste, wealth and poverty. Mirza Ghalib's lines on *ishq*—love—say it best:

'*No power can hold it back; it is a fire*
When you try to ignite it, it refuses to ignite,
When you want to put it out, it refuses to be put out.'

'Ishq-vishq, love-shove, all bullshit,' Boota cuts in. 'Baig Sahib, lust is real, love is the gloss romantics put on it. Lust is natural. It begins to build up in infancy, assumes compelling proportions in adolescence, and lasts till old age. Boys start getting erections and want to put them in other boys' bottoms or girls' bums;

girls start getting damp in their middles. Nature compels all of them to put their thighs together, fuck away till they are spent. Let me tell you what probably passed between the Bishnoi and the Brahmini. The Bishnoi wanted a new woman and was on the prowl, looking for a dainty dish. The Brahmini in her mid-thirties, fair-skinned, black curly hair hanging down to her shoulders, eyes of a gazelle, bosom like this Bara Gumbad in front of us. Their eyes meet. Lust is aroused. So they get down to the act: *Tamaam shud*—that's all.'

'Bhai Boota, no one can answer you,' protests Baig with a smile. 'You get down to the basics. Don't forget that love, not lust, has generated the greatest poetry in all languages of the world.'

Sharma cuts in impatiently: 'Forget love and lust, aren't you concerned about the harm such illicit liaisons do to society? A married man with a family and also deputy chief minister of Haryana should be setting an example in propriety. And that woman, a lawyer, advises him that the easiest way to avoid being charged with bigamy, which is a crime, is to convert to Islam which sanctions bigamy. Disgraceful!'

Baig is not one to let Sharma get away with a slur on Islam. 'Sharma Sahib, Islam does not sanction bigamy; it permits it if a marriage does not work out. You must know a lot of Muslims: can you name even one who has more than one wife? I can name several Hindus in important positions—chief ministers of states, MPs, film stars, dancers, business tycoons. Not one has been prosecuted for bigamy. Nevertheless, everyone blames Muslims for being bigamous. Here am I, who finds it hard enough to cope with one wife!'

'I am sorry if I hurt your feelings. But you take it from me that the Chandra Mohan–Anuradha drama is not yet over. There will be lots of ups and downs in the time to come.'

'I agree,' says Boota, slapping his thighs loudly with both hands. 'We are a people full of contradictions. On one side we have a couple who break all rules of propriety, on the other we have fundoos like those of the Ram Sena in Mangalore who beat up boys and girls for drinking beer in a pub. These goondas should be stripped naked and beaten with chappals on their bare bottoms. What do you say, Baig Sahib? You must have read about it in the papers.'

'Some people don't know how to mind their own business,' replies Baig. 'Unfortunately, we have lots of them in our country.'

'So you think we should ignore them or *joota maro* them? Spit on their bums before we smack their backside with chappals?'

Before they bid each other goodnight they generally allude to the subject uppermost in their minds; it is too delicate to be put bluntly. Baig quotes Ghalib:

Life goes at a galloping pace
Where it will stop, no one knows;
Our hands are not on the reins '
Our feet not in the stirrups.

Boota adds another couplet:

There is a day fixed for death
Why then spend sleepless nights thinking about it?

Sharma says, 'Cheerio.'

On that happy note they bid each other farewell for the day.

PLAY

TYGER TYGER BURNING BRIGHT

CAST

• Yasmeen Ahmed	(22)	Receptionist (Ex-Air-hostess)
• Sardool Singh	(60)	Commissionaire. Sikh (retired soldier and shikari)
• A.N. Mathur	(35)	Joint Secretary. Director of Tourism, Government of India
• H.H. Maharaja of Shamnagar	(30)	
• Jack Conran-Smith	(25)	English (long red hair and beard as worn by hippies)
• Alf Schneiderman	(60)	American Tourist
• Babette Schneiderman	(55)	Wife of Alf Schneiderman.
Hotel Staff		

ACT ONE
SCENE I

(*Scene: Foyer of a hotel in a national game preserve. On one side there is a reception desk with cubby-holes for keys and letters and a telephone switchboard. On the desk there is a large guest-book, a notice saying 'Dry, Day', a figure of the Air-India Maharaja, and other bric-a-brac typical of small hotels.*

The foyer is also the hotel lobby. Facing the reception desk are a sofa, three armchairs and a table. Potted palms, flowers, vases decorate the room.

On the top of the wall facing the stage and the entrance leading into

477

the hotel are framed posters: one of Jawaharlal Nehru with a caption about welcoming foreign visitors, the other of the Taj Mahal with the caption 'Visit India', between the posters there is a mounted head of a snarling tiger.

The receptionist is behind her desk, working at her accounts.

The Commissionaire is sitting on the steps of the entrance with a muzzle-loader between his legs.

N.B. : *Outer entrance to hotel can be closed by sliding iron trellis gates which are kept open during the daytime.)*

Commissionaire	:	Miss Sahibji, tell me one thing—is there any sense in building a hotel in the middle of a dense jungle? You have been all over the world and have read many books, does anything our government does make any sense to you?
Receptionist	:	*[Removing her glasses]* Be patient, man! This is only the first day. We expect people from all over the world to come here to see our wild animals . . .
		[Buzz on the switch board] You see what I mean.
		[Plugs in line] Hotel Wild Life. Good evening!
		[Crackling noise] Yes, Yes, Hotel Wild Life.
		[Turning to Commissionaire] It's the telephone people checking our line.
		[Disconnects] As I was telling you, Sardool Singh, we are expecting thousands of rich Sahiblog to come here.
Commissionaire	:	Then tell me another thing, why hire a shikari like your slave here, give him a gun, and then say, 'No, no, you must not shoot anything, this is a wildlife sanctuary?'

Receptionist	:	You will show them our white tigers and our maneless lions, our rhinoceros and elephants. You must see that they come to no harm. Your old bundook is to frighten off animals, not to kill them.
Commissionaire	:	*[Examining his single barrel muzzle-loader]* This is a new one, Miss Sahib. If a gun only made a noise—*thah*—and did not hurt, even the animals would lose respect for it. Where would you be then? I tell you . . . *[Buzz on switchboard]*
Receptionist	:	Hotel Wild Life, Good evening! *[Crackle. Puts hand on mouth of phone]* It's the telephone people again. They have no imagination. *[Imitating telephone people]* Testing, testing, testing. One, two, three, four. *[Speaking into phone]* Yes, yes,—what were you saying, Sardool Singh?
Commissionaire	:	Miss Sahibji, what I was saying is this: if you have a gun, have one which kills. What would you do if you ran into a man-eater?
Receptionist	:	A man-eater! Now that is an interesting phenomenon.
Commissionaire	:	A what?
Receptionist	:	An interesting phenomenon is something which interests everyone. Why should anyone want to eat human beings when there are so many other and nicer things to eat like tandoori chicken and ice-cream and . . . *[Buzz on switchboard]* Nuisance! *[Into telephone]* Yes, yes for the hundredth time this is the hotel in the jungle . . . Oh! I beg your

pardon, sir . . . Yes, sir, this is Hotel Wild Life, good evening. I thought . . . Yes. Three rooms. One single, one double and the suite for the Sahib . . . Yes, they will be ready. *[Puts down the phone. Brushes back her hair]* Phew! You see Sardool Singh, four guests on the very first day. And the Burra Sahib as well. *[Taps bell beside visitors' book. A bearer in uniform appears]* Get Numbers Two, Five, Six and Nine ready. Have flowers in Number Two for the Burra Sahib. And tell the cook to prepare the special VIP menu: tomato soup, chicken curry and rice, caramel custard, coffee to follow.

Bearer : Yes, Madam.

Receptionist : Sardool Singh, you will see how many people will come here. All you have to do is to get a few man-eaters to pose for them when they have their cameras ready. You will see how many people will want to take pictures of man-eaters. You see everyone in the world is interested in that kind of animal.

Commissionaire : Do you know what a man-eater is, Miss Sahib?

Receptionist : A man-eater is a man-eater. Eats men.

Commissionaire : Eats women too.

Receptionist : Well yes, eats women too.

Commissionaire : And children.

Receptionist : *Accha bhai* he eats men, women and children. He eats human beings.

Commissionaire : He is not always a he, Miss Sahib. A she-tiger often eats more humans than a he-tiger.

Receptionist : Oh, does she?

Commissionaire : She does. And the older she gets, the more man-hungry.

Receptionist	:	Now that is also an interesting phenomenon.
Commissionaire	:	A what?
Receptionist	:	I told you, an interesting phenomenon is something which is of interest to everyone.

[Buzz on switchboard]

Hotel Wild Life, Good evening! Suite of rooms? We have only one suite and that is taken. Singles or doubles . . . A double . . . Yes, sir, what name? The Maharaja of what? Oh Shamnagar . . . Yes, Your Highness. Yes, there are quarters for servants. Thank you. *[Puts down phone]* Now you believe me! A real Maharaja. A man who killed tigers by the dozen now wants to just look at them.

Commissionaire	:	Miss Sahib, when a man gets old he can only hunt with his eyes.
Receptionist	:	What do you mean?
Commissionaire	:	No powder in his bundook.
Receptionist	:	That is not a proper thing to say. Besides, how do you know he is old? He may be young and handsome. Listen—is that a car?

[Sound of a car approaching. Commissionaire stands up. Receptionist tidies her hair. Sound of car halting on gravel road. Opening and slamming of doors. Commissionaire puts away gun and goes to fetch luggage. Enter Mr and Mrs Schneiderman armed with cameras, field-glasses, etc. Sound of car driving away.]

Mrs Schneiderman	:	Oh boy! Isn't this great? And right in the centre of nowhere. Alfie, I know I am going to like this place. *[Turning to Receptionist]*

	And how are you this evening? *(Puts out her hand)* I am Mrs Schneiderman and this is my husband.
Receptionist	: Good evening, Madam. Good evening, sir. I hope you had a nice journey.
Mrs Schneiderman	: *[shaking hands]* Sure! Great ride through the jungle in that bucket of bolts. Some place you have here!
Receptionist	: Please sign the visitors' book. Your room is ready. Dinner will be served at seven o'clock.
Mrs Schneiderman	: *[Writing in visitors' book]* Honey, we are the very first guests in the hotel. Now isn't that something! Maybe we can tear off the first page and take it home to show it to the folks. *[Picks up notice saying 'Dry Day']* Aren't these Indians clever! They know when it's going to rain and when it's going to be dry.
Receptionist	: I am sorry, Madam, that only means we cannot serve alcoholic beverages today.
Mr Schneiderman	: We've brought our own booze. You don't mind us drinking our own stuff, do you?
Receptionist	: Not at all, sir. I will have soda and ice sent to your room. *[Taps bell. Bearer appears. Gives him a key]* Number Six. *[Bearer takes baggage from Commissionaire]* After dinner there will be an excursion to the jungle. We have a jeep fitted with searchlights. Our professional hunter will show you some of our wild life. If you care to join the party . . .
Mrs Schneiderman	: Sure, we'll join, that's what we are here for.

Receptionist	:	I hope you have a pleasant stay.
Mrs Schneiderman	:	You bet! See you later.

[The Schneidermans follow bearer. Pause. Sound of car approaching. Slamming of doors. Commissionaire goes to fetch luggage. Enter Conran-Smith, red-haired, bearded, dressed hippie-style, has sack on back.]

Receptionist	:	*[Startled]* You?
Conran-Smith	:	The name, Madam, is Conran-Smith. We've had the pleasure of earlier acquaintance. Have you a room for me?
Receptionist	:	What are you doing here? I thought I'd seen the last of you.
Conran-Smith	:	Come to study the nature of man and beast—and woman. Are you going to give me a nice room—maybe next door to your own?
Receptionist	:	*[Embarrassed, taps bell. Bearer appears]* Number Nine. Please sign the book.
Conran-Smith	:	With pleasure. *[Begins to make entry]* Name: Conran-Smith. Nationality: British . . . and proud of it.
Receptionist	:	Please, no comments in the visitors' book.
Conran-Smith	:	Occupation? Occupation . . . occupation . . .
Receptionist	:	Vagabond.
Conran-Smith	:	Occupation: Pursuit of love.
Receptionist	:	*[Snatching book out of his hand]* You are impossible. Just give me your passport number; I'll fill in the rest.
Conran-Smith	:	*[Handing her his passport]* Yours forever. Onward to Room Nine and thence to paradise. I take it you are in Number Ten?—yes? *[Exit]*
Commissionaire	:	Is the Sahib an old friend, Miss Sahib?
Receptionist	:	I met him once when I was an air-hostess. He is a bit mad. Most Sahibs are a bit mad.

Commissionaire : When I was in the army, our Colonel Sahib used to go out every evening armed with a mosquito net stuck to a pole and hunted butterflies and grasshoppers and beetles and bugs and other vermin. His Memsahib was even madder. She used to collect stray cats and dogs. One time she had fourteen in her house. I used to say to myself, 'How can these people rule an Empire!' You see how right I was. A king must look like a king, speak like a king, behave like a king.

[Sound of car approaching. Commissionaire goes to receive new visitor. Enter Mr Mathur dressed like a typical Indian civil servant with rose bud in his third button hole a la Nehru, transistor across shoulder, cigar in mouth.]

Receptionist : Good evening, sir.

Mathur : *[Ignores greeting—turns back to holler]* Hey Chowkidar! Don't pick the case by the handle, put it on your head. Really these Sikhs! Chaprasi, take my briefcase to my suite. What's your name . . . Miss . . . Miss . . .

Receptionist : Ahmed, sir.

Mathur : Oh yes, Yasmeen Ahmed. I am A.N. Mathur, IAS, joint secretary and director of tourism. You must have heard of me.

Receptionist : Yes, sir. I am new to the ministry. This is my first posting.
[Commissionaire and chaprasi go by with luggage]

Mathur : I'll see what I can do for you. Have you any visitors?

Receptionist : Yes, sir, an American couple and an English gentleman. And we are expecting one more, the Maharaja of Shamnagar. The suite has been reserved for you. I hope His Highness will not be offended.

Mathur : Why should he be offended? It is time these Maharajas learnt who the real rulers of the country are. I want tea in my room. And a couple of sodas and ice at 6.30 sharp.

Receptionist : Yes, sir. *[Mathur follows bearer who has come back to escort him]* Well, Sardool Singh, here's our new ruler—looking, speaking and behaving like a king.

Commissionaire : *[Wagging his head and spitting]* Thoo.

[Sound of car, slamming of doors, etc. Commissionaire looks up without getting up. Maharaja's servant brings in suitcases. Maharaja follows, dressed in jodhpurs and open collar shirt. Commissionaire stands up and salutes.]

Maharaja : *Sat Sri Akal,* Sardar Sahib. What a pleasure palace you have in this wilderness. *[Greets Receptionist Indian style]* Namaskar. I trust you have a room for me and my companion.

Receptionist : *[Pushing the visitors' book in front of him]* Yes, Your Highness. I apologize, the only suite we have was already booked.

Maharaja : What would I do with a suite! A charpoy and a chair are all I need. *[Fills in visitors' book]*

Receptionist : Would Your Highness like some tea—or soda sent up to your room?

Maharaja : No, thank you. I'll just have a wash and some rest and join the others for dinner. *[Follows bearer]*

Commissionaire : You see what I mean? Every inch a ruler.

Receptionist	: But he is no more a ruler. Sardool Singh, the rulers of today are people like our Burra Sahib and the Americans. The Maharaja and the Englishman were rulers of yesterday. They do not matter except in history books.
Commissionaire	: I cannot read books but you mark my words—when there's trouble of some kind, the fellow who has it in his blood will always come up on top. One day you will say Sardool Singh told me something worth a hundred thousand rupees.
Receptionist	: I will remember.

[Starts scribbling in her account book. Commissionaire retires. Lights slowly dim to produce effect of twilight. Sounds of jungle filter in—the chirp of crickets, cicadas, frogs; the roar of a tiger, first at a distance, then nearer.]

ACT ONE
SCENE II

(Scene: Same as in Scene I except for a standard oil lamp in a corner and another on the Receptionist's desk. The Receptionist and Commissionaire are in their respective places. The bearer brings tray with coffee percolator, cups, saucers, lays them on the table and retires.

Background sounds: jungle noises, mainly the cheep of crickets, and people talking in the dining-room. They come out talking loudly, led by Mathur and Mrs Schneiderman. Commissionaire stands up.)

Mathur	: As I was saying, Mrs Schneiderman, in our next Five Year Plan, we have made provision for building tourist bungalows in all our wildlife sanctuaries.
Mrs Schneiderman	: Isn't that nice! Did you hear that, Alfie, they're going to build lots of places like this one.

Mr Schneiderman : *[A little inebriated]* I am all for it. But you must do away with all this 'Dry Day' foolishness. Then you wouldn't have to go out into the dark forest to see all those damned animals.
[Polite laughter]

Mathur : Drinking is not in our tradition, Mr Schneiderman. Mahatma Gandhi, Father of our nation, considered it a great sin. We are hoping that by the end of the next Five Year Plan, most of India will be dry.

Mr Schneiderman : *[Produces a hip-flask and places it next to sign saying 'Dry Day']* I hope you won't object to my having some cognac with my coffee. Your Highness, it's three-star Napolean.

Maharaja : Thank you very much Mr Schneiderman, I don't drink.

Mr Schneiderman : You, sir, with the double-barrelled name.

Conran-Smith : If you mean me, the answer is no. I do not imbibe liquor. I prefer to smoke pot— guaranteed to produce visions of Valhalla, guaranteed to make you high without producing a hangover. Non-habit forming, much more fun than any three-hundred star brandy. And taken by the greatest people in the world. I am afraid I cannot offer it to anyone, too expensive and forbidden by the law. *[Proceeds to light his pipe]*

Maharaja : Bravo, Mr Conran-Smith! Freedom to break the law shall hereafter be recognized as a fundamental right of the greatest people in the world. *[Conran-Smith bows]*

Mr Schneiderman : Mister Mathoor, I take it you won't jail me for taking a few drops of brandy?

Mathur	: Ha! Ha! Just to prove that we are not a narrow-minded people I will join you—but very little, just a tear drop, as the French say.
Maharaja	: Shabash Mathur Sahib! You maintain the honoured tradition of the Civil Service which considers itself above the law. Besides, Mahatma Gandhi, Father of our nation, said it's the spirit and not the letter of the law that matters. And I am sure Mr Schneiderman's cognac is excellent spirit.
Mathur	: *[Ignoring Maharaja's sarcasm]* Mrs Schneiderman, you must visit some of our great dams. 'Temples of New India', as our late Prime Minister Mr Nehru called them. In the current Five Year Plan . . .
Mrs Schneiderman	: Coffee everyone? Do forgive my interruption—please go on with your temples. We saw some very nice old ones at Konarak and Khajuraho. Alfie was quite excited by them, weren't you, Alfie?
Mr Schneiderman	: Jesus! Never seen anything like it in all my sixty years. For making love, give it to the Hindoo. Standing up, sitting down, lying on a bed of nails, from the front, from the rear . . .
Mrs Schneiderman	: That's enough, Alfie! You don't have to go into the details.
Mr Schneiderman	: But really! How many ways of doing a woman does the Hindoo bible on sex mention . . . Sixty-nine?
Conran-Smith	: It doesn't matter how many ways they catalogue. You take it from me, Mr Schneiderman, they don't know the first thing about love or sex. Where in this

	benighted country does one find a place without a hundred eyes peering at you? Can you make love in public? I ask you.
Maharaja	: You sound like a very frustrated lover, Mr Conran-Smith.
Conran-Smith	: Indeed I am. Hence I seek the solitude of a Himalayan jungle.
Mrs Schneiderman	: I am not being anti-Indian or anything like that, but I do remember reading in a journal that Indians make lousy lovers. Alfie, you remember the name of the American girl who wrote the article?
Mr Schneiderman	: No I don't, but she must have been quite a girl.
Maharaja	: Remarkable achievement! Discovering the sexual potential of 500 million people would take many ages! But for instant research, give it to the Americans. Don't you agree, Mr Mathur?
Mathur	: I am sorry I do not like this kind of sexy talk in the presence of ladies. [*Turning to Mrs Schneiderman*] I was not talking of those kinds of temples; I meant the wonderful new things coming up in India—like our big steel plants at Durgapur, Rourkela and Bhilai.
Maharaja	: One built by the British, one by the Russians, one by the Germans.
Mathur	: Foreign aid is useful.
Maharaja	: [*In response to Mrs Schneiderman holding up coffee and cream jug*] Fifty-fifty.
Mathur	: Yes, fifty-fifty but no strings attached, mind you . . .
Maharaja	: I meant coffee and cream, Mr Mathur, not foreign aid. Do go on.

Mathur : Our economy will soon become self-expanding. You see, Mr Schneiderman, India is not properly understood abroad. Our propaganda is not very effective.

Maharaja : Famines make better stories than Five Year Plans.

Mathur : I do not care what you or anybody else says. I know India's millions are on the march. India will soon rise and become the leader of the free nations of the world.

Conran-Smith : [Loudly humming the Internationale] Indians of the world arise, you have nothing to lose but your loin cloths.

Maharaja : That will not help our family planning programmes, will it, Mr Mathur?

Mathur : All people like you can do is to make fun of everything. Even our birth control plans are forging ahead. In the next Five Year Plan . . .

Mr Schneiderman : [Turning to Receptionist] Come and join us for coffee. We can't have you standing there looking at us.

Receptionist : No thank you, sir, I am on duty.

Mrs Schneiderman : Come on, honey!

Conran-Smith : [Getting up and drawing up a chair] Remember the Indian maxim, Guest is God! The gods order you to have coffee with them.

[All men except Mathur stand up]

Mrs Schneiderman : How do you like it, my dear?

Receptionist : Just black, Mrs Schneiderman.

Maharaja : Must be very lonely for you in this jungle.

Mr Schneiderman : 'Queen of the Himalayan jungle': What do you think of that as a title for a movie?

Conran-Smith : 'The lonely lovely Queen of a lonely lovely forest'. Too long to be a title of anything, but very true.
[*Laughter. Mr Schneiderman slaps Conran-Smith on his shoulder*]

Mathur : This is no laughing matter. I will transfer her to another station. [*Turning to Receptionist*] Remind me about it when I get back to Delhi; I will pass orders.

Receptionist : I am very happy here, sir.

Mathur : That has nothing to do with it. A jungle is not a suitable station for a lady. Have you made arrangements to take us on a sightseeing tour?

Receptionist : Yes, sir. We have a jeep fitted with searchlights. Sardool Singh will escort you. He knows the jungle well. As soon as you have finished your coffee.

Mr Schneiderman : And our cigars. [*Taking tubes out of his pocket*] Anyone care for a genuine Havana? Can't get them back home—thanks to Comrade Fidel Castro. You, sir, Maharaja of whatever-it-is?

Maharaja : No, thank you, Mr Schneiderman. I do not smoke.

Mr Schneiderman : Hey what kind of Maharaja are you? You don't drink, you don't smoke. Next you'll be telling us you don't have a harem. How many wives do you have anyway?

Maharaja : Only one, Mr Schneiderman. By Maharaja's standards I am almost a bachelor.
[*All laugh*]

Mathur	: You see, the days of Maharajas with many wives are over. In new India . . .
Maharaja	: It's the days of ministers industrialists and civil servants with many mistresses.

[Louder laughter]

Mr Schneiderman	: *[To Conran-Smith]* You Mr British Empire, cigar?
Conran-Smith	: I've never smoked a Havana. I am sure it will improve with an injection of good Indian hashish. Thank you.
Mr Schneiderman	: Mr Government of India!
Mrs Schneiderman	: Don't mind him, Mr Mathoor, he's like that on one whisky.
Mathur	: Not at all. I'll try one if I may. Actually we make very good cigars in India. We have launched an export promotion scheme . . .

[Buzz on switchboard. Receptionist hurries to answer. Jungle noises begin to filter in—jackals, later tigers.]

Receptionist	: Hotel Wild Life, good evening. Who? Yes . . . Yes . . . police station? Yes. Oh! . . . Oh, I see . . . Actually we were planning to . . . Yes, we have a retired soldier who has also been a shikari . . . Old hand but only an old blunderbuss . . . yes . . . I'll let you know if anything happens. *[Puts back receiver]* *[Addressing guests]* Sir, a woman was lifted an hour ago in Badi village only half-a-mile from here.
Mathur	: Lifted? Who lifted her?
Receptionist	: A tiger. The police officer says it's the third

case this month. He says no one must go
out at night; doors and windows must be
kept shut. He says it's a man-eater.

*[Sounds of jungle are louder now—jackals howling, then roar of a tiger.
Lights fade slowly. Commissionaire draws trellis gate from either side.]*

ACT ONE
SCENE III

*[Scene: Same as in Scenes I and II. Standard oil lamp is now shedding
light on the table. Receptionist, in dressing gown is relaxing in armchair,
with legs on table; she, is reading. A transistor on the table plays sitar
music. Commissionaire is asleep on steps of the entrance, holding gun
against his chest. Occasional snore. Jungle noises in the background.*
*Conran-Smith comes down with tape-recorder slung across
shoulder.]*

Conran-Smith   : *[Comes in reciting]* 'At night upon my bed I
sought him whom my soul loveth. I sought
him, but I found him not. I called him but
he gave no answer. I will rise now and go
about the city, in the streets and in the
byways.'

Receptionist   : *[Startled]* Good god! Don't tell me you mean
to go out in the jungle?

Conran-Smith   : I do! To make the world's first recording
of a man-eater eating a woman.

Receptionist   : That's not funny. Besides, you cannot leave
the hotel without my permission. I forbid
it.

Conran-Smith   : O Queen of the Himalayan jungle, your
order will be obeyed. O Lovely Empress of
Hearts, can't you also command your slave
to hold your beautiful hands?

Receptionist : Stop this tomfoolery. How insensitive can you be! Half-a-mile—perhaps only a few yards—from here a woman is lying dead, her husband and children wailing and the countryside petrified with fear. None of this seems to concern you in the slightest. What kind of man are you?

Conran-Smith : A very ordinary, average kind of man. I too live in fear—some of it real, most of it imaginary. Give in to fear and you've had it. Ignore it or pretend it does not exist and carry on the business of life. That's my motto.

Receptionist : The business of life being smoking pot and making passes at women.

Conran-Smith : Precisely! Now may I take your hand in mine? [Extends hand]

Receptionist : [Slapping it] You may not. You do not realize I am on duty here and holding visitors' hands is not a part of my duties.

Conran-Smith : Then we must get Mr Mathur to amend your job description. 'In order to promote tourism during the fifth Five-Year Plan all lady receptionists will hereafter be expected to allow their hands to be held by visitors, and if further pressed, even allow them to be kissed'—signed A.N. Mathur for the Government of India. [Takes receptionist's hand and kisses it. She does not withdraw hand]

Receptionist : O Jack, I wish you'd stop playing the buffoon sometime.

Conran-Smith : Do you still doubt that I love you? Do you want me to prove it by walking into the jaws of a man-eater?

Receptionist	:	You don't know what the word 'love' means. Being in love and wanting to make love are not the same thing.
Conran-Smith	:	Conceded! But wanting to make love to the person you love is the ultimate expression of being in love. That represents the state of mind of Jack Conran-Smith towards Yasmeen Ahmed. Yasmeen, I love you and want to make love to you. Do you object?
Receptionist	:	I most certainly do. Love can't be a one-way traffic. I also have to be in love to permit anyone to make love to me. And I am not sure if I am in love with you, Jack. At the moment I am only aware of your desire for me; it boosts my self-esteem; I feel grateful and am at times impelled to make some gesture to express my gratitude. Something tells me there should be more to love than that.
Conran-Smith	:	My dear young lady, do not despise desire; desire that gives birth to love is more than lusting after a body. It is designed by the gods to fulfil the greatest need of human beings, the need to fill the aching void, the utter loneliness that is within us. Haven't you at times woken in the stillness of the night and heard a dog baying to the moon? *[Imitates dog baying]* Or heard a train go by from nowhere to nowhere? *[Imitates siren of a locomotive and rhythmic patter of train's wheels]* And haven't you suddenly felt absolutely alone in the huge, awesome, frightful world—so alone that it hurts? And haven't you then wanted some one person to share that inner solitude? I call that

		desire love. It is that kind of love I have for you.
Receptionist	:	Thank you, Jack. You've almost talked me into it—but not quite. In any case how pointless it all is in the face of death. Death is real. That dead woman with her bones being crunched by the tiger is real. The sobbing of her children is real. Being in love or making love to someone you love and who loves you is trivial and unimportant.
Conran-Smith	:	It is not. It is the only answer to all the ills that beset our daily lives. All you have to do is to let me make love to you and you will see how quickly your fears of the world outside will be dissipated.
Receptionist	:	Rubbish! Again you equate love with lust. It's like being drunk or stoned—only for a much shorter time.
Conran-Smith	:	You are wrong about the time. Love is like samsara of the Hindus. It is born, it dies only to be reborn again. It is reincarnated in different forms. It is the Creator, Preserver and Destroyer all rolled into one. What about that!
Receptionist	:	That is beyond me. In any case I am not Hindu. We Muslims are more earthy. We do not hold hands for spiritual communion. *[Freeing her hand]* What would Mr Mathur think if he were to come down now?
Conran-Smith	:	That's all that worries you? What will people think. To hell with people who think ill of people in love! Down with everyone and everything! Up with Prophet Messiah Conran-Smith, hashish addict and master fornicator!

Conran-Smith : *[Gets up, comes behind Receptionist's chair, takes her in his arms and kisses her]* Yasmeen Ahmed, I love you.

Receptionist : Coming from you love sounds like an obscene four-letter word. I cannot honestly say I mind very much. *[Kiss again]* Enough of that. You better get back to your room—please!

Conran-Smith : Okay—let me just record your voice for keeps. If I cannot record a woman-eating tiger, I'll settle for a man-eating tigress. *[Opens tape-recorder]*

Receptionist : Fi, Fie, Fo, Fum. I smell the blood of Englishmen. *[Growls]* I haven't a very good voice and I have very little to say for myself.

Conran-Smith : The moving tape moves on, recording a pregnant silence.

Receptionist : Oh dear! Let me think. Perhaps a little poem.
'*Tyger, tyger burning bright*
In the forest of the night
What immortal hand or eye
Framed thy fearful symmetry?'

Conran-Smith : Symmetraee, to rhyme with 'eye'.

Receptionist : Symmetraee, '*And what shoulder*'.

Conran-Smith : You are skipping a verse. '*In what distant deeps or skies*'.

Receptionist : Ah yes.
'*In what distant deeps or skies*
Burnt the fire of thine eyes?
On what wings dare he aspire
What the hand dare seize the fire?'
I don't remember the rest except something about 'stars throwing down their spears' and

'watering heaven with their tears' . . . and, 'twisting the sinews of the heart'.

Conran-Smith : [Switches off. Plays it back.]

Receptionist : What an awful cackle!

Conran-Smith : That happens when human beings don't speak straight . . . sounds like a debate of the United Nations, doesn't it? Now listen. [Plays back first verse]
Your voice is as beautiful as your face. I expect under your sari your body is more beautiful than either.

Receptionist : Lecherous bastard! I wonder how the legend of the English being cold-blooded was generated! You are the randiest nation on earth.

Conran-Smith : How true! For further proof of British randiness come to Room Nine. [Takes her hand]
Please!

Receptionist : Certainly not. Go back to bed and get some sleep. [Frees her hand] I beg of you. Do not embarrass me any more.

Conran-Smith : [Taking her in his arms and kissing her] Yasmeen, I love you. Won't you let me make love to you?

Receptionist : [Freeing herself and gently patting him on his beard] If I were really persuaded that your desire to make love is born of love I might—some day. Goodnight.

Conran-Smith : [Kisses her again] Goodnight. I'll leave the recorder here. If you have nothing better to do you can listen to some of the animals' calls I recorded, specially commend the mating call of the British lion. Goodnight. [Kisses her again]

[Exit. Receptionist resumes seat and fiddles with recorder. Enter Maharaja. Receptionist startled. Puts feet down from the table]

Maharaja	: I am sorry to disturb you. Please, please do not get up. I thought I heard that English boy's voice and came down to see if he was making a nuisance of himself.
Receptionist	: *[Switches off tape-recorder winding backwards]* Not at all, Your Highness. He is a very nice young man—only a little crazy. He wanted to go out to record calls of wild animals. I refused to let him out. Do sit down, Your Highness. Can I make you a cup of coffee?
Maharaja	: *[Takes chair]* No, thank you. No coffee. One can never be too sure of these evil-smelling, long-haired and bearded types who wear flowers and profess to make love all the time. 'Make love not war'—sounds very nice and all that. If everyone went about making love, the world would be in a worse mess than it is today.
Receptionist	: I don't think they mean the messy kind of love, Your Highness. They say what men of god have been saying all along: Love is stronger than hate. Love makes for a better world.
Maharaja	: Love might make for a better world but it is by no means stronger than hate. Hate rouses stronger passions than love; it produces the worst as well as the best in human beings. But all this is academic. As long as the destroyer is at large, someone must destroy him.

Receptionist	:	I may sound very stupid but I do not understand this logic of kill the killer
Maharaja	:	Let me explain. If I were to go out into the jungle now and say, 'Shri Man-eaterjee, I love you,' would it make him change his mind? What good would it do to anyone except the man-eater?
Receptionist	:	That's different, it's the law of the jungle.
Maharaja	:	Precisely! One nation produces a new kind of bomb, a man-eating bomb. What is its neighbouring nation to do except to produce a bigger man-eating bomb? It's the same, the law of the jungle.
Receptionist	:	And so we go on.
Maharaja	:	So we go on—from stones to spears, from bow and arrow to blunderbuss and bundook, from Big Berthas to doodle-bugs, from supersonic bombers to intercontinental ballistic missiles with megaton load of bomb-heads to devastate an entire country. That's how we'll go on. *[Mrs Schneiderman appear at the back and listens]*
Receptionist	:	No, Your Highness, that is not how we will go on. We are at the end of our road.
Mrs Schneiderman	:	*[Coming forward]* I heard that anti-American talk. We are Americans and proud of being American. *[Receptionist and Maharaja stand up]*
Receptionist	:	Do sit down.
Maharaja	:	We were not criticizing your country, Mrs Schneiderman. We were not criticizing any country. We were talking of the doom of the world.
Mrs Schneiderman	:	That's fine. It's not right to criticize the United States for everything that happens.

	We feed half the hungry people of the world, you know.
Maharaja	: Quite right, Mrs Schneiderman. You have much to be proud of. Tell me, have you any views on man-eating?
Mrs Schneiderman	: Really, Your Highness! What an odd question! You mean to ask me if I approve or disapprove of cannibalism? As an American citizen, I'd say I am definitely against it.
Receptionist	: *[Laughing]* His Highness has an odd way of putting things. He meant if you have any views on what to do with man-eating tigers.
Mrs Schneiderman	: Don't tell me a big, brave Maharaja like you is scared of over-sized pussy cats!
Maharaja	: As a matter of fact I am. That's why I came out of my room—looking for company and comfort. Isn't that why you came here too, Mrs Schneiderman?
Mrs Schneiderman	: *[Laughing nervously]* That's right. Why, every time that darned tiger growls, it scares the daylight out of me. Yasmeen dear—your name is Yasmeen, isn't it? You must be an awfully brave girl to live alone in a place like this. Doesn't it frighten you?
Receptionist	: I am terrified. I came down to talk to the Commissionaire. But he—just look at him.
Mrs Schneiderman	: He's worse than my Alfie. Alfie at least snores to let you know he's there—and alive.

[Commissionaire snores]

He's alive all right. Men are so insensitive. Begging your pardon, Your Highness.

Maharaja	:	Not at all, Mrs Schneiderman. Women are naturally more concerned when the lives of their children and their children's children are in danger.
Mrs Schneiderman	:	Now look at this situation. Here we are in the heart of a thick jungle, zillions of miles away from civilization, we are surrounded by wild beasts thirsting for our blood—the men sleep through, the only two women in the place are the only ones really concerned.
Maharaja	:	More scared than concerned Mrs Schneiderman.
Mrs Schneiderman	:	Put it any way you like. But it does make you think why the world is in such a mess.
Maharaja	:	I do not understand you.
Mrs Schneiderman	:	What I mean is this, if you men were really concerned about the world, you would do something about it. There are these Russians with their bombs floating about space; they could drop them anywhere they liked and kill millions of people.
Maharaja	:	I am told your own people have as many if not more missiles than the Russians.
Mrs Schneiderman	:	Sure we have! We have to, haven't we? We are a responsible people. But there are all these others—Russians and Chinese, English and French—and soon even Canadians and Indians and may be Arabs, *bang, bang*, and the show is over. What do you think men are doing about it? Making more bombs.
Receptionist	:	How right you are, Mrs Schneiderman. It's like getting tiger cubs from a zoo, training them to be killers and letting them loose in the city.

Mrs Schneiderman : Exactly! Like here—man-eater prowling about and look at that man!

[Commissionaire snores . . .]

Maharaja : His peace of mind comes from experience. He knows that a man-eater who has just made a kill will not make another for some days.

Mrs Schneiderman : There's my Alfie, snoring without a care in the world.

Maharaja : Perhaps he hasn't even heard of the man-eater. He doesn't know how close we are to it. When it comes to fears, the ignorant are as well off as the knowledgeable. It's the in-betweens who suffer.

Mrs Schneiderman : Your Highness is a philosopher.

Maharaja : Mrs Schneiderman, please do not address me like that. My name is Vijay—my friends calls me Bijjoo, the badger. I am not a philosopher. All I know is that if I went into the jungle and told this man-eater, 'I am His Highness the Maharaja of Shamnagar, please go away from here,' he would use some four-letter growl and tell me to buzz off. *[Mathur appears at the back]* He might have a little more respect for a real ruler, someone like our director of tourism.

Mathur : What were you saying about me?

Maharaja : We were wondering whether you as representative of the Government of India could go into the jungle and order the man-eater to go away.

Mathur : Maharaja Sahib has a strange sense of humour.

Maharaja	:	That is all that your government has left me with, Mr Mathur.
Mrs Schneiderman	:	Don't tell me, Mr Mathoor, you too are scared?
Mathur	:	Scared? Scared of what? I was working. You see I have so many files to dispose of and so many reports to write. When I am in station I never go to bed before midnight. When I am on tour I always bring work with me. I heard your voices and came down to see if all is well. You see, Mrs Schneiderman, I am responsible for your safety.
Maharaja	:	We are in safe hands, Mrs Schneiderman. As long as we stay in and barricade ourselves in Mr Mathur's hotel, we are assured by him that we will come to no harm. His guarantee does not extend into the realm of danger—the jungle.
Mathur	:	In the morning I'll get the police to organize a hunt for this man-eater. We will deal with the danger in the most appropriate way. We may need the co-operation of all the men—the shikari over there as well as yours, Maharaja Sahib. In your time, you must have killed many tigers.
Maharaja	:	I have never killed one, Mr Mathur, I do not know how they are killed, nor do I intend learning the art of killing. But I am willing to join any party under your command. Perhaps I can be with the beaters and shout *Ho, ho.*
Mathur	:	We'll see, we'll see. I don't suppose that English boy will be any good.
Maharaja	:	He does not look as if he had ever fired anything more powerful than a pop-gun.

Mrs Schneiderman	:	I don't care very much for the hippie types. We've a bunch of them back home; burning draft cards, taking drugs—just running away from every responsibility. What is the world coming to?
Maharaja	:	Chaos. That's what it is coming to, Mrs Schneiderman . . . chaos. If the brave new world is to be peopled with long-haired psychedelics, what can you expect.
Receptionist	:	Sir, Mr Conran-Smith is not a bad man. He only wants to be left alone in peace.
Mrs Schneiderman	:	I don't mean to be harsh, my dear, but this business of wanting to be alone to smoke pot . . .
Maharaja	:	And make love to anyone and everyone he can . . .
Mathur	:	That's very immoral.
Maharaja	:	And very inappropriate in a time like this.
Mrs Schneiderman	:	Doesn't sound very nice, does it? Let's not be too hard on the poor boy. May be he has his own point of view and his own philosophy of life. Well, I am going to turn in and try to get some sleep.
Maharaja	:	Me too. Goodnight.
Mathur	:	I suggest we all get some rest so that we can put the best of ourselves tomorrow. Goodnight.
Maharaja	:	Goodnight everyone. Sleep well.
Receptionist	:	Goodnight, sir, goodnight, Madam. I'll turn down the lights after you have got to your rooms.

[*Exit everyone except Receptionist. She dims the lights, lights a cigarette and fiddles with the tape-recorder. A little rewinding, then Conran-Smith's voice comes over clearly, reciting:*]

Love wakes men once a life-time each
They lift their heavy lids and look
And lo what one sweet page can teach
They read with joy, then shut the book,
And some give thanks and some blaspheme
But most forget. But either way
That and the child's unheeded dream
Is all the joy of all their day.

ACT TWO

(Time: Next morning.
  Scene : Same as before. The Commissionaire and the Receptionist are at their respective places—he sitting on the ground, she making entries in book. The bearer's dusting chairs, tables, emptying ashtrays, etc.)

Commissionaire : What a night that was! I wish I could do in the mother of that bastard tiger. Did you get any sleep, Miss Sahibji?

Receptionist : If you had gone visiting the tiger's mother, I might have had some sleep. Sardool Singh, it was not the roaring of the tiger that kept me awake, it was your snoring. How you could have slept through all the turmoil is beyond me.

Commissionaire : I am an old shikari. I know that a tiger who has made a kill will not hurt anyone else for many days. Not unless someone tries to rob him of his kill or pull his tail. Did you know that, Miss Sahibji?

Receptionist : No, I did not. But knowing it would not have made any difference. It's the thought of a woman lying dead not far from us—and the danger. No one got much sleep except you and that fat old American Sahib.

Commissionaire	: *[After a pause]* Miss Sahibji, that bearded Englishman, the one you said is a little mad, is he an old friend of your family?
Receptionist	: *[Looking up]* No, I told you I met him a few weeks ago when I was working in an airways company. Why do you ask?
Commissionaire	: For no reason at all, Miss Sahibji. He acts as if he had known you a long time.
Receptionist	: I don't know what you mean . . . *[Guests come out from dining-room talking loudly. Commissionaire stands up and salutes]*
Mr Schneiderman	: Never slept better in my life. Gimme the fresh air of the Indian jungle. No horns honking beep, beep . . . no roar of jets going whoosh. The great silence of a primeval forest, and bird-song to rouse me. Boy, it's good to be alive: Allah's in His heaven and all's right with the world. Cigar anyone? First of the day after breakfast tastes best. *[Only Mathur accepts]*
Mrs Schneiderman	: How selfish can you be, Alfie? You are the only one who got any sleep. The rest of us were up most of the night. We were worried to death, weren't we Mr Mathoor?
Mathur	: *[Nodding towards the Commissionaire]* Our guardian angel also slept through. The tiger could have devoured all of us without disturbing his sleep. Miss Ahmed, you must make a formal report of his conduct. For a watchman to sleep is grave dereliction of duty.
Maharaja	: Why not institute a committee of inquiry? Terms of reference, conduct in face of danger. I take it, Mr Mathur, you deported

		yourself as befits a senior official of the Government of India is expected to?
Mathur	:	*[Sharply]* My conduct is not in question, Your Highness. I have to see that no one comes to harm. That is why we employ a watchman.
Maharaja	:	Then you must order the detention of Mr Conran-Smith. He did wilfully and with intent scheme to go out into the jungle at night to do himself mischief. What about that?
Mr Schneiderman	:	*[Imitating British accent]* Did you really, Connie old boy! Whatever for?
Conran-Smith	:	*[Imitating American accent]* Yeah! To see whadda man-eater does to a dead dame.
Mr Schneiderman	:	I'll be damned!
Mathur	:	A very odd subject for investigation, if I may say so, Mr Conran-Smith.
Conran-Smith	:	You may say so, Mr Mathur, you may. We have our own ambitions. You no doubt hope to be the first Mathur to be the secretary of a department. My ambitions are more modest. One is to record the growl of the man-eater. So I can tell the world what he sounds like when he is on the rampage.
Mr Schneiderman	:	I don't doubt your other ambitions are just as crazy.
Conran-Smith	:	Even crazier, Mr Schneiderman. The only other ambition I have is to be the first man to sleep with a woman in an aeroplane.
Maharaja	:	A most laudable and unique ambition! You may however find that with so many planes flying empty, some slick captain or radio engineer or purser or steward may have pulled off the trick with a pliant air-hostess.

You may not be the first atop a woman at 30,000 feet.

Conran-Smith : Then I will be content to take the second or even third place. I may even settle for a grounded air-hostess.

Mrs Schneiderman : I don't approve of this kind of loose talk in front of a young lady; it's not nice.

Receptionist : Please don't let my presence bother you, Mrs Schneiderman. I have had to put up with much worse in mixed company.

Conran-Smith : I do not tailor my talk to suit the sex of my audience.

Maharaja : Freedom for the four-letter word Freedom from cant and humbug.

Mr Schneiderman : I don't know what you fellers are talking about. I want to know what we're gonna do today. If we can't go out into the jungle to see them wild animals, we may as well get back home and see them in a zoo. We've got a big one in Milwaukee.

Mathur : That's not the same thing, Mr Schneiderman. *[Turning to the receptionist]* Miss Ahmed, ring up the police station and ask them if it is safe to go out in the daytime.

Receptionist : Yes, sir. *[Plugs switch-board]*

Mathur : Mr Schneiderman, our ancients have wisely said that most human tears are imaginary, we mistake a rope for a serpent and panic.

Maharaja : Our ancients may have been right, Mr Mathur. But take it from me, if you picked up a serpent by the tail believing it to be a rope, the result may not be very pleasant.

Mr Schneiderman : I never understand anything you Indians say.

Conran-Smith : Mr Schneiderman, Indians have a genius for making simple things sound very complicated. My father who served in India for forty long years used to say that the Indians' mind is like a cork-screw.

Mr Schneiderman : That's not a very nice thing to say—in the middle of India.

Mathur : The British hated India and Indians.

Conran-Smith : Not India, Mr Mathur—and not all Indians either. My father (may his soul rest in peace) used to say, give me the Indian peasant—and you can have the half-baked university babu and the civil servant on his dirty chapatti! As a matter of fact, my father used very strange language, unfit for ladies' ears. He used to describe the educated Indians as 'arrogant little bottom-licking wogs'.

Mrs Schneiderman : Mr Conran-Smith! How absolutely outrageous! How can you . . .

Receptionist : [Interrupting] Excuse me, Madam . . . sir, it's the police station. They say they have no further information of the whereabouts of the man-eater except that he is somewhere in the vicinity of the hotel and if we go out, we will do so on our own responsibility.

Mathur : [Very sharply] Who says so? Tell the inspector I want to speak to him. Tell him who I am.

Receptionist : Yes, sir. [Turns to phone]

Maharaja : Spell it out—Shri A.N. Mathur, Joint Secretary of the Government of India.

Conran-Smith : Go tell it to the tiger. It might impress him.

Receptionist : Sir, the inspector is on leave. They say today is a holiday.

Maharaja	:	How wise! The wisdom of our new rulers never ceases to amaze me. They have devised so many holy days and holidays, and other occasions such as deaths of ministers and other VIPs as reasons for celebration, that now we can have 367 days of the year away from the dull routine of office.
Conran-Smith	:	All work and no play makes Jack a very dull boy. A British legacy most cherished by the Indians. *[Bows to the Maharaja]*
Maharaja	:	*[Returning the bow]* What foresight your honoured parents must have had to give you the name Jack!
Conran-Smith	:	*[Laughing]* Touché.
Mathur	:	This may be a laughing matter to you gentlemen, it is not for me. I have certain responsibilities.
Conran-Smith	:	So have all of us, Mr Mathur. We can't sit in this lobby for ever wasting time in idle gossip—or smoking Mr Schneiderman's Havana cigars. Let us venture forth into the jungle—on our own responsibility, as the policeman said. *[Stands up]*
Mathur	:	It is dangerous, Mr Conran-Smith.
Conran-Smith	:	I know.
Mr Schneiderman	:	You must be crazy.
Conran-Smith	:	All the world's crazy; I am only a little bit crazier.
Mrs Schneiderman	:	That's not a nice thing to say.
Conran-Smith	:	I am not a nice man, Mrs Schneiderman.
Maharaja	:	You are just trying to show off.
Conran-Smith	:	That is also true. *[Puts tape-recorder on shoulder and moves towards exit]* Well, *adios, amigos. [Turning to Mr Schneiderman]* See you later, alligator.

Receptionist : *[Stands in his way]* Don't be silly, Jack.

Conran-Smith : I take it you desire my company.

Receptionist : All right. I desire your company. Be a good boy and sit down.

Conran-Smith : *[Shrugs shoulder and goes back to his chair]* Maybe I'll accept one of your Havana cigars after all.

Maharaja : You do a great favour to the United States, Mr Conran-Smith.

Mr Schneiderman : Yeah. Everyone makes suckers of us Americans. I don't care. I'd rather be a sucker than a lousy sponger. *[Offers Conran-Smith a cigar who examines it, sniffs at it and lights it]*

Conran-Smith : Not bad! Not bad at all.

Maharaja : You've made a convert, Mr Schneiderman. I am sure hereafter Mr Conran-Smith will be an ardent supporter of the American Aid programme.

Conran-Smith : Sure! More and diversified aid. Wheat and rice to the starving Indians; rye, whisky, bourbon and cigars for the well-to-do.

Maharaja : *[Interrupting]* Bubble-gum for their brats.

Mrs Schneiderman : I declare I've never heard so much ungrateful talk in all my life.

Mr Schneiderman : That's okay, honey. Let 'em talk away. That's all some people can do. When somebody whips them they'll come running back to ole Uncle Sam. Like the Indians did when the Chinese took their pants off, when was it?

Mathur : 1962. But, Mr Schneiderman, they stabbed us in the back.

Mr Schneiderman : Somebody is always stabbing somebody else in the back. It's like your man-eating tiger.

Crawl up from behind, crouch, then spring to make the kill.

Mathur : You are right. The price of liberty is eternal vigilance.

Maharaja : A very original thought, Mr Mathur. I believe I read it first in an ancient Sanskrit classic. We understand there is some plan to 'vacate this agression', as it is usually expressed in bureaucratic jargon, without external assistance!

Mathur : *[Angrily]* Every inch of the soil of our motherland is sacred to those who love it.

Conran-Smith : *[Imitating Gujarati accent]* Jai Hind phor that.

[Fade in sounds of drum beating, the clanging of brass cymbals, and people yelling. The group in the foyer listens.]

Mathur : Chowkidar, what is that noise?

[Noise becomes louder]

Commissionaire : Sahib, I think someone has seen the body of the dead woman. The villagers must be going out to recover it.

Maharaja : The moral is, in the event of danger, face it all together.

Conran-Smith : Who is for joining the hunt? *[Gets up, picks up tape-recorder]* What a wonderful recording it will make! The world in arms against the man-eater.

Maharaja : They are not on a tiger hunt; they only want to reclaim the body of the dead woman.

Mr Schneiderman : Or whatever remains of it. Ugh!

Mrs Schneiderman : How horrible! Wouldn't it be wiser to forget

	about it? What's the sense of having half of someone you love? It will haunt the minds of the family for the rest of their days, won't it?
Mr Schneiderman :	Besides, if that old tiger is robbed of its supper, it will soon be looking for someone else to eat, won't it?
Maharaja :	You are right, Mr Schneiderman. It will have to make another kill soon.
Conran-Smith :	Perhaps one of us may have to provide him his tiffin. That'll be jolly, won't it?
Mathur :	I do not like this at all. Miss Ahmed, do try and get the police inspector on the phone.
Receptionist :	I'll try, sir, but . . .
Maharaja :	I am sure he has taken his family to see some film with a highly religious, moral theme. Try the cinemas in the town. Relax everyone. We have been told it is a holiday. Even the tiger respects government orders: he made the kill on a working day. If you disturb him on a holiday, his temper may be worse than that of a government official on a Sunday afternoon.
Mathur :	For people like you and Mr Conran-Smith, nothing is right with this country. That is because neither your kind, the princes, nor his, the British, count for a copper naya paisa. Thank god for that.
Conran-Smith :	Amen.
Maharaja :	*Ameen*—that's the same in this part of the world.
Mr Schneiderman :	Really, what kind of people are you? Here we are in a booby trap and all you can do is

talk, talk and more talk. You Indians must
be the biggest gas-bags in the world.

Maharaja : How right you are, Mr Schneiderman. Didn't
you know that humbug is our biggest earner
of foreign exchange? And the Americans are
our best customers.

Mr Schneiderman : I don't buy any of your spiritual poppy-
cock nor your yogi's meditations. You ask
foreigners to visit your country so you can
get their money. You put them in a goddamn
fox-hole in a goddamn jungle and yak, yak,
yak.

Mrs Schneiderman : Why, Alfie! What's the matter with you,
honey? Did you clear your stomach this
morning? Lemme see your tongue.

Mr Schneiderman : O shut up! You make me sick. I'll say what
I like. I am a free citizen of a free country.
Why, if this was in the United States I
would simply have to buzz for the police or
the fire brigade and they would settle this
man-eater's wagon in a jiffy—bang, bang,
bang—and leave me his skin to make a nice
rug.

Maharaja : Exactly as they are doing in Vietnam. Bang,
bang, and more bang. But no dead man-
eater, no tiger skin for a nice rug.

Mr Schneiderman : There you go again! More cunning yak yak.
Why don't you Indians do something about
those darned Commies? If they win, you're
next on their list. But all you can do is to
criticize those who try to do the job for
you.

Conran-Smith : How right you are. Didn't you know the
Indians' genius to get other people to do
their work? [*In sing-song*]

'Pick up the white man's burden. Send forth the best ye breed.'

A bard of the name of Kipling wrote that for his Empire-building compatriots. But now we've had our run we pass the baton to you. We hand over the care of 'the lesser breeds without the law'. Black, brown and yellow, they are all yours. Save them from each other and from other man-eaters. Of course, in the process you may have to eat them up yourself.

Mr Schneiderman : I don't go with this kind of clever anti-American talk. As Babette said, it's not nice.

Conran-Smith : As I have already admitted, I am not a nice man.

Maharaja : I am sure most people would agree with your opinion of yourself.

[Sounds of yelling, drums, cymbals. Roar of tiger retreating. Wailing of women.]

Mathur : Chowkidar, what are they wailing about?

Commissionaire : Sahib, it is very bad. They must have found the woman's corpse.

Mathur : Why is it very bad?

Commissionaire : Well, Sahib, it is simple commonsense. If the tiger is still hungry, it must kill someone else for its food.

ACT THREE
SCENE 1

(Time: Afternoon of second day.
  Scene: Same as in Acts I and II.

The trellis gate is drawn. When the curtain rises only the Receptionist is at her desk. Conran-Smith comes into the foyer.)

Conran-Smith : I cannot believe my eyes: a lonely, luscious bait for the ravenously hungry British lion. Not even the hirsute huntsman with his antique bundook on his lowly machan.

Receptionist : Sardool Singh has gone to the village to see if he can get beaters. He thinks they will help flush out the tiger and he may get a pot-shot at the beast.

Conran-Smith : With that Mutiny model blunderbuss! He must be an ass.

Receptionist : You know what these Sikhs are! Once they get a notion in their heads it is impossible to get it out.

Conran-Smith : I bet he'd rather face the man-eater than his brown Burra Sahib.

Receptionist : Give it to him, he is doing his bit, which is more than can be said of the others—not excluding present company.

Conran-Smith : What do you expect us to do? Offer ourselves as sacrifice to the tiger of Goddess Durga? You sound like the Roman pagans amusing themselves watching wild beasts devour Christians. I am not a Christian. I regret I cannot provide you with the same ghoulish pleasure. I have much to live for: amongst other things, you

Receptionist : All of us have someone or something to justify our desire for immortality.

Conran-Smith : What change of heart the mere passage of three watches wrings! Only yesternight when I sought to venture forth into the jaws of the man-eater, the figure of an angel barred my way. 'This is the angel of life,' I cried. 'She bids me live and love.' The same figure now orders me to my doom. It must be the angel of death. So be it.

Receptionist : Shut up! I do not mean anything of the sort—and you know it. All I ask is, 'Here we are in this mess. What is anyone doing about it?' Only an illiterate, retired sepoy has had the nerve to try. Neither Schniederman nor the Maharaja, nor Mathur nor indeed Shri Jack Conran-Smith.

Conran-Smith : What an indictment! Anyhow, where is everyone?

Receptionist : Mathur was sitting here a moment ago. When the Schneidermans asked for soda and ice to be sent to their room, he went back to his.

[Taps bell]

Conran-Smith : No Americans, no free Scotch or bourbon for the tired Indian civilian . . . what?

[Bearer appears]

Receptionist : Ice and two bottles of soda in the Burra Sahib's room. *[Bearer nods and goes back]* He will have to do with his own Indian whisky. Poor man.

Conran-Smith : Bloody awful stuff. I'd rather drink water from the holy Ganga and get dysentery than drink Indian whisky and get a hangover.

Receptionist :· Scratch a Britisher and you'll find an India-hater. Some of our stuff is as good as any in the world—all it needs is time to mature. I am sure in a few years people won't be able to tell our whisky from the best produce of Scotland.

Conran-Smith : Jai Hind phor that! Scratch an Indian and you'll find a patriotic tub-thumper. You almost sound like your boss. *[Imitating Mathur's voice and accent]* 'In the fifth Five Year Plan we propose to put up a distillery to produce instantly matured whisky. Purely for export,-mind you. Drinking is against our national tradition.'

[Bearer passes through with tray bearing ice and soda]

Conran-Smith : Bearer, one moment please. *[Conran-Smith puts 'Dry Day' sign on the tray]* Tell the Burra Sahib this is with the compliments of the 'Father of the Nation'.

Receptionist : No, no, bearer. Put the notice back in its place. *[Bearer obeys]* You want to have me sacked? I do not think Mr Mathur suffers from an acute sense of humour.

Conran-Smith : A very British understatement. Bearer, tell the Burra Sahib that the American Sahib and his wife would like him to join them for a drink in their room. *[Turning to Receptionist]* I hate to see a civil servant go thirsty. That should also keep them out of the way for a while. And, Bearer, take a glass of mango juice for the Maharaja. I'll sign for it. *[Bearer nods and returns to get juice]* We can have a few moments to ourselves.

Receptionist : The great messiah of love can't stand many people, can he?

Conran-Smith : I hate people who hate people like me.

Receptionist : Most people hate those who hate them. You are no different.

Conran-Smith	:	Hate is too strong a word; I don't really hate anyone. I simply cannot suffer some kinds: bores like the Schneidermans, smart alecs like the Maharaja, pipsqueaks like Mathur. I do not object in the slightest to the Yasmeen Ahmeds of the world.
Receptionist	:	*[Bowing]* How very, very generous of you, Mr Conran-Smith.
Conran-Smith	:	*[Bowing, hi haw-haw accent]* Not at all m'deah! Besides, wanting to be alone with someone you love does not mean you hate others. *[Pause in dialogue. Conran-Smith lights his pipe]*
Receptionist	:	Jack, that poem you put on tape—you know the one I mean? Something about love waking men once a lifetime each?
Conran-Smith	:	Oh yeah—I don't remember who wrote it.
Receptionist	:	It's lovely, but not really true, is it?
Conran-Smith	:	Of course not! Love wakes men many times in their sordid lives. They fall in and out of love all the time.
Receptionist	:	*[Sighing]* I thought so. I wonder if the poet had in mind some other kind of love.
Conran-Smith	:	What do you mean 'some other kind of love'?
Receptionist	:	I don't know, except that he could not have been writing of the love of a man for a woman. Maybe he was thinking of an all-consuming passion. Some other-worldly love which gives life a fresh orientation, without which living on would be living without meaning or purpose.
Conran-Smith	:	Fiddle-sticks!
Receptionist	:	I beg your pardon!

Conran-Smith   : Fiddle-sticks, tommy-rot and poppy-cock—all signifying the same thing. Something which adds up to nothing.

[Sounds of villagers jabbering. Sardool Singh's voice asks them to wait and keep quiet.]

Conran-Smith   : Here comes the hairy re-incarnation of Vishnu, the Preserver. Please enquire of him in a language he understands what steps have been taken to ensure the continuance of our earthly existence against the devilish machinations of the man-eater.

Receptionist   : Sardool Singh, did you have any luck with the villagers?

Commissionaire   : *[Wagging his head]* No, Miss Sahibji, they are an ignorant lot. Would you believe that when they went to recover the body of the woman one of them shot an arrow into the tiger. You know what a wounded tiger is like, don't you! Now they are huddled together in the panchayat ghar. They have lit fires all around and are beating drums and yelling to keep away the tiger. When I finally got the ear of the elders, they abused me and everyone else they could think of. They will not act as beaters for me alone: I am like one of them. You know what they say? They say we have sacrificed one life. It is the turn of the big Sahibs in the hotel. What do you say to that, Miss Sahibji?

[Lights begin to dim to create effect of twilight]

Receptionist	:	Surely, Sardool Singh, they don't really mean that! This sacrifice business sounds quite silly to me.
Commissionaire	:	Of course, Miss Sahib, they exaggerate. What they really mean is that the Sahibs in the hotel must help them. That is why they have come with me.
Conran-Smith	:	My Hindustani is not very good, but am I correct in understanding that the villagers want one of us to go and kill the wounded man-eater?
Receptionist	:	That is the general idea. They are willing to do their bit if the big Sahibs can lead them.
Conran-Smith	:	Preposterous nonsense!
Receptionist	:	[After a pause] Well, Jack, shall we tell them to go back to their houses and fend for themselves?
Conran-Smith	:	Why don't we put it to the little Lok Sabha of Hotel Wild Life?
Receptionist	:	Sardool Singh, ask the villagers to wait till the Sahibs have had time to discuss the matter.
Commissionaire	:	*Bahut accha*, Miss Sahib.

[*Fade in sounds of jungle, with bellowing of tiger first at a distance, getting nearer with each roar.*]

ACT THREE
SCENE II

(*Time: Same night after dinner.*

Scene: Same as before. The oil lamps are lit. In one corner near the Commissionaire's seat, four villagers are huddled up beside him. The Receptionist is at her desk.

*Sounds: Jungle noises and sounds of drums, yelling, etc. to be kept in
background throughout.*
*Guests emerge from the dining-room, led by Mathur and Schneiderman,
both smoking cigars. Schneiderman has a bottle of cognac in his hand.
They pause before coming to the foyer.)*

Mathur : Mr Schneiderman, you should read the
Gita—I think, everyone should read the Gita.
It is the philosophy of *Nishkama Karma.*

Mr Schneiderman : The philosophy of what?
[Conran-Smith joins them]

Mathur : Nishkama Karma—it implies that a man's
duty is to put in his best effort without
seeking the fruits of his labours.

Conran-Smith : Sounds like some kind of birth control
device—do all you can without worrying
about the results.

Mr Schneiderman : That's a dumb thing to say when somebody's
talking of his holy book! Don't you have
any respect for any religion?

Conran-Smith : Nope, not one. But I didn't mean to
hurt your feelings, Mr Mathur. Please tell
Mr Schneiderman what the Gita says.

Mathur : Mr Conran-Smith, you mock at everything.
You should read the Gita, it may change
your views on life.

Conran-Smith : I have no desire to change my views on life.
A man has but one. I believe in living that
life to the full—and no matter what any
prophet, messiah, redeemer or guru or holy
book of any religion says to the contrary I
will stick to my views.

Mathur : Certainly man lives but one life—also
man dies but once. The Gita tells us how
we should die in the performance of our
duties.

[Others come out of the dining-room]

Mr Schneiderman : I can't get on with this high falutin' talk. Let's have some coffee and cognac. Miss Ahmed, could you ask the bearer to get us brandy glasses when he brings in the coffee?

Receptionist : Certainly, sir. *[Taps bell]*

Mathur : *[Seeing the villagers who stand up and salaam]* Chowkidar, who are these people? What business have they in the hotel?

Receptionist : *[Intervening]* Sir, they are from Badi where the woman was killed. They have come for help. They are frightened so I let them sit inside the trellis gate till you had spoken to them.

Mathur : What am I supposed to do? Go and kill the tiger with my bare hands?

Maharaja : I thought I heard somebody say 'man dies but once' and how we should die in the performance of our duty, it would seem as if some people's only role in life was to preach sermons.

Mathur : It would seem as if some person's only role in life is to be sarcastic about everyone else.

Mrs Schneiderman: Now, now, now. I wish you men would stop sniping at each other.
[Bearer brings in tray of coffee and brandy glasses]

Mrs Schneiderman: Let's have coffee in peace. Yasmeen dear, you mind serving it? I don't feel up to it.

Receptionist : Certainly, Madam. I hope you are feeling well.

Mrs Schneiderman: I am all right—really. Just a little tired. Nerves, you know. All this talk about man-eaters and death. And of course I haven't slept a wink for the last twenty-four hours. I don't suppose anyone except my Alfie has had any sleep.

Mr Schneiderman : *[Holding up bottle of brandy]* Cognac anyone?

Mathur : It is very good brandy. You must be a connosheear.

Mr Schneiderman : A what?

Maharaja : Mr Mathur means connoisseur.

Mr Schneiderman : I don't know what that means, but I do know a good brandy from a bad one. *[Pours it for Mathur]* Maharaja, won't you change your mind? It's good stuff.

Maharaja : I might try a little. Thank you, Mr Schneiderman. *[Holds up his glass]*

Mr Schneiderman : You, Mr Smith?

Conran-Smith : I could do with a man-size dollop tonight.

Mr Schneiderman : *[Pouring it for Conran-Smith]* After the rude things you've been saying, I hope you get properly pickled. I am forgetting my manners. Pardon me ladies, can I tempt you with the grape? A few drops won't do you any harm.

Mrs Schneiderman : I could do with some. Yasmeen, do keep us company.

Receptionist : Thank you very much, Mrs Schneiderman. Only a very, very, tiny drop.

Mr Schneiderman : *[Pours brandy for everyone; then raises his glass]* I don't know what we are celebrating but I guess we are in a mood to get drunk. Here's to everyone. *[All except Conran-Smith raise their glasses]*

Conran-Smith : I can tell you why we are in a mood to get drunk. We are in a bloody funk.

Mr Schneiderman : A bloody what?

Conran-Smith : Funk. Don't you know what it means to be in a blue funk. We are plain scared.

Mr Schneiderman : *[Imitating British accent]* Speak for yourself, Smithy ole boy!

Conran-Smith : *[Irritated]* Don't you ole boy me. I am scared and I admit it. Otherwise I would not be drinking this foul brew of festering grape. Here's to the man-eater. *[Gulp down his drink and helps himself to another]*

Maharaja : There's an example of gratitude for you! I have been given to understand that the British were a phlegmatic race; courteous and cool in times of crisis, nerves of steel and what have you.

Mathur : There is nothing to be scared of. We are perfectly safe in the hotel. If you keep your doors and windows shut you won't even hear sounds from the jungle.

Conran-Smith : Nor the wailing from the village. We could shut out the world and drink ourselves silly—but the stupid world intrudes into our haven of refuge. What do we say to these villagers?

Mr Schneiderman : I dunno. It's not our country so I guess it's none of our business. We are visitors, you know! *[Pointing to the Nehru poster and reading loudly]* 'Foreign visitors are our honoured guests.' You don't expect guests to pick your chestnuts out of the fire, do you?

Conran-Smith : That would go for me too; erstwhile ruler, now a not-so-honoured guest. I don't think these villagers would understand why being American or British would free us of the obligation to help them. Of course they might expect a little more understanding and sympathy from their own countrymen.

[Mr Schneiderman pours himself a brandy, then holds it up to ask the others. In turn they all accept. They drink and smoke in silence for about a minute]

Mr Schneiderman : Well!

Conran-Smith : Well what?

Mr Schneiderman : Isn't somebody going to do something to help these people? Mr Government of India . . .

Mathur : What can I or any government do in this situation? We are perfectly safe in the hotel; the villagers are looking after their safety as best as they can. Tomorrow I will send for the armed police to restore confidence in these peoples' mind. There is no need for anyone to do anything immediately.

Maharaja : Also remember it's a gazetted holiday. That goes for the armed police as well as the joint secretary; only death takes no holiday.

Mathur : *[Angrily]* You have done nothing except criticize the government and poke fun at me. Don't you have any responsibilities any more? After all, all that you and your class have ever done in your lives is to drink and womanize and kill tigers. Why don't you go out and shoot another one and add to your collection of tiger skins?

Maharaja : There is no reason to lose your temper, Mr Mathur. I do not deny that the princely order acquired certain standards of excellence in the art of drinking, associating with women and destroying dangerous animals— but as I have already told you I disinherited myself from my legacy. I do not drink except under a strain; for reasons of health I do not fornicate; and I am so peace-loving that I refuse to shoot any living thing even with a camera. Surely, this is your domain. You are the officer-in-charge. This hotel is in your parish. Our lives and safety and those of the villagers are your responsibility.

Conran-Smith : This in common English parlance is known as passing the buck.

Maharaja : An art which your people have mastered to perfection. And you, Mr Conran-Smith, have surely inherited the trait in full measure. None of the ills that beset the common run of mankind disturb your pipe-dreams of flowers and love. You should be the last one to accuse people of passing the buck.

Mr Schneiderman : Gentlemen, gentlemen. Let's keep our tempers under control—and our heads on our shoulders. [Pours cognac in glasses] Let's drink to peace, goodwill and understanding. [All except Conran-Smith raise their glasses and drink]

Conran-Smith : You got them in the wrong order—first understanding, then goodwill and finally peace. [Pours cognac into glasses] Another toast to get the sequence right.

All : To understanding, goodwill and peace.

Conran-Smith : Hallelujah.

Mathur : What?

Conran-Smith : Hallelujah means praise be to god.

Mathur	:	I did not think you believed in god.
Conran-Smith	:	I do not. I just like the sound of the word. Nice mouthful like Mesopotamia or Chatanooga or Saskatoon or Marwar Mandooa. My favourite Indian word is the name for the monkey god, Veer Bajrang Bali. Here's to him.
All	:	To Veer Bajrang Bali.
Maharaja	:	In case you do not know. Veer Bajrang is our counter-part of your superman. He flew with a whole mountain on his shoulders so he could get a life-saving herb to Rama and Lakshman.
Mr Schneiderman	:	Sounds like a good guy. Let's drink another one to him—whatever his name is *[Pours cognac in glasses]*
All	:	Veer Bajrang Bali.
Mrs Schneiderman	:	I am afraid all of us have had too much to drink. And I guess no one is anxious to be alone in their room. Why don't we just relax here and keep each other company?
Conran-Smith	:	A jolly good idea. Maybe Miss Ahmed can get some nice sitar music on her radio. *[Men arrange chairs to stretch legs, Receptionist fiddles with transistor]*
Maharaja	:	If the music fails, Mr Mathur can tell us of the Five Year Plans—that will surely lull us to sleep. *[All laugh—a little drunk]*

[Receptionist finds station with sitar music and places transistor on the table.]

Receptionist	:	There. Lovely psychedelic music. What do we say to the villagers?

Mathur   : Nothing. They can wait. In any case they are sound asleep.

[*Receptionist lowers the light of the lamps and finds herself an easy chair. Guests drop off to sleep one by one. The jungle sounds are more distinct. Maintain scene for a minute or more. Conran-Smith gets up, makes sure everyone is asleep. He tiptoes towards the Commissionaire, slowly extricates the gun out of his grasp and goes out of the trellis gate. After another minute, the roar of the tiger becomes louder and closer. Guests begin to wake in alarm and look around. There is a loud roar as when a tiger springs to attack, and then the report of a gun.*]

JOKES

WHAT'S SO FUNNY?

Making up jokes is no laughing matter. It is a serious business requiring knowledge, insight and experience of what will make people laugh, what will go flat and fizzle out like a damp squib. First, we have to find out why people laugh. For some, the sight of a person with a big nose, a harelip or a stutter, a pot belly or a game leg is enough to set them laughing. Others want more action, like somebody slipping over a banana skin, to have the same reaction. One does not need to have a sense of humour to laugh at these. On the contrary, it betrays a total lack of it.

There are many things that make different people laugh. But trying to analyse laughter is like dissecting a frog. You may see its entrails and whatever else it has inside, but you will kill the frog in the process. You should just accept laughter as a phenomenon that releases tension and makes you feel lighter and happier. People of different ages react differently to different situations. A child will laugh when somebody stumbles down the stairs. A grown-up will feel sorry for the same man because he has been through a similar experience. Even among grown-ups, the stimuli for raising a laugh differ from nation to nation. Although Europeans have a corpus of ethnic jokes about Jews, Scotsmen, Irishmen and Poles, they regard them as bad form. On the other hand, many of our jokes are aimed at certain communities. We make fun of Marwaris, Banias, Bawajis (Parsees), Mianbhais and Sardarjis. All of them are based largely on ethnic stereotypes which have no factual basis. Europeans indulge in black humour making jokes about death and funerals; we in India consider them in bad taste.

However, we share the same interest in making jokes about our mothers-in-law and our wives. The wife's brother, saala, as the butt of humour is an Indian speciality.

There is a fund of humour in all of us. The more it is sought to be suppressed the more it manifests itself. You forbid a person to laugh and he will laugh all the louder. Thus jokes about Hitler, Stalin, fascism and communism flourished in Russia and Germany. When General Zia-ul Haq imposed military dictatorship on Pakistan, he became the object of ridicule in his country. It was the same in India during the Emergency regime. Indira Gandhi became a target of humour when she suppressed the freedom of speech.

Getting a laugh out of other people is easier than being able to laugh at oneself. Only people with self-confidence can afford to laugh at their foibles. At one time (before 'Operation Blue Star') Sikhs rightly boasted of manufacturing the best of Sardarji jokes. Since then they have developed chips on their shoulders and take offence at jokes aimed at them. Nevertheless Sardarji jokes continue to flourish. Another community which excels in making jokes about itself and continues to do so are the Parsees. There is a sizeable collection of Bawaji jokes but they need to be related in Parsee Gujarati. I do not know of any other Indian community which has the self-confidence to poke fun at itself.

Not many people are aware that India has a long tradition of humour right from the times of Kalidas and other Sanskrit writers. Every generation has produced great humorists like Birbal, Tenali Raman and Gopal Bhat. Our *bhands* kept this tradition alive throughout the ages.

I have my own targets to aim at. Besides the powerful and the self-opinionated, I find name-droppers extremely ludicrous. There is hardly an Indian who does not indulge in self-praise and not-so-subtle name-dropping. These diseases afflict our politicians who are forever dropping hints about their closeness to the Prime Minister, chief ministers and the people in seats of authority. In addition, our politicians are also sanctimonious humbugs proclaiming their sacrifices for the country and dedication to social service. It is not very difficult to deflate their self-esteem with a carefully aimed pinprick. Self-praise I regard as a form of vulgarity which is found commonly among my countrymen. They will invariably preface it by words like 'although I am saying it myself, out . . .'

The common man's humour is of a lower order than the humour of a man of sophistication. The educated aesthete will respond to literary allusions, puns and jokes about poets, authors, composers and painters. They will mean nothing to the hoi polloi, Our film-going public enjoys jokes of the broadest type. A simple reference to a wife as the home minister will bring peals of laughter in an Indian audience. Any situation where a head-strong woman is humbled makes them rear. Our people have to be educated to understand and enjoy subtle humour.

The most sophisticated journals on humour are *Punch* and the *New Yorker.* They are not merely comic, but have highly sophisticated forms of wit, irony, sarcasm which tickle one's fantasy. At times their cartoons are so subtle that it takes a long time pondering over them to catch what they are meant to convey.

There are not many jokes in print that will make you explode with laughter. The best that the print can hope to produce is a wistful smile. For explosions of laughter you have to have them told orally by a practitioner of the art of joke-telling. Fortunately they are to be found in every establishment and at every cocktail party. I am often asked to tell my favourite joke. I don't have a top favourite but over a dozen which improve with each telling. Unfortunately most of my favourites are unprintable because they are dirty and sex-based.

Nevertheless, here are some from my collection, which my grand-daughter, Naina, has helped me choose.

Delhi   *Khushwant Singh*

HEARD THIS ONE?

An American delegation on a visit to India were being shown round the capital. In the evening they were taken to the Secretariat for a panaromic view of Vijay Chowk and Rajpath. Came the closing hour and thousands of clerks poured out of their offices. The place was crammed with bicycles and pedestrians.

'Who are all these people?' asked the leader of the American delegation.

'They are the common people of India; the real rulers of the country,' proudly replied the minister accompanying the visitors.

A few minutes later came a fleet of flag-bearing limousines escorted by pilots on motorcycles followed by jeeps full of armed policemen. 'And who are these?' asked the American.

'These are us,' replied the minister with the same pride, 'the servants of the people.'

Kakey da Hotel is a very popular eating-place in Connaught Circus. It started off as a humble Kakey da Dhaaba with stools and charpoys laid out on the pavement and, the tandoor, *handees* and *pateelas* placed in the open. With prosperity the kitchen went into the rear and a dining-room was furnished with tables, chairs as well as wash basin. One evening, a patron having finished his meal went to rinse his mouth in the wash basin. He proceeded to do so with great vigour; gargling, spitting *thooh thooh* and blowing his nose. This ruined the appetites of other diners who protested to the proprietor. Kakaji went to the rinser–spitter and admonished him. 'Haven't you ever eaten in a good hotel before?' he demanded.

'Indeed, I have,' replied the errant mouth-rinser, 'I have eaten at the Taj, Maurya, Oberoi, Imperial, Hyatt.'

'What did they say to you when you rinsed your mouth making all these unpleasant sounds?'

'They asked: "You think this is Kakey da Hotel?" And threw me out.'

A rich lady had a family of four children, all of whom turned out to be very bright. She was always boasting of their records at school and was sure when they grew up they would bring credit to India. I asked her somewhat sarcastically if she had ever heard of the family planning slogan *hum do hamaarey do.* 'Yes,' she replied somewhat haughtily, 'that is for the *aira ghaira*—hoi poiloi—not for people like us who have highly intelligent children and can afford to give them the best of education.'

'In that case why don't you have five more and give India another *nau ratans*—nine gems?'

She ignored my sarcasm and replied: 'I have just read a book on population statistics. It says that every fifth child born in the world is a Chinese.'

Nurul Alam from Silchar sends me a few lovely samples of bureaucratic wit of the days of the British Raj. One is an entry made by an executive engineer in the visitors' book of a circuit house:

'The veranda of the circuit house badly needs railings. During my momentary absence, a cow ate up some estimates which I had left lying on a table in the veranda.' Below this note was the commissioner's observation: 'I find it hard to believe that even cows could swallow PWD estimates.'

In another circuit house book another executive engineer had noted: 'The washbasin should be immediately replaced. I could not wash my face properly for want of proper facilities.' Against this entry is a marginal note in the commissioner's beautiful hand: 'SDO will replace the washbasin at once. The executive engineer had to wash his face in tears during his last visit to this station.'

The prize remark is against a complaint that the latrine was too far away from the bungalow. 'He should have started earlier,' wrote the wit.

All these are attributed to one Mr Bentinck.

Two men met in heaven. 'What did you die of?' asked one.

'I died of extreme cold. And what about you?'

'I came home from work and thought I heard my wife talking to a stranger. On entering the house, I searched every nook and corner but could not find anyone anywhere. I felt so guilty of my suspicion that my heart failed.'

Hearing this, the other one said, 'Had you cared to open the fridge, neither of us would have died.'

A gentleman travelled all the way from Islamabad to Karachi to have an aching tooth taken out. The Karachi dentist said, 'Surely you have dentists in Islamabad! You did not have to come all the way to have your tooth attended to.'

'We have no choice. In Islamabad we are not allowed to open out mouths,' replied the man with the aching tooth.

A party of American pressmen were granted an interview with Chairman Mao Zedong. After having heard the denunciation of the Soviet Union and other imperialist powers, one of the party asked the Chairman: 'Sir, what in your opinion would have happened if, instead of John F. Kennedy, Mr Khrushchev had been assassinated?'

Chairman Mao pondered over the question for a while before he replied, 'I doubt very much if Aristotle Onassis would have married Mrs Khrushchev.'

Duleepsinhji was playing in a test match for England against Australia. An English spectator turned to an Australian sitting next to him and asked: 'Have you any princes in your team?' The Aussie admitted they had none. 'We have had many,' boasted the Englishman. 'Now take this fellow Duleep! As blue-blooded as any aristocrat in the world. And a damn fine cricketer too!' Just then Duleep hit a sixer. 'See what I mean?' exploded the Englishman. The next ball knocked Duleep's centre wicket. The Englishman yelled: 'He's out! The bloody nigger!'

You have to be a master of words to mix flattery with satire. Our ancestors knew the art better than we. Badauni in his *Mantakhab* records some incidents when recipients of rewards were able to combine their disappointment with the gift with flattery for the emperor in the hope of receiving more.

One was the poet Anwari who was presented with an old horse which gave up the ghost on the very night it had been delivered at Anwari's home. Next morning the poet came to court on foot. 'What happened to the horse we presented you yesterday?' asked the emperor.

Replied the poet: 'It was so fleet-footed that in one night it traversed the distance from the earth to heaven.'

No Offence Meant!

Two terrorists were driving their Maruti to the spot where they intended to place their bomb. The one in the driver's seat looked very worried. 'Natha, what happens if the bomb we have on the back seat blows up before we get to the site?'

'Not to worry,' replied Natha, 'I have a spare one in my attache case.'

When tenders were floated for the Channel Tunnel to connect England and France, many international building companies vied with one another to get the contract. The stakes were very high; the job of digging beneath the sea required great engineering skill and building expertise. Tenders were opened by the board of directors of the Anglo-French Corporation which had taken on the project. British builders' estimates were over 200 million dollars each; French and German builders' were marginally lower. There was one from India: Singh & Singh Builders whose estimate was only five million dollars. The board was for ignoring the Indian tender but out of curiosity invited Singh & Singh over to discuss the plans.

Banta Singh and Santa Singh of Singh & Singh Builders appeared before the board. The chairman asked them, 'Have you any experience of undertaking this kind of work?'

'Indeed we have,' replied the two Singhs. 'We bored a lot of tube wells in the Punjab and Haryana. We can bore holes anywhere.'

'This is not as simple. How will you connect the tunnel from the English side to the French?'

'Simple,' replied Santa Singh, 'Banta Singh will dig from the French end and I from the English.'

The chairman was flabbergasted. 'You don't realize that it will need a lot of accurate calculation to get the two tunnels to meet at the same point under the channel. Other companies' estimates are over 200 million dollars each and you think you can do the same job for five million dollars. How will that be possible?'

'What is bothering you?' demanded Singh & Singh. 'If our two tunnels don't meet, instead of one we will give you two tunnels.'

Contributed by Prem Khanna, Noida

Santa Singh and Banta Singh were always boasting of their parents' achievement to each other.

Santa Singh: 'Have you heard of the Suez Canal?'

Banta Singh: 'Yes, I have.'

Santa Singh: 'Well, my father dug it.'

Banta Singh: 'That's nothing. Have you heard of the Dead Sea?'

Santa Singh: 'Yes, I have.'

Banta Singh: 'Well, my father killed it.'

This I picked up in the Central Hall of Parliament. Apparently President Zail Singh was operated on in the same Texan hospital as his predecessor Sanjiva Reddy. When taken to the operating theatre, the chief surgeon asked our Rashtrapati, 'Are you ready?'

'No I am not Reddy,' replied Gyaniji, 'I am Zail Singh.'

A patriotic Sardarji saw the Indian tricolour fluttering in the breeze. He stood at attention and saluted. 'Why did you salute that flag?'

asked a passer-by. 'It has saffron for the Hindus, green for the Muslims and white for all the others. Nothing for the Sikhs.'

Prompt came the Sardarji's reply: 'And what do you think the danda on which the flag flutters represents? Only the Sikhs.'

A Hindu, a Muslim and a Sikh were discussing the marvellous achievements of their own brands of surgery. Said the Hindu, 'I know of a vaidji who joined a severed arm with the use of Ayurvedic glue. You can't even tell where the arm had been cut.' Not to be outdone, the Muslim spoke: 'A hakeem sahib has evolved a new kind of adhesive ointment. He used it on a fellow who had his head cut off. You can't tell where the neck was severed.' It was the Sardarji's turn to extol the latest developments in Sikh surgery. 'We have gone much further,' said the Sardarji thumping his chest proudly. There was this chacha of mine who was cut into two round his navel. Our Sikh surgeon immediately slaughtered a goat and joined its rear half to Chacha's upper half. So now we have our Chacha as well as two litres of milk every day.'

Actor–wrestler Dara Singh, taking a stroll along Juhu beach, was set upon by a dozen urchins who after beating him black and blue took away his purse which, fortunately for him, contained very little money. Dara who had floored the world's best wrestlers put up no resistance. When he arrived home with two black eyes, puffed cheeks and a torn shirt, his Sardarni asked him in great alarm what had happened. Dara Singh told her all. 'And why didn't you hit back? Surely you could have knocked the hell out of these skinny fellows!'

'Sure!' replied the Sardar. 'But my fee for flooring champions is Rs 25,000. I don't fight for free.'

Contributed by Wazir Chand Didi, Chandigarh

Banta Singh happened to be in a queue at a railway station ticket counter with a man ahead of him.

'*Ek* Punjab Mail *dena* (Give me one for the Punjab Mail),' demanded the man in front. He was given a ticket.

Then came the turn of Banta Singh, '*Ikk* Punjab female dena.'

'What do you mean by Punjab female?' asked the clerk.

'It is for my wife,' replied Banta Singh.

Contributed by J.P. Singh Kaka, New Delhi

Two Sardarjis, both students of IIT, Kanpur, were talking about the American astronauts. One said to the other, 'What's the big deal about going to the moon—anybody can go to the moon. We are Sikhs—we'll go direct to the sun.'

'But if we get within thirteen million miles of the sun, we'll melt.'

The first answered, 'So what, we'll go at night.'

Contributed by Judson K. Cornelius, Hyderabad

Banta Singh: 'Er, is that Air India office? Can you tell me how long it takes to fly from Delhi to Bombay?'

Booking clerk: 'Just a minute, sir . . .'

Banta: 'Okay. Thanks a lot.' And he hangs up.

Contributed by Kamal Sharma, Mukerian

A Sardarji and a Bengali were travelling in the same railway compartment. It was very hot and the Bengali was having trouble undoing the steel strap of his wrist-watch. The Sardar went across and with one mighty jerk undid the buckle. 'You Bengalis should eat *gehoon* (wheat). It makes you strong.'

The Bengali did not appreciate the advice. A few minutes later he grasped the alarm-chain and pretended to be unable to pull it. Once again the Sardarji leapt to his assistance and pulled down the chain with a triumphant yell: 'There! You Bengalis should eat . . .'

The train came to a halt. The conductor accompanied by a couple of policemen asked the Sardarji to explain why he had pulled the chain, and on his failure to do so, fined him fifty rupees.

After they had left, the Bengali gently advised the Sardarji, 'You Punjabis should eat rice. It is better for the brain.'

An elderly Punjabi admitted to the intensive care department of a hospital made a request that he should be allowed to take lessons in Urdu. The doctor in charge was very puzzled and asked him the reason why. 'Urdu is the language of angels,' replied the Punjabi. 'If I die I want to be able to converse with all the houris I will meet in paradise.'

'How can you be sure you will go to heaven?' asked the doctor. 'You may go down to hell, then what good will Urdu, which you call the language of angels, be to you?'

'That will be no problem. I am fluent in Punjabi.'

Gorkhas are famous for the discipline they observe in the army and the respect with which they treat their officers. Once there was a fire in a highrise building occupied by the army. No sooner had they heard the alarm, a batch of Gorkha jawans ran out with a heavy net to rescue those who jumped down from the upper storeys. Some clerks came down and were saved. Then their commanding officer leapt from the top floor. The soldiers saw him hurtling down. They dropped the net, sprang to attention and saluted. The colonel was not as lucky as the clerks.

Contributed by M.L. Batra, Karnal

A Haryana Jat, who had been irritated by his failure to answer any of the riddles put to him by a clever Bania, said angrily: 'All right, now you answer this riddle: What is hung on a wall, is red, drips and speaks?'

After a while the Bania admitted he did not know the answer.

'It is a picture!' said the Jat triumphantly.

'A picture? It can be hung on a wall but it is not always red,' protested the Bania.

'Then paint it red.'

'A picture doesn't drip; it's dry,' protested the Bania again.

'Put fresh paint on it and it will drip.'

'But whoever heard of a picture that talks!'

'That's right!' replied the Jat, 'I added that to make sure a cunning Bania like you would not get the answer.'

A wealthy Maheshwari, the richest of the Marwari community, was complaining about his wife's spendthrift habits to a friend. 'One day she asked me for ten rupees, the next day she asked me for twenty and this morning she wanted twenty-five. She is the limit.'

'She certainly is,' agreed the friend. 'What did she do with all that money?'

'*Main kya jaanoon* (How should I know),' replied the wealthy man. 'I never gave her any.'

A Muslim couple arrived in paradise and approached Allah for permission to have another nikah performed. Allah asked them to wait for some time. After waiting for some years, they again approached the Almighty with their request. Allah took them to His office and showed them a pile of thousands of pending applications asking for permission for a repeat marriage. 'You see

I can do nothing till some mullah is allowed to enter paradise; there hasn't been one for many decades.'

Contributed by Prof. Gurcharan Singh, Patiala

Sindhis are known both for their sharp practices as well as for their clannishness: they drive hard bargains but also help fellow-Sindhis find employment. The following story was told to me by a Sindhi businessman on a visit to Hong Kong. He wanted to have a silk suit made and went to a Sindhi tailor's shop at the airport which advertised suits made to measure in a couple of hours. The visiting businessman selected the material and asked how much it cost. The tailor replied: 'Sir, seeing you are a fellow Sindhi I will offer you a special price. A suit of this material costs 200 Hong Kong dollars as you can see clearly marked on the label. I charge everyone else $ 200 but not a fellow Sindhi. I won't ask for $ 199, not even $ 180. For you it will be $ 170, not a cent more.'

'Why should you lose money on me just because I happen to be a fellow-Sindhi,' replied the visitor. 'So what should I offer for this suit? Seventy dollars? That I would to a non-Sindhi brother. I offer you ninety dollars and not a cent less.'

'Okay. That's a deal,' replied the tailor.

HINDLISH

From the number of letters I receive, it would appear that linguistic bloomers are a very popular form of humour. Most of us who are Anglicized wogs switch from our native languages to English, interspersing each with words from the other. Even the uneducated make free use of English words. I heard a qawwali singer complain that because of her inattentive audience, 'Mood kharab ho gaya.' A labourer reprimanded the foreman: 'Mere kaam mein interfere mat karo.' And I hear the word 'bore' in almost all Indian languages.

Then there is the mauling of foreign words. A lady reluctant to give up a seat she had occupied proclaimed: 'I am not nicling from here.' Mr Pandu Chintamani of Bombay sends a report conveyed by the guard of a train in which the lights were on the blink. It read 'Bijlee is bajanging . . . if any haraj maraj ho gaya, guard is not jumevar.' I don't believe it. However, here is one of my favourites:

A minister for housing (name not disclosed for fear of causing 'hatred, ridicule or contempt') was presiding over a committee considering plans for building urinals. The plans were examined and passed. The honourable minister made the concluding address: 'Gentlemen, now that we have sanctioned plans for the construction of urinals, it is only appropriate that we should take up the scheme for raising arsenals.'

This is an anecdote about a student looking for a textbook prescribed for his English examination. He could not recollect the title of the book. 'I can tell you what the name of the book is in Hindi: *Maimney ki dum say hilti naashpaatee.*' The erudite bookstore owner was able to locate the required book: *Lamb's Tales from Shakespeare.*

Contributed by Shanti, Delhi

A young lady went to a hospital and told the receptionist that she wished to see an upturn. 'You mean an intern, don't you dear?' asked the kindly nurse. 'Well, whatever you call it, I want a contamination,' replied the girl. 'You mean examination,' corrected the nurse. 'Maybe so,' allowed the girl. 'I want to go to the fraternity ward.' 'Maternity ward,' said the nurse with a slight smile. 'Look,' insisted the girl, 'I don't know much about big words, but I do know that I haven't demonstrated for two months, and I think I'm stagnant.'

Brown sahibs have lots of fun spotting grammar and spelling bloomers on hoardings, ads and brochures put out by their countrymen whose command over English is not as good as theirs. An American friend, Leonard J. Baldgya of the US embassy, has sent a short compilation of items picked up by American students in different parts of Europe. They make as good reading as our Hindlish.

In a Bucharest hotel lobby: The lift is being fixed for the next day. During that time we regret that you will be unbearable.

In a Belgrade hotel elevator: To move the cabin, push button for wishing floor. If the cabin should enter more persons, each one should press a number of wishing floor. Driving is then going alphabetically by national order.

In a hotel in Athens: Visitors are expected to complain at the office between the hours of 9 and 11 a.m. daily.

In a Japanese hotel: You are invited to take advantage of the chamber-maid.

In the lobby of a Moscow hotel across from a Russian Orthodox monastery: You are welcome to visit the cemetery where famous Russian composers, artists and writers are buried daily except Thursday.

In an Austrian hotel catering to skiers: Not to perambulate the corridors in the hours of repose in the boots of ascension.

On the menu of Polish hotel: Salad a firm's own make; limpid red beet soup with cheesy dumplings in the form of a finger; roasted duck let loose; beef rashers beaten up in the country people's fashion.

In a Bangkok dry cleaner's shop: Drop your trousers here for best results.

Outside a Paris dress shop: Dresses for street-walking.

Outside a Hong Kong dress shop: Ladies have fits upstairs.

In an advertisement by a Hong Kong dentist: Teeth extracted by the latest Methodists.

In a Czechoslovakian tourist agency: Take one of our horse-driven city tours—we guarantee no miscarriages.

Detour sign in Kyushi, Japan: Stop—Drive Sideways.

In a Swiss mountain inn: Special today—no ice cream.

In a Bangkok temple: It is forbidden to enter a woman, even a foreigner, if dressed as a man.

In a Tokyo bar: Special cocktail for the ladies with nuts.

In a Copenhagen airline office: We take your bags and send them in all directions.

In a Rome laundry: Ladies, leave your clothes here and spend the afternoon having a good time.

A translated sentence from a Russian chess book: A lot of water has been passed under the bridge since this variation has been played.

In a Rhodes tailor shop: Order your summers suit. Because is big rush we will execute customers in strict rotation.

In an East African newspaper: A new swimming pool is rapidly taking shape since the contractors have thrown in the bulk of their workers.

Advertisement for donkey rides in Thailand: Would you like to ride on your own ass?

In the window of a Swedish furrier: Fur coats made for ladies from their own skin.

Two signs from a Majorcan shop entrance: English well talking. Here speeching American.

From a brochure of a car rental firm in Tokyo: When passenger of foot heave in sight, tootle the horn. Trumpet him melodiously at first, but if he still obstacles your passage then tootle him with vigour.

PAKI-BASHING

A joke that recently did the rounds of Delhi's diplomatic cocktail circuit, though slightly over the line of propriety, deserves to be told because it illustrates the kind of feelings that obtain between Indians and Pakistanis. The President of the Soviet Union was celebrating his silver jubilee. As head of state he desired that all countries accredited to it should present him with the best of their products. First came the American ambassador with a brand new Cadillac. The President graciously accepted the gift. It was followed by the British ambassador presenting the latest model of a Rolls-Royce. The President was delighted and desired that his thanks be conveyed to Queen Elizabeth II. The next was the ambassador of Israel. He had brought a new variety of elongated lemon developed in his country. The President was furious and ordered the lemon to be put up the Israeli's posterior. Then came the Indian ambassador. He presented a luscious Alphonso mango. The President was not amused and ordered the fruit to be stuffed up the Indian's behind. Having been subjected to this painful insult the Israeli and the Indian ambassadors met in the lobby of Kremlin Palace. The Israeli looked woebegone. The Indian was wreathed in smiles.

The Israeli asked the Indian, 'How can you manage to look so happy after what has been done to you?'

The Indian ambassador replied, 'You've no idea what is in store for the ambassador of Pakistan. He has brought the largest watermelon developed in his country.'

No sooner was General Zia buried than a whole lot of anti-Zia jokes which were whispered around began to be told openly. 'How did they recognize General Zia's body from the debris of the air crash?' Answer: 'It was the only one firmly clutching the chair it was seated on.'

The other one is more macabre in its black humour. Since all victims of the crash were mutilated beyond recognition, the workers putting bodies in coffins did the best they could, giving each a head, torso, arms and legs, without bothering what belonged to whom. The bodies were solemnly interred in different graves.

The General was summoned by god and reprimanded for the wrongs he had done to the people. 'You will receive a hundred lashes on your buttocks,' was the Divine sentence.

The General was duly tied to a post, his bottom exposed and the jailer began to apply the whip. With each stroke, the General roared with laughter. The Almighty was very surprised at his behaviour and asked, 'Why are you laughing while being beaten?'

'Because the buttocks receiving the lash belong to the American ambassador.'

President Zia-ul Haq's trusted barber seemed to have become infected by the popular demand for the restoration of democracy. One morning while clipping the President's hair he asked: *'Gareeb purwar!* When are you going to have elections in Pakistan?'

The President ignored the question with the contempt it deserved from a military dictator. At the next hair-cutting session, the barber asked: *'Aali jah!* Isn't it time you redeemed your promise to have elections?'

The President controlled his temper and remained silent.

On the third hair-clipping session the barber again blurted out: *'Banda Nawaz,* the *awam* (common people) are clamouring for elections, when will you order them?'

The President could not contain himself anymore and exploded: '*Gaddar!* I will have you taught a lesson you will never forget.' And ordered his minions to take away the barber and give him ten lashes on his buttocks.

The barber fell at the great man's feet and whined: '*Zill-i-Ilahi* (shadow of God) I eat your salt; how can I become a *gaddar*? I only mentioned elections to make my job easier.'

'What do you mean?' demanded Zia-ul Haq.

'Every time I utter the word election, Your Excellency's hair stands on edge and is much easier to clip.'

After the last summit meeting between Rajiv Gandhi and President Zia-ul Haq, the two met privately for a friendly exchange of views. 'What is your favourite hobby?' Zia-ul Haq asked Rajiv Gandhi.

'I collect jokes people tell about me,' replied Rajiv. 'And what is your favourite hobby, Mr President?'

'I collect people who make jokes about me,' replied Zia-ul Haq.

Yahya Khan, the former Pakistan President, trying to persuade a yokel to volunteer for the Pakistani Air Force, took him inside the aircraft and explained: 'You press this yellow button and the engine will start. Then you press the red one and the plane will fly off. It is all very simple.'

'But how do I bring it down?' asked the yokel, puzzled.

'You don't have to bother about that,' explained Yahya Khan. 'Leave that to the Indian Air Force.'

Recently I received an anonymous letter from Islamabad containing an unsigned poem entitled, 'A User's Guide to Indian Causology'. I found it extremely witty and biting in its satire. I reproduce it in full for Indian readers:

When the monsoon fails and the sun drums down
On the parched Gangetic plain
And the tanks dry up and dust-storms blow
Where once were fields of grain.
When hunger stalks each village hut
And famine grips the land,
It isn't Mother Nature's fault
It is the Foreign Hand!
For this is India, you see,
Not Germany or France,
And nothing here is blamed on god
Much less on quirky chance.
Here evil has a fingered form
Both alien and planned.
It is the Foreign Hand!
When Hindu lads hack Sikhs to death
In peaceful Delhi town.
When Rajiv's corns are acting up
Or the Bombay bourse goes down,
When the pesky little Nepalese
Insist on things like borders.
When once-tame Tamil Tigers balk
At taking South Block orders.
The reasons for this mischief
I think you'll understand
It's those meddling foreign digits
It is the Foreign Hand!
So when you're in a Delhi lift
Beside a buxom dame
And you give in to the natural urge
To pinch her husky frame,
Confront her adamantine glare
With a visage mildly bland,
And say: 'It wasn't me, my dear
It was the Foreign Hand!'

With Due Disrespect

An anti-establishment joke: A vagrant, finding no place on the pavement, parked himself at the feet of the statue of Mahatma Gandhi. At midnight he was awakened by someone gently tapping him with his stick. It was the Mahatma himself. 'You Indians have been unfair to me,' complained the benign spirit. 'You put my statues everywhere that show me standing or walking. My feet are very tired. Why can't I have a horse like the one Shivaji has? Surely, I did as much for the nation as he! And you still call me your Bapu.'

Next morning the vagrant went round calling on the ministers. At long last he persuaded one to join him for a night-long vigil at the feet of the Mahatma's statue. Lo and behold, as the iron tongue of the neighbouring police station gong struck the midnight hour, the Mahatma emerged from his statue to converse with the vagrant. He repeated his complaint of having to stand or walk and his request to be provided a mount like the Chhatrapati's.

'Bapu,' replied the vagrant, 'I am too poor to buy you a horse, but I have brought this minister of government for you. He . . .'

Bapu looked at the minister and remarked: 'I asked for a horse, not a donkey.'

This was a favourite story during the Emergency imposed by Indira Gandhi in 1975. Bapu Gandhi, up in heaven, was troubled by the thought that after all he had done for his country, no one even remembered his name. He sent for Jawaharlal Nehru and

555

said: 'Nehru beta, you ruled the country for many years. What did you do to perpetuate the memory of your Bapu Gandhi?'

'Bapu, I did everything I could. I had a samadhi built on the spot where we cremated your body. On your birthdays and death anniversaries we gathered at the samadhi, sang *Ram Dhun* and *Vaishnav Jan.* What more could I do?'

'Who came after you?' asked Bapu.

'I am told Lal Bahadur became Prime Minister after me,' replied Nehru.

So Bapu Gandhi sent for Lal Bahadur and put him the same question. Shastri replied: 'Bapu, I had a very short time as Prime Minister—only one-and-half years, but I had your statues put up in every town and village. I had all your speeches published in all languages and distributed free. What more could I have done?'

'Who came after you?' asked Bapu.

'It's Nehru's chhokree, Indira. She is now ruling India.'

So Bapu sent for Indira Gandhi, who had just imposed Emergency on the country and put the same question to her. Indira Gandhi replied: 'I have done more to perpetuate your memory than either Shastri or my father. I have made the entire country like you. I have left the people nothing more than their langotis and a staff like you have.'

Bapu was horrified. 'Beti, this is very wrong. The people will rise against you for depriving them of everything.'

'Not to worry, Bapu,' replied Indira. 'I have taken care of that. I have put the langoti in their hands and put the danda up their bottoms.'

An argument arose as to which state government excelled in corruption. The following story settled the issue.

Six years ago an MLA from Kerala visited Chandigarh and called on a Punjab minister at his house. He was amazed at the ostentation and asked his old friend. 'How did you manage to acquire so much wealth?'

'Are you really interested to know?'

'Of course, yes. A little extra knowledge always helps.'

'Then wait till tomorrow, and I shall explain fully.'

The next day the minister drove the MLA down the highway for several kilometers in his personal Honda.

He stopped the car, both of them got out and the minister pointed his finger to a spot down the beautiful valley.

'Do you see the big bridge over there?' he asked.

'Yes,' replied the MLA.

'Half the cost of the bridge went into my pocket.'

Four years later the Punjabi who in the meantime had lost his ministership, went on a holiday to Trivandrum and called on his old friend, who had now become a minister. 'By god,' said the Punjabi, 'you have beaten me flat. Crystal chandeliers, Italian marble, Mercedes. Tell me how you managed it.'

'I will tell you tomorrow,' said the minister. Next day the minister drove him down the highway, stopped the car at a spot overlooking a valley and the minister pointed his finger to a spot down the valley, and asked:

'Do you see the bridge over there?'

'I see no bridge,' said the Punjabi.

'Quite right,' said the minister. 'The entire cost of the bridge went into my pocket.'

A minister due to go on a foreign tour had a lot of cash lying with him. He thought it would be safest left with the Prime Minister and requested him to keep it for him till he returned. The Prime Minister agreed but insisted that the transaction be witnessed by two of his senior advisers. 'Money matters can lead to misunderstanding,' said the PM. 'It is always wise to have two witnesses.'

The minister saw the wisdom of the advice. The cash was handed over to the PM in the presence of two of his senior advisers.

Some weeks later when the minister returned home, he called on the PM and asked for the return of the money.

'What money?' asked the PM. 'I don't know what you are talking about.'

'The cash I left with you,' pleaded the minister. 'You even had two of your senior advisers as witnesses.' 'Let's ask them,' replied the PM. The senior advisers were sent for. 'Do you know anything about this minister leaving money with me?' asked the PM.

'No, sir, I know nothing,' replied one. 'No, sir, he did not leave any money with you,' said the other. The senior advisers left the room. The PM opened his safe and gave back the minister his cash.

'Why did you first say you knew nothing about my money?' asked the bewildered minister.

'I just wanted you to know what kind of advisers I have,' replied the PM.

A minister of government whose knowledge of English was very poor was provided with a secretary to write speeches for him.

'Give me a fifteen-minute speech on the non-aligned movement,' ordered the boss.

The text was prepared to last exactly fifteen minutes. But when the minister proceeded to make his oration it took him half-an-hour to do so. The organizers of the conference were upset because their schedule went awry. And the minister was upset because his secretary had let him down. He upbraided him: 'I asked for a fifteen-minute speech; you gave me a half-hour speech. Why?' he demanded.

'Sir, I gave you a fifteen-minute speech. But you read out its carbon copy as well.'

Two tigers disappeared from the Delhi zoo. Not a trace could be found of them anywhere. Then suddenly one day six months later, they were back in their cages. One was skin and bones; the other had put on a lot of weight. They began to compare notes. Said the thin tiger: 'I was very unlucky. I found my way to Rajasthan. There was a famine and I couldn't find anything to eat. The cattle had died and even the humans I ate had hardly any flesh on them. So I decided to get back to the zoo. Here at least I get one square meal every day. But you look healthy enough. Why did you come back?'

Replied the fat tiger, 'To start with I was very lucky. I found my way to the government secretariat. I hid myself under a staircase. Every evening as the clerks came out of their offices, I caught and ate one of them. For six months no one noticed anything. Then yesterday I made the mistake of eating the fellow who serves them their morning tea. Then all hell broke loose. They looked for him everywhere and found me hiding under the staircase. They chased me out.

'So I am back at the zoo. It is safer here.'

This comes from a young entrant to the Indian Administrative Service. His first posting was as a junior assistant to the secretary of the ministry. One morning he took some important files to discuss with his boss. After knocking on the door and receiving no reply, he gently pushed open the door to find his senior standing by the window deeply engrossed in his thoughts. He tip-toed out of the room. Since the files were marked 'Immediate', he went back to the secretary's room and, again receiving no reply to the knock, went in. The boss was still standing where he had been and intently looking out of the window. Junior sahib coughed lightly to make his presence known. The secretary turned round and remarked, 'How can this country go forward! For the last one hour I have been watching the workmen on the road. They haven't done a stroke of work.'

The Kashmir militants tried to kidnap one of Devi Lal's loved ones but gave up: they couldn't decide which buffalo to take hostage.

PUNCHLINE

Question: What did the little boy tell his father when the radiator of their new Maruti Suzuki developed a leak?
Answer: Maruti nay soo soo kee.

Question: What do you call a very well-dressed man in Kerala?
Answer: Debo Nair

Contributed by Joydeep Ghosh, Calcutta

A visitor having tea at a restaurant complained about the quality of the tea.

'Sahib, we have got this tea from Darjeeling,' explained the waiter.

'Is that why it is so cold?' asked the customer.

Contributed by J.P. Singh Kaka, New Delhi

Customer: Waiter! I asked for *alu paratha* but I find no potatoes in it!'

Waiter: 'What's in a name, sir! If you ask for Kashmiri pulao, will you expect to find Kashmir in it?'

Contributed by Rajib Bhattacharjee

Seen inside a DTC bus:
Aana free
Jaana free
Pakray gaye to
Khana free

Contributed by J.P. Singh Kaka, New Delhi

An anti-smoking enthusiast addressed a person who had just lit a cigarette. 'Do you realize that one-third of the smoke from your cigarette is inhaled by me?'

'Is that so?' replied the smoker. 'Every cigarette costs me sixty paise. So you owe me twenty paise for this one.'

Contributed by Manoj Datta, New Delhi

It was the morning after, and he sat groaning and holding his head.

'Well, if you hadn't drunk so much last night you wouldn't feel so bad now,' the wife said tartly.

'My drinking had nothing to do with it,' he answered. 'I went to bed feeling wonderful and woke up feeling awful. It was the sleep that did it!'

A passenger from Bombay on a visit to Singapore picked up uncomplimentary acronyms on the subcontinent's two major international carriers: Pakistan International Airways and Air India.

PIA: Please Inform Allah.
AI: Already Informed.

A gambler's three-year-old son learned to count upto thirteen. It went as follows: One, two, three, four, five, six, seven, eight, nine, ten, jack, queen, king.

The three stages of sickness:
  Ill
  Pill
  Bill
Sometimes these is a fourth:
Will

First man: 'Call me a doctor, call me a doctor!'
  Second man: 'What's the matter? Are you sick?'
  First man: 'No, I've just graduated from medical school!'